THE EVOLUTION OF SOVIET OPERATIONAL ART
1927–1991

VOLUME II

CASS SERIES ON THE SOVIET STUDY OF WAR

(Selected Translations)

Series Editor: David M. Glantz

This series examines what Soviet military theorists and commanders have learned from the study of their own military operations. Separate volumes contain annotated translations of Soviet works analysing their own experiences, as well as the works of important Soviet military theorists and collections of Soviet articles concerning specific campaigns, operations or military techniques.

1. Harold S. Orenstein, translator and editor, *Soviet Documents on the Use of War Experience*, Volume I, *The Initial Period of War 1941*, with an Introduction by David M. Glantz.
2. Harold S. Orenstein, translator and editor, *Soviet Documents on the Use of War Experience*, Volume II, *The Winter Campaign 1941–1942*, with an Introduction by David M. Glantz.
3. Joseph G. Welsh, translator, *Red Armor Combat Orders: Combat Regulations for Tank and Mechanized Forces 1944*, edited and with an Introduction by Richard N. Armstrong.
4. Harold S. Orenstein, translator and editor, *Soviet Documents on the Use of War Experience*, Volume III, *Military Operations 1941 and 1942*, with an Introduction by David M. Glantz.
5. William A. Burhans, translator, *The Nature of the Operations of Modern Armies* by V. K. Triandafillov, edited by Jacob W. Kipp, with an Introduction by James J. Schneider.
6. Harold S. Orenstein, translator, *The Evolution of Soviet Operational Art, 1927–1991: The Documentary Basis*, Volume I, *Operational Art, 1927–1964*, with an Introduction by David M. Glantz.
7. Harold S. Orenstein, translator, *The Evolution of Soviet Operational Art, 1927–1991: The Documentary Basis*, Volume II, *Operational Art, 1965–1991*, with an Introduction by David M. Glantz.

THE EVOLUTION OF SOVIET OPERATIONAL ART
1927–1991:
The Documentary Basis

In two volumes
VOLUME II
OPERATIONAL ART, 1965–1991

Translated by
Harold S. Orenstein

With a foreword and introduction (Volume I) by
David M. Glantz

FRANK CASS

First published in 1995 in Great Britain by
FRANK CASS & CO. LTD.
Newbury House, 900 Eastern Avenue,
London, IG2 7HH

and in the United States of America by
FRANK CASS
c/o ISBS
5804 N.E. Hassalo Street, Portland, Oregon 97213-3644

British Library Cataloguing in Publication Data

Evolution of Soviet Operational Art,
1927–91: Documentary Basis. – Vol.2:
Operational Art, 1965–91. – (Cass Series
on the Soviet Study of War; No.7)
I. Orenstein, Harold S.   I. Series
355.00947

ISBN 0-7146-4548-6 (cloth)
ISBN 0-7146-4229-0 (paper)

Library of Congress Cataloging in Publication Data

The evolution of Soviet operational art, 1927–1991.
    p.   cm. — (Cass series on the Soviet study of war; 6–7)
Includes index.
Contents: v. 1. Operational Art, 1927–1964 — v. 2. Operational
art, 1965–1991.
    ISBN 0-7146-4547-8 (v. 1) — ISBN 0-7146-4548-6 (v. 2) (cloth)
    ISBN 0-7146-4228-2 (v. 1) — ISBN 0-7146-4229-0 (v.2) (paper)
1. Operational art (Military science)—History—20th century.
2. Soviet Union—History, Military.   I. Series
U162.E96   1995
355.02—dc20   94-39330
                                                     CIP

pesetting, London
Britain by
Midsomer Norton

Contents

List of Sketches and Figures

List of Tables

CHAPTER SIX

The Reinvigoration of Operational Art, 1965–70

Articles and studies published during the period after 1964 evidence movement away from preoccupation with nuclear questions, first through an examination of the historical roots of operational art, and finally, by 1968, by demonstrating acute awareness that traditional operational techniques applied within a modern context. These articles were, in fact, precursors to the period of the 1970s, when operational art and conventional operations in a "nuclear scared" context again became preeminent Soviet military concerns.

A capstone Soviet work on the development of operational art appeared in 1965. Entitled *Problemy strategii i voyennogo iskusstva v sovetskikh voyennykh trudakh (1917–1940)* [Problems of strategy and operational art in Soviet military works (1917–1940)], the two-volume work contained selections from the writings of a host of interwar theorists, many of which had not been available to readers since the 1930s. The introduction to the book by the then Chief of the Soviet Army General Staff, Marshal of the Soviet Union M. V. Zakharov, emphasized the importance of the writings and officially sanctioned the rehabilitation process of such writers as Svechin, Tukhachevsky, and a host of forgotten or scarcely remembered theorists on operational art.

Also during 1965, *VIZh* published a lengthy retrospective account of the development of operational art in the 1930s by the surviving theorist of the interwar years, G. Isserson. The article provided fresh details on the process by which operational art was developed, exposed the views and contributions of those who were purged in the late 1930s, and candidly explained for the first time how Stalinism had adversely affected the process.

A subsequent 1965 article by Colonel A. Golubev complimented and critiqued the piece by Isserson and also fully rehabilitated the key strategic and operational theorist, A. Svechin. Golubev resurrected the great strategic debate of the 1920s regarding the contending strategic schools of "attrition" and "annihiliation," examined the works of Tukhachevsky, Triandafillov and others, and cast new light on the concept of successive operations.

The following year, Major General N. Pavlenko, writing in *VIZh*, authored a substantial piece addressing the strategic context for the development of operational art in the 1920s, again reviewing in detail the writings and views of purged military theorists, in particular Svechin and Tukhachevsky. Pavlenko's article focused on the evolution of strategic offensive concepts within the parameters of the strategic debate and highlighted the role of successive operations.

The 1968 article by Chief of Soviet Ground Forces and Deputy Minister of Defense Army General I. Pavlovskiy applied the same critical eye to the development of operational art in the Great Patriotic War and reflected a broader new trend as major new books appeared on the subject (for example, Colonel General P. A. Kurochkin's *Obshchevoyskovaya armiya v nastuplenii* [The combined-arms army on the offensive]).

Completing the process of reinvigorating the analytical basis of operational art, in 1970 a key article appeared by Chief of the General Staff, Marshal of the Soviet Union M. V. Zakharov that reviewed in detail the historical development of the concept of "the deep operation," the core element of historical operational maneuver. Zakharov underscored the contemporary utility of the deep operation and paved the way for Soviet fixation on operational maneuver, which dominated the next decade and a half. The intellectual ferment is clear in these articles, as is the steady movement away from fixation on nuclear warfare to an increased faith in the utility of conventional operations, a faith which undergirded renewed Soviet interest in operational art.

Problems of Strategy and Operational Art in Soviet Military Works (1917–40)[1]

CHIEF OF THE GENERAL STAFF, MARSHAL OF THE SOVIET UNION M. V. ZAKHAROV

The collection *Voprosy strategii i operativnogo iskusstva v sovetskikh voyennykh trudakh (1917–1940)* [Problems of strategy and operational art in Soviet military works] acquaints the reader with the most significant works revealing the content and development of the strategy and operational art of the Soviet Army and Navy up to the Great Patriotic War.

This is the first time that such a collection has been published. Many of the scientific works contained in it are not known to the modern generation of officers, inasmuch as during Stalin's cult of personality they were destroyed or preserved in single copies. Nevertheless, the basic tenets of Soviet military-theoretical thought are distinctly formulated in them.

It should be emphasized that Soviet military theory is reflected not only in military-scientific works. It was developed in the practical activity of prominent Soviet military leaders and personalities, who published scientific works in the field of strategy and operational art. Among them, I. Ye. Yakir, V. K. Blyukher, A. I. Sedyakin, R. P. Eydeman and others played a notable role.

A number of instructions, manuals, directives, and regulations, which set forth principles for conducting battle and operations, were produced with the participation of these eminent military leaders, who occupied high positions in the army and navy. Analyses of maneuvers and war games, proposals and instructions of military leaders – all this developed the theoretical tenets for the use of armed forces in war.

In order that the reader may more thoroughly understand the materials in the given collection, I would like to examine briefly the overall course of development of Soviet military-theoretical thought up to the Great Patriotic War.

On the day after the victory of the Great October Socialist Revolution, the practical tasks of organizing the defense of the proletarian revolution's gains against foreign enemies and domestic counterrevolution lay before the Communist Party and the Soviet country. The old Russian Army was not suited for this. It was necessary to organize new armed forces, which, in their class make-up and ideological preparation, would conform to proletarian revolution's aims, and would be capable of protecting the Soviet state. It was necessary also to develop principally new theoretical foundations for the development of the army, its combat training, and the conduct of combat operations. These difficult tasks were not immediately resolved by the Central Committee of the Party, headed by V. I. Lenin, but only during the war, on the basis of its experience in accordance with the critical situational requirements.

Not only organizational problems of Soviet Armed Forces development arose in a new way at that time. Combat leadership required no less attention. The features of the military-political situation, equipment, supply, the Red Army's limited materiel potential, inadequate command personnel experience, low level of force combat training, and many, many other things – all these affected the forms and methods of conducting armed combat. Thus, in the fire of the Civil War not only were the Soviet Armed Forces created, but also new foundations of military art were developed.

During the Civil War the most important tenets concerning the nature and character of modern war and factors which would provide victory in war, theoretically worked out by Lenin even before the October Revolution, were fully confirmed and developed further. Creatively developing Marx and Engels' study of war and the army, Lenin substantiated a number of decisive features of modern wars.

The springboard of Marxist-Leninist study on war and the army was Lenin's position on the social essence of war and its class nature, which included a basic difference from Clausewitz's well-known formulation: war is the continuation of politics by violent means. Lenin taught that war is the continuation not only of foreign, but also of domestic politics of states, conditioned by the social system and class interests. The place and role of politics and strategy in war, its preparation, and its leadership are determined by this. Politics not only determine the war's aim, but also guide the war for its entire duration. Military strategy is called upon by the armed forces to achieve its assigned aim.

But modern wars are not limited to armed combat. They encompass all fields of activity of a state. In some form or another broad masses of the population participate in war. The struggle is also conducted in the field of economics, diplomacy, ideology, etc. It is apparent that only consolidation of all state activities into a single leadership organ during a war will make it possible to conduct it most successfully (the Council of Worker and Peasant Defense in the Civil War, the State Defense Committee in the Great Patriotic War).

In practice, this unity of war leadership was implemented by the Central Committee of the Party, headed by V. I. Lenin during the Civil War, and by the Central Committee of the Party in the Great Patriotic War. In 1918 the Central Committee of the Party already established that all "policies of the war department, and all other departments and institutions, are carried out on the precise basis of general directives issued by the Party in the person of the Central Committee and under its direct control."[2] This position on the leading role of the Party in the military development of the army and its combat activity, proceeding from Marxist-Leninist study on war and the army, was of primary significance in the achievement of victory, and became one of the most important principles of Soviet military science after the Civil War. Experience in the development of the Soviet Armed Forces and their combat leadership in the several years that followed fully confirmed the correctness of this tenet.

In the Party program adopted by the XXII Congress, it was noted that "the principal foundation of military development is the Communist Party's leadership of the Armed Forces, and the increased role and influence of Party organizations in the army and navy."[3]

Marxism-Leninism examines not only the social essence of war, but also what distinguishes war from other forms of struggle. Lenin wrote that "armed revolt is a special type of political struggle, subject to special laws which must be considered attentively. Karl Marx expressed this truth in a remarkably bold way, writing that armed 'uprising, like war, is an art.' "[4] The Communist Party always attached great significance to the study and mastery of this art as one of the most important factors of victory in war. Already in 1905 Lenin indicated that

> not one Social-Democrat who is even barely familiar with history and who has studied this theme of Engels can ever question the enormous significance of military knowledge, the enormous importance of military equipment, such as guns, and military organization, which the masses and classes of people use to resolve great historical conflicts.[5]

Lenin subsequently returned to this theme more than once, emphasizing the necessity of using all past experience and military learning, critically reworking and interpreting them. Lenin said that without military science and without using military knowledge, victory was impossible.

In this respect, one of the most important problems was the use of military specialists of the old army in the interests of the new Red Army. On the one hand, the old intelligentsia was the bearer of achievements and experience of bourgeois science; on the other hand, it was burdened with a petty bourgeois world view and conservatism created by education and the entire tenor of life. And in the Soviet Armed Forces the role of the leader and commander is especially crucial. Consequently, the problem of creating prepared and experienced officer cadres became exceptionally important.

It should be noted that a complete misunderstanding of the problem of using military specialists, their military knowledge, and their combat experience was characteristic for the "military opposition," which came forth before the VIII Congress and at the Congress itself. Overcoming this "opposition" created the necessary foundations for strengthening the army's combat capabilities, its development, and successful combat activity. Resolutions of the VIII Party Congress on military questions played an exceptional role in this respect. They were based on Lenin's instructions that our army was to be trained, armed, and organized according to the latest word in military science and technology. Only under these conditions could it fulfill its missions for protecting the socialist Fatherland. Use of modern war experience, accumulation of knowledge of bourgeois military science, and its critical reworking without weakening the struggle against bourgeois ideology – all this required strict application of the Marxist-Leninist method in the field of military-scientific knowledge.

Attaching great significance to a scientific approach to the resolution of tasks before the Party in all fields of development of the Soviet State, including the military field, Lenin steadfastly demanded of military workers that they study military affairs and in all possible ways increase the quality of military leadership. With the development of military affairs, the role of science in this increases as well, and leadership methods become more complex and improve. And only those military leaders who master solid military knowledge and a broad world view, and who correctly use the Marxist-Leninist method will be capable of successfully resolving their missions.

Lenin's guidelines, duly noted in the resolutions of the VIII Party Congress, became the principal requirements in our army's development, the training of its cadres, and the development of Soviet military-theoretical thought.

In determining the nature and essence of military art, Engels, and Lenin after him, indicated that methods of conducting war change and depend on the level of production and the development of technology, and that each epoch has its own corresponding military art and its own method of conducting war. But within the limits of a given epoch there is not a single strategy which is common for all countries and people. Strategy is determined by politics; it is concrete and depends on the level of the economy of the given state, its social system, geographic position, condition of the armed forces, population, and materiel capabilities, and on those very features of the states of probable enemies. The development of Soviet military art, in turn, was determined by all these data.

The Civil War proceeded on a weak economic base, with the absence of new military-technical means and a large shortage of trained command personnel. Under conditions of devastation, hunger, and cold, Soviet troops experienced great difficulties, and trained on the battlefields on the basis of experience of battles won and lost. In addition, the emancipation of creative labor forces as a result of the Great October Socialist Revolution could not fail to affect the course of military operations and the development of Soviet military art. Revolutionary enthusiasm of the working masses attached to old forms of combat operations qualities inherent in the struggle of the proletariat – decisiveness, boldness, and dynamism based on a profound faith in their strength and the greatness of the aims of the proletarian revolution. Therefore, it is not by chance that decisive forms of combat operations of the Soviet Armed Forces – flank attacks, envelopment, encirclement, and others – were displayed during the Civil War with an unprecedented upsurge. During this war, Soviet military art reached a wide expanse of maneuverability, which, as M. V. Frunze justly observed, was the result not only of purely objective conditions of the Civil War, but also of intrinsic Red Army characterisitcs, its revolutionary spirit, and its class nature.

The great experience of the war, then critically generalized, served as a basis for the subsequent development of Soviet military theory. Lenin's direct leadership in the defense of the Soviet Republic, the creative generalizations he made of past war experience, especially the Civil War, and his statements and directives concerning the most important questions concerning defense and Armed Forces development played a decisive role here.

Civil War conditions did not permit weighty theoretical generalizations about the experience of conducting combat operations. Nevertheless, military-theoretical problems, although in their limited aspect, were also studied at that time. Here researchers attempted to analyze and generalize theoretically everything new which the Great October Socialist Revolution and the Civil War had introduced into the field of military science. In 1919, 5th Army (commanded by M. N. Tukhachevsky) on the Eastern Front came out with its first collection, *Grazhdanskaya voyna* [The Civil War], containing "*Soobshcheniya po strategii grazhdanskoy voyny, chitannyye sotrudnikam shtaba 5-y armii*" [Reports on Civil War strategy given by 5th Army staff workers].[6] This collection examined problems of preparation and conduct of Civil War operations. Almost all *fronts* in 1919–20 published their own military-scientific journals. At the end of 1919 Tukhachevsky gave a lecture on strategy at the Military Academy,[7] in which Civil War experience in this area was generalized. In 1920 this lecture was published in a separate pamphlet in Rostov-on-the-Don.

In the Civil War period, scientific research and generalization could not be shaped in the form of official documents, regulations, instructions and manuals. Manuals and regulations published at that time were, in essence, the old Russian Army regulations, reprinted with minor changes.

After the Civil War, the possibility presented itself for more extensively developing military-technical work. Its main content was the universal study and generalization of the experience of the Civil War and World War, taking into account the conditions assumed for future imperialist wars against the Soviet republic.

M. V. Frunze's practical activity and printed works had particular influence on the development of Soviet military-theoretical thought in the first half of the 1920s. A talented organizer and military leader in the Civil War, and then leader of the War Department, Frunze provided the theoretical grounds for the most important problems of Armed Forces development and the country's defensive preparation. He considered the achievement of uniformity of views on the principal questions of military development, methods of combat training, and means of conducting combat operations to be the decisive condition for a high level of national combat might. Frunze proposed these ideas in the article "*Yedinaya voyennaya doktrina i Krasnaya Armiya*" [Unified military doctrine and the Red Army], and in "*Doklad na soveshchanii komandnogo i komissarskogo sostava Ukrainy i Kryma v marte 1920 g.*" [Lecture at the meeting of command and commissar personnel of the Ukraine and Crimea in March 1920].[8] The positions stated in these articles elicited sharp and heated arguments. This was natural. The establishment of a uniformity of views on basic questions of army development and military art had enormous educational significance, and became a vital necessity and basis for the conduct of the 1924–28 military reforms. In addition, erroneous conclusions on the possibility of creating a new theory of proletarian military art at that time and in that situation came to light during the discussion process. Lenin came out against the untimeliness of such conclusions, warning about the danger of falling into communist self-conceit.

Concerning the nature of future war, Frunze said that war would have a class character and would inevitably aggravate the class struggle within the hostile capitalist state that initiated aggression against the Soviet Republic. Without rejecting the possibility of lightning blows, he also considered that future conflicts would lead to a protracted war.

In evaluating the nature of operations in a future war, Frunze proceeded from an assumption of its high degree of maneuver; however, he did not exclude the possibility of using positional combat forms in separate sectors. Steadfastly cultivating the idea of maneuver, he viewed this as one of the ways of overcoming the military-technical superiority of our potential enemies.

Frunze put the defense and offense in close connection with maneuver. He reached the following conclusions: all things being equal, the offense is more advantageous than the defense; as its mission, the defense has to provide for successfully shifting to the offense; the Red Army must be educated in an offensive spirit.

Frunze's views greatly influenced the development of Soviet military-theoretical thought in the mid-1920s. They were reflected in official manuals, particularly in the *Field Regulations of 1925*, in the manual "*Vyssheye komandovaniye*" [Higher command], approved by Frunze and published in 1924, and in combat regulations for infantry and other combat arms which appeared in 1924. The publication of these documents had enormous significance for establishing uniformity of views in the field of operational-tactical thought.

Much work on reorganizing our Armed Forces was conducted with Frunze's direct participation; this work became history under the title of Military Reform. These measures concerned all aspects of the military organism. Principal attention was directed toward mobilization readiness, coordination of operational-strategic proposals with the state's actual capabilities, and the raising of the country's combat capability on the whole.

In the first order, the central military apparatus was reorganized. All functions not peculiar to the Staff of the *RKKA* [Workers' and Peasants' Red Army] were singled out. Here, Frunze indicated that the formulation of operational issues and mobilization plans should be carried out with consideration of the Soviet Union's economic, political, and strategic capabilities. In his opinion, this operational staff was to become "not only the brains of the Red Army – it should become the military brain for the entire Soviet state and should supply the material which will be the basis of the Defense Council's work."[9]

In 1925 the Directorate for Research and Use of War Experience was created as part of the *RKKA* Staff. In a short time it published many valuable military-historical works, thereby creating a base for potential development of military theory. The rejuvenation of the War Department's central apparatus was also of substantial significance. Young cadres with Civil War experience, who had graduated from the Military Academy and Higher Academic Courses, came to the *RKKA* Staff and the main directorates. They brought along a freshness, inquisitiveness, and boldness of thought, will and energy in work, and a passionate loyalty to Soviet power. The attraction of young officers and the simultaneous broad use of the experience of senior cadres made it possible to combine theory with practice successfully in the work of the central apparatus and attach a purposeful nature to it.

During that period the army was structured according to a territorial-militia principle. In 1926 territorial formations comprised 65 per cent of all Soviet Armed Forces. This fully met the demands of the Party program and the resolution on the military question adopted by the VIII Party Congress. A mixed system of cadre and militia formations was laid at the foundation of Armed Forces development. In practice, the mixed system was conditioned by the military budget, consideration of reliable and operationally efficient protection of the country, and mobilization plan calculations for supporting deployment of the necessary number of first-line divisions and creating a sufficient reserve of a militarily trained manpower contingent in the country. Economic needs were also taken into account: short periods for combat training in Red Army territorial units did not tear men away from their practical activities.

In the 1920s the Military-Scientific Society [*Voyenno-nauchnoye obshchestvo/VNO*], created on 13 October 1920 as part of the Military Academy of the General Staff, had a prominent place in military-scientific work. It had as its task the study and use of class war experiences in the epoch of the proletarian revolution.

The creation of this society was dictated, in particular, by academic instruction being removed to a considerable degree from reality, that is, it bore an abstract nature. The professor-instructor staff, consisting almost entirely of military specialists from the old army, were not able to restructure themselves. In 1920 there was not yet a course given on the history of the Civil War, or even on the history of the World War on the Russian front.

Moreover, the Academy's student body had sharply changed. In it were more than 50 per cent of workers and peasants and as many as 80 per cent of Communists who had extensive combat experience in the Civil War, and some with experience in the World War; they required practical training in military activities in a new situation on the basis of an all-round comprehension of recent war experience from new, Marxist-Leninist methodological positions. This is why the Military-Scientific Society became widely recognized and its activities very useful. At the same time, it personified the struggle of the new against the old, a progressive attempt to coordinate theory with revolutionary practice and to develop military affairs and art on the basis of Marxist-Leninist study on war and the army. These extensive tasks led young military-scientific cadres onto the broad path of creative generalization of past experience, and of scientific searches for the new in accordance with the changed social situation in the Soviet republic.

The Military-Scientific Society created its own periodical printing organs and published collections and other literature. Having originated in the Academy of the General Staff, it soon embraced other military academies and forces throughout the entire territory of the Soviet republic, with its own departments and organizations. To unify and guide *VNO* activities, in May 1925 an all-union conference of the society's departments took place, at which the *VNO* Provisional Central Council was created, headed by Frunze. The Society became a broad, mass organization, and by 1926 had up to 300,000 members. In 1926 an all-union congress of this society took place. Among those who presented papers at it were M. N. Tukhachevsky – "Voprosy sovremennoy strategii" [Problems of modern strategy]; V. K. Triandafillov – "Razmakh operatsiy sovremennykh armiy" [The scope of operations of modern armies]; S. S. Kamenev and R. S. Tsiffer – "Osnovnyye voprosy sovremennoy taktiki" [Basic problems of modern tactics]; and S. A. Pugachev – "Osnovy podgotovki strany k oborone" [Foundations of preparing the country for defense]. These and other papers reflected the success of Soviet military-theoretical thought. The congress not only summed up past military-theoretical work, but also noted prospects for its future development.

By this time many military-theoretical works had come out, which made it possible to generalize more fully the rich experience of recent wars. Included among these were the works of V. Novitsky, I. Vatsetis, A. Bazarevsky, A. Zayonchkovsky, B. Shaposhnikov, A. Kolenkovsky, and others on the First World War, and the works of M. Tukhachevsky, A. Bubnov, S. Gusev, V. Melikov, N. Kakurin, G. Gay, Ye. Shilovsky, N. Varfolomeyev, and others on the Civil War.

One of the most important results of studying previous war experience was the theory of conducting successive operations. In his work *Pokhod za Vislu* [The campaign for the Vistula] published in 1923, Tukhachevsky laid the foundations in the following way:

> the impossibility in the presence of modern wide fronts to destroy an enemy army by a single blow compels us to achieve this by a series of successive operations. . . . A series of annihilating operations, introduced successively and combined by continuous pursuit, can replace the annihilating engagement, which in former armies was a better type of combat.[10]

This theory of successive operations was further developed in a series of military-scientific works of the 1920s, especially by N. N. Movchin,[11] N. Ye. Varfolomeyev,[12] V. K. Triandafillov,[13] and others. These authors considered that successive operations always had and will have superiority, inasmuch as they make it possible to shift from one particular target to another, while at the same time maintaining unity of a common aim. They also considered that with an average duration in that period of six to seven days, an army operation could have a depth of 75–90 kilometers, while a *front* operation could be within the limits of up to 200 kilometers. The opinion was expressed that a grouping of army operations should directly evolve from the *front* command's plan. The study of the problem of conducting successive operations was, to a certain degree, a prerequisite for the subsequent development (in the 1930s) of the deep operation.

A very substantial phenomenon which affected the successful development of military-theoretical thought in the 1920s was the separation of operational art from the field of strategy and its becoming an independent field of military theory. The two-part formula "strategy – tactics," which had been dominant until the beginning of the 1920s, was divided into three parts: "strategy – operational art – tactics." This most favorably affected the entire methodology of teaching and studying urgent problems of military art. A separate department, "Conduct of Operations," was created in 1924 at the Military Academy. Before, lectures on the conduct of operations made up only part of the overall course on the conduct of war, that is, strategy in its former understanding. The creation of such an independent academic discipline made it possible to approach more thoroughly the all-round study of preparing and conducting operations. The system of successive operations was a subject in the study of operational art of this period.

According to N. Ye. Varfolomeyev, this system was characterized by the following design: operational aim – annihilation, complete rout of enemy personnel; operational method – uninterrupted offensive; means – prolonged operational pursuit, avoiding pauses and stops, implemented by a series of successive operations, each of which is an intermediary link on the path toward the ultimate aim, which is achieved in the final, concluding, decisive operation.[14]

Another component of the investigation of the modern operation was the study of its materiel support. This was especially furthered by assimilating the experience of the Soviet–Polish campaign of 1920. In the system of successive operations, which did not allow pauses or stops, materiel support acquired particular significance. However, both in academic study and in operational problems and games, materiel calculation for conducting an operation still did not receive the attention it deserved. Past war experience demonstrated the continuously increasing role of the rear in war. The problem of organizing the rear and its particular significance in preparing the country's defense and in combat operations became one of the most important tasks of strategy and operational art. In his talk at the Military Academy in 1924, Frunze focused special attention on this and demanded that the study of problems of organizing the rear and supply be included in strategy. For this purpose, according to Frunze's instructions, a special Department of Supply was created at the Military Academy in 1924. It was called upon to prepare highly qualified workers for the operational rear, with a broad strategic world view, capable also of directing the national economy's preparation and mobilization in the interests of the country's defense.

The theoretical development of questions concerning organization and conduct of operations was improved in its subsequent evolution in full accordance with the changing materiel-technical base and with the conditions of developing the Soviet state's Armed Forces. Problems of operational art at the end of the 1920s were most fully reflected in Triandafillov's work, *Kharakter operatsiy sovremennykh armiy* [The nature of operations of modern armies], published in 1929.[15] A characteristic feature of this book is the author's attempt to avoid general discussions. He substantiates his theoretical generalizations and conclusions with concrete practical data – the materiel condition of the Red Army and armies of probable enemies, and probable tactical and operational norms under those conditions. In his theoretical conclusions he attempts to demonstrate in which direction military affairs were developing. It is in this that the book's scientific value lies.

Regulations and manuals published during that period were practical handbooks on troop training and combat preparation, and reflected the corresponding level of their materiel support. At the same time, however, they proceeded in their principal tenets from the prognosis of an increasing influence of technology and its role in future wars (in the new *Field Regulations of 1929*, much attention was focused on the role of tanks and aviation in future wars. The long-range action tank group was introduced, the significance of massed aviation was emphasized, and problems of antiair, antitank, and anti-chemical defense were posed).

But if in the field of the formation and development of operational art in the 1920s a certain uniformity of views and opinions on its basic problems was observed, then this was not so in the field of military strategy. There were many reasons for this. The most substantial was that after the October Revolution and the creation of the Soviet state the correlation of social forces in the international arena and within the state, as well as the correlation of possible military groupings, had profoundly changed, and strategy in its broad understanding required radical reworking on the basis of Marxist-Leninist methodology. Here a single consideration of past experience alone was not adequate. As an example, the "Strategy" course which Professor A. A. Svechin taught at the Military Academy (and then published in a separate book) can be used as a model. In the section where the problem of conducting armed combat on fronts was examined, the author provided useful material, but as soon as he began to discuss the preparation and conduct of war as a whole, he fell into scholasticism. An active follower of the well-known German historian Hans Delbrueck, an advocate of the superiority of the "strategy of attrition" [*strategiya izmora*, literally, "strategy of starvation"], the idealist Svechin was unable to go further than generalizations of recent war experience and strategic theories of his predecessors. He was unable to understand the new phenomena in our social life and in the development of the Soviet state and its Armed Forces; he did not perceive the prospects of their development or, consequently, the possible development of military art. He attempted to provide a general, abstract strategy valid for any country. His thinking, although sometimes original, remained conservative in its spirit. Nevertheless, Svechin's book, in essence, was at that time the single, unclassified serious work on strategy.[16] It was broadly disseminated and had a positive effect on the development of military-theoretical questions, if only because it provided a great deal of material for thought and discussions, at times very keen and long, in the process of which a correct Marxist-Leninist understanding and interpretation of the actual essence and tasks of military art were elaborated.

Most of all, arguments emerged around the question of the "strategy of attrition" and the "strategy of annihilation" [*strategiya sokrusheniya*].

According to Svechin's definition, the strategy of annihilation attempts to achieve the assigned aim by a single rush, and it views a series of successive operations as a single whole. The strategy of annihilation strives for decisive victories by an annihilating rout of enemy personnel. It operates by means of elements of speed and direct linearity of operations, and by means of the enormity of the blow. A general engagement is not viewed as a means of conducting war; it is of self-sufficing significance. Everything is subordinated to the basic idea of the strategy of annihilation, which should assure decisive success. And this determines the strategic line of conduct.

The "strategy of attrition" is based on gradually exhausting and weakening the enemy. It combines the successive resolution of limited missions with flexible maneuver tactics to create necessary superiority in the interests of the latest decisive blow. Here, it is not destruction of enemy personnel (this is only part of an armed front's mission), but weakening of the enemy in every possible way, politically and economically, which has prevailing significance. This determines the line of conduct of a strategy of attrition in war.

In essence, these categories in Svechin's definition were a particular treatment of Clausewitz's well-known tenets on wars with decisive and limited aims as applied to the new conditions of the twentieth century. In the widely developed discussion, however, they acquired a different interpretation and began to be viewed in light of the nature of future wars and tasks of revolutionary armies. In this aspect the primary objections against a strategy of attrition were reduced to its being directed against decisive, revolutionary, offensive wars, supported by an outburst of exacerbated class contradictions in the enemy camp. But advocates of a strategy of annihilation had to admit, all the same, that under those conditions of conducting war it was necessary to be oriented not toward lightning, annihilating blows, but prolonged, stubborn war, which could not always be a mobile one, and one in which the tasks of exhausting the enemy were to play no small role.

Generally speaking, it is foolish to juxtapose the above-mentioned categories of strategy one against the other. The one-act Napoleonic annihilating blows had already long ago retreated into the realm of history. Modern wars do not adhere to a single method of conducting war, and "annihilation" and "attrition" as strategic forms can even complement one another and be changed during a war. But all the same, this discussion, which at that time took on a broad character, in sum furthered the strengthening of an offensive beginning in Soviet military doctrine and confirmed its superiority over the defense. It led to further development of views, already stated by Frunze, on the necessity of educating army cadres in the spirit of a maneuver strategy, dynamism, initiative, and decisive actions in offensive operations.

There were also presentations on the advantages of a defensive form of operation as a method of armed combat with insufficient forces and poor rear organization. But these views did not meet with great support. A. I. Verkhovsky, for example, came forward with such a position. Having joined together concepts varied in their content – the defense as a form of combat operation, and defensive war in a political regard – he concluded that a defensive engagement provides enormous political advantages and makes it possible to augment force strength. From this point of view, he concluded, it is more advantageous for us to give up Minsk and Kiev in the first battles than to take Belostok and Brest. The strong choose "Cannae," the weak – "Poltava." Such a strategic concept, in sharp contradiction to the spirit of Soviet military doctrine, was, of course, decisively rejected.

At that time bourgeois military science was experiencing a severe crisis. In searching for expedient forms of developing armed forces, bourgeois military writers proceeded from two positions: an attempt to make maximum use of growing military technology, and a fear of creating and arming mass armies. On this basis there arose the popular (at that time) theories of de Gaulle, Seekt, Zoldan and others on the expediency of organizing small, professional, select armies, well-armed and capable of providing support for the bourgeoisie and the principal force for deploying a mass army in a future war. Other theories, for example, Douhet's and Fuller's, overstated the significance of technology in future war. They correctly noted the great role of large aviation and tank formations in future war, but completely incorrectly assumed that aviation and tanks would be able to decide the outcome of a war in a short time by independent operations.

In reality, not one of the capitalist states set off on the path of these modernist theories; in general they did not find their place in our military-theoretical thought either. Some prominent military writers who did not stand on Marxist-Leninist ideological positions attempted, nevertheless, to substantiate the possibility of substituting in future wars a mass army by a small, technologically equipped and select (with regard to class) army of "knights."[17]

Basing itself on the development of military technology abroad in the 1920s and on the outfitting of the Red Army with it, our military-theoretical thought correctly oriented itself on the profound effect which new military technology could have on army structure and military art. But at the same time it did not reject the principle of mass armies. It should be noted that by the end of the 1920s the army had already been considerably strengthened by new and modern forms of artillery weapons, which sharply increased its fire power.

The five-year plan for the country's industrialization, adopted by the XVI Party Conference in 1929, made it possible to envision the real possibility of reorganizing the army in the near future on principles of broadly mechanizing it and equipping it with aviation technology. The army's technical rearmament, which had already commenced, played an exceptional role in the development of Soviet military theory, which then led to extensive development of the deep operation.

The rudiments of deep battle tactics could be seen in Tukhachevsky's lectures at the end of the 1920s, Triandafillov's work, and I. P. Uborevich's

articles. Tukhachevsky and Triandafillov, in special lecture notes, substantiated the requirement that the Red Army be equipped with tanks and
aviation to conduct combat operations more successfully. Triandafillov considered it expedient to have three tank echelons (direct infantry support,
long-range infantry support, and long-range action), making it possible to
attack the enemy to the entire depth of his combat formation. In 1929,
Uborevich, evaluating the tactical-technical properties of tanks, indicated the
possibility of boldly and swiftly striking the enemy's combat formation in
the shortest possible time and over the greatest depth.[18] Thus, Soviet military-
theoretical thought, outdistancing the development of the Soviet state's
economy, provided the army with a purposeful perspective.

A significant phenomenon in the development of Soviet military-scientific
work in this period was the creation of the Military Section at the
Communist Academy, which began its planned work in 1929 and played a
notable progressive role. It was headed by the well-known Party and military
personality, A. S. Bubnov, and members of its Presidium included M. N.
Pokrovsky, Ya. B. Gamarnik, I. P. Uborevich, R. P. Eydeman, K. A.
Mekhonoshin, and A. M. Vol'pe. The Military Section's mission was to
consolidate the Marxist-Leninist cadres of different specialties who were
working on military-theoretical and military-historical problems.

Two principal factors in these years directly influenced the development
of Soviet military-theoretical thought. A powerful socialist industry began to
develop successfully in the country, and the collectivization of agriculture
was successfully initiated; this created a new, broader materiel-technical and
social base for the Soviet Armed Forces. At the same time, the threat of a
new armed attack against the Soviet Union intensified. The XVI Congress of
the CPSU, in 1930, emphasized the increasing preparation of the imperialists
for war against the USSR. All this demanded new, broad military-theoretical
research. Tukhachevsky wrote at that time:

> we, of course, cannot remain at the former level of our military-
> theoretical thinking ... we cannot fail to take the five-year plan into
> consideration in the Red Army's theory of military affairs ... [we can-
> not fail] to react to it with the appropriate restructuring of military-
> theoretical tenets.[19]

Military-theoretical thought at that time proceeded from the following
general political line, written into the *Field Regulations of 1936*:

> Any attack against the socialist state of workers and peasants will be
> repelled with all the might of the Armed Forces of the Soviet Union,
> with a shift of military operations to the territory of the enemy who
> has attacked. Red Army combat operations will be conducted for
> annihilation. The achievement of a decisive victory and the complete

destruction of the enemy are the primary aim in a war into which the Soviet Union has been drawn.

Soviet military-theoretical thought visualized future war as an armed conflict of enormous, million-man armies in which the opposing sides would pursue decisive aims – complete annihilation of the enemy. War would attain colossal scope and force. It could not be a blitzkrieg, that is, it could not be decided by a single, albeit gigantic strategic operation. It was considered that armed combat would consist of a series of successive blows, which would form a system of successive operations of enormous strategic significance. Soviet military thought reached the conclusion that deployed mass armies would form a continuous strategic front, with its flanks up against inaccessible areas (seas, neutral states, etc.).

It follows from all this that tested armed combat forms and methods, based on past war experience and the old materiel-technical base, even if old equipment were modernized, could not be used without changes to achieve victory. The necessity arose of using those forms and methods of armed combat which would make it possible to surmount the strong fire of a continuous front and destroy the enemy's operational groupings in the interests of achieving strategic success. "The main and principal mission of military art," wrote A. I. Yegorov, Chief of the *RKKA* Staff, "is to prevent the formation of a continuous front by applying an annihilating blow and swift tempo to operations and battle."[20] This meant an attempt to give armed combat a maneuver character and to avoid positional war. Soviet military thought acknowledged the most effective method of resolving this task as being that in which blows of enormous penetrating power were inflicted against the enemy to the entire depth of his formation. Inflicting such blows would be possible only with the help of deep echelonment of the mass of interacting rifle forces, tanks, and artillery, supported by aviation. This method of combat operations acquired the name "deep operation."

The deep operation as a process included several stages: penetration of the tactical defense by the joint efforts of infantry, tanks, artillery and aviation, and the formation of a breach in it; development of tactical success into operational success by introducing a mass of tanks, motorized infantry, and mechanized cavalry through this breach, and also by landing air-assault forces (the routing of reserves and the elimination of the enemy's operational defense); exploitation of operational success (operational pursuit) until the complete rout of the enemy grouping selected as the objective of the operation, and the occupation of a favorable initial position for a new operation. The first stage is the foundation of the deep operation, since without penetration of the tactical defense, the deep operation, in general, cannot take place, that is, it is thwarted. But its essence rests in the fact that cooperating artillery, tanks (several echelons), aviation, and infantry deliver simultaneous strikes against the enemy combat formation to his entire depth, as if to penetrate his defense with a single, deep and powerful surprise blow, forming a breach in the defense and then attempting to reach operational space. Here, all combat arms operate in the interests of the infantry.

The main thing in this method of offensive battle is a rejection of linear combat forms, that is, not striking the enemy on a line of direct contact and pushing him back, but rather pressuring him deeply, expressed by simultaneously destroying, suppressing, and pinning down his main grouping, encircling it, and completely routing him.

The second condition for success of the deep operation is the arrival of mobile forces (tanks, motorized infantry, mechanized cavalry, air-assault forces) in the operational depth of the enemy defense. Only under this condition could a stationary front be penetrated from within; only by using rifle forces and direct and long-range infantry support tanks could a maneuver character be imparted to armed combat.

Accordingly, it was considered that the shock group's operational formation should always include the following: a penetration echelon consisting of rifle forces (reinforced rifle corps); an echelon for developing the penetration, consisting of mobile forces (tanks, motorized infantry, motorized cavalry), and possessing great mobility and shock force; an aviation group and an air-assault group. It was recommended to create shock armies (corps) on the main axis, generously outfitted with combat equipment, transport, and communications means. Another important condition for success of the main operation was gaining air superiority, isolating the engagement region from approaching enemy reserves, and preventing the delivery of materiel to his forces under attack.

The theory of the deep operation affirmed the method of conducting an operation in which operations by shock, holding, and other groups, and penetration echelons and echelons for developing the penetration,[21] tactically unrelated to one another, are combined with respect to front and depth, on the ground and in the air, into an attack mechanism which provides for single purposeful action against the enemy's operational grouping until its complete defeat. Here, possible forms of operational maneuver in offensive operations could be frontal attack; attack on converging axes (dual penetration exploiting a favorable front configuration); combined attack – the organization of several attacks of varied strength on a broad front (so-called "splintering strikes" [drobyashchiy udar]); envelopment (of one or both flanks); and encirclement. All these forms of operational maneuver were subsequently employed extensively during the Great Patriotic War.

Such, in general outline, is the theory of the deep operation, or, in other words, the theory of deep forms of armed combat. Its practicality was assured by the materiel-technical base created by the rapidly developed industry of the Soviet Union.

The technical reconstruction of the army in all fields of development achieved great success. By 1939 its overall result was reflected by the following indicators, cited in the speech by the People's Commissar for Military and Naval Affairs at the 4th Session of the Supreme Soviet in 1939: since 1930, the number of tanks rose 43 times; aircraft – 6.5 times; heavy, medium, and light artillery – 7 times; antitank and tank artillery – 70 times; and machine guns – 5.5 times. If 3.7 horsepower was needed for each soldier in 1930, then in 1939, 13 horsepower was required, despite the fact that during this time overall army strength increased 3.5 times.

At the same time, the system of Armed Forces development was also reexamined. The 1 September 1939 Law on Universal Military Service rejected militia-territorial formations and implemented a complete shift to a cadre army. By 1936 army cadre strength amounted to 1,300,000 men, and by 1937 – 1,433,000 men. The majority were workers and collective farmers who had obtained a general education and were familiar with various kinds of equipment.

Thus, Soviet military theory, reflecting the practical work of Armed Forces development, remained the theory of a mass army equipped with the latest technical combat means.

The theory of deep forms of armed combat occupied an important place in the scientific preparation of officer cadres in the 1930s. The Operations Department of the Frunze Military Academy, and then the General Staff Academy, as well as the Combat Training Directorate, focused much attention on systematization of its tenets and to applied and calculated implementation (as applied to the *front* and army).

In February 1933, the Red Army had already received official guidance, *Vremennyye ukazaniya po organizatsii glubokogo boya* [Provisional instructions for organizing deep battle]. It was issued under the leadership of the Chief of the Combat Training Directorate, A. I. Sedyakin, and published by the General Staff.

In 1936 new Field Regulations came out (*Provisional Field Regulations-36*), which already reflected deep battle tactics and some elements of the deep operation. The field regulations were worked out under the direct leadership of Tukhachevsky and Yegorov. At that time an operations manual was also being prepared, which, however, never saw the light, because of the mass repressions which soon began in the army, engendered by Stalin's cult of personality.

The repressions of 1937 and subsequent years brought enormous harm to the army and to the entire country. They deprived the Red Army and Navy of its most experienced and military-theoretically prepared cadres, talented researchers, and highly qualified military leaders. This had a negative effect on the further development of military-theoretical thought. Thorough study of military-scientific problems and the working out of the principal issues of troop leadership were replaced by narrow, neatly applied solutions – creeping empiricism. And, in general, strategy was not studied as a science and academic discipline. All this was a result not only of the unfounded repressions, but also of the blind alley in which social science, including military science, found itself. Military science was essentially reduced to the compilation of a mosaic from Stalin's statements on military questions. The theory of the deep operation was subjected to doubt on the basis that Stalin had made no statements about it, and that its creators were "enemies of the people." Such elements as, for example, independent operations of motor-mechanized and cavalry formations ahead of the front and in the enemy's operational depth were even called "harmful", and for this ridiculous reason were rejected.

The reasons enumerated above, as well as incorrectly understood limited experience in Spain in 1936–39, led at the end of 1939 to the dismemberment of all mechanized corps – the shock forces of the deep operation. At the same time, there were attempts to change the missions of aviation sharply, essentially reducing them to operations only over the battlefield in close tactical connection with ground forces conducting the battle.

Such measures attested to the backward turn of military theory to linear combat forms on an operational scale.

For these reasons Soviet military-theoretical thought could not properly generalize the combat experience in the Lake Khasan region at the Khalkhin-Gol River, or in the war against the White Finns. Of special significance was the experience of penetrating the Mannerheim Line, whose success was achieved by a structure of deeply echeloned force combat formations and continuous intensification of the attack by reserves from the depth. All this underscored the necessity of new organizational forms and methods for using artillery, tanks, and aviation, which had not been implemented.

The Second World War demonstrated that Fascist Germany was using deep operational methods we had earlier developed. The Germans borrowed the achievements of Soviet military-theoretical thought and applied them, not without success, in the war against Poland and in the West.

Taking into account the experience of the Second World War, which had already begun, the regeneration of mechanized corps was begun in summer 1940. However, time had been wasted. Moreover, by the beginning of the war, the army had not yet been rearmed with new materiel of improved design. The majority of tanks, aircraft, and antitank and antiaircraft guns in the border forces were still old models. They were inferior to German Army equipment with respect to tactical-technical qualities. This was felt especially keenly in vehicular transport and mechanical towing means, which sharply affected force maneuver capabilities.

All this created a definite discrepancy between practical force capabilities and theoretical and academic recommendations with respect to their operational and tactical use.

On the eve of the Great Patriotic War our operational-strategic views were most fully expounded at a meeting conducted by the Main Military Council in December 1940. Their basic tenets were formulated in the concluding speech at this meeting by the USSR People's Commissar for Defense. It was pointed out that our Armed Forces had to be prepared for both maneuver operations and penetration of modern, strongly fortified defensive sectors. The latter was especially emphasized. The experience of penetrating the Mannerheim Line in 1940 strongly influenced these instructions, and a conclusion was reached that with the modern technical outfitting of armies and means for organizing a prolonged defense, the principal type of offensive operation is the penetration, concluding with the enemy's encirclement and complete defeat. The experience of penetrating the Mannerheim Line was cited as an example of organizing the penetration of fortified regions. This tenet on the necessity of organizing the penetration of enemy fortified regions was also widespread in the initial period of the war. Proceeding from the circumstance that a state's borders, especially on the most important axes, are strongly fortified beforehand, and that their envelopment would not always be possible, it was thought that military operations from the beginning of a war would not assume the nature of a meeting engagement, but from the very beginning of the war would require the organization of a penetration of the front right up to the fortified region.

The problem of the initial period of conducting war, with its high level of dynamic combat operations and the struggle for seizing operational and strategic initiative, remained in the shadows. The theory of maneuver operations in the initial period of conducting war was not developed, although by this time there was already the sufficiently extensive experience of Second World War maneuver operations in the West, including the experience of the French Army's positional struggle for the Maginot Line, on which many hopes had been placed and which, as is known, was unsuccessful.

In working out problems of Soviet military theory in our publications, extensive maneuver operations and their peculiarities were undervalued and did not receive proper illumination. It was considered that maneuver could be developed into the enemy's operational depth, after the penetration of his continuous front. Little attention was given to developing methods for conducting defensive operations, particularly a strategic defense, or, in connection with this, methods of conducting combat operations under conditions of withdrawal, encirclement, or breaking out of an encirclement. The process itself of conducting the deep operation was limited by a specifically established design, but reality, as we afterward confirmed, turned out to be more varied and more complex, and, above all, required of all command personnel, from bottom to top, a high level of training, solid skills, and great flexibility in planning and controlling maneuver operations and force actions, especially during the initial period of war.

War confirmed the correctness of views on conducting deep operations, primarily on the use of echelons for operational development of success, especially in 1943, when our offensive operations, in accordance with the existing situation, began with a penetration of the enemy defense, into which mobile forces, tank armies, and tank and mechanized corps were subsequently introduced.

The Great Patriotic War demonstrated that the basic principal tenets of Soviet military theory were correct. They were founded on a correct prognosis of the nature of future war and, accordingly, on a correct system of organizing the Armed Forces and the defense of the Soviet Union.

NOTES

1. *Voprosy strategii i operativnogo iskusstva v sovetskikh voyennykh trudakh (1917–1940)* [Problems of strategy and operational art in Soviet military works (1917–1940)] (Moscow: Voyennoye Izdatel'stvo Ministerstva Oborony SSSR, 1965), pp. 3–24.
2. *KPSS o Vooruzhennykh Silakh Sovetskogo Soyuza. "Sbornik dokumentov" (1917–1958)* [CPSU on the Armed Forces of the Soviet Union. Collection of documents (1917–1958)] (Moscow: Gospolitizdat, 1958), p. 47.
3. *Programma Kommunisticheskoy partii Sovetskogo Soyuza* [Program of the Communist Party of the Soviet Union] (Izdatel'stvo "Pravda"), 1961, p. 112.
4. V. I. Lenin, *Sochineniya* [Works], Vol. 26, p. 151.
5. V. I. Lenin, *Sochineniya* [Works], 5th edition, Vol. 10, p. 340.
6. This collection has been kept in Lenin's personal library in the Kremlin. On the title page of the book there is the inscription, "Copy of V. Lenin. 24/IV – 1920."
7. See the article in this collection [i.e., *Problems of Strategy and Operational Art in Soviet Military Works 1917–1940*] by M. N. Tukhachevsky, "*Strategiya natsional'naya i klassovaya*" [National and class strategy].
8. These articles appear in *Problems of Strategy and Operational Art in Soviet Military Works 1917–1940*.
9. M. V. Frunze, *Sobraniye sochineniy* [Collected works], Vol. 11, p. 32.
10. M. Tukhachevsky, *Pokhod za Vislu* [The campaign for the Vistula] (Smolensk, 1923), pp. 25–7.
11. N. Movchin, *Posledovatel'nyye operatsii po opytu Marny i Visly* [Successive operations on the example of the Marne and Vistula] (Moscow: 1928).
12. N. Varfolomeyev, *Udarnaya armiya* [The shock army] (Moscow: GIZ, 1933). Part of this book is included in *Problems of Strategy and Operational Art in Soviet Military Works 1917–1940*.
13. V. Triandafillov, *Kharakter operatsiy sovremennykh armiy* [The nature of operations of modern armies] (Moscow: GIZ, 1929).
14. N. Ye. Varfolomeyev, "Strategiya v akademicheskoy postanovke" [Strategy in an academic formulation], *Voyna i revolyutsiya* [War and revolution], 11 (1928), p. 88. [Translator's note: the translation of this article appears in this current collection].
15. The primary part of this book is given in *Problems of Strategy and Operational Art in Soviet Military Works 1917–1940*.
16. The most interesting sections of this book are given in *Problems of Strategy and Operational Art in Soviet Military Works 1917–1940*.
17. See the section in A. I. Verkhovsky's work, *Kharakteristika srazheniya budushchego*

[Characteristics of a future engagement], in *Problems of Strategy and Operational Art in Soviet Military Works 1917–1940*.

18. See I. P. Uborevich, *"Operativnoye ispol'zovaniye tankov"* [Operational use of tanks] in *Problems of Strategy and Operational Art in Soviet Military Works 1917–1940*.

19. M. N. Tukhachevsky, *O kharaktere sovremennykh voyn v svete resheniy VI kongressa Kominterna. Zapiski* [On the nature of modern wars in light of the decisions of the VI Comintern Congress. Notes], Vol. 1 (Komakademiya, 1930), p. 20.

20. A. I. Yegorov's article is contained in the collection *Problems of Strategy and Operational Art in Soviet Military Works 1917–1940*.

21. In the Great Patriotic War, the echelon for developing the penetration included mobile troops – tank armies, tank and mechanized troops, and cavalry.

The Development of the Theory of Soviet Operational Art in the 1930s[1]

G. ISSERSON[2]

Soviet military theory, based on Marxist-Leninist study and exploitation of rich past combat experience, was born in the Civil War years and covered a great path of development in the two decades up to 1941.

The military-theoretical views of the 1930s, with which we entered the Great Patriotic War, are of particularly great interest. If in the 1920s our military-theoretical thought relied mainly on the experience of the First World War and was, to a significant degree, focused on the past, then in the 1930s it turned forward, toward an investigation of the problems of future war and methods of conducting it.

This period has special significance in the development of our military theory. It provides a clear picture of vast research work, extensive creative thought, and important principal decisions. Namely, the fundamentals of deep battle and the deep operation, which opened a new page in the theory of operational art, were developed in these years.

The deep form of combat was conditioned by the entire socio-economic development of the Soviet Union and the reconstruction of the Red Army. It was necessary for the solution of the problem of conducting annihilating operations, overcoming a continuous front, and penetrating it to the entire operational depth, that is, achieving an aim which was not and could not be achieved in the First World War.

THE HISTORY OF DEEP BATTLE

For the sake of historical truth it must be mentioned that the issue of deep battle was put forward for the first time by the English military theorist Fuller at the end of 1918. In anticipation of the decisive offensive in 1919 (the Entente did not count on a victorious conclusion to the war in 1918), at that time Fuller proposed that an attack of fast-moving tanks be organized against the depth of the enemy's tactical disposition simultaneously with a tank attack against the forward edge of the defense. It is true that he had not yet formed the concept of a long-range action tank group, although all the tactical prerequisites existed in his proposal.

However, Fuller's theoretical views on the question of deep battle were based on this. The conditions of capitalist development of bourgeois armies compelled him to shift to a theory of small professional armies in which the problem of the offensive was generally decided in a different way. This theory, reflecting the class nature of the capitalist military system, was in clear contradiction to the actual nature of modern war. For Fuller, deep battle was not a battle of combined combat arms. He wrote that "a formation [*soyedineniye*] of tanks with infantry is tantamount to harnessing a tractor in tandem with a cart horse."[3] Of course, such a point of view was, for us, completely unacceptable.

Foreign regulations of the 1930s did not, in general, contain instructions on deep battle in the sense of simultaneous suppression of the enemy's entire tactical depth. This idea belonged to our military-theoretical thought.

If we are to focus on the sources of our first concrete impressions on deep forms of struggle, it is impossible not to mention two 1928–29 documents of great significance.

The first document is a report by M. N. Tukhachevsky on reconstructing the Red Army and supplying it with new, modern armaments, mainly tanks and aviation.[4] Having unfolded in this report an expansive program for the rearmament of the army, Tukhachevsky wrote in conclusion that on the new materiel-technical base one could successfully reject the former wasteful, laborious form of combat against each critical element of the enemy's battle formation individually and shift to new, more effective ways and means of conducting battle, *simultaneously suppressing the entire depth of an enemy deployment.*

The second document is a report by V. K. Triandafillov on the use of tanks in an offensive battle, composed of three groups echeloned according to the range of group actions: *NPP* [*neposredstvennaya poderzhka pekhoty*/direct infantry support], *DPP* [*dal'nyaya poderzhka pekhoty*/long-range infantry support], and *DD* [*dal'nego deystviya*/long-range action],[5] penetrating to varied depths right up to enemy artillery positions and headquarters, thus suppressing the entire tactical depth of enemy deployment, cooperating with long-range artillery and aviation. This method of using tanks was already a practical realization of Tukhachevsky's concept that new, modern means of combat – tanks, long-range artillery, aviation, and air assault landings – made it possible to reject old, slow methods of subsequently striking the enemy piecemeal, and to shift to new forms of simultaneous deep strike. With his report Triandafillov personally laid concrete foundations for new forms of battle and presented the principal sketch of its organization and conduct.

Thus, in the above-mentioned documents Tukhachevsky and Triandafillov for the first time articulated the concept of deep battle and, by this, enormously influenced the path of our army's development and the formation of the principal views of our military-theoretical thought.

This idea had already been reflected in the *Field Regulations of 1929*, which looked far ahead and was the most progressive of the European manuals of that time. Article 191 of the Regulations mentioned the allocation of special battalions to be thrust directly into the second defensive belt. Article 207 precisely established the concept of a long-range action tank echelon designated to go into the depth of the defense simultaneously with the attack on the forward edge. Thus, *Field Regulations-29* already contained the first prerequisites for shifting to deep tactics based on the operations of large combined-arms formations.

In creating the theory of forms of deep combat, Tukhachevsky's and Triandafillov's merit lies in their not lagging behind changing historical conditions, but foreseeing the potentials of new technical combat means at a time when our army did not have them, when it had not yet been reconstructed.

K. B. Kalinovsky (first chief of motor-mechanized troops) carefully worked out the tactics for actions by *NPP*, *DPP*, and *DD* tank groups, and thus placed a practical foundation under the entire concept of deep battle. This foundation can be considered to have been laid in 1930.

The concept of deep battle received recognition at first in academic circles. At the beginning of 1930, the Frunze Military Academy was working on tactical map and terrain problems concerning the new foundations of deep battle, and played a large role in their dissemination in the army. R. P. Eydeman (Chief of the Academy), N. Ya. Kotov, K. A. Chaykovsky, P. I. Vakulich, S. N. Krasil'nikov, P. G. Ponedelin, I. P. Kit-Viytenko, R. S. Tsiffer, and others did significant work in this field at the Academy at that time.

Soviet military theorists were pioneers in this field at a time when the West were still not talking about the tactics of deep battle.

At the beginning of the 1930s, based on real exercise and maneuver experience, Tukhachevsky wrote in one of his service reports:

> Modern means of suppression, used on a massive scale, make it possible to achieve simultaneous attack and destruction of the entire depth of the enemy tactical defensive deployment. These means – in the first place tanks – make it possible to:
>
> (a) suppress the enemy's defensive fire system so that a large part of the artillery and machine guns is not able to take part in repelling the attack and the penetration of the advancing infantry and *NPP* tanks into the depth of the defensive belt;
>
> (b) destroy the system of control, and pin down and isolate enemy reserves so as to rout various echelons of the enemy battle formation in the depth of the defensive belt during the battle.

Tukhachevsky was absolutely clear in his definition of the missions of deep battle. However, they were not all immediately understood. At a plenum of the USSR's Revolutionary Military Council [*RVS*], K. Ye. Voroshilov came out against Tukhachevsky. His criticism disclosed a clear lack of understanding of the essence of the issue, which Voroshilov reduced to a single type of battle, the offensive against an enemy who has halted.

Deep tactics were, of course, basically developed for a more complex type of battle, an offensive against an enemy defense. By its very essence, however, deep tactics were not a type of battle, but a new form and new method of conducting battle, and were to be used in any type of offensive.

Tukhachevsky patiently explained this to Voroshilov in a special report in order to eliminate confusion in the minds of command personnel.[6] I. E. Yakir, I. P. Uborevich, and S. S. Kamenev, representatives of the Higher Command, supported Tukhachevsky, and correct understanding of the essence of deep tactics as a new form and method of modern battle was affirmed.

FIRST BASIC TENETS OF THE DEEP OPERATION

Only half the problem was solved by the establishment of the fundamentals of deep battle. Tactical penetrations were also successful in the First World War with the help of old tactical procedures. The primary essence of the entire problem was how to crown tactical success with operational development of the penetration and, having penetrated a ruptured breech of the front into maneuver space, how to destroy enemy personnel on an operational scale.

Thus, the idea of deep battle immediately touched the very cardinal problem of operational art and defined it by means of a new solution.

Tactics were triumphant, but proponents of the deep operation remained concerned. Then a major misfortune occurred. In the summer of 1931, V. K. Triandafillov and K. B. Kalinovsky perished in an air crash. The family of operational art proponents seemed to be orphaned, and at first operational thought did not find a new path.

Expressing a concern at that time due to the fact that "our military theory lags far behind the country's successful execution of the general party line"; Tukhachevsky said that "in connection with the growth of our socialist economy we cannot remain at the former level of our military-theoretical thought, but should strive for the decisive development of our military-theoretical thought on the basis of Marxism."

After Triandafillov's death, Tukhachevsky continued to work intensively on deep forms of combat. In 1932 he completed the first part of his work, *Novyye voprosy voyny* [New issues of war], conceived on a broad scale, in which he investigated the influence of modern technical combat means on the change in forms and methods of conducting battle and operations.[7] However, the first part of this work contained mainly technical and tactical issues. Apparently, Tukhachevsky intended to treat operational and strategic questions in the second and third parts of the work, in which he proposed to investigate the fundamentals of modern war and the struggle against imperialist coalitions. This work was not considered to be completed.

Nevertheless, it was absolutely clear that changes in tactics also had to be reflected in operational art. The necessity of a decisive step along the path of creating a new theory of conducting operations was recognized by everyone. Pointing to the importance of this mission, Tukhachevsky wrote: "reconstruction of the Army calls for new forms of operational art."[8] The first kernel of truth ripened for this in the concept of deep battle; then new operational thought penetrated into consciousness. Our army attained a degree of development and capabilities for use which authoritatively put forward the demand for new use of forces and means in large-scale, decisive ground and air operations.

All fundamental issues of operational art as a study of the conduct of operations had first to be reexamined from the point of view of completely changed conditions. Such a statement of the question advanced a series of new problems, opening an enormous field for Marxist military-scientific investigation. All the fundamentals existed for stating that the main mission of our operational art consisted of creating new forms and means for decisive, annihilating operations under new historical conditions, with a new army, and on a new materiel-technical base.

Of course, here there was no complete analogy with the tactical resolution of the question, since battle (tactics) and the operation (operational art) have their own qualitative differences determined by spatial and temporal scale and by the differentiation of the force operational force formation from the tactical combat formation, which is a single, connected system of direct interaction. The organization of a deep operational strike, in this respect, was to have an essential distinction from the organization of deep battle, and this posed a number of new problems. The simultaneity of the deep strike could not, on an operational scale, receive such direct expression.

However, one thing was certain: aviation, air-assault landings, and mechanized and motorized formations organized accordingly for independent operational use could also extend their long-range strike to the enemy's operational depth, measured approximately as a distance of 50–60 kilometers, that is, to the line of deployment of operational reserves and forward airfields and headquarters. Here, the problem consisted not only of modern long-range and fast-paced combat means making it possible to organize a deep enemy strike, but also because this is necessary in order to solve fundamentally the problem of operational penetration, which, without a strike to the entire operational depth, cannot be resolved.

It was necessary to translate the principal plan of deep battle into an operational scale. This required, first, motor-mechanized formations capable, with respect to their organization and arms, of resolving independent operational missions. Second, the problem was how to project the efforts of these formations into enemy operational depths. Thus, the main problem of organizing a deep operation was reduced, in essence, to solving the problem of how to convert a tactical penetration into an operational one, that is, how to commit independent motor-mechanized formations into a penetration through a ruptured breach in the tactical defense.

These were the first basic tenets of the theory of the deep operation. But, while only general arguments, they required thorough investigation and needed a theoretical foundation and concrete formulation. The vast work in this direction, begun in 1931–32, was related to the creation of the Frunze Military Academy's Operations Department, which played a definite role in the development of our operational art.

THE OPERATIONS DEPARTMENT OF THE FRUNZE MILITARY ACADEMY

The very establishment of a department signified a new step in the development of the theory of operational art, which had grown out of a tight framework. Thorough study of the problem of conducting modern operations was required. In addition, the current need arose for well-trained and broadly educated personnel possessing the operational perspectives for higher staffs. The Frunze Military Academy's Operations Department, called on to resolve these problems, began its work in autumn 1931. It proposed the commencement of a reexamination of the fundamentals of operational art and established a vast amount of scientific research work, posing and solving a number of new problems. The guiding idea was deep operational forms of combat. Now these began to receive a theoretical foundation and concrete formation.

A collective of intelligent and capable instructors worked in the department, including old military specialists, who thoroughly understood the necessity of reexamining their own opinions on the nature of modern operations and were permeated by new ideas of deep forms of combat. Among the department collective were the instructors A. V. Fedotov (my department assistant), S. N. Krasil'nikov, Ye. N. Sergeyev, and A. M. Peremytov, and technical leaders in various specialties A. N. Lapchinskiy, D. M. Karbyshev, I. I. Trutko, and B. K. Leonardov (from the Military-Medical Academy). Lapchinskiy worked on problems of the use of aviation in an operation. Karbyshev, by means of his work on the organization of modern enemy defense, brilliant in depth and detail, provided the ability to study carefully conditions of a deep penetration. Trutko was in charge of work on the rear, and Leonardov was in charge of the organization of medical evacuation. Having scientifically based calculations of possible losses in a modern operation and the requirement for hospitals and evacuation means, he reworked the entire scheme of medical evacuation in a deep operation. Unfortunately, many of the enumerated department leadership personnel are no longer alive today. A. N. Lapchinskiy died in 1938, D. M. Karbyshev died a hero's death in a Fascist camp; Fedotov, Sergeyev, Peremytov, and Trutko were victims of the anarchy in the years of Stalin's cult of personality.

It should be noted that exceptionally favorable conditions for work in the department were created by the Chief of the Academy, R. P. Eydeman, who knew how to value and respect a young, creatively operating cadre, protect it, and help it.

The instructions of M. N. Tukhachevsky and A. I. Sedyakin (at that time Chief of the Combat Preparation Directorate) had great, inestimable significance for the direction of the Operations Department's work. The broad scope of Tukhachevsky's operational thought and Sedyakin's inquisitive mind were directed at many questions and pointed out the path of their solution.

A. I. Yegorov (then *RKKA* Chief of Staff) also adhered to progressive opinions regarding the new nature of modern operations. He liked and supported any new idea. In 1931 he presented a massive report at the military academy on the "spatial operation" (as he called the deep operation). The report was illustrated by a mobile schematic developed by V. I. Mikulin, instructor at the Academy. The term "spatial operation" was, of course, imprecise, because any space has two measurements on one plane, that is, along the front and in the depth. Maximum spatial sweep had already been achieved during the First World War. Characteristic for the development of operational forms in future war was their extension into the depth. Therefore, the distinction from operations of the past was better and more correctly expressed by the concept of the deep operation. This definition was established for it in Soviet military theory, and was then adopted by all bourgeois military literature.

With respect to Tukhachevsky, Sedyakin, and Yegorov, who occupied leading army posts, the Operations Department met with the broadest support, and this was especially valuable, for we know how difficult it is to lay a new path and make the first breach in opinions already rooted and to which many of the old military specialists in the Academy tenaciously held. One need only recall the disbelief and ironic comments that greeted the works of the Operations Department. This, of course, made work difficult, but it could not halt the development of our military theory. Some of the old specialists simply stayed on the sidelines of this process. However, the majority soon understood the very progressiveness of the idea of the deep operation and firmly stood on the new path, having brought great favor to the development of our operational art. Among them were N. Ye. Varfolomeyev, Ye. A. Shilovsky, N. N. Shvarts, F. P. Shafalovich, A. I. Gotovtsev, and a number of others. Even A. A. Svechin, in the final analysis, agreed with the inevitability of a shift to new combat forms and supported the concept of the deep operation, examining it, however, within the framework of a strategy of attrition [*strategiya izmora*, literally "strategy of starvation"].

Not everything was smooth in the department's work, and acceptance of the new ideas was far from immediate.

Even at the *RKKA* Staff itself there was not, at first, complete unity on the question of the new nature of modern operations. Some Operations Directorate workers (S. A. Mezheninov, and P. S. Obysov) did not support the principal bases of the deep operation. They objected, in particular, to the independent use of motor-mechanized forces before the front and in the depth of a penetration separated from combined-arms formations. However, on these issues the Operations Department had the full support of the *RKKA* Chief of Staff, Marshal Yegorov.

DEVELOPMENT OF THE THEORY OF THE DEEP OPERATION

The entire development of the theory of the deep operation was conducted on an operational scale; at that time we did not concern ourselves with problems of military strategy, such as the conduct of armed conflict on the scale of war as a whole.

Suppression of the enemy's operational depth undoubtedly affected the strategic sphere of armed conflict; however, this required, first of all, the resolution of practical questions concerning the use of motor-mechanized formations and their cooperation with aviation and air-assault landings, which were limited to operational scales.

At the beginning of the 1930s, we had three mechanized corps in all, not enough to combine into larger groups (or armies) of *frontal* designation. Therefore, their use at first was conceived as separate corps jointly operating with motorized divisions and cavalry on an army scale, and the initial step in the development of the theory of the deep operation was the army operation as the operation of a shock army.

In developing this theory two possible situations were kept in mind: when the enemy is approaching in free maneuver movement; and when the enemy, having assumed an organized defensive deployment, forms a dense front of resistance.

In the first instance, when there is extensive dispersal between opposing sides, it was considered possible to organize a deep strike on a selected axis by advancing a group of highly mobile troops (motor-mechanized formations and cavalry), supported by aviation. This group was to be landed in the rear jointly with aviation and an air-assault landing, attack and wrest from the enemy, who was approaching the front, a specific portion of the operational formation, and form in it a breach with bare flanks, causing hesitation on the enemy's part. The principal mission was to prevent the enemy from forming a continuous front and digging in. Those foundations on which a continuous front was structured and held had to be knocked out. The group operating before the front was called the *advance guard echelon*.

Approaching combined-arms formations, comprising the *main echelon*, could be directed to the existing flank and conduct the attack with a decisive aim. Here, the operational depth was not to be left undefended, since it could be subject to a deep enemy penetration. Therefore, it was considered necessary to bring up an army reserve group, in two to three days' march behind the main echelon; this group was called the *reserve echelon*.

Thus, the entire army operational formation during an offensive against an approaching enemy consisted of three echelons (advance guard, main, and reserve) and could occupy as much as 200 kilometers and more in the depth. In this formation deep operational forms were already rather fully expressed.

Resolution of the problem of a deep operation against an established enemy front in a defensive position was more complex.

Four problems required practical resolution to achieve the deep operational aims of a penetration:

(a) What should the operational formation and the operational use of various combat arms (basically, motor-mechanized, combined arms, aviation, and air-assault landing) be?

(b) To what operational depth could and should the operational efforts be projected, keeping in mind their supply situation? (This issue related mainly to the permitted depth of separation of a motor-mechanized group from the front of the combined-arms formations.)

(c) How to organize the operational development of a penetration so that the tactical break in the front immediately develops into an operational break to the entire operational depth, and into complete destruction.

(d) How to isolate the penetrated enemy front in the operational depth so as to prevent concentration of new reserves able to hinder operational development of the penetration, and so as not to allow reestablishment of the penetrated front.

The theoretical and practical development of these problems in a series of map exercises led to the following solutions, which were posited as the foundation of the preliminary concept of the deep operation:

(a) the operational formation of a penetrating army should consist of two echelons: an attack echelon, consisting of combined-arms formations, reinforced by artillery and tanks, penetrating the tactical defense, reinforced by artillery and tanks; and an echelon for developing the penetration, consisting of highly mobile mechanized, motorized, and cavalry formations, developing the penetration through the broken tactical breach of the defense into its operational depth;

(b) the echelon for developing the penetration should be committed shortly after the penetration of the first defensive belt, if it has been broken in a six to eight kilometer-wide sector; in favorable circumstances this can be done even earlier. In this case, the echelon itself suppresses the last resistance in the tactical depth of the enemy defense. In any case, it should intercept the enemy's second defensive belt before he is able to withdraw to it or have his reserves occupy it;

(c) all operational development of the penetration on an army scale is conducted at a depth of 60–100 kilometers – to the line of deployment of the enemy's forward storage facilities and army headquarters;

(d) army aviation (light bomber and ground attack) is used to prepare the penetration and subsequently in operational cooperation with the echelon for development of the penetration, to deprive enemy reserves of the ability to operate and resist in the depth;

(e) *frontal* aviation (long-range bomber) is used to isolate the penetrated enemy front completely from his strategic depth and prevent the approach of strategic reserves;

(f) an air-assault landing is thrust into the depth of deployment of the enemy's forward storage facilities and army headquarters to interact with the echelon for development of the penetration in the operational depth.

This was, in general, the initial principal outline of the deep operation, which was accepted in practice at the Academy in 1932. On this basis, the first operational assignment on the theme "A Deep Offensive Operation Of A Shock Army" was worked out on a map; it was published and distributed to other academies and district headquarters.

In 1932, lectures were given in the Department on deep battle tactics. They expanded the concept, whose foundations were laid by Triandafillov. The Academy published these lectures. In the same year lectures were presented on new problems of the modern deep operation. At first they bore a general theoretical character, but in 1933 they received a more specific, designed formulation. The work *Osnovy glubokoy operatsii* [Fundamentals of the deep operation], published by the Academy, set forth the already applied theory of forms and methods of conducting the deep operation and its development in the depth to a decisive, ultimate result. Its chapters about the work of army headquarters and control of deep operation at each stage of its development acquired important significance.

By order of M. N. Tukhachevsky (then Deputy People's Commissar for Defense), the work was examined by a commission of the *RKKA*'s Staff under the chairmanship of A. I. Yegorov. The commission recognized the necessity of distributing the work as an unofficial manual to all academies and district headquarters. *Fundamentals of the Deep Operation* was published by the Frunze Military Academy in 100 copies, and soon became the text-guide on operational art, playing a specific role in forming the views of our military theory.[9] In this work the theory of the deep operation was simplified for the first time into concrete forms and received applied exposition. It was used as a textbook in 1936 at the then General Staff Academy.

Of course, *Fundamentals of the Deep Operation*, as the first work in this field, written during the first five-year plan when army technical reconstruction was still in its initial stages, far from fully foresaw (or, therefore, solved) all the complex problems of organizing and conducting a deep operation. However, the initial, principal foundations were laid. Subsequently, the theory of the deep operation received further theoretical development, and in the brilliant operations of the Great Patriotic War a number of substantial corrections were introduced into it.

In 1933, an enormous, two-sided operational war game was conducted in the Operations Department. This game reflected the differences of opinion regarding separate principal questions of the deep operation. The argument mainly concerned a mechanized group's capability for independent actions before the front and in the operational depth of the enemy separated from combined-arms formations.

The student playing the role of army commander during the game, under the influence of the present *RKKA* Staff Operations Directorate commanders, refused to advance his mechanized group ahead of the front to attack decisively the approaching enemy. It required persistent interference from those in the role of front command for the course of events to take the desired direction for the aims of the game.

Marshal Yegorov was present during the entire game, which lasted three days. He attentively followed the game's course, and through his guiding questions supported bold use of the mechanized group, full of initiative, to solve independent operational missions. In summing up, the Marshal provided concluding words and said that for the first time in our army the question of the deep operation received such full and developed treatment in a war game. This was an acknowledgement of the specific results achieved in the development of new foundations of our operational art.

PRACTICAL WORK IN THE ARMY

But military theory is never created by a single piece of theoretical research. It is born of practical experience of training an army in peacetime and during its wartime operation. Therefore, it would be completely incorrect to suppose that the theory of the deep operation was engendered and created by a single, closed collective of a military academy's Operations Department.

Deep forms of combat matured so much with the appearance of new armaments, that this theory simultaneously was engendered in the army on the initiative of a number of military figures. Independent of the Operations Department, work on the theory of the deep operation was done at other academies as well, in particular the Armor Academy, Zhukovsky Air Academy, and the Chemical Defense Academy, and in military districts, especially the Belorussian and Ukrainian Military Districts and in the Special Red Banner Far East Army. I. P. Uborevich (Commander of the Belorussian Military District) and I. E. Yakir (Commander of the Ukrainian Military District) and their Chiefs of Staff – Bobrov and D. A. Kuchinsky; the then Deputy Chief of Armored Forces, I. K. Gryaznov; Chief of the Armor Academy M. Ya. Germanovich; Chief of Chemical Troops, Ya. M. Fishman, and other comrades from the armor and artillery academies introduced a number of new tenets into the theory of the deep operation, adding to and developing it.

Experimental exercises with tanks and air-assault landings, conducted by Uborevich, Yakir, and Gryaznov, provided much of value. Troop maneuvers in the 1930s and district war games were, in this respect, a great school and provided a number of valuable theoretical and practical conclusions.

It should be especially noted that Uborevich and his staff developed the combat formation of a motor-mechanized group during its commitment into a penetration and its actions in the operational depth. Uborevich also resolved in a new way the question regarding the battle of an advance guard reinforced by tanks before the approach of the main forces. Yakir and his staff particularly worked out the problem of cooperation between a motor-mechanized group and an air-assault landing in the operational depth. V. K. Blyukher, I. F. Fed'ko, and M. V. Sangursky worked out in practice problems of deep battle as applied to Far Eastern conditions. Under Gryaznov's leadership a number of exercises with tanks were conducted in the Transbaykal region. An enormous amount of work was carried out among the troops, which enriched and deepened our military theory.

In general, if in the Frunze Military Academy's Operations Department the development of questions concerning deep forms of combat inevitably took on a more theoretical character, then in the military districts questions concerning this theory were made all the more concrete and received practical development.

Thus, from the beginning of the 1930s our military theory developed and was generalized, having later taken on the nature of a polished concept of deep forms of combat in the field of tactics and operational art with the completion of army reconstruction and the introduction of more improved armaments into it.

Many comrades, in addition to those mentioned, took part in this work; among them, S. N. Bogomyakov, V. D. Grendal', A. V. Kirpichnikov, V. K.

Mordvinov, P. D. Korkodinov, and B. L. Teplinsky should be mentioned. Basically these were all young cadres filled with enormous enthusiasm and faith in the success of the work on the development of Soviet military theory.

During these years the troops began to retrain on the basis of the new principles for conducting battle. Already in 1931 Uborevich published the first unofficial instructions on deep battle. In 1933, the official instructions of the *RKKA* Staff, developed by A. I. Sedyakin, appeared.

The *Field Regulations of 1929* was already obsolete; under M. N. Tukhachevsky's leadership, the new *Field Regulations of 1936* were developed, fully reflecting for the first time the fundamentals of deep tactics.

One of the leading articles of these regulations stated that ". . . the enemy should be pinned down through the entire depth of his deployment, encircled, and destroyed" (article 164).

During these years the first significant scientific-research work on strategy and operational art and independent use of motor-mechanized formations, aviation, and air-assault landings appeared.[10]

Turning now to the brilliant deep operations conducted by the Soviet Army during the last war, we should recall the period of the 1930s which has been examined. It was then that the foundations of the deep operation were developed and formulated for the first time. Of course, this was only the beginning, and of course the initial concept of the deep operation was far from perfect and required even greater development. However, the beginning was set and it brought a strong foundation to the further development of our operational art. This occurred already in the second half of the 1930s and on the eve of the Great Patriotic War.[11]

In the second half of the 1930s, the development of Soviet military theory continued within the context of the growing threat of war and a series of military events in Europe and other parts of the world. This stage was complex, contradictory, and unstable. The influence of Stalin's cult of personality, which brought the Red Army grievous trials, adversely affected this. However, during these years our military theory continued to improve and expand.

In 1936 the problem of reconstructing the Red Army and rearming it was basically solved, although this process, in connection with continuous technological development and the appearance of new, improved combat means, could never be considered terminated.

New deep forms of battle and operations continued to improve and develop. With the entire course of events of the 1930s, characterized by enormous growth of armed forces on the European continent, these forms received even greater acknowledgement and confirmation. Now Western bourgeois military-theoretical thought, having clearly borrowed this concept from us, began to speak with determination about it and develop it on the pages of its official presses. Behind its general discussions, the German-

Fascist command's already fully concrete views on the use of tank formations and deep echeloning of the battle formation were disclosed.

In 1936 General Guderian, the Fascist theorist of tank war, established the following sequence of using tank formations on the offensive: the first echelon passes directly through the tactical defensive depth and attacks its reserves (this is our echelon for development of the penetration); the second echelon attacks enemy artillery (this is our long-range action group); the third echelon attacks the infantry within the limits of the tactical defensive depth (this is our immediate and long-range infantry support groups). Here, in Guderian's opinion, the use of armored divisions was to be particularly effective when the defense was already detected in a specific sector and the sudden appearance of tanks at that moment would make it possible for them to penetrate immediately beyond the defensive belt into maneuverable space. This entire system of attack, with some changes in sequence, was a copy of our principal outline of deep battle already approved in 1932–33.

Thus, the deep structure of an operation and the operational depth of combat actions were being more and more acknowledged as characteristic of modern conditions. But we had already shifted from these principal tenets to a higher class of mastery of the art of conducting deep operations. This task advanced the necessity for establishing a special institute for expanding the development of operational art and preparing educated higher headquarters commanders. The framework of the Frunze Military Academy's Operations Department was too narrow for this, and at the beginning of 1936 the question of establishing a special military academy as a higher operations school was already posed. It was established in autumn 1936 and named the General Staff Academy. This had great significance for the further development of the theory of operational art. The training of our command cadres was raised to a higher level and entered a new phase.

THE GENERAL STAFF ACADEMY

Work on the theory of the deep operation at the new Academy developed further; however, the work kept to an operational scale and the Academy's academic plan pursued the aim of preparing experts in organizing and conducting modern operations. In essence, this turned the Academy into a technical school for preparing higher staff cadres. From the point of view of practical army needs in a period of establishing new forms of operation, this was correct. However, this narrow mission assignment contained a negative aspect. In 1936 the theory of the deep operation had attained such a level of evolution that it was already impossible to exclude the strategic sphere of its development, and only the strategic scale and situation in an entire theater of military operations could give it a sensible, purposeful significance, warranted under existing conditions.

In the Operations Department, which was the first step in the development of new operational combat forms, the deep operation could still be studied outside of its relationship to the overall strategic situation. However, after the principal outline of the deep operation had been developed, another approach was required. At the General Staff Academy it was necessary to examine the deep operation as a means of carrying out a specific strategic mission and to give it concrete direction, depending on the situation in which it could arise and be developed at the given theater of military operations. In other words, so that the developed scheme of the deep operation could be turned into an actual phenomenon, it was necessary to underpin it with a specific strategic background and inject strategic content into it.

All this was completely clear when the General Staff Academy started its work. However, the smallest hint of the necessity in some way or another of introducing into the Academy a strategy course as a base for operational art met with objections from above. When this issue was raised at one of the meetings before the opening of the Academy, Marshal Yegorov, Chief of the General Staff, with some irritation directly asked Academy representatives, "What are you going to study concerning strategy? A war plan? Strategic deployment? Conduct of war? No one will allow you to do this because this is the business of the General Staff!"

There was, of course, no objection to asking such a question, and the Chief of the Academy, D. A. Kuchinsky, a man with a very lively and practical mind and a great organizer, agreed with the marshal and rejected the conduct of a strategy course at the Academy. But the issue, of course, was not one of studying at the Academy the development of practical problems of a strategic nature, which were the purview of the General Staff. It was a matter of bringing the operational art course closer to the actual military-political situation, created in connection with the deployment in the center of Europe of a large, aggressive army in Fascist Germany. To do this it was necessary to evaluate the new correlation and grouping of forces on the new western border, and to analyze and study the possible situation of war erupting and the nature of its initial period. All this brought the operational art course closer to the scale and problems of strategy, and required enormous research work.

M. N. Tukhachevsky indicated the importance of this task. He believed that it was impossible to answer the question of what the nature of all future war would be, because war changes its forms and nature as a measure of development, which was impossible to divine in advance. But he stated: "The first period of war should be correctly foreseen in peacetime, and it is necessary to prepare for this correctly."[12] Unfortunately, there was no place for such work in the Academy. This was one of the reasons that our military-theoretical thought before the war did not receive proper and flexible strategic orientation relative to those possibilities and conditions under which military operations could begin on our borders. Higher Command representatives were also disinclined to lecture at the Academy on strategic issues, and only Tukhachevsky spoke once at the beginning of 1937 on general problems of modern war. It should be noted, however, that district commanders I. E. Yakir and I. P. Uborevich spoke at the Academy on the question of deep battle and use of motor-mechanized forces in an operation, and conducted war games with the instructors. Corps commander G. P. Sofronov, at that time chairman of a commission working out problems of the use of air-assault landing units, conducted exercises with students and acquainted instructors with this new problem.

Thus, with respect to strategy, the establishment of the General Staff Academy in 1936 changed nothing in our higher military education system. The actual roots of this situation lay in Stalin's cult of personality; policy and strategy questions were considered the exclusive realm of the higher political and military leadership. The negative consequences of this were felt at the beginning of the war in 1941, when many within the high chain of command (of *fronts* and armies) were confronted with the necessity of independently examining a large-scale situation and making serious decisions of strategic significance. A certain confusion, and an inability to grasp a complex situation in its totality, make expedient decisions on a large scale, and subordinate the entire course of events to this were, to a significant degree, the result of a lack of strategic orientation and a lack of training to think in terms of large categories of strategic significance. We paid a heavy price in 1941 for our narrow view on the tasks of preparing cadres and for the inadequate development of our military-theoretical thought in the field of strategy.

The leading Academy departments (operational art and tactics of higher formations) understood the significance of strategic issues for the proper direction of their work. In winter 1936-37, their chiefs turned to M. N. Tukhachevsky, First Deputy People's Commissar for Defense, with a request to clarify a number of strategic questions. The meeting with Tukhachevsky concerned important problems of modern war, its initial period, and forms and methods of conducting modern operations.[13] It had great significance for the structure of the Academy's operational art course, introduced clarity into the understanding of many important problems, and pointed out in which direction our military-theoretical thought should develop. Of course, the academic course plan was dictated by General Staff directives, but Tukhachevsky played a large role in posing a number of operational problems.

The Operational Art Department worked out operational tasks based on the actual perspective of the initial period of war it was able at that time to imagine. This representation was, of course, far from the situation in 1941, impossible to foresee at that time. It is true that the forces of Fascist Germany and her probable allies were viewed as the principal enemy; however, strategic conditions and operational forms of deployment on our western border in the initial period of war were far from sufficiently investigated.

It was suggested that during initial strategic deployment a continuous front would be formed, requiring penetration and making a frontal attack unavoidable. From the point of view of force calculations and theater capacity, this was, in general, correct. However, here the new capabilities of motor-mechanized forces to penetrate the front before it could be organized and established, thus bringing it into confusion at a great depth, were not taken into consideration.

The development of a maneuver course of operations was, of course, foreseen, but mainly after the penetration of a front. In the operational depth maneuver actions were to attain the widest development and decisive result. To acquire this capability, however, it was considered necessary first to penetrate the front. Principal attention was concentrated on the resolution of this most difficult task.

According to views accepted at that time, supported by Marshal Yegorov, it was proposed during the initial period of war to invade the enemy's border territory, disrupt his mobilization and concentration, and support one's own force deployment, all by dynamic air and ground operations. These missions were to be carried out along the most important operational axes by invasion groups consisting of motor-mechanized and cavalry formations and border forces supported by strong aviation. Operations by these invasion groups thus took the form of separate operations conducted before the deployment of the main forces. Their nature recalled old methods of operations not unlike the invasion by the German group into Belgium at the beginning of the First World War to capture Liège.

This was the initial point of view. Tukhachevsky came out against it with good reason. According to his weighty considerations, separate invasion group operations in the presence of fortified borders, heavy composition, and a high degree of readiness of border forces could not be counted on for success and could lead to great losses. In 1934, Tukhachevsky in one of his service lectures had already written that

> the conduct of war by means of old methods, that is, in previous forms of strategic deployment, is impossible … the old usual notions of concentrating mass armies along the railroads leading to the border and on the mass nature of border engagements no longer correspond to actual conditions.[14]

Foreseeing the great vulnerability of border theaters of war with respect to enemy aviation, he considered the entire accepted plan for mobilization and concentration of mass armies to be obsolete, requiring fundamental changes. Tukhachevsky proposed maintaining heavy forward armies in the border sector as the main forces' first operational echelon. In his opinion, in a period of threatening war these armies should be covertly concentrated in areas occupying, if possible, flank positions with respect to those axes along which the enemy was most likely to initiate military operations.

Tukhachevsky attached great significance to fortified regions constructed on the border. In his view, fortified regions were to be a shield, absorbing the enemy advance themselves and covering the concentration of forward armies – a hammer inflicting a flank strike on the enemy. However, a passive-defensive significance should in no way be attached to fortified regions. They were, in Tukhachevsky's opinion, an operational factor organically connected with dynamic field army operations, and a fulcrum for their maneuver in the overall offensive operation.

These were the principal theoretical views on the nature of operations in the initial period of war. Unfortunately, we did not use them, due to the different political-strategic situation in which we found ourselves in June 1941.

Proceeding from these views, which at that time had weighty foundation, in 1936 the General Staff Academy began work on developing our military theory and preparing higher command personnel. The Academy's primary operational task encompassed the successive development of the deep army offensive operation in the Belorussian–Polish theater of military operations. It was worked on at the Academy for two to three consecutive years. In working out this task, the entire collective of the Operations Department participated, as did student M. V. Zakharov (now Marshal of the Soviet Union), who was attached to the department.

Questions concerning the deep operation received more detailed and multi-sided treatment. Three variants were envisioned for committing an echelon for developing the penetration:

First variant – with a weakly occupied defense and in the absence of large enemy reserves, the echelon for developing the penetration is committed at the very beginning of the attack or before complete penetration of the tactical depth of the enemy defense. In this case the echelon for developing the penetration should itself make a breach in the defense and penetrate into its depth. Such a variant provides, of course, the most rapid offensive tempo, but it can be used only against a weak enemy.

Second variant – this is considered to be the most normal case: the echelon for developing the penetration is committed after the tactical depth of the enemy defense has been penetrated and a breach opened in it. It was suggested that with an average-strength defense and the presence of adequate offensive means, this could be achieved at the end of the first day of battle.

Third variant – the most complex, when it is necessary to penetrate a strongly-fortified sector, and the penetration of the tactical depth of the defense itself can lead to serious battles lasting several days. In this case the commitment of the echelon for developing the penetration is possible to reinforce a tactical attack in the depth, followed by complete penetration of the defense jointly with advancing troops. Such a variant for using an echelon for developing the penetration is considered the least desirable, since it leads to the exhaustion of forces before the principal mission has begun to be carried out in the operational depth. However, this variant cannot be excluded in penetrating a permanently fortified sector.

Several variants of actions by an echelon for developing the penetration into the operational depth were also worked out.

The first is the so-called *short* variant: in the absence of significant enemy reserves, a comparatively weak echelon for developing the penetration, having intercepted the second defensive belt, immediately turns to the rear of the defense to encircle and destroy defending garrisons jointly with forces attacking from the front. In this case only forward motorized detachments and reconnaissance are thrown into the operational rear (up to 50 kilometers).

The second is the so-called *deep* variant: a strong echelon for developing the penetration immediately rushes against enemy operational reserves to attack and destroy them, cooperating with aviation and an air-assault landing in the deep rear. In this case the entire attack can extend to a depth of as much as 100 kilometers, while separate blocking motorized infantry detachments are left in the rear of enemy garrisons still defending from the front.

Finally, the third is the *combined* variant: the echelon for developing the penetration interacts with another echelon for development committed by a neighboring army. In this case, the two echelons for developing the penetration, operating from various directions and heading toward each other, should close the ring of encirclement around a large enemy group and destroy it.

In one way or another, all these variants were used in the Great Patriotic War.

After this, the entire theme of the offensive operation was broadened by the commitment of a cavalry-mechanized army [*konnomekhanizirovannaya armiya*], controlled by *front* command.[15] Thus, the development of the deep operation took on a strategic character. However, since this pursued only the aim of studying the activities of a cavalry-mechanized army consisting of several mechanized and cavalry corps and motorized divisions, supported by aviation and an air-assault landing, the sphere of the strategic operation was still far from being grasped.

In any case, the deep operation received further development at the General Staff Academy, posing for our military-theoretical thought a number of new questions. In this respect, 1936–37 were the years of its take-off and animation. Unfortunately, this ascent did not last long.

A DIFFICULT PERIOD

In spring 1937, events shook the Red Army to its very foundations. Arbitrariness and anarchy engendered by Stalin's cult of personality spread over a large part of the higher and senior command personnel. The victims were honored and experienced cadres, and the army was, in essence, beheaded. For many years these cadres had been in charge of army training and the operational preparation of its command personnel, advancing Soviet military theory by indicating the path for its development. Now they were declared "enemies of the people," while the military-theoretical work they created on new forms of battle and operations were called into question and declared all but sabotage. All textbooks, official and unofficial military literature, whose authors had been repressed, were removed, and it was not known by what one could or could not be guided in military theory. Even at the General Staff Academy they began to sound the retreat on the basic issues of the deep operation, taking exception to motor-mechanized formation operations before the front and their use to develop the penetration into the depth. And all this occurred one year before the maneuver operation fully revealed its new nature in the autumn 1939 German–Polish campaign.

The incorrectly understood and generalized experience of the war in Spain also had a negative influence on acknowledging the new ideas. A thoroughly mistaken, historically near-sighted conclusion was drawn from this that the new combat means only provided the ability to conduct a modern attack, but they changed nothing in its nature and forms.

After the war in Spain and our marches of liberation into Western Belorussia and the Western Ukraine, mechanized corps – the main shock forces of the deep operation on the ground – were even disbanded in the Red Army, and the development of bomber aviation – the main shock force in the air – was curtailed. Such incorrect measures deprived the theory of the deep operation of the primary material base upon which it was being developed. The disbanding of mechanized formations did great harm to the army.

Everything mentioned above could not help but affect the development of our theoretical views. Creative initiative was rigidly paralyzed for a time. The seed of doubt was sown in military thought, and instead of expanding and developing the theory of the deep operation, already knocking on the door of history, it began to be repudiated by unspoken impediments.

This, of course, could not help but kindle certain confusion in the minds of young command personnel who, after 1937, were advanced to high command positions and in 1941 were to bear the first blows inflicted by the German-Fascist command in the style of the deep operation. The fact that these young, honorable, brave chiefs could not correctly act in the whirlpool of events into which they were suddenly drawn at the beginning of the war was explained, to a certain degree, by the fact that they were not adequately oriented to the new nature of the deep operation which they were encountering.

In summary, during 1937–38 a certain deviation from the correct line of development of our military theory occurred, causing a certain stagnation and uncertainty in this field. Although this set-back left serious consequences, it was, however, only temporary.

A NEW ASCENT

The cult of personality could not stop the general forward movement in the development of Soviet military theory. In 1939 military-theoretical thought took new steps in its further development, taking into consideration the experience of ongoing military events. It is true that the "Phony War" in the West and the Soviet–Finnish War in winter 1939–40 hid the actual forms of a large modern war and even could have been misleading. The Maginot Line was still unassailable and inevitably determined the positional nature of war. The war in Finland seemed to confirm this.

Thus, in reality the forms of deep operations remained undisclosed. Only the German–Polish War in September 1939 was the first implementation in action of new deep forms of combat. Of course, this was only a separate campaign, and conclusions from it could not yet have ultimate significance.[16] However, in eight months events broke in the West which fully revealed the nature of deep operations at the high level of a large, modern European war.

Initial events of the Second World War in Poland and France already demonstrated that Soviet military-theoretical thought was following the true path and correctly envisioned deep forms of modern operations. However, their clearly expressed maneuver nature and unprecedented scope (with respect to depth) exceeded all the most optimistic suppositions. The campaigns of 1939 in Poland and 1940 in France revealed the new nature of the initial period of modern war. They demonstrated that military operations begin with an invasion by the armed forces' main mass, concentrated beforehand. They imparted to the initial period of war a picture of suddenly developing, large strategic-scale operations, and required their examination from a strategic point of view. Under these conditions operational art not only moved closer to strategy, but also intertwined with it in organic interdependence.

However, our operational art was locked, to a certain degree, within its own framework, while the strategic sphere, unfortunately, chiefly remained outside of military theoretical research. Requisite attention was not directed to revealing the initial period of war, and necessary theoretical conclusions were not made applicable to our Western Theater of Military Operations. This was an indisputable problem of our military theory and, of course, was evident at the beginning of the war in 1941.

During the last years before the war, forms and methods of conducting operations continued to be studied at the General Staff Academy chiefly on an operational scale, irrespective of the strategic situation which could arise at the beginning of war. However, under the influence of ongoing events in military-theoretical thought, a definite shift occurred. First, the study of maneuver operations occupied a significantly greater place. Second, the problem of operational-scale defense attracted general attention. Young commanders remaining at the Academy after graduation infused a fresh spirit into creative work. They comprised the principal cadre of instructional personnel. Among them were I. Kh. Bagramyan (now Marshal of the Soviet Union), F. P. Isayev, V. Ye. Klimovskikh, N. V. Korneyev, A. V. Sukhomlin, N. I. Trubetskoy, A. M. Shimonayev, P. G. Yarchevsky, and others. The older generation of specialists – A. I. Gotovtsev, A. V. Kirpichnikov, S. N. Krasil'nikov, F. P. Shafalovich, N. N. Shvarts, Ye. A. Shilovsky, and others – also contributed during these years their vast experience and knowledge in solving new problems.[17]

THE THEORY OF OPERATIONAL DEFENSE

In 1938, for the first time in the General Staff Academy's existence, the question of a defensive operation was put forth. The reasons for this were not openly discussed in academic circles. However, every operational art proponent understood that in encounters with the strong, aggressive army of German Fascism in specific front sectors, and during specific time periods, defense would be a natural, and in some cases unavoidable, method of operation in order to stop the onslaught of a strong enemy and exhaust him. Meanwhile, defense on an operational scale presented less of a research problem. Over the entire history of the Frunze Military Academy and the General Staff Academy, the theme of "The Army On The Defense" had not once been studied. Tactically, the defense had been well developed by us and occupied a place in all the field regulations befitting its significance. However, to speak about army defense on an operational scale in a significant sector of a theater of military operations was considered somehow improper and all but contradictory to our offensive doctrine. There was no consideration here that the latter did not exclude defensive operations as a type and method of military action. One could adhere to an offensive doctrine and have a theoretically well-developed defense. Conversely, one could, in fact, adhere to a defensive doctrine and neglect careful development of defensive questions on an operational scale, as the French did. That is the dialectic of this issue, which, unfortunately, was not clarified properly.

During the First World War, the defense, despite exceptionally strong engineer-tactical development, did not achieve operational organization. Everything was reduced to fighting only to maintain the tactical defensive zone. Reserves were designated to resolve this mission only by counter-attacks and counterstrokes. When the tactical zone was penetrated, the defense moved back and resistance was organized on a new line. With the fall of a tactical zone, all operational capabilities of the defense were exhausted, and concentration of new reserves, who either reestablished the former position if possible, or created a new defensive front, was required.

Now it was considered necessary to resolve the question of defense and its forms in a new way. Depending on offensive methods, the operational-scale defense was to assume a deep nature and be capable of holding, even in case of penetration by enemy tank formations into its rear. For this purpose, it was suggested the army organize, within its framework, a tactical defense zone out of two defensive belts joined by a series of cut-off antitank lines, and to turn every populated area and every convenient sector in the army rear (with respect to relief) enclosed by the army defensive belt into an antitank "fortress." An army defensive region could occupy up to 75–100 kilometers in depth. This concept envisaged an enemy tank group, having penetrated through the tactical defense zone, falling into a labyrinth consisting of anti-tank regions ("fortresses") in the operational depth, against which it would be destroyed. The defensive formation itself was to force the enemy to develop the offensive in the depth not as was planned, but as predetermined by the entire system of created lines and antitank "fortresses." Namely in this respect the defense was to impose its will on the attacker; it would be conducted in an area of great depth and would be a uniform operational system.

The theory of operational defense was set forth in a work published by the Academy, *Osnovy oboronitel'noy operatsii* [Fundamentals of the defensive operation]. A large operational task was also worked out on a map at the Academy, whose theme was "Army Defense with Delivery of a Counterstroke." The development of a defensive operation in a new way undoubtedly enriched Soviet military theory and had similar significance for the development of defensive forms as the deep operation had for the development of offensive forms.

ON THE EVE OF THE WAR

Thus, during the last years before the war, the circle of operational questions significantly broadened. This notably affected the vigor of our military-theoretical thought.

The December 1940 meeting of the Higher Military Council had great significance for the development of Soviet military theory on the eve of the war; here the results of the military events of 1939 and spring 1940 were discussed, important talks on the nature of modern operations were heard, and a decision was made to create anew the mechanized corps.

At the end of the 1930s, enormous work was carried out in publishing new official instructions, regulations, and directives. New draft *Field Regulations*, worked out in 1939, corrected the *Field Regulations of 1936* on the basis of the latest experience, and significantly broadened the concept of deep battle. For example, a new article (No. 294) on the development of the penetration with an indication of those missions which fell to combined-arms formations at the moment that units of the echelon for developing the penetration passed through a breached defense was included in the draft Regulations. Also new in the draft *Field Regulations-39* was the chapter "On The Foundations Of Troop Control In Battle," which set forth principal questions concerning operational decision-making and execution. While clearly expressing offensive ideas, the draft Regulations at the same time assigned a significant place to the defense, particularly pointing out the necessity for its deep echelonment.

The draft *Field Regulations-39*, reworked in spring 1941, was the last regulations before the war. It concluded the process of enormous work on regulations, reflecting the rapid and stormy development of our military-theoretical thought.[18] From 1925 through 1940, four Field Regulations (1925, 1929, 1936, and the draft *Field Regulations-39*) appeared. Each of these developed deep battle forms even more broadly, and the results determined a specific stage in the development of our military theory, which clearly reflected the overall nature of its forward motion.

DEVELOPMENT OF MANUALS AND QUESTIONS REGARDING THE CONDUCT OF OPERATIONS

It was significantly more complex to develop manuals on the conduct of operations. The necessity of such a manual, which did not exist in the past, arose from the new nature of the deep operation as a complex system of using qualitatively different combat efforts in a single, centralized, uniform joint operation on the ground and in the air. In 1934, a draft manual on the conduct of operations was worked out by A. V. Fedotov according to tasking by Marshal Yegorov; however, the General Staff did not accept the draft plan. At the end of summer 1936, a new draft of a manual was worked out according to tasking from Marshal Yegorov. This task was complex and its expediency doubtful. The theory of the deep operation was still in the process of development; it was still not stable enough to be settled conclusively. In addition, it was necessary to base the manual for the conduct of operations on the foundation of a definite strategic concept, at least for the initial period of war, and a prognosis of the principal lines of its subsequent development. But this complex, higher realm of strategy was poorly researched. Therefore, the draft manual took the form of only an account of techniques of conducting, supporting, and controlling an operation. Throughout the winter of 1936–37, the draft which had been worked out stayed with A. I. Yegorov; afterwards, in connection with the events of 1937, it remained within his sphere.

Once again, work on the manual helped in thinking through all the principal tenets of the deep operation, formulating them more precisely, and editorially refining them. In the draft manual they received more mature, clearer, and more established expression. One copy of this draft was sent to the General Staff Academy and used as the basis of instruction for the Academy's operational art course. Its separate sections were issued for use as an unofficial textbook under the title, *Osnovy vedeniya operatsii* [Fundamentals of conducting operations].

An attempt to publish the manual on conducting operations was not resumed before the war. In sum, before the war we did not have any operational instructions or official manual on operational art. There was no such handbook in any European army, even the German Army. In general, there was doubt as to whether a stable, official manual on the conduct of operations could play a positive role in a period of great changes in forms and methods of conducting armed combat. It was much more important to continue the comprehensive study of the problems of operational art in their further development, and to inculcate new ideas of deep combat forms to the broad contingent of operational art proponents. This mission was carried out by the General Staff Academy, whose students were directly trained and educated in the spirit of the concept of the deep operation, which was at the basis of their military thought. From this medium, a number of prominent commanders and organizers of triumphant deep operations came forward during the Great Patriotic War.

Along with the principal tenets of our operational art, higher command personnel were familiar with instructions and large-scale war games and maneuvers conducted in the districts. Therefore, despite the absence of official instructions on conducting operations, the fundamentals of operational art were well known to higher command personnel, and this was felt in full measure when the Soviet Army, after the difficult initial period of war, shifted to conducting decisive offensive operations. The enormous significance of the vast creative work in the field of military theory which was conducted before the war came to light. At the beginning of the war, however, on the strength of existing conditions, this theory could not be effective or applicable.

CONCLUSIONS

An investigation of the history of the development of Soviet military-theoretical thought would be incomplete and would not achieve its aim if the question were not disclosed and explained as to why our military theory, which envisioned to such a great extent and so correctly the nature of future operations, was not able to play a positive role in the difficult situation which unfolded during the initial period of the war. Serious conclusions should be drawn from this.

Despite a number of operational-strategic questions, including the problem of the initial period of war, remaining unresearched, on the eve of war we had a progressive military theory, with respect to its principal tenets. It proceeded from, above all, a correct prognosis of future war as an attack against the Soviet Union by a coalition of capitalist countries, and as a struggle against them not for life, but to the death.

It foresaw the stubborn and prolonged nature of this struggle, requiring the enormous effort of all the country's moral and material forces. Tukhachevsky wrote, "We must take into account the fact that a difficult, prolonged war lies before us, we must be able to distinguish periods of the war, and we must be able to consistently dismember and eliminate the coalition of capital."[19] It was namely this initial position which required of our military theory a clear solution of the problems of the subsequent conduct of offensive operations with the most decisive aims, right up to routing the enemy on his own territory, and which imparted to our military doctrine a clearly expressed offensive character. However, keeping in mind the prolonged and intense course of the struggle against its unavoidably changeable flow, our military theory foresaw a series of consecutive stages and war campaigns of the most varied operational-strategic nature and content.

In no way was it thought that the war would end by a single lightning blow, and it was namely this realistic point of view, and many others, which distinguished our military theory from the Fascist adventuristic strategy of a total lightning war (blitzkrieg). The entire course of the Great Patriotic War demonstrated the correctness of our point of view and completely confirmed it by its actual development from beginning to end.

In the field of operational art, our military theory structured the conduct of an operation on the deep strike against the enemy, achieved by means of joint use of combat arms and types of weapons, each of which, depending on the given concrete situation and available assets, was accorded more or less significance. The reliable strike against the entire operational depth expressed the main idea of our theory of operational art.

Our theory acknowledged the offensive operation as the principal type of operation. However, a deeply echeloned defense found its place in the theory and design of the draft *Field Regulations of 1939* and was completely elaborated. Military-theoretical research, in general, provided sufficient foundation for the conduct of various types of operations: penetration, maneuver actions, envelopment, encirclement, actions in the operational depth of various types of defense, and breaking out of an encirclement. In our operational art theory, army and *front* commands were able to find an adequate foundation for expedient operational-strategic decisions and organization of operations under the most complex situational conditions. Another question concerned what type of operation and which operational forms and methods were to be selected. This depended on the concrete situation and required its correct clarification and great flexibility of thought not bound by any dogma. But it was namely here that our school of operational training was not at a sufficiently high level.

We were bound by specific tenets of a declaratory nature on the offensive conduct of war; on the fact that we would shift military operations to enemy territory, etc. These tenets were presented from the top as immutable guiding directives of our military policy and strategy, and were placed at the foundation of all military thought of command personnel. During Stalin's cult of personality, they acquired the significance of law and were not subject to theoretical discussion. In sum, the entire military frame of mind imagined future war no differently than a rapid shift to the offensive. All other possibile strategic situations were excluded and not examined by theory.

Even the events unfolding in 1939 in Poland and in 1940 in France did not change or shake these dominating official views. Not that in the depth of consciousness the higher General Staff officers did not understand that the situation in the initial period of war could unfold completely differently. In some General Staff and General Staff Academy circles they even spoke about this rather concretely, with appropriate calculations in their hands. However, these conversations were conducted only behind closed doors and went no further than the offices.

Therefore, the circumstances in which the Great Patriotic War commenced in June 1941 were unexpected for our higher command's entire subjective strategic and military-theoretical orientation, which gave birth to definite confusion and an inability to understand events thoroughly, subordinate them to the will of the command, and seize the initiative. The orientation of military-theoretical thought, on which our command was nurtured over the years, continued through its own inertia to influence military speculation, although it had long since come to contradict the actual facts of strategic actions which had arisen on our western borders, at least from autumn 1940, when Hitler began to concentrate his forces in Western Poland and East Prussia.

The situation existing at the beginning of the Great Patriotic War required a completely different strategic orientation. But rapid change in the mind-set of the military command, already involved in deadly engagements with the invading enemy, was not supported by inculcation of flexible thought free to make necessary operational decisions under existing conditions. It was namely this that explains the reasons for the failure of the command of higher formations to extract benefits from our advanced military theory, which it could have acquired in the initial period of the war.

In addition, at the beginning of the war there were no older, experienced military leaders who had created Soviet military theory and would have been able to implement it with a high degree of skill, nor was there an adequate number of operationally prepared commanders. Therefore, the serious drama played out in summer 1941 had deep-seated roots of political and strategic significance associated with Stalin's cult of personality. The consequences of this were immeasurably severe. They required tremendous sacrifices and caused enormous losses.

But the heroic Soviet people, led by the great Communist Party, were able to overcome the serious consequences of the initial period of war. And when this occurred, the Soviet Army opened a brilliant series of deep operations of unprecedented strategic scope. These operations received such splendid implementation because, in addition to other decisive factors, their principal foundations were worked out before the war by advanced Soviet military theory. They enriched it, contributed much that was new, and created a rich fund of Soviet military art.

NOTES

1. G. Isserson, *"Razvitiye teorii sovetskogo operativnogo iskusstva v 30–ye gody,"* *Voyenno-istoricheskiy zhurnal* [Military-historical journal], 1 (January 1965), pp 36–46.
2. G. S. Isserson in the 1930s occupied the post of chief of the operations department at the Frunze Military Academy, and was then the chief of the department of operational art at the General Staff Academy. In the present article, the author, using personal recollections, summarizes his views on the development of the theory of Soviet operational art in the 1930s.
3. J. F. Fuller, *Operations Of Mechanized Forces*, translated from the English (Moscow: Voyenizdat, 1933), p. 13.
4. This report was known to a narrow circle of workers of the Staff of the Workers' And Peasants' Red Army (*RKKA*). It is discussed in greater detail in "Zapiski sovremmenika o M. N. Tukhachevskom" [Notes of a contemporary on M. N. Tukhachevsky], *Voyenno-istoricheskiy zhurnal*, 4 (1963).
5. At first, Triandafillov called the two latter groups *TIP* (*tanki – istrebiteli pulemetov*/tanks – machine gun destroyers) and *TIA* (*tanki – istrebiteli artillerii*/tanks – artillery destroyers).
6. In November 1933, Tukhachevsky again turned to Voroshilov on this issue, and in a service report wrote:

   > . . . after your speech at the Plenum of the Revolutionary Military Council, an impression was created among many people that, despite new weapons in the army, tactics should remain old. . . . After the Plenum there began a complete fermentation in the minds of the commanders. Conversations are taking place concerning the rejection of new forms of tactics, rejection of their development . . .
   > (See M. N. Tukhachevsky, *Izbrannyye proizvedeniya* [Selected works], Vol. 1 (Moscow: Voyenizdat, 1964) p. 18.)

7. In 1936, Tukhachevsky significantly reworked the first part of his work, having in mind the rebirth of a large aggressive army in Fascist Germany. Unfortunately, the reworked manuscript has been lost.

8. Tukhachevsky, *Selected Works*, Vol. I, p. 12.

9. Unfortunately, not a single copy of this work exists today – all were destroyed in the period of Stalin's cult of personality.

10. Among the scientific works published at this time, the following should be mentioned: N. Ye. Varfolomeyev, *Udarnaya armiya* [The Shock Army]; M. R. Galaktionov, *Temp operatsiy* [Rates Of Operations]; V. A. Melikov, *Problemy strategicheskogo razvertyvaniya* [Problems Of Strategic Deployment]; Ya. M. Zhigur, *Sovremennyye operatsii* [Modern Operations] (this work was not published and the manuscript was lost); A. N. Lapchinsky, and a number of others.

    In 1932 there appeared the first edition of G. S. Isserson's *Evolyutsiya operativnogo iskusstva* [Evolution Of Operational Art] (the second, supplemented edition appeared in 1937), in which the development of forms and methods of armed struggle in modern war was researched and a foundation for the theory of deep operation was given. In it, the fact was emphasized that we are on the threshold of a new epoch of military art and should transfer from a linear strategy to a deep strategy.

    In December 1932, an analysis of this book was made in the Central Club of the Red Army named for Frunze. The Chief of the Combat Preparation Directorate, A. I. Sedyakin made the primary report, saying that ". . . the book is very instructive, providing a useful creative exercise and correct direction for operational thought."

    According to Sedyakin's conclusion, ". . . the work on the whole, with a few corrections, quite correctly illuminates the problem of operational art" and "is for this great matter the first and very valuable contribution" (*Voyna i revolyutsiya* [War and revolution], 1–2 [1933], pp. 113–18).

11. Translator's note: the first part of the article ends here; it is continued in *Voyenno-istoricheskiy zhurnal* [Military-historical journal], March 1965, pp. 48–61.

12. M. N. Tukhachevsky, *Selected Works*, Vol. 1 (Moscow: Voyenizdat, 1964), p. 261.

13. This conversation is given in more detail in "Notes of a Contemporary on M. N. Tukhachevsky." See *Voyenno-istoricheskiy zhurnal*, 4 (1963).

14. Tukhachevsky, *Selected Works*, Vol. 1, p. 24.

15. This task was worked out by A. V. Kirpichnikov, now Lieutenant General (retired).

16. In the German–Polish war of 1939 there were many specific conditions favorable to the conduct of a deep operation. At first the German deployment occupied an enveloping position with respect to Poland. The Polish theater was not fortified and represented full freedom of maneuver. The front was not continuous, and the Germans had a great superiority in forces and equipment, with complete dominance in the air.

17. In the first part of the article, in enumerating military personalities contributing to the development of the theory of deep operation, the author made an omission by not naming A. Ya. Lapin, who worked in the beginning of the 1930s in the Military Preparation Directorate of the *RKKA*. A. Ya. Lapin actively participated in the development of the theory of deep battle and contributed many substantive suggestions to it.

    It was also mistakenly indicated that I. I. Trutko was a victim of the anarchy during the years of Stalin's cult of personality. In actuality, Major General I. I. Trutko perished in September 1941 while breaking out of the encirclement in the area north of Bedanovko, Lokhgistkiy region, Poltava *oblast'*, Southwestern Front.

18. Translator's note: the Russian word *burnyy* can mean "stormy," "impetuous," "rapid"; in light of the direct references to the cult of personality and indirect references by the author to the purges throughout the article, the term was probably deliberately chosen for its possible double meaning to describe the development of Soviet military thought.

19. M. N. Tukhachevsky, *Selected Works*, Vol. 1, p. 261.

Was Our Military Theory in the 1920s Turned to the Past?

A. GOLUBEV[1]

An article by G. Isserson, *"Razvitiye teorii sovetskogo operativnogo iskusstva v 30-e gody"* [Development of the theory of Soviet operational art in the 1930s] was published in 1965 in the first and third issues of *Voyenno-istoricheskiy zhurnal* [Military-Historical Journal]. From the point of view of the history of Soviet military thought, this article is, undoubtedly, of substantial interest. The author imparts a number of new historical facts and, on the whole, correctly evaluates the concrete achievements of the theory of operational art during these years. But at the same time, Comrade Isserson also advances a number of debatable positions. For example, he writes:

> If in the 1920s our military-theoretical thought rested mainly on the experience of the First World War and was, to a significant degree, turned toward the past, then from the 1930s it turns forward to the investigation of issues of a future war and methods of conducting it.[2]

Such an evaluation of the development of Soviet military theory does not reflect actual facts and processes. It seems to us that it is impossible to draw such a sharp boundary between the two prewar decades. Each of them was connected with both study of the "past" and an analysis of a possible "future." And on the whole, a continuous link existed between them.

In this article we will examine the principal ideas of the military theory of the 1920s as reflected by the outstanding military-scientific works of that period. The development of Soviet military thought in the 1920s is basically defined by two facts. First, these years were the period of its establishment as a special military theory, based on the principles of Marxism-Leninism. Second, this was a time of great military reforms which determined the Soviet Armed Forces' developmental path, with broad prospects for the future.

Both required a thorough theoretical foundation. The 1920s was a period of stormy military-theoretical discussions unprecedented at a single stage in the subsequent development of Soviet military theory. In the course of discussions methodological foundations of Soviet military theory unfolded, its content was determined, and the first Soviet military-scientific cadres were formed. A new basic classification of the theory of Soviet military art was also accepted in this period. Instead of the former subdivision into only strategy and tactics, Soviet theory of military art began to include three relatively independent categories – strategy, operational art, and tactics – and the content of each of them was determined. Without resolving these problems, the further development of Soviet military theory, in general, would have been impossible. In actual fact, what kind of development of the theory of Soviet operational art could have been discussed in the 1930s if the concept itself of this theory and its object and content had not been established in the 1920s?

It is true that in the 1920s, especially at the beginning, Soviet military theory was engaged in studying the experience of the First World War, then still completely contemporary. But no less attention was focused on Civil War experience. And this had great significance, since the combat forms in these two wars were different. The First World War basically was a positional one, while the Civil War proceeded in the form of large maneuver operations. In the study of war experience, research on the history of the First World War by V. F. Novitsky, A. M. Zayonchkovsky, A. S. Beloy, A. B. Bazarevsky, A. A. Svechin, A. M. Neznamov, M. D. Bonch-Bruyevich, and others had great significance,[3] as did research on the history of the Civil War by M. N. Tukhachevsky, B. M. Shaposhnikov, N. Ye. Kakurin, V. A. Melikov, and others.[4]

Points of view on the experience of each of these wars were varied. But gradually the overall opinion emerged that future wars of the Soviet Union would fundamentally bear a broad, maneuver nature.

At the beginning of the 1920s, increasingly greater attention began to be focused on problems of future wars, and determining their nature and the methods and forms for conducting them. These received the greatest elaboration in the works of M. V. Frunze, whose opinions provided the foundation of all military reforms carried out at that time. Proceeding from an analysis of the contemporary international and domestic situation, in his works and presentations Frunze defined future possible wars of the Soviet Union as decisive and all-embracing clashes of two different socio-economic systems, which would draw upon all the productive forces of the opposing sides. In this connection, he considered inevitable the participation in them of mass armies and masses of new technical combat means to such an extent as permitted by the productive capabilities of the contending sides.

Pointing out that the armies of the most technically advanced bourgeois countries would arrive on the future battlefield with weapons for the most part different from those they had in the First World War, Frunze stated, "Future war, to a significant degree, if not as a whole, will be a war of machines."[5] Consequently, he considered one of the most important recurrent tasks the overall acceleration of the Red Army's technical outfitting within the limits of those opportunities provided by the Soviet government's economic growth.

He suggested that such wars could not be concluded within a short period by a single "lightning," crushing blow by either side in the style of the previous "strategy of annihilation" [*strategiya sokrusheniya*], a proponent of which always was the Prussian General Staff, but would take on an extended and stubborn character which would exhaust the contending sides' forces and means. He required that the country's defensive preparation, theory of military art, and, in the first order, its main part – the theory of strategy – be oriented on such a nature of war.

He wrote:

> In the case of first-class enemies, resolution cannot be achieved by one blow. War will take on the nature of a prolonged and fierce contest putting to the test all economic and political foundations of the opposing countries. Expressed in the language of strategy, this means shifting from a strategy of lightning, decisive blows to a strategy of attrition.[6]

The term "strategy of attrition" [*strategiya izmora*, literally "strategy of starvation"] was not acknowledged in Soviet military theory, although Frunze repeated it in each of his major presentations. Such an understanding of strategy directly issued from Lenin's definition of modern wars as a test of "all economic and organizational forces of each nation."[7] It coincided as well with the definition of the exhaustive nature of wars of the coming imperialist era, which Engels provided in the 1890s.[8]

The unpopularity of this term at that time and later was explained by two circumstances. First, among leading Red Army command personnel was an influential group which overvalued Civil War experience, especially its offensive operations, and was inclined to view future war from the point of view of the experience of these operations. Also significant were "theoretical" considerations that only the "strategy of annihilation" was peculiar to the Soviet state by its very nature as a progressive revolutionary class state. But it was understood that our Civil War did not consist only of victorious operations. In its separate stages, Soviet forces more than once were forced to execute deep withdrawals, shift to the defense, and lose enormous territory; any subsequent shift to the offensive required new mobilizations, new efforts of all the materiel and spiritual forces of the Soviet republic.

The same segment of command personnel held the conviction that, in case of war against us, capitalist country rear areas would be as precarious as White government rear areas during the Civil War; therefore, after the first attacks the Red Army would develop a victorious offensive as it had in the latter stages of the Civil War, and namely for this reason it seemed that the "strategy of attrition" was, in principle, inapplicable to the Soviet State.

In introducing the concept of "strategy of attrition," emerging from the nature of all great wars of the twentieth century, M. V. Frunze proceeded from the fact that in these wars victory was not achieved by a single attack or a single, continuous offensive. It became possible as a result of conducting many operations and campaigns, inevitably drawn out over an extended period, and requiring not only the participation of massive armies in the conflict, but also the efforts of all forces and means of the deep rear areas of the opposing countries. And only when all the enemy's forces and means were exhausted in the struggle, and when he was unable to continue armed opposition, only then could final victory over the enemy be counted on.

Citing the unavoidability of precisely this strategic characteristic in possible wars involving the Soviet Union at that time, he said that if the matter came to a large, grave war between the Soviet Union and a coalition of large bourgeois states, then there would be no limited war aims, "the war will be to the death of the opposing sides." In such a war, the efforts of all forces, not only of the front, but also of the country's entire rear, would be compulsory. Frunze wrote:

> This conclusion is not new; it was acquired from the experience of the past Imperilalist War. When the strategy of annihilation went bankrupt, when the first operational plans, which counted on immediately delivering a crushing blow to the opposing side, was not crowned with success, when the strategy of annihilation was replaced by the strategy of attrition it was then that all states, and in the first order the military machinery, had to pose before themselves the question of decisively enlisting all forces and means of the rear for the matter of defense. . . . We should now take these data into consideration so as not to be in a state of unpreparedness at the moment of a future military clash.[9]

Frunze himself did not reach this conclusion immediately. In his works of 1921–22, there was no concept of "strategy of attrition"; moreover, in their very substance they were directed against such a notion. This concept appeared in Frunze's works of 1924–25 and was substantiated in them. His conversation with Lenin in spring 1922, in connection with a discussion on a unified military doctrine, had substantial significance in Frunze's turn of strategic thought.

In summer 1921, Frunze came out with the article "*Yedinaya voyennaya doktrina i Krasnaya Armiya*" [Unified military doctrine and the Red Army], in which he stated in principle the correct position on the necessity of working out unified views on the development of the Soviet Armed Forces, their missions, and combat forms and methods. He named this system of views "unified military doctrine." The organization and preparation of the Soviet State's armed forces were to be structured on this basis.

But he provided the first definitions of the concrete content of doctrine while still under the fresh influence of just-completed victorious Civil War operations. In this period he conceived of future revolutionary war of the Soviet State also basically as a civil or semi-civil war "under conditions of the developing world revolution,"[10] and considered that a special military theory, defined only by its class features and inapplicable under any other conditions, was necessary for the Soviet State.

Frunze's article elicited stormy discussion. Its final stage was the meeting of military delegates of the XI Party Congress and Frunze's discussion with Lenin. The reason this discussion was not carried to its conclusion was subsequently explained thus by Frunze:

> What was the essence of my proposals? It amounted to a reexamination of all issues of military science and art from the point of view of the proletariat, to the establishment of a proletarian study of war. . . . At that time I had not begun to develop the broad struggle. . . . My conversation with Comrade Lenin played a decisive role. I told him my point of view, and he answered me: "From the point of view of perspectives, your approach is, of course, correct. Of course, you should be prepared for the task of fully mastering military affairs and conducting corresponding work. Please, study, put forth youthful efforts, but if you now begin to come forth with a theory of proletarian art, then you run the risk of swaggering. It seems to me that our military communists are still not mature enough to claim leadership of all military affairs."[11]

The instructions which Lenin gave to Frunze reflected Lenin's attitude toward science in general, and to the cultural and scientific legacy of the past as a whole. Beginning in 1918, Lenin conducted an irreconcilable struggle against at first the "left" communists, then against proletarian cult currents headed by empiriocritic A. A. Bogdanov, who came out against the use of past cultural and scientific legacies and for the creation of special, proletarian-class sciences in all fields of knowledge. Lenin called for the study and assimilation of the entire cultural and scientific legacy of the past, as well as scientific and cultural achievements of modern capitalist states, on the basis of Marxist methodology. This also applied to the field of military knowledge. During the Civil War, Lenin more than once said that without military science it was impossible to create a combat-ready Red Army. But he called not for the rapid creation of a new, special "proletarian" military theory," but for rapid use of the already-existing military science, developed for centuries, and for its mastery and use in the interests of the Soviet State to defend against its enemies. Summing up in March 1920 the experience of two years of Civil War, he explained:

> You know that to study military affairs immediately is impossible . . . only the officers – colonels and generals who remain from the tsarist army – know military science.

> [It] was necessary to assemble command personnel from former officers so that the workers and peasants could learn from them, for without science it is impossible to build a modern army. . . . This task is a difficult one, but we will surmount it.[12]

Lenin understood Soviet military science, not in the sense that it rejects all past military knowledge and recreates it proceeding from "the class interests of the proletariat," but in the sense that it first assimilates all past military knowledge and then develops it as applicable to new historical conditions based on Marxist-Leninist principles. From these tenets came his instructions to Frunze in connection with questions raised in the discussion on "unified military doctrine."

Frunze completely mastered Lenin's instructions, and his theoretical works of 1924–25 greatly differed from his works of 1921 and those at the beginning of 1922. If in the works of the first years he strove to develop the principal tenets of Soviet military theory only from the peculiarities of the Soviet State and the military tasks confronting it, then in the works of the second period the center of gravity of his analysis lay in objective study of the nature of modern wars and those tasks which they presented to modern military art and the practice of Soviet military development.

Frunze saw the principal path to victory in future war in routing the enemy's armed forces and depriving him of all those strategic bases on which he relies to create, restore, and supply his armed forces. But for him this path did not take the form of a continuous chain of offensive efforts, but the form of a long and stubborn struggle, including many operations and campaigns, each of which resolved only a particular mission of war and required most careful organization, preparation, and planned conduct.

Frunze's conclusion that future wars would be long and stubborn was based not only on the fact that in these wars massive armies would participate which would be impossible to shatter by a single blow, but also on the new role the deep rear had begun to play in wars. He wrote:

> The primary and most important conclusion from the experience of the past Imperialist War of 1914–18 is the reevaluation of the issue of the role and significance of the rear in the overall course of military operations. . . . War experience demonstrated that the achievement of war aims under modern conditions has become a significantly more

complex matter than before. Modern armies have enormous survivability. This survivability, as a whole, is connected with the general
condition of the country. Even the complete destruction of enemy
armies, achieved at a specific moment, still does not guarantee ultimate
victory, inasmuch as the destroyed parts have behind them an
economically and morally strong rear area. In the presence of time and
space supporting a new mobilization of human and materiel resources
necessary to restore the army's combat capability, the latter can easily
recreate the front and, with hope of success, conduct the struggle
further . . . . The life and work of a front at a given moment is
determined by the work and condition of the rear.[13]

From this it followed that to achieve final victory in war it was necessary
not only to destroy enemy forces at the front, but also to exhaust all state
resources and assets necessary to continue the war. At that time, Frunze
already quite distinctly also noted existing new combat forms, which
necessitated simultaneous destruction of the enemy both on his front and in
the deep rear, in connection with the development of equipment and means
of destruction.

However, under the conditions of the 1920s, this was still viewed only as
an outlook on an overall tendency in the development of forms of armed
conflict. Capabilities for attacking an enemy's deep rear areas were limited
and could not play a decisive role during war as a whole. The center of
gravity of armed combat lay in continental theaters of military operations. At
that time, only here could the forces of an opposing state really be exhausted,
and Frunze's main attention was concentrated on the development of forms
of combat in these theaters.

Frunze's conclusions regarding the inevitability of the protracted nature of
war and the strategy corresponding to it did not raise doubts among other
great military theorists of that time. Tukhachevsky, who never used the term
itself "strategy of attrition" [*strategiya istoshcheniya*, literally, "strategy of
exhaustion"] came out sharply against the "strategy of starvation" and with
all his nature gravitated toward calling for only a "strategy of annihilation";
nevertheless, in full agreement with Frunze's basic tenets in the mid-1920s
he wrote:

> We must be prepared for a protracted war. . . . The world situation is
> already such, that a future war cannot be decided by a single stroke.
> But in individual periods of a war, in individual moments of tension,
> our country should strive to resolve those combat missions which stand
> before it by the most economic, rapid, and decisive means.[14]

But this was exactly what Frunze called the "strategy of attrition." He did
not fully exclude the possibility of a "strategy of annihilation" either, that is,

the possibility of ending the war by a single continuous blow or a series of blows rapidly following one another, giving the war a fast-moving character. Moreover, he considered that objectively the imperialist states would strive for just such a type of strategy in the struggle against the Soviet Union, attempting to avoid a protracted nature. He also did not exclude the fact that under certain conditions the Soviet State could have recourse to such a strategy. But he associated the possibility of such a strategy under those circumstances with the presence of especially favorable conditions. He considered protracted war with the strategy peculiar to it as typical for that time. But in return, under all circumstances he excluded the possibility of striking the Soviet State by means of a lightning war or blitzkrieg. He said:

> Even if the situation unfolded very unfavorably for us, we have a whole series of conditions which do not permit the possibility of rapid violence against us. Here, in the first order, we have, apart from external allies, such a powerful ally in the size of our own territory. The chance of inflicting on us a mortal blow in the first period of the campaign, in the presence of any number of enemies who would come out against us, must be considered absolutely impossible.[15]

Soviet military theory's acknowledgement in the 1920s of the inevitability of a long, protracted war prompted the necessity of dividing the war into periods, campaigns, and operations, and determining the nature and scale of those missions which could be resolved in each of these forms of struggle on the path to ultimate war aims.

In light of these requirements, Tukhachevsky continued to work on the theory of successive operations, implying by these a group of operations developing continuously along one axis, at the maximum possible depth, having, as a whole, a propensity for that type of "ram" strategy which allowed the Red Army to surmount the entire territory of Belorussia rapidly during the 1920 Summer Campaign, but which did not yield success on the Vistula.

Frunze advanced to the forefront the necessity of thorough study of the organizational side of modern operations – techniques of their organization, preparation, and conduct on the basis of the most precise possible materiel-calculation data. He considered that organizational questions were advanced to the forefront by the entire course of the development of military art, especially in connection with the use of massive combat forces and means. He said:

> I personally think that now the successful outcome of military operations, the outcome of the war depends to a much lesser degree on correct operational leadership than on the correct establishment of organization of the rear area and all that prepares the conduct of mili-

tary operations. At least three-quarters of all matters are resolved by preliminary work, strictly thought out on the basis of completely accurate data. Of course, all this work will not provide results with poor operational leadership, but the center of gravity is still being shifted more and more here.[16]

Hence emerged the requirement for that time: "Fewer general discussions, more work on details and techniques of conducting operations!"[17]

Implementation of this requirement obliged Soviet military theory to reveal concretely the material content of modern operations; otherwise, the further development of the theory of strategy and operational art would be impossible. This was important for the theory of strategy because the potentials of each separate operation had to be the basis of all strategic plans. For the theory of operational art, the materiel side of the operation, its preparation, organization, and conduct comprised the very subject and content of the given theory.

The practical significance of this requirement arose because at this time in army command circles there was still strong gravitation toward conducting operations not on the basis of precise, calculated materiel data, but mainly on the basis of taking into account the moral and revolutionary superiority of Red Army soldiers over the soldiers of capitalist countries. The extent to which such attitudes were strong and influential is reflected in this episode. One of the well-known military-political workers of that time, F. Blyumental', the author of a number of voluminous books on army political work, in discussing the calculated norms of shells necessary to destroy one machine gun nest, seriously stated that such norms were significant only when applied to bourgeois armies, since the conscientious Red Army soldier protected in a trench could withstand a significantly greater quantity of shells.[18]

The task posed by Frunze for studying the materiel side of operations and associated requirements for their organization and conduct was, on the whole, resolved in the second half of the 1920s by V. K. Triandafillov in the book *Kharakter operatsiy sovremennykh armiy* [The nature of operations of modern armies]. The significance of this book in the history of the development of the Soviet theory of strategy and operational art was enormous. For the first time in a single concept, which coordinated the combat operations of troops, their maneuver, and work of the rear in an operation, this book provided a completely distinct, current, and concrete representation concerning the materiel side and structure of an operation within the framework of those capabilities which the army had at its disposal at that time; it also convincingly demonstrated the role of materiel-technical calculations in formulating and realizing operational plans, established the maximum capabilities of separate operations of that time, and indicated the correct, scientific method for resolving similar theoretical and practical problems in the future.

Then and later it was said that this book taught a broad cadre of Red Army command personnel to "think," to structure their concepts and plans not on the basis of intuition and consideration of only moral advantages of the conscientious Red Army soldier, but on precise materiel-technical calculations.

Triandafillov's book was structured on the basis of Marxist-Leninist methodology, for it took for analysis and subsequent generalization the objective, material aspect of the phenomena being studied. It approached these phenomena not from the point of view of whose interests they corresponded to, but from the point of view of what these phenomena actually were, and what they could provide in accordance with their material nature.

Having investigated the materiel basis of an operation, Triandafillov clarified its resultant forms. He demonstrated that materiel requirements of modern operations were enormous, while their potentials were limited. Based on this conclusion, he dispelled the hopes, still maintained by some people, concerning the reality under these conditions of a "strategy of annihilation," which envisioned (if this term is understood properly) putting any enemy out of action by a single, continuous offensive to the entire depth of his resistance, on the scale of war as a whole.

It was indisputably proven that large modern operations required careful materiel-organizational preparation, that it was impossible to conduct them continuously, that between them interruptions no less protracted than the operation itself were unavoidable, and that these interruptions would be filled with preparations for new operations or with the repulsion of attacks by enemy reserves being brought up from the depth of the country or from other sectors of the front not being attacked at all, or being attacked by fewer forces than in the main operations sector.

Triandafillov revealed the very close dependence of operations on their rear area, having shown the rear as a factor which limited the scope of an operation, its depth being no less, and sometimes even of greater importance than the combat resistance of enemy forces. Forces participating in an operation, even if they fully destroyed the enemy, at a certain stage would be forced to cease their advance as a result of separation from the rear areas which were feeding and supplying them. If advancing forces disregarded the disposition and organization of their rear area during an operation, they could, in turn, find themselves in a critical or even catastrophic position, fraught with the danger of obliteration of all their previous successes.

Triandafillov also worked out the problem of the possible spatial scope of operations. He established that the most decisive operations of that time were possible in a sector no greater than 150–250 kilometers, with a maximum materially supported advance to a depth of also 150–250 kilometers, and this under the condition that advancing shock armies were not restricted in motor vehicles; in their absence, the scope of the operation was reduced by several times. The principal factor limiting the scope of an operation under these conditions was railroad transport, since the tempo of restoring railroads sharply lagged behind the tempo of troop movement possible and necessary to destroy the enemy in an offensive operation.

But with that spatial scope of operations, significant enemy armed forces groupings (15–20 divisions) could be destroyed, and territorial sectors important to the enemy could be occupied. Such a depth of operation was sufficient to put small states (which entered as members of an opposing coalition) out of action as a whole (if the depth of their territory did not exceed 200–250 kilometers). But in a conflict against a strong state having at its disposal great territorial depth, and especially in a conflict against a large coalition, such operations were conducted for the achievement of only partial success, which did not decide the fate of the war as a whole.

On the scale of a large war, the scope of a single operation was insufficient to destroy enemy forces decisively, even within the framework of the single theater of military operations (or front), unique to the enemy. To destroy an enemy in an entire specific theater of military operations (for example, Belorussian, Ukrainian), Triandafillov considered it necessary to conduct an operation in a 350–400-kilometer sector, with an advance to roughly the same depth and tempos of advance which outstripped the possible tempo of enemy force withdrawal. The materiel-technical conditions of the 1920s did not yet support such depth of operation. However, taking into account the continuous development of combat and transport means, Triandafillov considered such a scope of operations possible in the near future, and actually noted that it was necessary to work during these years so that such operations would become possible.

The book assigned the theory of operational art the concrete task of developing forms and conditions for conducting such operations in the near future.

The achievement of a depth of operations of 350–400 kilometers still did not create conditions for a strategic shift to destroying the enemy on the scale of war as a whole, but such a large operation did provide the potential for inflicting destruction on large enemy groupings operating on a strategic axis or even in a theater of military operations. This made it possible to conduct a war by larger strategic leaps and reduce its time, but it could not endow war with a "blitzkrieg" character, when everything depended on a single blow or a series of blows following one another continuously and fusing together into an uninterrupted offensive on the scale of war as a whole.

Triandafillov refined the notion of army offensive operations, having determined the depth of each of them as 30–50 kilometers, and also of successive operations, that is, continuously following one another, having combined army operations into a group of operations conducted on the scale of a *front*. For the first time, his book formulated the concept of the deep operation, in accordance with indices of the depth of space embraced by the operation and the force advance during it.

Speaking critically about the "ram" strategy, characterized by conduct of the entire operation, from beginning to end, in a single "ram" grouping, Triandafillov convincingly proved the advantages of conducting an operation along convergent axes, creating the opportunity to encircle the enemy and facilitating force advance and formation and operation of their rear area. He called for maximum force efforts and means to inflict the deepest blows against the enemy, whose limitations were to be determined only by force technical capabilities. Triandafillov proved that deep and shattering blows were "the most decisive strategic means for achieving assigned war aims,"[19] and they precisely "are the most reliable means for the rapid exhaustion of the enemy's human and materiel resources, and for the creation of objectively favorable conditions for a socio-political shake-up in the enemy country."[20]

The author did not limit himself to an analysis of offensive operations; he focused great attention on questions concerning operational defense on a broad scale, considering it a necessary form of action and an integral part of war as a whole.

Triandafillov's entire book was based on and proceeded from materiel calculations. This was its special strength, its clarity and persuasiveness. But at the same time, the book warned that war was not bookkeeping, that calculations gave only a method of work, and that in and of themselves they would not provide victory if they were not used for operational-strategic guidance based on the correct evaluation of the situation and on correctly drafted operational plans.

In reexamining all the issues, however, Triandafillov basically limited himself to the initial situation for an operation and almost did not touch upon the dynamics of its conduct; he did not subdivide the operation into the various stages through which it inevitably had to pass, and very superficially spoke about the maneuver of forces and technical combat means during the operation itself. He did not broadly pose the question of combat against large enemy shock groupings, as if excluding the possibility of such operations, or of the nature of cooperation during an operation by combined-arms and mobile formations, represented at this time basically by large cavalry formations. There is no doubt that powerful mechanized formations could resolve similar missions better than cavalry, but at that time the Red Army still did not have them, and in the near future equipment would not be part of the armaments in the necessary quantity.

A shortcoming of the book was that, practically speaking, in it the operation was examined basically only on an army scale (only successive operations of a shock army); it did not raise its concrete analysis and generalization to operations on a *front* scale. Even the very term "*front* operation" was absent from it, and there was still no concept of air force operations. The investigation of these issues was, naturally, a future task for the Soviet theory of strategy and operational art, but the book created an initial position for the resolution of this task.

Triandafillov's book won recognition in wide circles of our army's command structure. It could not be evaluated only as the author's individual research; it was an objective expression of the level at which the Soviet theory of strategy and operational art stood at the end of the 1920s and beginning of the 1930s. In addition, in the second half of the 1920s this book was not the only work in Soviet military literature on the theory of strategy and operational art. There were other works: for example, a number of long articles by M. N. Tukhachevsky and the 1928 book by N. N. Movchin, *Posledovatel'nyye operatsii po opytu Marny i Visly* [Successive operations according to the experience of the Marne and the Vistula], which analyzed the theory of this issue, using examples of the march of German armies to the Marne in 1914 and of Soviet forces to the Vistula in 1920, and raised the analysis of these questions to *front*-scale operations, especially regarding the arrangement of their rear areas. Important materials on strategic and operational art questions were contained in a large work by B. M. Shaposhnikov, *Mozg armii* [The brain of an army]. It investigated the work of the General Staff primarily based on activities of the Austro-Hungarian Army.

The book *Strategiya* [Strategy] by Professor A. A. Svechin, published in two editions in 1926 and 1927, provided a large amount of factual material and many correct propositions. Despite the author's enthusiasm for the "strategy of attrition,"[21] this book, in view of the abundance of its factual material and the broad formulation of questions concerning the relationship between military strategy and economic and political questions, even today is a unique work in comparison with all preceding works on issues of strategy in the old Russian Army and abroad. The sharp polemics which developed with the publication of this book proceeded during the second half of the 1920s and beginning of the 1930s under the loud slogan of struggle "against reactionary currents on the military-scientific front," and bore, to a significant degree, a subjective character, while ignoring the fact that Svechin's book basically was written from materialistic positions. Although the author himself was not even a Marxist, in a number of places in his book he provided principally reliable materialistic concepts and carried them through with greater consistency than some of his critics who came forth in the course of discussions.

A most important positive feature of this book was that all strategic questions in it were examined in close connection with the political and economic aspects of wars. Svechin argued that modern wars are not only conducted by armed forces, but that all political and economic forces and means of the opposing sides participate in them. In this connection, he advocated the idea that the aims, nature, and forms of strategy in such wars were not arbitrary, but determined by the political, economic, and military-technical capabilities of the opposing sides; these capabilities under modern conditions are such that wars, when powerful sides clash, inevitably take on a protracted character in which the forms of combat are inevitably also extremely varied. Svechin also did not consider the term itself, "strategy of starvation," completely apt. He indicated that this term "very poorly reflects the entire variety of nuances of various strategic methods which lie beyond the limits of annihilation."[22] He emphasized that "strategy of starvation" in its understanding "in no way negates, in principle, the destruction of enemy personnel as an operational aim, but sees in this only part of an armed front's mission, and not the entire mission," and that under modern conditions "it is necessary to think not only about projected efforts, but also about their 'dosage'."[23] In the book it is decisively stated that "a strategy of annihilation," that is, that of a lightning, fast-paced war, if there are the objective prerequisites for this, is always more acceptable than a "strategy of attrition"; that the latter, "in general, is chosen only when the war cannot be brought to an end by a single procedure";[24] with such a strategy, such decisive aims as with the "strategy of annihilation" can be pursued in the war as a whole.[25] Nevertheless, all polemics around this book were conducted from the point of view that the theory of "strategy of attrition" being developed by Svechin was a strategy of limited war aims, and this did not correspond with the very nature of the Soviet State, which in all wars had to pursue only the most decisive aims.

At the heart of Svechin's book were lectures he gave at the Military Academy when it was directly headed by M. V. Frunze, and many of his tenets coincided with those ideas which Frunze had developed as the foundation of his concept of "strategy of attrition." However, sharp polemics developed only after Frunze's death, and in the heat of them attempts were made in passing to question not only what Svechin had said, but also Frunze's statements. Until the beginning of the 1960s, Svechin's book *Strategy* was the only systematic work which analyzed strategy in wars of the first quarter of the twentieth century.

Questions of strategy and operational art were widely posed and analyzed in the 1920s in military-historical works as well. The prominent works of V. F. Novitsky on the maneuver period of the 1914 war on the Franco-German front, A. M. Zayonchkovsky on Russia's preparation for the First World War and an overall strategic survey of this war, A. Bazarevsky on the campaigns of 1918, and others contained abundant material on this war's strategy and operational art. The works of N. Ye. Kakurin, *Kak srazhalas' revolyutsiya* [How the revolution was fought], N. Ye. Kakurin and V. A. Melikov, *Voyna s belopolyakami* [The war against the White Poles], V. A. Melikov, *Marna – 1914, Visla – 1920, Smirna – 1922 goda* [The Marne –

1914, the Vistula – 1920, Smyrna – 1922], and others provided material applicable to our Civil War. All these works were not simple surveys of past historical events. They contained conclusions for modern times, and enriched Soviet operational-strategic thought and influenced its development, at times no less, and sometimes even more, than the simple, dry transpositions of statements in regulations and instructions which had a place in some works, or abstract discussions claiming to be statements of the theory of operational art and tactics.

In general it should be kept in mind that thorough military-historical research is never limited only to knowledge of the past. In disclosing the regularities of past events, it always influences the development of modern military-theoretical thought as well. To disclose these regularities and to explain the modern era's idiosyncracies correctly is possible only with a thorough study of the history of wars and military art as a whole. Modern times do not change the inherent regularities of wars and military art; they only make their forms concrete as applicable to new historical conditions, to new combat means and trends in their development.

Such, in general terms, was the state of Soviet military theory in the 1920s and immediately on the threshold of the 1930s. Can it be said that the theory in its foundation was "turned to the past" and "rested mainly on the experience of the First World War"? Such an understanding would be historically incorrect. Soviet military theory in the 1920s developed in an unusually tempestuous fashion, and approached the 1930s with a correct strategic orientation, with a basically developed theory of operational art and correct tenets in the field of tactics and organization of forces, and with a developed program for the country's further defensive preparation on the whole. Military-theoretical tasks of the 1930s consisted then not of simply thrusting aside the achievements of military theory of the preceding decade, that is, turned mainly "to the past," but of using them as a starting point and developing them as applicable to the situation and the new conditions unfolding in the 1930s.

NOTES

1. A. Golubev, "Obrashchena li byla v proshloye nasha voyennaya teoriya v 20-ye gody?," *Voyenno-istoricheskiy zhurnal* [Military-historical journal], 10 (October 1965), pp. 35–47.
2. *Voyenno-istoricheskiy zhurnal* [Military-historical journal], 1 (1965), p. 36.
3. V. F. Novitsky, *Mirovaya voyna 1914–1918 gg. Kampaniya 1914 goda v Bel'gii i Frantsii* [The world war 1914–1918. The 1914 campaign in Belgium and France], Vol. 1–2 (Moscow: GVIZ, 1924); A. Zayonchkovsky, *Mirovaya voyna 1914–1918 gg. Obshchiy strategicheskiy ocherk* [The world war 1914–1918. General strategic essay] (Moscow:

GVIZ, 1924); *Podgotovka Rossii k imperialisticheskoy voyne. Ocherki voyennoy podgotovki i pervonachal'nykh planov* [Russia's preparation for the imperialist war. Essays on military preparation and initial plans] (Moscow: GVIZ, 1926); A. Beloy, *Galitsiyskaya bitva* [The Battle of Galicia] (Moscow–Leningrad: GIZ, 1929); A. Bazarevsky, *Mirovaya voyna 1914–1918 gg. Kampaniya 1918 goda vo Frantsii i v Bel'gii* [The world war 1914–1918. The 1918 campaign in France and Belgium], Vol. 1, 2 (GIZ, 1927); A. A. Svechin, *Obshchiy obzor sukhoputnykh operatsiy mirovoy voyny.* "*Entsyklopedicheskiy slovar'* [General survey of ground forces operation of the world war. Encyclopedic dictionary] (Moscow: Granat) 7th edition, Vol. 46; A. Neznamov, *Kampaniya 1915 goda* [The 1915 campaign] (Moscow: VVRS, 1922); M. Bonch-Bruyevich, *Poterya nami Galitsii v 1915 goda* [Our loss of Galicia in 1915], parts I, II (Moscow: 1920, 1926).

4. M. Tukhachevsky, *Politika i strategiya v grazhdanskoy voyne* [Politics and strategy in the civil war] in the book M. Tukhachevsky, *Sbornik izdannykh trudov, lektsiy, i statey po voprosam strategii* [Collection of selected works, lectures, and articles on issues of strategy] (Moscow: 1924); B. Shaposhnikov, *Na Visle. K istorii kampanii 1920 g.* [On the Vistula. On the history of the 1920 campaign] (Moscow: GVIZ, 1924); N. Kakurin, *Kak srazhalas' revolyutsiya* [How the revolution was fought], Vol. 1–2 (Moscow–Leningrad: GIZ, 1925–1926); N. Kakurin and V. Melikov, *Voyna s belopolyakami* [War with the White Poles] (Moscow: GVIZ, 1925); V. Melikov, *Marna – 1914 goda, Visla – 1920 goda, Smirna – 1922 goda* [The Marne – 1914, the Vistula – 1920, Smyrna – 1922] (Moscow–Leningrad: GIZ, 1928).

5. M. V. Frunze, *Izbrannyye proizvedeniya* [Selected works], Vol. II (Moscow: Voyenizdat, 1957), p. 343.

6. Ibid., p. 133.

7. V. I. Lenin, *Polnoye sobraniye sochineniy* [Complete collection of works], Vol. 39, p. 321.

8. F. Engels, *Izbrannyye voyennyye proizvedeniya* [Selected military works] (Moscow: Voyenizdat, 1957), pp. 610–12; K. Marx and F. Engels, *Pis'ma* [Letters] (Moscow–Leningrad: Sotsekonomizdat), 1932, 4th edition, pp. 360–1, 387–8.

9. M. V. Frunze, *Selected Works*, Vol. II, pp. 221–2.

10. Ibid., p. 3.

11. M. V. Frunze, *Sobraniye sochineniy* [Collected works], Vol. III (Moscow–Leningrad: GIZ, 1927), p. 150.

12. Lenin, Vol. 40, pp. 182–3.

13. Frunze, *Selected Works*, Vol. II, pp. 133, 134.

14. M. N. Tukhachevsky, *Izbrannyye proizvedeniya* [Selected works], Vol. 1 (Moscow: Voyenizdat), pp. 177–8.

15. Frunze, *Collected Works*, Vol. III, p. 113.

16. Frunze, *Selected Works*, Vol. II, pp. 177–8.

17. Ibid., p. 352.

18. *Krasnaya Zvezda* [Red Star], 7 February 1930.

19. V. K. Triandafillov, *Kharakter operatsiy sovremennykh armiy* [The nature of operations of modern armies], 2d edition (Moscow: GVIZ, 1932), p. 152. The first edition of this book appeared in 1929.

20. Ibid., p. 154.

21. A. A. Svechin borrowed the term "strategy of attrition" [*izmora*] from the German military historian Hans Delbrueck. Svechin's opponents, in the heat of sharp polemics, attributed to him an understanding of the "strategy of attrition" in which acknowledgement of any role whatsoever of combat operations of armed forces was excluded, and the center of gravity of conducting war was shifted only onto the economic exhaustion of the enemy, onto his internal collapse and decomposition. Svechin himself was far from such a limited definition of "strategy of attrition."

22. A. Svechin, *Strategiya* [Strategy], 2d edition (Moscow: Voyennyy Vestnik, 1927), p. 178.

23. Ibid., p. 179.

24. Ibid., p. 180.

25. Ibid., p. 41.

Some Questions Concerning the Development of Strategic Theory in the 1920s

MAJOR GENERAL N. PAVLENKO[1]

Soviet strategy, as all its military science, began to develop during the Civil War, during the severe struggle against internal and external enemies. The Communist Party and V. I. Lenin personally focused great attention on the formation of the Red Army and development of Soviet military science, which had absorbed the rich experience of the revolutionary struggle and military knowledge and experience accumulated in the bosom of the old society. In March 1920 at the 1st All-Russian Congress of Worker Cossacks, Lenin said:

> You know that it is impossible to learn military affairs immediately. You also know that only the officers – colonels and generals who remain from the Tsarist Army – know military science. . . . It is necessary to recruit command cadres from former officers, so that workers and peasants can learn from them, for without science it is impossible to build a modern army.[2]

Among those officers and generals of the old Russian Army who went over to the service of the Soviet State were also military scholars with enormous military knowledge and experience. But together with useful scientific wares, many brought with them into the Red Army outdated views, old traditions, and, mainly, a methodology inappropriate for the progressive class, a methodology against which it was necessary to struggle for a long time.

A little more than two decades separate the Civil War from the Great Patriotic War. Each of these decades has its own specific features in the development of our country's military-theoretical thought.

The 1920s represent an important stage in the development of Soviet military science. This was the time of its establishment as a science, whose method was dialectical materialism. The process was suffused with struggle, arguments, and discussions in which not only purely military theory but also methodological questions were drawn in. An important task was overcoming one-sided concepts of foreign bourgeois authors. Thorough study of war experience, improvement of combat means and the outfitting of the armed forces with them, discussions on the most important military-theoretical and military-historical questions, and mastery by military cadres of Marxist-Leninist methodology facilitated the development of Soviet military-theoretical thought in the 1920s. During these years there were more than a few special works on military strategy. Above all, among these should be included the works of M. V. Frunze,[3] M. N. Tukhachevsky,[4] A. A. Svechin,[5] A. A. Neznamov,[6] A. M. Zayonchkovsky,[7] and others.

Questions concerning strategic theory were also drawn into works devoted to operational art[8] and military history.[9] The ideas expressed in them make it possible not only to establish the level of strategic theory of this time, but also to determine the degree of its influence on the subsequent development of military science.

Soviet strategic theory in the 1920s, in essence, correctly defined the nature of armed conflict in future war, envisioned growth in the role of the rear in this, and focused much attention on the development of methods for conducting successive operations into the depth. The foregoing far from exhausted the circle of issues our military theory was working on. But this period's strategic theory also had serious shortcomings. Many important problems of military strategy were treated in passing, without thoroughly investigating them. Above all, this applied to questions concerning the conduct of coalition war, organization and conduct of strategic offensives during campaigns, organization of a strategic defense, cooperation of *fronts,* strategic leadership, and a number of others. Necessary attention was not given to terminology. The terms "campaign," "approach," "strategic offensive," "strategic defense," and others were used, but their definitions very often were not given, which led to various understandings and interpretations.

The 1930s were marked by enormous successes in the development and improvement of combat means, especially tanks and aviation; the might of the armed forces grew considerably. Serious changes also occurred in the camp of possible enemies. With Fascism coming to power in Germany, it became more and more evident that it was namely this state that would be the most probable enemy to perpetrate aggression against our Motherland.

In the 1930s, Stalin's cult of personality, with all its negative manifestations and consequences, had an increasingly stronger influence on strategic theory, as most closely connected with the political realm of knowledge. At first this influence was expressed in the circle of personalities who were studying strategic theory becoming extremely narrow. The situation was complicated by a significant segment of the most prepared cadres of military theoreticians being subjected to unfounded repressions. An especially strong blow was inflicted against that small but very talented group of scholars developing strategic theory. This applied to M. N. Tukhachevsky, A. A. Svechin, R. P. Eydeman, N. Ye. Varfolomeyev, and others. Their works were not only placed in doubt, but were also declared as sabotage. Therefore, many interesting ideas on questions concerning the organization and conduct of the strategic offensive, stated in the 1920s and beginning of the 1930s, were not developed in the second half of the 1930s.

An enormous mistake was also made in excluding the strategic theory course from military academy programs.[10] This inflicted serious damage on our military science. Finally, in the prewar decade local wars became more frequent, and in 1939 the Second World War began, which was a severe trial for peoples and states, their armed forces, and various prewar theories. Careful study of all these conditions and an analysis of their influence on the development of strategic theory are the tasks of military-historical science.

In this article the author intends to examine, on the basis of works published at various times, only separate issues in the development of strategic theory in the 1920s, concerning mainly foresight into the nature of armed combat and the theory of the strategic offensive. Of course, even these issues can be examined only in general outline within the framework of a journal article.

The materiel-technical base, the point of departure for the military theory of the 1920s, did not stray far from the level of the First World War. It is true that at that time trends and prospects for the development of combat means were already distinctly exhibited: the improvement of automatic weapons, an increase in the range of artillery fire, and a qualitative improvement in tanks, aviation, communications means, and transport. Military-scientific thought took into account these trends. But, as always in similar situations, some overestimated the influence of the use of improved combat means on future battlefields, while others, on the contrary, underestimated it, clinging to outmoded types of forces and combat forms.

Armies of many millions of men seemed to some foreign theoreticians (Fuller, Seekt, Zoldan, and others) a sheer "nightmare." They dreamed of a small but classically reliable army. These views found their individual supporters even among us. Thus, the author of a generally interesting work stated at the end of the 1920s that "the mass army will disappear, and will be replaced by a small army of knights [*rytsar'*] which can be structured on class principles."[11] During these years some military personalities continued after the old way to idealize cavalry, without noting that with the massive appearance of automatic weapons, tanks, and aviation on the battlefield, this once very effective combat arm now had no future. Theories of creating small armored "knight" armies were not, however, disseminated among us. Enthusiasm for cavalry was still unusually prolonged. For a long time it was considered "a triumphant and annihilating force,"[12] although its time had already passed.

Soviet military theory also naturally took into account probable enemies who could oppose our Motherland. In the 1920s it was reckoned that the border bourgeois states of Poland, Romania, and the Baltic countries (Finland, Estonia, Latvia, and Lithuania) would be in the first echelon of the Entente acting against the USSR. It was assumed that at the end of the 1920s all these countries would be able to field 106 first-line[13] and 50–70 second-line infantry divisions with technical equipment that was not high-grade. Triandafillov also included among probable enemies France, which, according to his calculations, could field 57–64 first-line and 82–90 second-line infantry divisions.[14]

The length of our western border (from the Arctic Ocean to the Black Sea) amounted to around 3,000 kilometers; of this, the border with Finland was around 1,500 kilometers, with Estonia and Latvia around 380 kilometers, and with Poland around 800 kilometers; the Romanian sector of the border was 320 kilometers.[15] Thus, it was assumed that in case of war a single large *front* formation [*ob"yedineniye*], which under those conditions was considered to be strategic, could be deployed in each of the sectors.

In the 1920s, strategic theory, and military affairs on the whole, developed under the enormous influence of the First World War and the Civil War. A strenuous process of trying to understand the experience of these wars took place; lessons and conclusions were drawn. During the Civil War great attention was given to the use of the experience of the First World War. Thus, in the Communist Party Program accepted at the VIII Congress, it was pointed out that

> the widest use and application of the last World War's operational-technical experience is necessary. In connection with this, it is necessary to attract military specialists who have gone through the school of the old army for the matter of organizing the army and its operational leadership.[16]

Many military specialists' experience and knowledge and their active participation in military development played a significant role in Red Army victories during the Civil War, training of young Red commanders, the generalization of past war experience, and the development of the military theory of the 1920s.

Of course, old military specialists producing works on military theory and military history were far from Marxism and were prisoners of the old metaphysical and idealistic concepts and views which reflected the nineteenth century level of science. Therefore, for the successful development of Soviet military science, overcoming obsolete views and affirming Marxist-Leninist methodology, acquired exceptionally important significance. The military-scientific activity of Frunze, who brilliantly combined the qualities of states-man, military leader, and preeminent military theorist, played an important role in this matter. His works were distinguished by their high scientific level and greatly influenced the development of Soviet military science.

In studying the experience of the First World War and the Civil War, Soviet researchers distinctly presented the features of armed combat in these wars: in the First World War – a continuous, positional front, high troop and combat equipment density, limited scope for the majority of operations, low rates of penetration; in the Civil War – the presence of a front "full of holes," low troop and combat equipment density, decisive nature of operations, their great spatial scope, and high maneuverability. It is completely obvious that military theorists investigating problems of future war could not fail to consider the experience of wars recently ended.

In analyzing historical experience, trends in the development of military affairs, and policies of imperialist states, Frunze viewed a future war of the Soviet state against capitalist countries as a class struggle.[17] He associated extreme dynamism, decisiveness, and maneuverability with the most characteristic features of Red Army actions in such a war. It is curious to note that strategic questions in class wars also attracted the attention of A. M. Zayonchkovsky, a representative of the old Russian school. In lectures given at the *RKKA* Military Academy in 1922 and 1923, he said that it was impossible to develop a theory of strategy in future class wars based on limited Civil War experience, and that from this experience only preliminary appraisals could be drawn. Zayonchkovsky wrote, "Defensive strategy, which is not decisive, does not correspond to the idea of class wars." In his opinion, the offensive would expand across wide fronts. Strategic cavalry, an air fleet, and armored forces would actively operate on the enemy's flanks and in his rear. However, he also recommended not to forget in class wars "cold calculation and complete consideration of the unchanging foundations of military affairs."[18] In analyzing historical experience, Zayonchkovsky concluded that twentieth century armed combat conditions had changed fundamentally. At the beginning of the nineteenth century, campaigns, if not wars, were won by one or two general engagements. In the Franco-Prussian War, three operations (Sedan, Metz, and Paris) brought the Germans a victorious conclusion to the war. Another situation was observed in twentieth century wars. The Mukden victory did not open the road to peace for the Japanese, and two months later an even more powerful Russian Army stood before them. In the First World War, "defeat and victory alternated with each other, prisoners were numbered in the hundreds of thousands, but armies suffering defeat were reborn as if from the ashes."[19] Former Commander-in-Chief of the Red Army S. S. Kamenev also noted this very feature of twentieth century wars. In his work *Ocherednyye voyennyye zadachi* [The next military tasks], he wrote:

> A characteristic feature of wars with massive armies is the enormous routs of large military formations [*soyedineniye*] (corps, armies, *fronts*); these routs, despite their sometimes even catastrophic dimensions, nevertheless do not bring with them either decisive defeat or decisive victory for the corresponding sides. The struggle continues after such routs with the same obstinacy and intensity.

For decisive victory, he continued, it was not enough to produce utter defeat in one particular sector of a colossal front. This rout in no way would signal a catastrophe for the enemy.

> The routed sector will be easily reestablished by a new army and new materiel, after which the game will begin anew. In a war of modern armies, the sum of continuous and systematic victories on the entire front of the struggle, successively added one to the other and connected to each other with respect to time, is necessary for a decisive rout of the enemy. Only with the help of such a chain of victories can the will of the enemy be considered shattered, where he is not able to use personnel and materiel available in his deployment to reestablish the routed sector.[20]

Thus, our military-scientific thought correctly reckoned that even a serious victory in one front particular sector could not lead to the destruction of the enemy. A series of *continuous and systematic victories* are necessary to achieve this aim. This indicated a completely new phenomenon in military theory, elicited by the fact that million-man armies relying on the entire economic might of the warring states joined the struggle. Following behind first echelons, second and then even subsequent echelons were introduced into combat. Industry and transport continuously and very intensively worked for the needs of the war. Victory demanded prolonged and stubborn efforts. Frunze wrote that modern armies possess a colossal survivability.

> Even the complete defeat of enemy armies achieved at a specific time still does not guarantee ultimate victory. . . . With time and space supporting a new mobilization of human and materiel resources necessary to reestablish the combat capability of an army, the latter can easily recreate a front and conduct combat further with hope for success.[21]

If the armies of strong enemies had such an enormous survivability in past wars, then there was no basis for supposing that the situation could be radically changed in the near future. The basic might of warring armies at the front was the country's rear area, with its enormous human and materiel resources. At that time there were no combat means for any kind of effective action against the rear. The enemy's might had to be shattered on the battlefields.

Inasmuch as our theory acknowledged that a strong enemy had enormous survivability and that a number of "continuous and systematic victories" were necessary for his complete destruction, naturally there arose the question: Which large strategic stages lie on the path to final victory over the enemy? Researchers acknowledged that campaigns were such strategic stages of war. However, there was no clear definition of a military campaign as a strategic category. Thus, Tukhachevsky wrote in his work *Voprosy sovremennoy strategii* [Problems of modern strategy], "Campaigns have lost the characteristic aspect they formerly possessed. They can characterize either the entire period of the war or part of it, or coincide with a series of successive operations."[22] It cannot be said that this formulation was distinguished by particular clarity, but from this it is still evident that Tukhachevsky recognized both periods of a war and military campaigns which could "coincide with a series of successive operations." Svechin also adhered to roughly the same opinion. He considered that, "several operations united by time and place form a campaign [*kampaniya*]; the totality of campaigns in the course of an entire year is called a crusade [*pokhod*]."[23] Of course, the concept of a "crusade" for twentieth century wars was an anachronism. N. Movchin, the author of the interesting book *Posledo-vatel'nyye operatsii po opytu Marny i Visly* [Successive operations according to the experience of the Marne and Vistula], expressed an original view on the essence of the campaign. He wrote that a campaign was "a collective concept, which encompasses the entire totality of actions in a specific theater of military operations during a large interval of time."[24] He considered the principal portion of a campaign to be the totality of successive operations which developed on the main attack axis. As is evident from Svechin's and Movchin's definitions, we viewed a campaign as the totality of military actions united by place and time. Such an interpretation of a campaign was a step backwards, even in comparison with the definition of a campaign given in Sytin's encyclopedia, which noted that a campaign is "the totality of military actions directly connected to one another."[25] Indication of a direct connection of events assumed the presence of some general campaign plan.[26] But it was not only a matter of terminology. A great shortcoming of our military theory in the 1920s was that it poorly investigated the problem of planning and organizing armed combat in campaigns. The ideas stated in Svechin's work *Strategy* bore a very general character.

In investigating the possible nature of future war, considerable attention in military theory was focused on questions concerning the strategy of "annihilation" [*strategiya sokrasheniya*] and the strategy of "attrition" [*strategiya izmora*]. Frunze, Zayonchkovsky,[27] Svechin, Shaposhnikov, Tukhachevsky, and others touched upon these issues in their works.

Posing the question of a strategy of "annihilation" and a strategy of "attrition" ensued directly from the experience of the First World War. At the beginning, Germany and Russia, in part, attempted to bring the war to an end before the autumn snowfall by means of annihilating blows. This strategy was bankrupt. For various reasons the war took on a prolonged, exhausting character. Our military thought focused attention on this very instructive fact.

In analyzing the economic and military capabilities of probable enemies, our theory considered that future war could assume a prolonged and stubborn character. In the mid-1920s Frunze wrote:

> War will take on the character of a prolonged and fierce competition subjecting all the economic and political foundations of the warring sides to a test. Expressed in the language of strategy, this means a shift from a strategy of lightning, decisive blows to a strategy of attrition.

However, Frunze further stressed that "from this in no way does the necessity arise for rejecting absolutely the strategy of lightning blows."[28]

Svechin devoted much attention to the strategies of "annihilation" and "attrition"; he considered that the term "attrition" poorly expressed the variety of all nuances of strategic methods found beyond the limits of a strategy of "annihilation." Despite such reservations, Svechin preferred, following Delbrueck, to use the term "attrition."

We will attempt to analyze the essence of Svechin's views on this issue.

1. The strategy of annihilation, in his opinion, was characteristic of wars at the beginning of the nineteenth century, when a campaign, if not the war, was won as a result of one or several engagements. In the twentieth century the situation had radically changed. In a struggle between strong enemies, armies which entered war were only the first echelon. Svechin wrote, "The beginning of war in our time is not the culmination point of strategic tension. Second and third echelons of mobilized and equipped personnel represent military and economic mobilization."[29] Such a situation exists when it is impossible to win a war by means of a single effort.

2. If there are objective conditions for lightning wars, then the strategy of "annihilation" is a more preferable form of struggle than the strategy of "attrition." The latter is used when war cannot be ended by a single method.[30] A struggle of attrition is typical for those states economically stronger than their enemies, have a stable rear, and are not torn apart by class and national conflicts.[31] A strategy of "annihilation" will be the most efficient form of struggle against that state "whose territory can be crossed on foot from end to end in a week."[32] This form can also be used in a war against a large state which is "in a state of political decay."[33] A war of annihilation will be conducted predominantly using materiel resources accumulated in peacetime.

"A large state can base the struggle of attrition exclusively on the work of its industry during the war itself."[34]

3. The political leadership, in advancing war aims, should indicate how to conduct it: Will it be in the form of "annihilation" or in the form of "attrition"? Here, Svechin emphasized that

> in the political mission which establishes the political aim, a compromise will be suggested – either brief annihilation or prolonged attrition; preparation for war receives the same compromise solution, including an attempt to prepare part of the forces for swift operations and the tendency to provide for the possibility of a prolonged struggle.[35]

4. In his opinion, the struggle of attrition can be conducted "for the achievement of the most energetic, ultimate aims, until the complete physical annihilation of the enemy." On the strength of this circumstance he did not agree with the term "war with a limited aim."[36] The strategy of "attrition" in no way rejects annihilation of the enemy, which is the aim of an operation. "But," he wrote, "it sees in this only part of an armed front's missions, and not the entire mission."[37] Within the framework of the strategy of "attrition," all operations have a limited aim; in his opinion, it is as though the main theater loses its dominant significance, and the role of the struggle for geographic points which embody the economic interests of the warring states increases.[38]

Only some of Svechin's views on the strategy of "annihilation" and "attrition" have been summarized here. They raise questions related to the nature of armed conflict in which million-man armies take part. In Svechin's opinion, the principal aim of the struggle of attrition is to deprive the enemy of his economic capabilities as a basis for further conduct of the war. Stressing attention on the strategy of "attrition," he considered that a small state could be defeated by a shattering blow. As for war against large states which have large materiel and human resources, it would inevitably take the form of a struggle of attrition and exhaustion. In such a war, the main role in supplying the front with arms, combat equipment, and ammunition will be played by the intensive work of industry during the war. Peacetime reserves will not be enough. They will be sufficient only for a rapid, lightning war. The very interesting idea which had been stated about the combination of "brief annihilation and prolonged attrition" unfortunately was not developed by Svechin.

Many of his tenets were poorly substantiated and one-sided, especially in polemical statements; therefore, they contained errors of a methodological nature which his opponents could not fail to notice. One of Svechin's critics on the issue of the strategy of "annihilation" and "attrition" was Tukhachevsky. In the preface to Delbrueck's book *The History of Military*

Art Within the Framework Of Political History, he criticized the author of *Strategy* for the fact that he rejected "the influence of the political aim on the form of war,"[39] ignored the class nature of states, and did not "see the difference between working class politics and bourgeois politics."[40] Having stated a number of correct critical observations, Tukhachevsky then pointed out that he did not wish to belittle the service of the author of *Strategy*.[41] At the same time, criticism of a number of this work's theoretical positions were far from always being objective and correct. For example, Svechin's statement that even the strategy of "attrition" in war could achieve "the complete physical annihilation of the enemy" was called "an absurdity." Being a fervent advocate of the strategy of "annihilation," Tukhachevsky cleanly rejected the strategy of "attrition." Such an attitude was explained to a significant degree by Tukhachevsky acknowledging the possibility of exporting revolution. In one of his early articles, called *Revolyutsiya izvne* [Revolution from without] he wrote, "The advance of a working class revolutionary army to the borders of a neighboring bourgeois state can depose the power of the bourgeoisie there and transfer dictatorship into the hands of the proletariat."[42] This mistaken view of Tukhachevsky was also reflected in other works of his.[43]

The rejection of the strategy of "attrition" willingly or unwillingly reflected the view that in case of war against us the rear of capitalist countries will be unstable, that with the first strong blows of the Red Army, class conflicts will be exacerbated in such countries, the working class will rise up, and a civil war will begin. And once the matter takes such shape, what, it may be asked, is the strategy of "attrition" that we are talking about? One cannot fail to agree with A. V. Golubev that at that time, namely for these considerations, it seemed that the strategy of "attrition" was, in principle, inapplicable to the Soviet state.[44] It is true that not everyone adhered to such an extreme point of view. B. M. Shaposhnikov, for example, considered that "*a future war will take on the character of a struggle of attrition*, but, depending on the size of the enemy's country, his domestic condition, and the class struggle developing there, the possibility of a strategy of annihilation is not excluded either."[45]

Unfortunately, the opinion which envisioned a combination of the strategy of "annihilation" and the strategy of "attrition" was not developed in our literature in the 1920s and 1930s. In the final analysis, the concrete practice of the Second World War resolved this problem. In rapidly paced wars, the complete defeat of the enemy was achieved by one or two shattering blows; in prolonged wars, the strategy of "attrition" applied its laws, with all the resulting consequences.[46] We fully share the idea of Marshal of the Soviet Union M. V. Zakharov, which amounts to the fact that it is senseless to oppose the strategy of "annihilation" and the strategy of "attrition."

Single, Napoleonic annihilating blows have already long ago receded into the field of history. Modern wars do not know a single method for conducting war, and "annihilation" and "attrition" as strategic forms can also supplement one another and change in the course of a war.[47]

From the course of the discussion on the strategy of "annihilation" and "attrition," an important conclusion is that it is extremely dangerous in resolving theoretical questions to ignore the conclusions of one's opponents and to support an extreme point of view.

The First World War and the Civil War introduced significant changes in the forms and methods of conducting armed combat. In these wars the scale of military operations grew atypically, leading to a significant widening of the functions of strategy.

Our analytical thought on the whole correctly took into account the strategic experience of these wars. But there were also shortcomings. One of them must be kept in mind. Military theory in the nineteenth century identified the strategic offensive with the strategic offensive operation.[48] Practical experience of the First World War and the Civil War showed that the strategic offensive cannot be reduced to one offensive operation, however large. For example, in 1914 Russian troops simultaneously conducted two strategic offensive operations (one in East Prussia, the other in Galicia); in 1920, the Red Army simultaneously conducted two strategic offensive operations (on the Warsaw and L'vov axes). It is true that the experience of conducting a strategic offensive simultaneously within two theaters of military operations for various reasons did not have positive results. But at the same time, from this experience the conclusion also arose that under specific conditions (the presence of sufficient forces and means, a high level of art, and others) a strategic offensive was possible even in several theaters. Nevertheless, our military theory, following nineteenth century traditions, did not digress from the framework of the strategic offensive operation implemented in a theater of military operations. As before, it identified the strategic offensive with the strategic operation. In this connection it is appropriate to note that in some scientific works published in the 1920s, the possibility of simultaneously conducting offensive operations in several theaters was envisioned.[49] Triandafillov expressed a very interesting idea on this issue. He wrote that in the development of operations on a wide front and in directing an attack against intersecting operational axes, "it will be useful to have two fronts," and the operational leadership of the operations should be "left directly to the commander-in-chief in the main theater of military operations."[50]

It is completely natural that offensive operations by several *fronts* should encompass several theaters of military operations as well, that is, the greater or, in any case, a significant part of a strategic front. The conduct of such operations presents high demands for their guidance on the part of the High Command. However, individual thoughts about the scales and nature of the strategic offensive were not developed in theoretical works.[51] Traditions of the nineteenth century were alive. One of the reasons for such a situation was the fact that the students of G. Leer, who examined strategy as the study of operations, were the authors of the first works on strategy.[52] In these works tribute was given (by some authors to a greater degree, by others to a lesser degree) to Leer's basic concepts. Svechin made a serious attempt to overcome Leer's scheme of the strategic operation. More than once he emphasized that in our time operation "with a capital O" was inapplicable, that the scale of the struggle had overgrown the framework of even the largest operations. The criticism of obsolete views which attempted to enclose armed combat within the framework of a single strategic operation was justified, but, unfortunately, was not given any attention. The strategic offensive, as before, was identified with the strategic operation, which was conceived as conducted by the forces of a single *front*. This view not only was dominant in the 1920s, but also, in general, was maintained right up until the beginning of the Second World War. It is true that on the eve of the Great Patriotic War individual ideas were expressed about the possibility of conducting a strategic operation with forces of more than one *front*.

What then was understood as the strategic offensive operation from the point of view of aims and methods of conducting it?

In the 1920s, it was considered that the defeat of an enemy's entire strategic front, extending thousands of kilometers, was a task beyond one's means. Thus, Zayonchkovsky wrote, "To destroy personnel on the entire expanse from, for example, the Baltic to the Black Sea is an unthinkable matter."[53] Therefore, he suggested that the strategic offensive would unfold in one of the theaters and take the shape of a large strategic operation.[54]

A strategic operational aim is understood as that final result for whose sake the operation is undertaken.[55] Hence, it was considered that such operational aims could be varied. In studying historical experience, military researchers completely naturally reached the conclusion that the most typical aim of a strategic offensive operation developing in a theater of military operations is the decisive defeat of the enemy. Zayonchkovsky wrote:

> Napoleon's principle of defeating personnel remains inviolable today. . . . Territory and lines are ultimately only intermediate stages and a kind of background for leading to the complete lack of combat capability of the enemy's armed forces, which, as before, is the only true success in war.[56]

Tukhachevsky formulated this idea even more categorically. He wrote,

"The aim of war is economic and political acquisitions for one side and the struggle against such acquisitions for the other side." But to achieve these aims it is necessary to destroy the enemy's armed forces. "The more fully such destruction is, the greater the degree of guarantee for the achievement of war aims."[57] In Tukhachevsky's work *Voprosy vysshego komandovaniya* [Problems of higher command], there is a small section on the annihilating operation [*unichtozhayushchaya operatsiya*]. In it he wrote:

> Operations are conducted to annihilate the enemy's vital armed forces; this is necessary to achieve war aims. The most advantageous annihilation is achieved by taking the enemy prisoner, since, in addition to weakening the enemy's army, prisoners economically reinforce the victor's rear. If taking prisoners is difficult or unsuccessful, the operation should achieve annihilation by physically destroying the enemy. . . . An attempt to annihilate enemy personnel forces the chief conducting the operation *to barely consider or completely disregard the acquisition or maintenance of territory.*[58]

In arguments Tukhachevsky correctly emphasized the idea that defeat (annihilation) of the enemy is the truest path to decisive victory. But it is, of course, impossible to agree with the statement that in conducting an operation "the acquisition or maintenance of territory" cannot be considered. At least two objections can be raised against this. *First*, the struggle against the enemy is not conducted in a vacuum, but on specific territory. The defeat of large strategic groupings operating on large expanses seriously influences the course of the war. Therefore, the question of capturing territory is also resolved automatically with the successful resolution of this mission. *Second*, territory is a concrete source of human and materiel resources. Important economic and political centers are located on it. Therefore, for the attacker it makes no difference in whose disposition these resources and centers are located. It also makes no difference for politics and strategy on whose territory the war is conducted. In theaters of military operations where battles and operations are taking place, the population experiences enormous hardships. The maximum easing of the situation for the population in the zone near the front is one of the important tasks for military-political leadership. Thus, the statement that in conducting operations acquisition or loss of territory should not be taken into account cannot be considered correct. Even during the Napoleonic Wars, when the economic significance of territory was different, much attention was given to capturing capitals and other important centers where considerable materiel resources were concentrated.

In later works Tukhachevsky changed his view on the significance of territory. In the work *Voprosy sovremennoy strategii* [Problems of modern strategy], published in 1926, he wrote that Germany held out so long during the First World War because she "seized a whole series of productive regions: Romania, Poland, the Baltic area, etc. In addition, she seized a whole series of areas with fuel, iron, etc. All this increased her capability to conduct war."[59] Later he pointed out that capturing territory has an exceptionally important significance for the Red Army too, since this widens the "war base."[60]

Proceeding from war experience, some authors (Gutor, for example) considered that in the course of armed combat other aims can arise as well for strategic offensive operations. Thus, in his opinion the ultimate operational aim of the Western Front in 1920 was to capture a political and economic center (Warsaw); the ultimate aim of the Northwestern Front at the beginning of the 1914 campaign was to capture an important portion of enemy territory (East Prussia); in the Russo-Turkish Wars it was to capture a strategic line, an inaccessible obstacle, after which favorable conditions were created for the development of the offense (the Danube and the Balkans). The posing of such aims in strategic operations could take place in those wars in which it was not possible to put an end to the enemy with one blow, where it was consequently necessary to proceed step by step to victory over the enemy.

Soviet military-scientific thought viewed a future war of the Soviet state against capitalist countries as a struggle against coalitions of bourgeois states. Under these conditions it was suggested that the most important mission would be cutting off any of the countries from hostile coalitions. Tukhachevsky said that in conducting a war against a coalition, we must build "a plan for the liquidation of the entire coalition, not at once, but piecemeal, successively and systematically."[61] With such a nature of armed combat, taking one or another of the participants of the hostile coalition out of the war could require the conduct of a large offensive operation.

Thus, our military theory in the 1920s proceeded from the fact that, depending on war aims and situational conditions, the aims of strategic offensive operations could be varied. Decisive defeat of the enemy and capture of a specific area was considered one of the most typical operational aims. Such a view of operational aims was proven completely correct during the last war.

Our analytical thought focused great attention during these years on the question of methods for conducting armed combat. It was completely evident that operations could be implemented between the Baltic and Black Seas (an expanse of 1,500 kilometers) in four theaters of military operations: Northwestern, Western, Southwestern, and Southern. It was considered that one large *front* formation [*ob"yedineniye*] would operate in each of these theaters (as in 1916–17). The simultaneous development of a strategic offensive against an enemy coalition along the entire expanse from the Baltic to the Black Sea was considered an impossible task as a consequence of insufficient forces and means. Tukhachevsky wrote:

Therefore, in conducting a war against a coalition, it is necessary . . . to note the significance of one, or another, or a third member of this coalition and correctly formulate a plan for their successive elimination until a favorable correlation of forces, overwhelmingly in our favor, has been created – all this is a fundamental difficulty, and together with this the fundamental art of modern strategy.[62]

With the great expanse of strategic fronts (2,000–3,000-plus kilometers), armed combat can be conducted simultaneously by several states belonging to a hostile coalition: on the right flank – one state, in the center – a second, and on the left flank – a third state. Successively putting them out of the war, as was suggested by Tukhachevsky, was connected with conducting a series of successive operations along the front. This method of conducting offensive operations was acknowledged, but was not worked out theoretically. And this was a substantial shortcoming of our theory.

In developing methods of conducting combat in theaters of military operations, our military theory focused great attention on questions of organizing and conducting successive offensive operations into the depth. Many military researchers, including Tukhachevsky, Svechin, Triandafillov, Varfolomeyev, Movchin, and others, studied this problem.

Tukhachevsky considered that to fully defeat the enemy it was necessary that one offensive operation develop into another without any loss of time whatsoever. The conduct of an offensive should provide the capability of completing the annihilation of enemy forces which have slipped out from under a blow. Therefore, a new annihilating operation should begin directly from the march, without the slightest loss of time. He considered all successive operations as parts of one large operation.[63] Svechin also supported this point of view. Under conditions which had become complex, the destructive offensive, he wrote, is

> a series of successive operations which, however, are internally connected in such a way that they merge into one gigantic operation. The initial position for the following operation proceeds directly from the achieved aim of the operation which has been completed.[64]

And so, in the opinion of Svechin and Tukhachevsky, the strategic offensive was enclosed within the framework of one large, or in Svechin's terminology "gigantic" operation. What, then, was the scope suggested for this operation?

In the work *Novyye voprosy voyny* [New questions of war], Tukhachevsky wrote that to destroy the enemy it was necessary to develop the offense over a significant expanse. "A wide front is necessary to defeat a large, or in any case, a significant part of the enemy forces, and to be able to commit one's own even greater overwhelming forces into battle."[65] In his opinion the offense had to include hundreds of kilometers of front and to be executed by forces of up to 100 divisions. The main attack was to be delivered by forces of up to 60 divisions on a front of up to 120 kilometers.

Interesting thoughts on this question were expressed by Triandafillov. He considered that with a large extension of the front line and stability of the defense, operations could not be executed in narrow sectors. He wrote:

> One shock army can decisively attack in a sector of only 25–30 kilo-meters. With respect to a 400-km front, this is literally a pin-prick. Such an operation can have only limited local aims. For decisive success on fronts of the above-mentioned lengths, an attack in a sector of no less than 150–200 kilometers is required, for which it is necessary to deploy forces numbering 50 divisions or more in the first echelon alone.[66]

And further: "Operations reckoned against the enemy and occupying a front of 350–400 kilometers require depths of no less than these 350–400 kilo-meters and an accelerated tempo of advance."[67] Triandafillov put the achievement of such a depth in dependence on the operation of railroad transport. He considered that its development would make it possible in the near future to resolve the problem of deep and annihilating attacks by executing a series of successive operations conducted within the framework of one larger operation.

Thus, both Tukhachevsky and Triandafillov, speaking about a 400–km offensive front, had in mind the conduct of one large *front* operation. Such a view of the scope of an offensive *front* operation remained, in essence, right up until the beginning of the Great Patriotic War.[68]

N. Movchin devoted a special book to the problems of conducting successive operations.[69] In it he investigated the advance of German forces to the Marne in 1914 and the advance of our Western Front forces to the Vistula in 1920, and on the basis of the experience of these greatest of mili-tary events he made very interesting judgements about the possible nature of successive operations under modern conditions. He considered that successive operations in depth could be conducted in the following sequence: *first operation* – initial; *second operation* – pursuit operation; *third operation* – decisive.

He envisioned that in practice "various combinations of the principal types (two or three initial operations) which end with pursuit, etc., are possible."[70] Movchin identified the pursuit operation as strategic pursuit. He considered that a front could conduct two or three successive operations; the depth of the first two was determined as being from 120–150 kilometers. He suggested that it was necessary either to stop at a convenient line or to con-tinue to the exhaustion of forces and means in a decisive operation (in some cases risk was possible, and even necessary) to conduct the third *front* operation.[71]

Such a conclusion resulted, to a significant degree, from the experience of engagements lost by German forces on the Marne in 1914 and by our forces on the Vistula in 1920. These lessons strongly influenced many of Movchin's conclusions. He considered that under modern conditions (the end of the 1920s) the achievement of a depth of 500–600 kilometers was definitely impossible "if it proceeds from an assumption about the stability of the enemy."[72] Here the author emphasized that "a series of successive operations are of themselves a rare occurrence, and much preliminary data are required to make their execution possible."[73] He associated these data with superiority over the enemy in forces and means (within the main theater of military operations), good troop training and their high moral condition, the presence of manpower reserves, a sufficient quantity of materiel reserves, etc.

Thus, if one speaks about methods of armed combat, our military theory had done much to work out questions of organizing and conducting offensive operations into the depth. As for investigating the question of conducting successive operations along a front, this was only posed, and was not researched theoretically. Questions of conducting a system of successive offensive operations unfolding simultaneously both along a front and into the depth remained in the same condition.

Summing up what has been said, it should be noted that in the 1920s our military-scientific thought achieved considerable successes in working out many important strategic theory questions. One of the serious achievements was that, in principle, the possible nature of armed combat in future war was correctly determined. Considerable success was also achieved in developing the theory of strategic offensive operations. Views on these questions were basically vital in subsequent years as well. It should also be considered that strategic theory in the 1920s developed under conditions of a narrow material-technical base, taking into account fully defined probable enemies. This, naturally, put its stamp on the possible framework and methods of armed combat in a future war.

NOTES

1. N. Pavlenko, "Nekotoryye voprosy razvitiya teorii strategii v 20-kh godakh," *Voyenno-istoricheskiy zhurnal* [Military-historical journal], 5 (May 1966), pp. 10–26.
2. V. I. Lenin, *Polnoye sobraniye sochineniy* [Complete collection of works], Vol. 40, pp. 182–3.
3. M. V. Frunze, *Yedinaya voyennaya doktrina i Krasnaya Armiya* [Unified military doctrine and the Red Army]; *Front i tyl v voyne budushchego* [Front and rear in future war]; *Osnovnyye voyennyye zadachi momenta* [The primary military tasks of the moment]; *Lenin*

i Krasnaya Armiya [Lenin and the Red Army]; and others (see M. V. Frunze, *Izbrannyye proizvedeniya* [Selected works], Vols I and II (Moscow: Voyenizdat, 1957).

4. M. N. Tukhachevsky, *Voyna kak problema vooruzhennoy bor'by* [War a question of armed struggle]; Preface to H. Delbrueck's book *Istoriya voyennogo iskusstva v ramkakh politicheskoy istorii* [The history of military art within the framework of political history], and others (see M. N. Tukhachevsky, *Izbrannyye proizvedeniya* [Selected works], Vols 1, 2 (Moscow: Voyenizdat, 1964).

5. A. A. Svechin, *Strategiya* [Strategy], 1st edition (Moscow–Leningrad: Gosvoyenizdat, 1926); 2d edition (Moscow: Voyennyy Vestnik, 1927).

A. A. Svechin (1878–1938) was a major general in the old army. He took part in the Russo-Japanese War and the First World War. From March 1918 he was military leader of the Smolensk region of the Western [Defensive] Screen, and later was the chief of the All Russian Main Staff (*Vseroglavshtab*), chairman of the Military-History Commission, instructor at the *RKKA* Military Academy from 28 November 1918, and then instructor at the General Staff Academy. He was the author of many works on questions of military theory and military history.

6. A. A. Neznamov, *Sovremennaya voyna* [Modern war], parts I and II (Higher Military Editorial Council, 1922).

A. A. Neznamov (1872–1928) was a major general in the old army; he graduated from the General Staff Academy ànd was a professor at the Academy and served at important posts in staffs. In 1918 he entered the Red Army and taught strategy and tactics at military academies. He was the author of a number of scientific works on strategic issues.

7. A. M. Zayonchkovsky, *Lektsii po strategii, chitannyye na voyenno-akademicheskikh kursakh vysshego komsostava v Voyennoy akademii RKKA v 1922–1923 gg.* [Lectures on strategy given in military-academic courses for higher command personnel at the *RKKA* Military Academy in 1922–1923], parts I, II, 1923.

A. M. Zayonchkovsky (1862–1926) was an infantry general; he graduated from the General Staff Academy, took part in the Russo-Japanese War and the First World War. In 1918 he entered the Red Army. After the Civil War he became a professor at the *RKKA* Military Academy. He left a rich literary legacy on the history of the Crimean War and the First World War.

8. V. K. Triandafillov, *Kharakter operatsiy sovremennykh armiy* [The nature of operations of modern armies], 2d edition (Moscow: GVIZ, 1932).

9. S. S. Kamenev, *Operatsiya (Voprosy strategii i operativnogo iskusstva v sovetskikh voyennykh trudakh 1917–1940)* [The operation (Questions of strategy and operational art in Soviet military works 1917–1940)] (Moscow: Voyenizdat, 1965); B. M. Shaposhnikov, *Mozg armii* [The brain of the army], Books I, II, III (Moscow: Voyennyy Vestnik, 1927); N. N. Movchin, *Posledovatel'nyye operatsii po opytu Marna i Visly* [Successive operations according to the experience of the Marne and the Vistula] (Moscow–Leningrad: Gosizdat, 1928).

N. N. Movchin (1896–1938) took part in the Civil War, served on the *RKKA* Staff, and graduated from the *RKKA* Military Academy. In the 1920s he published works on the investigation of war experience.

10. The attitude toward strategy is characterized by the following. In 1935, the military-history department was organized at the Frunze Military Academy. According to the testimony of the department head, A. V. Golubev, a 32-hour course of lectures on strategic theory was envisioned in its academic program. The deputy chief of the academy, Ye. A. Shchadenko, in examining the program, announced to Golubev, "What kind of a strategy course is this? Comrade Stalin personally studies strategy, and it is not a matter for us." It is true that the chief of the Frunze Military Academy, B. M. Shaposhnikov, did not agree with his deputy's opinion. According to Golubev's testimony, Shaposhnikov told him, "The question of giving lectures on strategy is in agreement with the Political Directorate of the *RKKA*; there will be a lecture course on strategy in the department, and your task is to prepare it." Lectures were prepared, but they were not given. The department was in existence all of one year, and then it was included in the newly created General Staff Academy, in the program of which was no cycle of lectures on strategy. Attempts were made to advocate a strategy course in the General Staff Academy. However, as former head of the department of opera-

tional art of this academy, G. S. Isserson, recalls, the slightest hint of a necessity to introduce into the academy in one form or another a strategy course as a foundation for operational art ran into objections from above. When this issue was raised at one of the meetings before the opening of the academy, Chief of the General Staff Marshal A. I. Yegorov, with some irritation, directly asked the President of the Academy, "Well, what would you study about strategy? The war plan? Strategic deployment? Or the conduct of war? No one will allow you to do this, because this is a matter for the General Staff." (*Voyenno-istoricheskiy zhurnal* [Military-historical journal], 3 (March 1965), pp. 49–50). Of course, no one posing the question was encroaching upon the prerogatives of the General Staff in the area of practical development of the issues of planning and conducting a war. It was a matter of investigating issues of strategic theory.

11. A. I. Verkhovsky, *Ogon', manevr, i maskirovka* [Fire, maneuver, and *maskirovka*] (Moscow: Voyennyy Vestnik, 1928), p. 231.
12. In a speech dedicated to the 20th anniversary of the Red Army and Navy, K. Ye. Voroshilov in 1938 said, "The cavalry in all armies of the world is undergoing, or more correctly has undergone, a crisis, and in many armies has almost been reduced to nothing. . . We advocate another point of view . . . We are convinced that our excellent cavalry will continue to be spoken of as the powerful and triumphant Red Cavalry. As before, the Red Cavalry is a triumphant and annihilating armed force and can and will resolve great missions on all combat fronts" (K. Ye. Voroshilov, *XX let Raboche-Krest'yanskoy Krasnoy Armii i Voyenno-Morskogo Flota* [20 years of the Workers' and Peasants' Red Army and Navy] (Moscow: Gospolizdat, 1938), p. 14.
13. Poland – 48, Romania – 36, Estonia – 5, Latvia – 6, Finland – 6, and Lithuania – 5 (Triandafillov, p. 34).
14. Triandafillov, p. 38.
15. Ibid., p. 69.
16. *Vos'moy s"yezd RKP(b). Mart 1919g. Protokoly* [Eighth Congress of the *RKP(b)*. March 1919. Protocols] (Gospolitizdat, 1959), p. 345.
17. See Frunze, Selected Works, Vol. II, p. 44.
18. Zayonchkovsky, p. 37.
19. Ibid., p. 44
20. *Problems of Strategy and Operational Art in Soviet Military Works* (1917–1940), pp. 149–50.
21. Frunze, Vol. II, p. 133.
22. Tukhachevsky, Vol. I, p. 260.
23. Svechin, p. 296.
24. Movchin, p. 116.
25. *Voyennaya entsiklopediya* [Military encyclopedia], published by the Association of I. D. Sytin, Vol. XII, 1913, p. 331.
26. In the middle of the nineteenth century a precise definition of a campaign was given in the article "The Campaign" by Engels. He wrote, "The campaign indicates a number of military operations which are closely connected to one another by a single strategic plan and directed toward the achievement of a single strategic aim" (K. Marx and F. Engels, Works, 2d edition, Vol. XIV, p. 242).
27. Zayonchkovsky in his lectures given at the *RKKA* Military Academy in 1922–23 (part 2, p. 25) spoke "about a strategy of decisive operations and a strategy of exhaustion." The first, in his opinion, searched for a rapid solution by means of a decisive advance and battle, the second "is expressed in isolating the enemy from the external world and depriving him of means of existence."
28. Frunze, Vol. II, p. 133.
29. Svechin, pp. 258–9.
30. Ibid, p. 263.
31. Ibid., p. 56.
32. Ibid., p. 259.
33. Ibid.
34. Ibid., p. 58.
35. Ibid., p. 59.

36. Ibid., p. 57.
37. Ibid., p. 262.
38. Ibid., p. 264.
39. Tukhachevsky, Vol. II, p. 137.
40. Ibid., pp. 137–8.
41. An analysis of Svechin's works was conducted differently at the beginning of the 1930s. Here it was not so much evidence as unsubstantiated accusations which prevailed. Characteristic in this respect was the stenogram of the open meeting of the plenum of the section for studying war issues of the Leningrad Section of the Communist Academy of the USSR Central Institute of Communism dated 25 April 1931. Speaking at this meeting, Tukhachevsky directly called the theory of "attrition" a "defeatist theory" (*Protiv reaktsionnykh teoriy na voyenno-nauchnom fronte* [Against reactionary theories on the military-scientific front] (Moscow: Gosvoyenizdat, 1931), p. 10). He also very unjustly evaluated the author of *Strategy.* Svechin's theory was declared an integral link in the intervention being prepared against us. About the author himself, it was said that he "in fact is leading the Red Army to defeat," that he "objectively is an agent of the bourgeoisie" (against reactionary theories, pp. 7, 8, 10).

Of course, after similar "discussions," theoretical questions posed by Svechin on the problem of "annihilation" and "exhaustion" ceased to be discussed. The strategy of "attrition" was buried in oblivion, and opposing, one-sided points of view remained beyond criticism.
42. *"Revolyutsiya i voyna." Sbornik tretiy* ["Revolution and war." Third collection] (Directorate of Military-Educational Institutions of the Western Front, Publications Department, 1920), p. 46. In publishing Tukhachevsky's article, the editorial board of this journal noted that the article expressed the subjective views of the author, and that "the RSFSR conducted and can conduct only defensive wars."
43. Tukhachevsky, Vol. I, pp. 168, 252, 258.
44. *Voyenno-istoricheskiy zhurnal* [Military-historical journal], 10 (October 1965), p. 37.
45. Shaposhnikov, Book 1, p. 245.
46. Fascist Germany achieved victory in the war against Poland as a result of a single operation. Victory in Yugoslavia was gained by one blow. The rout of the armed forces of the Western powers was achieved in two successive operations. In the first operation, implemented in May 1940, German-Fascist forces succeeded in splitting the Allies' strategic front and reached the Channel; in the second operation, which unfolded in June from the Aisne River, French forces suffered complete defeat. In these wars, for a number of reasons favorable to the Germans, her forces succeeded in achieving victories by conducting one or two annihilating operations.

Fascist Germany's war against the Soviet Union acquired a completely different, prolonged, and exhausting character. German-Fascist forces had great successes in the 1941 and 1942 operations, but they were very far from victory.

During the last war a majority of offensive operations and campaigns conducted by the Soviet Army bore an exclusively decisive character. In order to bring the war to a victorious conclusion, it was necessary to disembowel the enemy, in the literal sense of the word, and exhaust his human and materiel resources by the skillful conduct of annihilating operations. The following figures convincingly attest to losses of German-Fascist forces. At the beginning of the war the German-Fascist forces had on the Soviet–German front 4.4 million men (3.3 million in the ground forces), 50,000 guns and mortars, 3,400 tanks and 4,000 aircraft (*Istoriya Velikoy Otechestvennoy voyny Sovetskogo Soyuza 1941–1945* [History of the Great Patriotic War of the Soviet Union 1941–1945], Volume I (Moscow: Voyenizdat, 1963), p. 384). During the war against the Soviet Union, German forces lost (dead, wounded, prisoners, and missing in action) around 10 million men, 167,000 guns and mortars, 48,000 tanks (*History of The Great Patriotic War*, Vol. VI, p. 29) and 62,000 aircraft (*Porazheniye germanskogo imperializma vo vtoroy mirovoy voyne* [Defeat of German imperialism in World War II] (Moscow: Voyenizdat, 1960), p. 115). Consequently, Germany lost 2.3 times more men, 3.3 times more guns and mortars, 14 times more tanks and assault guns, and 15.5 times more aircraft than it had on the Soviet–German front at the beginning of the war.

During the war the strategies of "annihilation" and "attrition" were combined in practice. Strategic offensive operations and campaigns skillfully conducted by the Soviet command were, in truth, a clear expression of the strategy of "annihilation," which Tukhachevsky had so favored in the prewar years. Annihilating routs of enemy strategic groupings in each campaign undermined the military, economic, and political might of the enemy. The human, materiel, and spiritual strength of Fascist Germany was gradually worn down. It was unswervingly approaching a catastrophe. If the offensive operations and campaigns of the Soviet Army had an annihilating nature, in the full sense of the word, the war of the Soviet Union against Fascist Germany and her allies was a war of complete exhaustion of human and materiel resources. The close intertwining of the strategy of "annihilation" with the strategy of "attrition" of the warring sides is one of the characteristic markers of the last war.

47. *Problems of Strategy and Operational Art in Soviet Military Works (1917–1940)*, p. 16.
48. See *Military-Historical Journal*, 10 (October 1964), pp. 104–16.
49. Svechin, p. 317.
50. Triandafillov, p. 171.
51. The question of the possibility of simultaneous development of a strategic offensive by forces of several fronts was raised at the meeting of the Higher Command in December 1940. Thus, in summing up the results of the work of the meeting, People's Commissar for Defense Marshal S. K. Timoshenko said in his concluding remarks on 31 December, "It is necessary to keep in mind the possibility of simultaneously conducting two, if not three offensive operations of various fronts on a theater of war with the intention of strategically shaking the enemy's entire combat capability as extensively as possible."
52. A. A. Neznamov, *Osnovy sovremennoy strategii* [Foundations of modern strategy], General Staff Academy of the *RKKA* (Moscow: 1919); *Sovremennaya strategiya* [Modern strategy], part I, 1921, part II, 1922; A. M. Zayonchkovsky, *Lectures*; A. Ye. Gutor, *Lektsii po strategii chitannyye v Voyennoy akademii RKKA v 1922–1923 uch. godu* [Lectures on strategy given at the Military Academy of the *RKKA* in the 1922–1923 academic year] (Moscow: 1923).
53. Zayonchkovsky, *Lectures on Strategy*, part 2, p. 44.
54. Zayonchkovsky understood strategic operations as "successive rapid stages in the armed forces' execution of the overall war plan" (*Lectures on strategy*, p. 41). Gutor gave the following definition of a strategic operation: "We understand the strategic operation as some completed period of troop activities or movement in a theater of military actions" (*Lectures*, p. 1).
55. Gutor, *Lectures*, p. 13. A. Ye. Gutor (1868–1938) was a lieutenant general in the old army; he commanded a corps and army in the First World War. He was a member of the special session under the commander-in-chief during the Soviet–Polish War. He was a senior instructor at the Frunze Military Academy and the author of a number of works on military theory and history.
56. Zayonchkovsky, *Lectures*, p. 45.
57. Tukhachevsky, Vol. I, p. 107.
58. Ibid., p, 185.
59. Ibid., p. 256.
60. Ibid., p. 259.
61. Ibid., p. 256.
62. Ibid.
63. Ibid., p. 186.
64. Svechin, p. 256.
65. *Problems of Strategy and Operational Art in Soviet Military Works (1917–1940)*, p. 119.
66. Triandafillov, p. 115.
67. Ibid., p. 151.
68. In this connection it is appropriate to note that the basic ideas stated by Triandafillov converged with those observations stated at the meeting of the higher command staff in December 1940. From the talk by General of Army G. K. Zhukov and the concluding words of Marshal of the Soviet Union S. K. Timoshenko, it is evident that it was suggested conducting a front offensive operation in a 300–400-kilometer sector and at a depth of 200–300

kilometers and more. The main attack in the operation was to be implemented on a front of 60–100 kilometers. To conduct such an operation, it was suggested having 60–75 rifle divisions, 4–5 mechanized corps, 2–3 cavalry corps, 15–30 aviation divisions, and other reinforcement assets as part of the front.

69. N. Movchin, *Posledovatel'nyye operatsii po opytu Marny i Visly* [Successive operations according to the experience of the Marne and the Vistula] (Moscow–Leningrad: Gosizdat, Military Literature Department, 1928).
70. Ibid., 118.
71. Ibid., p. 11
72. Ibid., p. 114
73. Ibid., p. 121.

Soviet Operational Art in the Great Patriotic War

GENERAL OF THE ARMY I. PAVLOVSKIY[1]

Twenty-three years ago the Great Patriotic War – the most brutal and fierce of all wars ever experienced by our Motherland – concluded with the glorious victory of the Soviet nation. The war, imposed upon us by a perfidious, treacherous, strong, and experienced enemy, was a severe and awesome test of our nation's entire moral and physical strength, and of the survivability of the economic and political organization of socialist society and the fortress of the Soviet Armed Forces.

The Soviet Union's victory in this gigantic encounter against the shock forces of imperialist reaction was the best proof of the invincibility and superiority of the new socialist state and social system, of Marxist-Leninist ideology, and of our military science. This great superiority was realized thanks to the wise and far-seeing leadership of the Communist Party, which confidently directed our nation's efforts toward a complete victory over the enemy.

The historic Soviet Armed Forces victory was, at the same time, a triumph for our Soviet military art and its component – operational art, which was developed and perfected during the Great Patriotic War. Together with the growth of our forces and combat experience, the art of conducting joint and independent operations by different armed forces services grew, and new, more improved methods and forms were found for conducting operations under maneuver conditions and the extremely intense nature of battle during the entire war.

The Soviet Armed Forces entered the war with a completely progressive theory of operational art, corresponding to the level of our armed forces' development and combat experience at that time. However, the treacherous surprise attack of superior enemy forces at the very beginning of the war advanced a series of new tasks and problems for Soviet operational art, and required reexamination of several principles established on the eve of the war.

This relates, above all, to the *problem of defense*, which our forces were compelled to wage from the first days of the war, conducting arduous battles against large enemy tank and mechanized groupings along the entire expanse of the Soviet–German front.

Despite the fact that our doctrine envisioned dynamic offensive actions with decisive aims from the beginning of a war, in the initial period of this war (June 1941–October 1942) our army was forced twice to resort to a strategic defense, resolving the especially difficult and complex task of creating a continuous and stable front with inadequate forces and means, faced with a dynamic and strong enemy.

Front and army defensive operations had the aim of preventing enemy penetration to important objectives; bleeding the enemy dry by firmly holding positions and lines, in combination with counterstrokes; exhausting his offensive capabilities and forcing him to abandon his offensive; and gaining time to deploy forces and means and bring up substantial reserves from the depth of the country. A feature of offensive operations was the fact that they were prepared hastily, under pressure from superior, dynamically operating enemy forces, and were conducted on a broad front with inadequate forces and means, especially artillery, tanks, and aviation. The defensive formation bore a linear, shallow nature. *Fronts* having a single-echelon formation defended, as a rule, in sectors with a width of 300–600 kilometers; armies defended in sectors with a width of 120–180 kilometers, with a density of five to ten guns and mortars and one to two tanks per kilometer of front. Forces occupied beforehand only the main defensive belt, with a depth of three to four kilometers and having a fragmented character. *Front* reserves were deployed 20–30 kilometers, and army reserves 10–15 kilometers from the forward edge. Such a nature of the defense, as well as the inadequate massing of forces on decisive axes, did not ensure the thwarting of the enemy offensive. Our forces were compelled to conduct a defense on the principles of mobile actions to parry enemy penetrations and envelopments, by which they were able to wear out the enemy while maintaining their own strength, without taking into account losses of territory.

As forces accumulated, *fronts* and army combat compositions increased, operational densities grew, force dynamism and defensive stability, which acquired positional forms, matured, and efforts on the enemy's main attack axes were more boldly concentrated. Defensive operations were prepared more carefully, forces and means were echeloned with respect to depth, engagements became longer and more stubborn, and the enemy suffered heavy losses without always achieving his offensive aims.

In 1942, serious qualitative changes occurred in our forces. Tank and mechanized corps were created, and tank armies (of mixed composition), air armies, and formations of other combat arms were also included in the *fronts'* composition. All this made it possible to create a deeper defensive operational formation of forces, which ensured the repulsion of massive enemy ground forces and air attacks.

On the whole, experience obtained in organizing and conducting defensive operations in 1941–42 demonstrated that only large *front* formations had the strength necessary to create a stable and dynamic operational defense, capable of stopping an enemy offensive by massing these forces on the enemy's main attack axes.

Under conditions of the enemy's mass employment of tanks and aviation, operational art resolved the problem of creating a stable *antitank* and effective *air defense*. Experience showed that existing antitank artillery densities of two to five guns per kilometer of front, the equal distribution of antitank defense means along the front, and their grouping in regions inaccessible to tanks did not ensure the repulsion of massed enemy tank attacks. Therefore, from autumn 1941, all combat arms and aviation were enlisted to fight against tank groupings. Here, means for fighting against tanks were used in mass quantities and echeloned into the depth along the main axes. The most advantageous method of employing them was constructing antitank regions and strongpoints, increasing the density of engineer antitank obstacles, and creating antitank reserves in *fronts* and armies to reinforce likely tank approaches. All this significantly increased defensive stability.

In 1942, *air defense* was considerably strengthened by the creation of antiaircraft artillery divisions and air defense army regiments, and with the strengthening of *front* fighter aviation.

Views on the operational use of *artillery and tanks in the defense* also underwent changes. The inadequacy of artillery at the beginning of the war led to infantry support artillery groups being created in rifle divisions, which were weak with respect to their composition (one to three battalions); the same was true of long-range artillery groups to fight against enemy artillery. As artillery grew in size and was improved, and as experience was accumulated, its role in repelling enemy attacks increased, and, in the concluding operations of the 1942 summer and autumn campaigns, it became the decisive defensive fire force.

As a consequence of their small numbers, tanks were used as separate units in 1941 defensive operations, in close cooperation with infantry and cavalry, mainly for tactical purposes. In 1942, the number of tanks grew, and existing tank and mechanized corps began to be used as *front* and army reserves to deliver counterstrokes.

Because of heavy losses in the first months of the war, *front* aviation did not have the necessary force to deliver effective strikes against the enemy or protect its own forces against enemy aviation. However, in 1942 the combat capabilities of air armies increased considerably. They began to intensify the force of their strikes, which also led to an increase in the dynamism of the operational defense.

Serious searches were made for ways to improve the *engineer preparation* of terrain occupied for defense. Difficulties in resolving this problem arose from the fact that *front* and army forces had neither the time nor means to prepare defense zones in accordance with our prewar views. In 1941, forces managed the engineer preparation of only the main defensive belt and army reserve positions. And only beginning with the second half of 1942 did the forces of some *fronts* gradually shift to the preparation of a multi-belt defense with a developed system of trenches and obstacles. The defensive formation included main and secondary belts, regions of special and com-bined-arms army and *front* reserves, and a *front* line of defense. Based on these belts and lines prepared in an engineer sense, forces were able not only to repel the enemy offensive, but also to force him to abandon the offensive.

Thus, as the combat and numerical composition of *fronts* and armies grew and armaments and combat equipment increased, the depth of the operational defensive formation increased, higher operational densities were created, defensive stability and dynamism increased, maneuver of forces and means along threatened axes were executed more boldly, and problems of coopera-tion were more carefully worked out. All this had a decisive impact on the improvement of defensive methods and on the more successful conduct of *fronts* and army defensive operations. As a result, by the end of 1942, large-scale enemy offensive operations across the entire Soviet–German front were incomplete, and the real possibility arose for seizing the strategic initiative, which was done by the Soviet command on the Stalingrad and Caucasus strategic axes.

During the first period of the war, Soviet forces and commands acquired some experience in organizing and conducting *offensive* operations. They were undertaken under conditions where the strategic initiative already belonged to the enemy. Operations were prepared in a complex situation of fierce defensive battles, and began without pauses, directly after defensive engagements (the Moscow, Tikhvin, and Kalinin operations). This was the first experience of such operations, but it had great significance for the development of operational art.

Despite limited forces and means, *fronts* and armies had decisive offensive operational aims. Main attacks were delivered against the most vulnerable areas of the enemy defense, occupied with the least density, while auxiliary attacks were along axes where it was possible to disrupt defensive stability and tie down enemy reserves.

The predominant operational form was the frontal attack with penetration of the enemy defense, which in this period bore a non-continuous, interrupted character and lacked depth. Penetration was executed on one or two axes. To achieve a greater operational result, from 1942 they began to conduct more frequent coordinated operations by two and more fronts, upon which the foundations of future offensive operations by groups of fronts were based.

As the enemy defensive depth increased and the technical outfitting of our forces improved, the form and depth of the operational formation changed and operational force densities increased. If in 1941 an army operational formation was a single echelon to support the initial attack, in 1942 it was structured in two echelons, with mobile forces and reserves. However, the *fronts* had, as a rule, a single-echelon formation, mobile forces, and reserves. In 1942 the depth of the operational formation increased to up to 40 kilometers in *fronts* and 12–16 (sometimes up to 30) kilometers in armies. In the majority of operations, the overall operational density, although amounting to four to nine kilometers per rifle division, was, on the whole, clearly inadequate to ensure a rapid penetration of the enemy defense and successful development of the offensive.

Inadequate densities were also created in penetration sectors. Sometimes *fronts* shifted to the offensive with a twofold superiority in infantry, but an equal or disadvantageous correlation of forces with respect to artillery and tanks. The absence in a *front's* operational formation of sizable forces to exploit success limited the scope of operations, and, in a number of instances, the successful penetration of the defense was not developed as required. This was taken into account. New organizational forms were developed for mobile forces and artillery. Beginning in 1942, in connection with the creation of tank and mechanized corps, artillery formations of the Reserve of the Supreme High Command (RVGK), and then tank armies, *fronts* began to receive powerful means capable of successfully completing the penetration of the tactical zone and exploiting success into the operational depth.

On the whole, our forces, commanders, and operational staffs acquired considerable combat experience during the first period of the war, and operational art developed further.

During this period, shifting from linear forms of combat action to deep forms was characteristic of Soviet offensive operations. This was achieved by massing forces and means on the main attack axes and more carefully organizing cooperation among all combat arms and armed forces services. During 1941–42 engagements, methods were initially developed for preparing and organizing timely *front* and army operations, and for conducting them with limited forces, foundations were laid for fighting against counterattacking enemy groupings, and very important individual questions were resolved concerning operational troop support. In *front* and army operations, however, our forces did not manage to resolve fully the problems of repelling enemy counterstrokes, fortifying captured lines during the offensive, or rapidly creating a stable external and internal front for encirclement and destruction of encircled groupings. All this was successfully resolved in subsequent periods of the war. Working out methods of continuous artillery and aviation offensive support, and finding effective methods for our aviation operations against enemy airfields were important for the development of operational art. At this time, practical foundations were laid for employing groups of mobile forces in army and *front* operations. The problem of preparing and conducting operations by groups of *fronts,* which at subsequent stages of the war became the crown of our operational art and strategy, was completely new and not yet researched.

During the second period of the Great Patriotic War (November 1942–December 1943), further development of operational art was based on firmly established military-economic potential, the ever increasing volume of combat equipment production, and the thorough and all-round generalization of military operations of the first period of the war. Armaments entering the force inventory made it possible to increase sharply shock and fire power, as well as the mobility of formations and large formations of all armed forces services and combat arms. Re-establishment of rifle corps, creation of uniform tank armies, increase in the number of tank and mechanized corps, and establishment of artillery penetration formations, new air armies, and aviation corps and divisions had especially important significance for the increase in operational capabilities, mobility, and stability of troop control. All this made it necessary for operational art to find effective forms and methods for conducting offensive operations with decisive aims.

During this period, *offensive operations* were the predominant form for Soviet force actions. As a rule, offensive operations by a group of *fronts,* in which large *front* formations carried out part of the overall strategic mission, were conducted to defeat large enemy strategic groupings (30–60 divisions). In separate instances, *fronts* conducted independent offensive operations to defeat an enemy grouping (up to 10–12 divisions) and liberate important economic regions. Operations were prepared carefully, and the most decisive objectives and effective forms of maneuver were determined. The conduct of successive operations into the depth, without operational pauses, was most typical for army offensive operations. Here, the depth of the initial offensive operation usually included the immediate *front* mission, while the subsequent operation included its subsequent mission. Some experience was acquired as well in conducting successive operations across a front.

The most widespread form of *front* offensive operation was the frontal attack along one axis, and its development into the depth or in the direction of one of the flanks, to encircle and defeat enemy groupings in cooperation with forces of a neighboring *front.* A deep frontal attack was sometimes delivered to split an enemy grouping and destroy it piecemeal (Belgorod–Khar'kov Operation). Soviet forces succeeded in mastering the art of organizing and executing the penetration of the enemy defense at high tempos, and encircling and destroying large enemy groupings (Stalingrad operation).

The number of elements in the operational formation of forces were increased and their combat composition strengthened to resolve operational missions successfully. From summer 1943, in the majority of operations, *fronts* had more powerful first echelons (three to four armies) and second echelons (one to two combined-arms armies), mobile force groups (from two tank corps to two tank armies), and strong reserves. Combined-arms armies attacked in single-echelon formation, with the rifle corps combat formation in two echelons and reserves. Such a force formation was appropriate for new combat conditions and the changed nature of the enemy defense, and made it possible not only to deliver powerful attacks, but also to intensify their force from the depth, which led to an increase in the scope and offensive tempo of the operation. Operational formation was not a stereotypical pattern, and each time it was designed in accordance with the concrete situation.

Main attacks were delivered in narrow sectors, not exceeding 10–20 per cent of the overall front width, where 50–70 per cent of rifle forces, 70–80 per cent of guns and mortars, and up to 90 per cent of tanks and aviation were concentrated. This made it possible to conduct more powerful artillery and aviation offensives, having doubled the depth of suppression of the enemy defense during the artillery preparation for the attack, while supporting the infantry and tank attack by means of a fire barrage to a depth of up to three kilometers. The artillery and aviation offensive was an important achievement in the theory and practice of employing artillery and aviation in battles and operations. From summer 1943, this offensive acquired an operational character, and was fully executed to the entire depth of army and *front* operations.

Decisive massing of forces and means, as well as mastery of the art of selecting main attack axes and capably determining the time for shifting to the offensive, made it possible for Soviet forces to conduct offensive operations with significantly greater results, with respect to the defeat of large enemy forces, than during the first period of the war. Penetration of the enemy's main defense belt was now already completed on the first day of the offensive. Mobile forces, which ensured penetration of the entire tactical zone, were introduced to complete the penetration of the tactical zone, and conditions were created to exploit tactical success into operational success, shift to a swift pursuit, capture advantageous lines from the march, and rapidly form internal and external encirclement fronts. Improvement in organizing close cooperation, implemented with respect to time and lines, both tactically and operationally, had important significance in improving the effectiveness of coordinated attacks by all armed forces services and combat arms participating in the operation.

The changed nature of the enemy defense required the conduct of *reconnaissance in force* by forward battalions. As a rule, this preceded an offensive, and was conducted on a broad front with powerful artillery fire support. This was a new and very important operational support measure, which made it easier to penetrate the main enemy defensive belt successfully.

Combined-arms, tank, and artillery reserves and mobile obstacle detachments, which, together with first-echelon forces, destroyed the enemy who had shifted to the offensive, took on the main burden of battles to repel enemy *counterstrokes*. All ground attack and bomber aviation forces were enlisted to repel counterstrokes.

Considerable experience was acquired in organizing and conducting pursuit. Here, parallel pursuit provided the best results; this was conducted continuously, day and night, with maximum force intensity. The leading role in pursuit belonged to tank forces, which advanced at a tempo of up to 50–70 kilometers per day. Aviation also played an important role in successful pursuit of the enemy. It delivered massive strikes against withdrawing columns, road junctions, crossings, and defiles. At this time, the important problem of forcing large water obstacles and capturing and holding bridgeheads was resolved. Rivers were forced from the march on a broad front, using both authorized crossing means and local means on hand. Captured tactical bridgeheads were swiftly expanded to operational scales.

Despite having seized the strategic initiative, *defense* continued to occupy a significant place in our armed forces operations, since the enemy was still attempting to resume the offensive on separate axes. However, the growth in the Soviet Army's combat composition, and acquired experience and expertise, made it possible to prepare and conduct defensive operations in a much more organized fashion than during the first period of the war. In the majority of operations, enemy attacks were parried promptly and successfully by bold and swift concentration of forces on these axes.

It was characteristic that defensive operations were conducted along separate axes and in narrower sectors. However, the quantity of participating forces and means and operational densities grew significantly. The problem of creating a dynamic *antitank, antiaircraft, insurmountable* defense was successfully resolved. Insurmountability was achieved by a deeper operational formation of forces; creation of a dense system of fire and multi-belt defense with a dense network of trenches, communications trenches, and obstacles; great troop dynamism; and decisive and flexible maneuver of second echelons and reserves. Defensive stability particularly increased in connection with the growth in antitank means and use of tanks to fight in the tactical zone.

As a rule, a *front* had an operational formation of two echelons and strong reserves. In *front* sectors where an enemy offensive was expected, five to six defensive belts were prepared to an overall depth of 100–120 kilometers, and sometimes up to 150 kilometers (the defense in the Kursk salient). As a rule, antitank ditches were dug out in front of the third belt, and cut-off positions were outfitted in a number of sectors.

An army, in single-echelon formation, was deployed in three defensive belts with an overall depth of up to 25 kilometers, with rifle corps in two echelons. Special attention was focused on outfitting the tactical zone of defense, which included two defensive belts and cut-off positions. Two or three positions were created in each belt, each outfitted with two or three trenches and a bifurcated network of communications trenches. More than two-thirds of the first-echelon army forces were deployed in the tactical zone. Consequently, the enemy did not succeed in breaking through or deeply penetrating our defense. The offensive tempo of enemy forces on the main attack axes decreased to 1.5–3.5 kilometers per day.

An *antitank* defense was constructed to the entire depth of the *front's* operational formation on the basis of creating antitank strongpoints and regions and extensively using all types of artillery, rocket mortars, tank reserves, aviation, and engineer forces to fight against enemy tank groupings. Antitank artillery densities on the main axes reached 18 guns per kilometer of front. The success of the struggle against enemy tanks was ensured not only by the high density of antitank means and their concentration on important likely tank approaches, but also by skillful maneuver of strong antitank reserves and mobile obstacle detachments.

One of the most important measures for increasing the dynamism of the defense was careful preparation and conduct of the *counterpreparation*. The artillery and aviation counterpreparation began to be employed not only on tactical, but also on operational scales. Considerable *front* forces and means were used for this (density reached from 35 to 60 guns and mortars per kilometer of front), which, to a significant degree, ruined enemy plans and inflicted heavy personnel and equipment losses.

The high degree of dynamism of the operational defense was exhibited to the greatest degree by delivery of *counterstrokes,* conducted in greater strength and more organized. The power and effectiveness of counterstrokes especially increased in connection with the use of tank formations and large tank formations, used massively in cooperation with artillery, aviation, and combined-arms armies. As a result of powerful counterstrokes, a turning point was created during defensive operations: the enemy was forced to cease his offensive and shift to the defense, without having achieved his intended aims. In the majority of cases, successfully conducted *front* counterstrokes developed into general counteroffensives, planned beforehand by the *Stavka* of the High Command. Here, selection of the moment for shifting to the counteroffensive had especially important significance. This required precise determination of the culminating point of the enemy offensive.

Soviet commanders resolved all these problems skillfully, and the high moral spirit and offensive passion of the forces ensured the realization of all operational plans associated with shifting from the defense to a decisive counteroffensive.

Reliable *aviation preparation and support* of attacking forces by ground attack and bomber aviation acquired special significance for successful *front* force operations. Aviation began to be massed on decisive axes and execute rapid maneuver and closer cooperation with ground forces. Having superiority over the enemy in fighters, aviation reliably covered operations of the principal ground forces groupings.

Increased power of our *aviation* and accumulated combat experience in gaining air superiority also made it possible in this period to begin to conduct air operations, to defeat enemy aviation groupings. Large long-range aviation and *front* aviation forces were used to conduct such operations, which in a short time (one and a half to three days) delivered powerful massive strikes against enemy airfields. At the same time, the problem of organizing the repulsion of massive enemy aviation raids was also resolved positively.

The *Navy* received combat experience in organizing and conducting amphibious assault landings, artillery and aviation support of their operations at sea, executing troop transfers, fighting against enemy naval forces, and supporting ground forces operating along the coast. At this time, new tactical procedures appeared for using ships and weapons, and the art of conducting amphibious assaults and other operations was improved.

Thus, during the second period of the war, Soviet operational art resolved a number of complex problems. Forms of organizing and conducting *front* and army offensive and defensive operations, and methods for using combat arms and armed forces services were developed further, and forms of organizing cooperation, control, and all types of operational and materiel support of combat operations were improved. This made it possible for our armed forces to enter the concluding stage of the war even stronger, and to resolve confidently large-scale operational-strategic missions at an even higher level.

During the third period of the Great Patriotic War (January 1944–August 1945), decisive victories were achieved, Fascist Germany was decisively defeated, and the Japanese Kwantung Army in the Far East was routed. By the beginning of this period, Soviet forces firmly held the strategic initiative and were able independently, without Allied assistance, to defeat the Fascist war machine. These actual capabilities were conditioned by the steady rise and development of our country's economy, and the further strengthening of the might of the Soviet State and its Armed Forces. The war economy, in ever growing scales, provided the army and navy with combat equipment, weapons, ammunition, fuel, and food. New heavy tanks and self-propelled artillery (IS-122, ISU-152, SAU-122, and SAU-100), artillery guns and mortars (57mm, 85mm, and 100mm cannons, and 160mm mortars), and combat aircraft (YaK-3, LA-7, IL-10, and TU-2) appeared. The technical outfitting of forces improved continuously, and the growth of combat experience conditioned the improvement of organizational forms, the increase in combat capabilities of formations and large formations, growth in their mobility, and expansion of operational independence in resolving large-scale combat missions.

One of the most important conditions affecting the development and improvement of operational art was the subsequent change in the correlation of forces to our benefit.

As a result of the quantitative and qualitative growth of the armed forces and troop and command cadre combat expertise, operational art, whose mission was to find ways and methods to use large operational formations effectively to defeat the enemy decisively, improved and developed on the basis of generalizing combat experience. In operations of this period, the superiority of Soviet command personnel's strategic and operational thought, the flexibility and firmness of leadership of large groupings of all armed forces services, Soviet force mobility, and the troops' unsurpassed moral-combat qualities were clearly manifested.

The nature of the strategic missions assigned to the Soviet Armed Forces in the 1944 and 1945 campaigns determined the necessity for employing decisive methods and forms for conducting offensive operations, which in this period were distinguished by originality of concept, decisiveness of aims, great scope, initiative actions, bold maneuver, and skillful massing of forces and means on main axes.

At this stage of the war, all issues associated with operational and strategic employment of armed forces services in close cooperation during an armed struggle on an enormous front were further developed. It should be mentioned that by this time the roles of the air force and navy in resolving large-scale operational-strategic missions had sharply increased. Increased air force capabilities made it possible to fight against enemy aviation, execute an aviation offensive, and reliably support ground forces operations in the offensive and in the defeat of large encircled enemy groupings. Expedient methods and forms were developed for conducting combat operations by large aviation formations, directed toward thwarting massive enemy operational and supply transports and toward demolishing enemy military-industrial objectives, ports, and naval bases.

The navy acquired great experience in fighting at sea. Together with operations to assist ground forces on coastal axes, it also resolved independent missions to demolish enemy maritime communications and protect its own communications; support maritime transports and Allied convoys in the navy's operational zone; and assist Allies in fighting against enemy surface and submarine forces.

Front offensive operations were conducted, as a rule, within the framework of operations of a group of *fronts*, which delivered interconnected, successive, and simultaneous attacks on various axes of the entire enormous strategic front. The employment of a system of successive attacks in 1944 led to wrecking the enemy's entire strategic front, and made it extremely difficult for him to protect or withdraw his forces and create in his own rear a new line of strategic defense. In 1945, the delivery of attacks, which continued uninterruptedly during the entire campaign until the complete defeat of the enemy, expressed a new step in the development of Soviet strategy and operational art.

The most typical offensive forms were operations for encirclement and destruction of large enemy groupings under the most varied conditions, both during the penetration of tactical and operational defense zones, and during pursuit. Encirclement and destruction of the enemy ensued as a single process (without pauses). This was achieved by creating a stable internal and external front of encirclement, reliably blocking encircled groupings from the air, and isolating and destroying them piecemeal. Dynamic offensive operations were undertaken to move back the external front to prevent relief of the encircled forces. In fact, dynamic force operations on the external encirclement front developed into a continuous offensive. Soviet operational art successfully resolved the problem of the operational penetration of a deeply echeloned positional enemy defense. Penetration of the defense and creation of conditions to conduct extensive maneuvers for a shallow and wide envelopment of isolated enemy groupings in the depth were carried out by main *front* forces. Forms of penetration were distinguished by their wide variety. In one case, a *front* broke through the defense in one sector and subsequently developed the penetration into the depth and in the direction of the flanks; in another case, a *front* penetrated the defense in two sectors to develop the offensive along converging directions; in a third case, a *front* delivered deep, cleaving strikes.

To ensure successful penetration of a positional, deeply echeloned enemy defense, by massing forces and means in penetration sectors, a decisive superiority was created: 2–6 times in infantry, 6–10 times in artillery, 3–9 times in tanks, and 2–3.5 times in aircraft.

A powerful artillery offensive, in which second-echelon and reserve artillery participated, had special significance for the penetration of a defense. Increased artillery density made it possible to reduce the overall duration of the artillery preparation and support the infantry and tank attack with a double fire barrage at a depth of two to four kilometers. All these changes led to the tempo of penetrating the enemy defense in the third period increasing to 16 kilometers per day.

The high tempo of penetrating the tactical defense zone permitted successful introduction of *front* mobile groups into the penetration to exploit success. Here, they were supported by a strong aviation grouping and conducted skillful and swift combat operations in the operational depth (with an offensive tempo of 30–40, and sometimes 50–80 kilometers per day), separated from combined-arms armies by 40–70 or more kilometers. They completed the encirclement of large enemy groupings, created an external front, threatened deep operational reserves, and achieved the ultimate operational aims. The overall operational depth of advance of mobile groups was 300–500 and more kilometers. Second echelons (large combined-arms formations) were introduced into the engagement after the mobile groups to penetrate intermediate positions, roll up the defense from the flanks or complete the encirclement of an enemy grouping, create an internal encirclement front, rout enemy reserves, and repel counterstrokes.

An important condition for successful development of the offensive and achievement of ultimate operational aims was the skillful *repulsion of enemy counterstrokes* during the operation. The most widespread method of repelling strong counterstrokes was for a portion of *front* forces to shift to the defense along existing positions, while main forces exploited success into the depth. If strong reserves and second echelons were present, meeting attacks were delivered to repel counterstrokes, and enemy counterstroke groupings were crushed in a meeting engagement. Here, a decisive condition for success was forestalling the enemy in launching the attack, achieved by timely movement of necessary forces and means to the threatened axes.

Questions of organizing and executing unceasing operational *pursuit* were successfully resolved. *Front* forces pursued the withdrawing enemy on a wide front, at high tempos (combined-arms armies – 25–40 kilometers per day; tank formations – 40–70 kilometers), and at great depth, which reached 250–800 kilometers (the Belorussian, Vistula-Oder, and Khingan-Mukden operations). Both frontal and parallel pursuit were conducted. However, parallel pursuit provided greater operational results.

During pursuit, battling *front* forces penetrated intermediate enemy defensive positions, bypassed his centers of resistance, enveloped isolated groupings, and encircled and destroyed them. Thus, for example, in 1944, during pursuit *front* forces in Belorussia encircled an enemy grouping numbering 100,000 men in the Minsk region. Experience demonstrated that for successful pursuit at high tempos, it was necessary to have tank forces in *front* first echelons, and operations by forward formations and pursuit detachments had to be decisive, audacious, and continuous (day and night), with maximum intensification of efforts. Massing of bomber and ground attack aviation strikes against withdrawing enemy columns, eliminating enemy obstacles, and re-establishing routes of movement for one's own forces had important significance for successful pursuit.

An important achievement of Soviet operational art was the further development of the theory of *forcing* large water obstacles from the march. Success in forced crossings was ensured by timely concentration of crossing means to overcome rivers simultaneously on a wide front, and by rapid seizure of bridgeheads by forward detachments. Captured bridgeheads on the opposite shore were widened to dimensions which would support the concentration and deployment of a strong shock grouping for a decisive offensive. A well-organized antitank and antiair defense and prompt consolidation of these bridgeheads in an engineer respect had decisive significance in holding captured bridgeheads.

In the concluding stage of the war, our operational art was enriched by the enormous experience of storming large cities, penetrating fortified regions, and conducting offensive operations under special conditions: mountainous-forested, forested-swampy, and desert regions, and in the Zapolyar'ye [Polar region]; correct generalizations and recommendations were made.

Soviet operational art succeeded completely in resolving problems of operational force protection during offensive operations. Among problems resolved positively were *operational maskirovka*, conducted in the interests of ensuring surprise actions and misleading the enemy relative to the true intentions, time, and place attacks were to be delivered. Its success was achieved by covertly and rapidly concentrating forces in the staging area; regrouping under conditions of limited visibility; dynamically operating along auxiliary axes; creating false artillery, tank, and aviation groupings in secondary sectors and regions; strictly observing the secrecy of all developed operational and tactical plans for force operations; employing a strictly limited number of personnel to work out these plans; using radio-*maskirovka*; prohibiting conversations on technical means of communication concerning issues of preparing forces for the forthcoming offensive; resettling the local population from regions adjacent to the front line, etc. Using operational procedures and methods which the enemy did not expect had important significance for ensuring a surprise attack.

Front and army defensive operations occupied an insignificant place at this time in the overall course of armed struggle. *Front* forces went over to the defense after successfully completing offensive operations to hold captured lines and bridgeheads, or during an offensive operation to repel enemy counterstrokes and counteroffensives. In all cases, the defense's purpose was to gain time to regroup, prepare, and develop new offensive operations.

The defense fully ensured the repulsion of enemy attacks, and in a *front* usually consisted of four belts. The center of gravity of defensive battles shifted into the tactical zone. As much as 70–90 per cent of army rifle divisions and more than 60 per cent of all *front* artillery (the Balaton operation) were deployed in the main defense belt. As a rule, *front* tank reserves (two to three tank and mechanized corps), 10–30 kilometers from the forward edge, were deployed in the army belt. Strong *front* second echelons not only guaranteed the defeat of the enemy in case he penetrated into the operational depth, but also supported the transition of the *front* to a counter-offensive.

Since tanks comprised the main shock force of enemy offensive group-ings, the art of organizing an antitank defense, whose basis was a system of powerful antitank regions and engineer obstacles echeloned to the entire depth of the army defensive belt, acquired increasingly greater significance. All types of artillery were used against tanks. For this purpose, the principal mass of artillery firing positions were located on likely axes of tank advance, which made it possible to increase the antitank defensive depth. The average density of direct-fire artillery in the fight against tanks amounted to 25 guns per kilometer of front.

During defensive engagements, it was characteristic to intensify rapidly the defensive density in the tactical zone by maneuvering forces and means from sectors not under attack, and army and *front* reserves. Air strikes were directed against the most dangerous enemy groupings at decisive moments during defensive engagements. When the enemy had penetrated the defense to a depth of 20 or more kilometers, strong flank attacks were delivered. In the majority of defensive operations, front second echelons were not used to repel enemy attacks, but rather were held to conduct subsequent offensive operations.

During the Great Patriotic War, the Soviet Armed Forces acquired enormous experience in preparing and conducting operations under the most varied conditions. This combat experience reached a high level, and essentially was the crown in the development of operational art for the first half of the twentieth century. The victory of our army and navy in the war over a strong enemy demonstrated to the entire world the progressive nature of Soviet operational art, and showed that it was the highest achievement in the theory and practice of *front* and army operations. Responding to the plans and decisions of Soviet strategy, it ensured the crushing defeat of the most powerful coalition of Fascist states, a shock force of world imperialism.

The outstanding victories gained by Soviet forces during the second and third periods of the war eloquently attest to the indisputable superiority of our military art over the military art of the German-Fascist Army. Soviet forces demonstrated on the battlefields their superiority over a strong enemy, both in the offense and the defense. The German-Fascist defense could not withstand our powerful offensive, and attacking German shock groupings were powerless to surmount our operational defense.

The innovative nature of Soviet operational art was manifested with enormous force in all large-scale operations, especially commencing with the second half of the war, when Soviet forces had the necessary materiel-technical capabilities to employ the most effective methods and forms of conducting military actions. If during the first period of the war (1941–42) operational art and creative thought of military leaders were directed toward finding methods and means to conduct successful operations with insufficient forces and means, then, beginning in 1943, Soviet operational art sought capabilities for most fully using the ever increasing combat might of large operational formations.

During the entire war, operational art developed not only on the basis of enormous combat experience, but also under the influence of our military theory, which skillfully generalized experience and paved the way to practice, taking into account the changed forces, means, and conditions for waging war. The brilliant victories at the concluding stage of the war were achieved thanks to skillful employment of all combat arms and armed forces services participating in an operation; selection of expedient operational methods and forms; precisely organized and maintained cooperation; reliable troop control; all-round support of combat operations; and combination of the high offensive passion of our forces with expert employment of powerful Soviet combat equipment on the battlefields.

The rich experience acquired by Soviet forces in the fiercest battles, and its creative employment made it possible to develop operational art rapidly in the postwar period and further develop the Soviet Armed Forces and armies of all socialist countries. In this sense, our experience in conducting armed struggle and the creative method of resolving problems of operational art under specific historical conditions have an international nature.

During the postwar period, especially with the massive introduction of nuclear and rocket weapons, resulting in a radical change in military affairs, operational art has broadly led in working out problems concerning the conduct of operations, principles of employing nuclear means, and use of combat arms and weapons as applicable to conditions of nuclear war. On the basis of troop exercises and scientific research, operational thought recognized that at the foundation of any method of defeating the enemy must lie a combination of nuclear strikes and a swift offensive, predominantly by forces from the march, along axes, and under conditions of swift and sharp changes of the situation, and absence of continuous fronts and linearity in force formations and operations. Analysis of combat capabilities of new weapons made it possible to develop and substantiate an increase in the scope of operations, methods and forms of their conduct, the depth of the operational formation of forces, and many other issues, taking into account the development of combat means and the achievements of military science.

Presently, Soviet military-theoretical thought is called upon to interpret continually and thoroughly the essence of changes taking place, analyze creatively troop training practice in employing modern combat means, take into consideration the experience of foreign armies, study carefully everything new which advances and develops military affairs, and develop and master modern methods and forms of conducting armed struggle, operations, and battle. Constant consideration of probable enemy's strengths and weaknesses, thorough research of national-liberation, local, and past world wars, and scientific forecasting will have substantive influence on the successful development of Soviet military theory.

The inexhaustible, vital power of the Soviet State and social structure, the might of the socialist economy, the far-seeing wisdom of Lenin's party, the greatness of the spirit of the Soviet people, the bravery and indomitable heroism of Soviet soldiers, and the triumph of Soviet strategy, operational art, and tactics were embodied in the victorious operations of the Great Patriotic War.

The historical lessons of the Second World War are an awesome warning to aggressive forces nurturing plans for a new war against the powerful commonwealth of socialist countries. The perfidious surprise attack by the Fascist bloc against our Motherland in 1941 is a lesson for all progressive nations of the world. It demonstrates what insidiousness and cunning imperialist reactionary forces are capable of in the struggle against socialist states, and how necessary are the greatest vigilance of nations and maximum combat readiness of armies of the socialist commonwealth to repel a surprise attack by aggressors and rapidly defeat them.

The Soviet Armed Forces, enriched by the exceptionally valuable and grim experience of great historical battles, and outfitted with awesome modern combat equipment, are vigilantly standing on guard for the peaceful labor of the Soviet people, who are successfully carrying out Communist Party plans for building communism. Our powerful Motherland, striving toward a communist future, constantly remembers past victories and lessons.

In observing the 23d anniversary of the historic victory of our socialist state in the Great Patriotic War, the Soviet people, under the leadership of Lenin's Communist Party, are tirelessly increasing the defensive might of their Motherland, and are always recalling Lenin's instructions: ". . . be on the alert, cherish the defensive capability of our country and our Red Army as the apple of our eye. . ."

NOTE

1 I. Pavlovskiy, *"Sovetskoye operativnoye iskusstvo v Velikoy Otechestvennoy voyne,"* *Voyennaya mysl'* [Military thought], 3 (1968), pp. 18–32.

On the Theory of the Deep Operation

MARSHAL OF THE SOVIET UNION M. ZAKHAROV[1]

In the country's period of socialist development, the Communist Party and the Soviet State did not forget for a minute the country's defense or the strengthening of its military might. Great attention was given to the further development of military theory, whose cornerstone was Lenin's tenets, beginning with his definition of the nature of future war.

The practical activity and scientific works of M. V. Frunze – *Yedinaya voyennaya doktrina i Krasnaya Armiya* [Unified military doctrine and the Red Army] and *Front i tyl v voyne budushchego* [The front and rear in a future war] – had important significance for the development of Soviet analytical thought. They developed Lenin's tenets on the nature of future war and underscored the most important problems of developing the Armed Forces and preparing the country for war.

Future war, Frunze said, will be class war; it will inevitably exacerbate the class struggle within a hostile capitalist state which has begun aggression against the Soviet republic. Without rejecting the possibility of lightning blows, he considered that future clashes could lead to a protracted war.[2]

Frunze assumed high force maneuverability in conducting operations, while not excluding the possibility of using positional combat forms in separate sectors. He viewed high maneuverability as one of the ways of overcoming our forces' military-technical backwardness.

Frunze considered that, all things being equal, the offense is more advantageous than the defense; a successful transition to the offense is the mission of the defense; the Red Army had to be indoctrinated in an offensive spirit.

Frunze's views, supported by the Central Committee of the Party and the military community, greatly influenced the development of Soviet military-theoretical thought and were reflected in official documents, in particular in the *1925 Field Regulations*, in the instructions, *Higher Commands*, professed by Frunze and issued in 1924, and also in combat regulations for infantry and other combat arms which came to light in the same year. These documents had enormous significance for establishing uniformity of views on many operational-tactical questions.

The greatest achievement of military-theoretical thought was the development of the theory of the deep operation, which was the foremost theory of that time.

This article examines the history of the birth and development of that theory.

Based on the development of military equipment abroad in the 1920s and prospects for outfitting the Red Army, Soviet military-technical and analytical thought correctly evaluated the influence of new military equipment on the structure of the army and military art, and considered it expedient to have a massive army. Consequently, it searched for a way of developing the organization of the Soviet Armed Forces, their technical outfitting, and combat training, and attempted to determine scientifically the nature of future war, the operation, and battle on the basis of Marxist-Leninist teaching and past war experiences.

Prewar five-year plans played a large role in the successful solution of these vital problems, allowing for the creation of a stable materiel-technical base for army reorganization. Technical rearmament of the Soviet Armed Forces fundamentally changed the old concept about battle and the operation, and greatly influenced the development of Soviet military theory, which later arrived at the development of the foundations of the deep operation and deep battle tactics.

As a result of economic transformations mapped out by the five-year plan and continuous industrial growth, the technical outfitting of the Red Army improved as well. Thus, if in 1930–31 the aviation industry produced a yearly average of 860 aircraft and the tank industry 740 tanks, then in 1932–33 they produced around 2,600 aircraft and 3,770 tanks respectively. During this period the output of small arms and artillery grew from 1,911 guns and 174,000 rifles to 3,778 guns and 256,000 rifles. These rather tangible indicators brought our army to the level of the foremost modern armies. It changed its appearance qualitatively and quantitatively. New combat arms were created and their share increased. Massive training of technical cadres took place. The Communist Party slogan, "Technology in the period of reconstruction resolves everything" found living embodiment in the army as well.

By the end of the second five-year plan, the Red Army already had at its disposal a stable materiel-technical base. Our industry was able to produce all modern technical combat means, not lagging behind armies of capitalist states in quality. The quantity of arms and combat equipment for the army and navy, especially small arms, artillery, and aircraft, grew sharply. Thus, 5,469 aircraft, 12,687 guns, around 75,000 machine guns, and as many as 1,200,000 rifles came from industry in 1938. The army obtained new small-arms artillery armaments, tanks, and aircraft; the mechanization and motorization of ground forces proceeded; and the number of tank and mechanized formations [*soyedineniye*] and units making up the principal shock force increased. Air-assault forces came into being and successfully developed.

Army and navy personnel changed. Following the Communist Party slogan, "Cadres resolve everything," the country's academic institutions grabbed millions of highly-qualified specialists. Technically prepared young men not only from cities, but also from small villages were drafted into the army. Tractor and combine operators and drivers became tankmen and drivers of other combat vehicles. Replenishments prepared by *Osoaviakhim [Obshchestvo sodeystviya oborone i aviatsionno-khimicheskomu stroitel'stvu SSSR*/Society for Assistance to Defense and Aviation Development of the USSR] arrived for aviation. There were no illiterate soldiers in the Red Army.

All this had a positive influence on force combat and political training, and created favorable conditions for extensive military-theoretical research, taking into account the achievements of the national economy and science, new army technical capabilities, and the level of personnel training.

Soviet military thought conceived of future war as an armed conflict of enormous armies in which the opposing sides pursued decisive aims – the complete destruction of the enemy. War acquired a colossal scope and extreme tension. It could not be a lightning one, that is, brought to an end by a single, albeit gigantic strategic operation. Armed combat was considered to consist of a series of blows forming a system of successive operations of strategic significance. When deployed, massive armies can create a continuous defensive front, relying on natural lines, obstacles, fortified regions, or field defensive structures. Under these conditions, the necessity arose for organizing a penetration of the defense with the help of modern combat means to overcome the defense rapidly.

As is generally known, during the First World War a tactical penetration usually did not develop into an operational one. Operations remained incomplete and, consequently, did not achieve projected aims. The theory of successive offensive operations in the 1920s envisioned the delivery of two attacks or one main attack by front forces. Several more auxiliary strikes were planned so that the enemy could not throw his reserves into penetration sectors on secondary axes. Here, the overall attack frontage was not to exceed half the width of the entire *front* offensive sector. It was thought that uninterrupted combat operations could continue for a month and achieve a depth of 150–250 kilometers, after which forces would cease the advance for two to four weeks to bring forward the rear areas and replenishments. Such an offensive sequence permitted the enemy to withdraw forces into the depth and organize a defense along new lines. This theory, based on the experience of the First World War, was obsolete and did not respond to the new demands of future war.

Therefore, it was necessary to develop a principally new theory of offensive operation and find combat forms and methods which would make it possible to overcome the strong fire of a continuous front and annihilate enemy operational groupings to achieve strategic success.

Soviet military thought considered that it was necessary to inflict blows of enormous penetrating force to the entire depth of the enemy's defensive operational formation to resolve these missions. Such blows could be implemented only by deeply echeloned masses of cooperating infantry forces, tanks, and artillery, with aviation support. This method of combat operations was named the deep operation.

The rudiments of this theory can already be seen in the research conducted in the second half of the 1920s by M. N. Tukhachevsky, N. Ye. Varfolomeyev, A. K. Kolenkovsky, I. P. Uborevich, V. K. Triandafillov, and others,[3] whose ideas were reflected in the *1929 Field Regulations*. A great contribution to the creation of the foundations for the theory of the deep operation was made by scholars of the Frunze Military Academy and *RKKA* Staff workers: G. S. Isserson, Ye. A. Shilovsky, S. N. Ammosov, A. N. Lapchinsky, A. I. Sedyakin, K. B. Kalinovsky, S. M. Belitsky, and others working under the leadership of the Chief of the General Staff, A. I. Yegorov, and the Chief of the Academy, B. M. Shaposhnikov.

With the acceptance in 1929 of the first five-year plan for Soviet Armed Forces reconstruction, a search began for new paths of further military development, formation of military theory, and more effective methods of armed combat for the defense of the socialist Fatherland responding to the demands of the times. By decree of the Revolutionary Military Council of the USSR, these important and urgent tasks were assigned to the *RKKA* Staff, above all to its Operations Directorate. By the beginning of 1931, the first stage of this work had already been basically completed.

Several months before his tragic death in 1931, Triandafillov gave a lecture to the *RKKA* staff entitled *Osnovnyye voprosy taktiki i operativnogo iskusstva v svyazi s rekonstruktsiyey armii* [Basic issues of tactics and operational art in connection with army reconstruction],[4] in which his basic views on the nature of deep battle and operations were stated in the form of theses, and, as he wrote, an attempt was made "to find an overall, general line in the development of tactics and operational art and new combat means."

In Triandafillov's opinion, "the major and decisive tactical question lies in the fact that using new types of armaments and combat equipment opens the possibility of attacking the enemy to the entire depth of his tactical dispositions,"[5] simultaneously employing several echelons of tanks (long-range action/*DD*, long-range infantry support/*DPP*, and immediate infantry support/*NPP*) attacking jointly with infantry and supported by artillery and assault aviation against the enemy deployed in the first defensive belt. Such a powerful blow accorded speed and urgency to the attack. Deep tactical operations against enemy combat formations also opened prospects for operational art, creating conditions for preparing and conducting modern operations on great expanses; the depth of a simultaneous string of engagements did not have to yield to the width of the front.

Triandafillov's lecture was discussed extensively in the circle of higher command personnel. *RKKA* Chief of Staff Yegorov and the Operations Directorate under the leadership of I. P. Obysov concluded the matter begun by Triandafillov. On 20 April and 20 May 1932, *Taktika i operativnoye iskusstvo RKKA na novom etape* [Tactics and operational art of the *RKKA* at a new stage] was heard in the Revolutionary Military Council of the USSR.[6] The ideas stated were of great interest and an important summation of scientific, military-theoretical research being conducted at the beginning of the 1930s. Soon after, on the basis of the tenets advanced in the speech and of opinions and observations coming from the forces, *Vremennyye ukazaniya po organizatsii glubokogo boya* [Temporary instructions for organizing deep battle] were worked out;[7] in February 1933, after confirmation by the People's Commissar for Military and Naval Affairs, they were sent to the forces as an official guide.

It should be noted that this was a turning point when military art, relying on the experience of the First World War and the Civil War, for the most part did not respond to the new level of armed forces development.

The step forward made by Soviet military-theoretical thought found the correct perspective of development of combat means, although by this time not a single army in the world had experience in massed use of armor equipment, aviation, or artillery.

The newly developed theory was not immediately freed from the burden of old, uncommonly tenacious views. Together with bold and scientifically substantiated conclusions, erroneous positions, obsolete for that time, were expressed. Other extremes were also observed: some comrades gave preference to the most fashionable combat arms (*BTMV* [*bronetankovyye i mekhanizirovannyye voyska*/armored and mechanized troops]) and were distracted by an "arch-revolutionary nature" [*arkhirevolyustionnost'*], striving after super-originality. Thus, for example, Chief of the Combat Training Directorate A. I. Sedyakin in his *Vremennyye instruktsii po glubokomu boyu* [Temporary instructions for deep battle] attempted to reduce the offensive to a single type of operation – the penetration.

To achieve simultaneous penetration of the entire depth of the enemy's tactical defense, M. N. Tukhachevsky staunchly proposed that right up to the moment of attack there be a successive commitment into battle of various tank groups at various times: first a long-range action tank group, then a long-range infantry support group, and finally a direct infantry support group.[8]

Here he stated that

> one of the main missions of offensive battle is support of the long-range action and long-range infantry support tank advance by all means and support of the suppression of objectives assigned to them

. . . . Artillery and aviation . . . in the period preceding the infantry attack are used to assist and support tanks.[9]

Speaking with words he often used in discussions, this was "beginning at the beginning," that is, the First World War. Tukhachevsky's point of view, which gave priority to tanks in battle, held predominance for some time.

K. Ye. Voroshilov made erroneous statements when he announced that he understood "deep battle as one of the varieties of battle and only advantageous for a positional war, where it would often be necessary to penetrate the enemy's defensive front."[10]

However, in the course of an extensive search and experimental exercises and maneuvers, the most correct views and tenets were found which served as a firm foundation for the subsequent development of Soviet military science.

At the expanded Military Council of the National Defense Committee [*NKO*] in December 1934, deep battle tactics were determined to be not a type but a new form, a new method for conducting various types of combat operations. In his concluding speech Voroshilov rejected his former views and acknowledged that

> any battle is called deep battle . . . modern battle cannot be anything but deep battle. . . . And the issue is not how to understand deep battle, but how to conduct this deep battle in all of its varieties, in all its many manifestations. . . . This is the main task, and to learn this is more difficult than to conduct scholastic arguments. . .[11]

At this meeting, in a speech which summed up the results of the development of deep battle theory, A. I. Yegorov recognized as erroneous the statement that tanks are the pivotal unit in deep battle. Experience showed that infantry played the decisive role and, consequently, it was necessary to use all technical means to support its combat actions.[12] The speaker pointed out the inexpediency of the cumbersome three-level tank formation, which had not justified itself in battle. The creation of two tank groups (long-range action and direct infantry support) made it possible to attain a more compact battle formation and to advance into the attack along the entire front simultaneously to penetrate enemy positions.[13]

Based on decisions of the *NKO* Military Council, taking into account observations of military districts, and verifying in practice a series of tenets in the forces, the *RKKA* Staff ultimately produced *Instruktsiya po glubokomu boyu* [Instructions on deep battle], which was approved by the USSR People's Commissariat for Defense on 9 March 1935.

The well-known military leaders P. A. Belov, N. D. Kashirin, P. Ye. Dybenko, I. F. Fed'ko, I. P. Uborevich, I. E. Yakir, D. A. Kuchinsky, K. A. Meretskov, B. M. Shaposhnikov, and others played an enormous, definitive, even leading role in verifying the theoretical postulates of deep battle tactics in exercises and maneuvers, and substantiating this theory's generalized views.

The 1936 issuance of the new *Field Regulations (Temporary PU-36)* can be considered the concluding step in the development of the theory of deep battle and operation, fully expressing its basic tenets for all types of combat operations. The first draft of an operations manual was prepared at this time.

Having thoroughly analyzed strategic requirements, the Red Army's re-armament prospects, and the experience of the First World War in penetrat-ing a strongly prepared defense, and also having taken into account the maneuver nature and deep raids of cavalry in the Civil War, Soviet military science embarked on the correct path, focusing great attention on the development of the theory of the deep operation and the tactics of deep battle. It equipped the army with a purposeful outlook.

Above all, various new, powerful combat means – artillery, tanks, avia-tion, and air-assault forces – served as the basis for the development of this theory. These means were capable not only of suppressing and penetrating the tactical depth of the enemy defense and acting against his immediate reserves, but also of exploiting tactical success into operational success with the help of fast-moving, motor-mechanized and cavalry formations inter-acting with aviation, and of isolating penetration sectors from enemy opera-tional reserves approaching from the depth, acting against them by using super-long-range artillery, aviation, and air-assault forces.

In light of this, at the end of the 1920s and beginning of the 1930s we reexamined our views on *front* and army operations, and developed new forms and methods for conducting them.

The deep operation included several stages: *penetration* of the tactical defense was accompished by the joint efforts of infantry, tanks, artillery, and aviation; *exploitation of tactical success into operational success* was achieved by introduction of masses of tanks, motorized infantry, and mechanized cavalry through the breach formed in the defense, by long-range aviation actions, and by the landing of air-assault forces to destroy reserves and liquidate the enemy's operational defense; *exploitation of operational success* (operational pursuit) was carried out until the complete defeat of the enemy grouping selected as the operational objective, and the occupation of the next staging position for a new operation. The first stage was the primary one, since without penetration of the tactical defense a deep operation, in general, could not take place, that is, it was thwarted. In executing the pene-tration, infantry, artillery, tanks (several echelons) and aviation, cooperating with each other, simultaneously strike enemy combat formations to his entire depth; break his defense with one sudden deep and powerful strike, forming a breach in it; and rush forward to reach operational space. Here all combat arms act in the interests of infantry.

The main thing in the penetration is to reject linear combat forms in favor of deep actions against the enemy, which consists of simultaneous annihilation, suppression, immobilization, encirclement, and complete defeat of the main grouping, but not pushing the enemy back.

It is necessary to bring up mobile troops (tanks, motorized infantry, mechanized cavalry) and to land air-assault forces into the operational depth of the enemy defense *to develop a deep operation from the first stage into the subsequent ones.* Only under this condition can a stationary front be penetrated and armed combat take on a maneuver nature.

For a successful offensive, the shock group operational formation should always include a penetration echelon – rifle forces (reinforced rifle corps); an echelon for development of the penetration – mobile forces (tanks, motorized infantry, mechanized cavalry) possessing high mobility and shock force; and an aviation group and air-assault group. Shock armies, well outfitted with combat equipment, transport, and means of communications were recommended for use on the main axes.

Other important conditions considered necessary for the success of a deep operation are gaining air superiority, isolating combat areas from approaching enemy reserves, and preventing the supply of materiel to his attacking forces.

The theory of the deep offensive operation proposed a method of conducting combat operations in which shock, holding, and other groups, and tactically disconnected echelons for penetration and development of the penetration,[14] were united along the front and in the depth, on the ground and in the air, into a single shock mechanism providing purposeful action against the entire enemy operational grouping until his complete defeat. Here, possible forms of maneuver in offensive operations could be a *frontal* attack, an attack along converging axes (double penetration using favorable *front* configurations), a combined attack (organization of several so-called splintering attacks of various strengths across a broad front), envelopment (of one or both flanks), and encirclement.

Working out an offensive operation did not overshadow the development of tactical and operational forms of defense, although this was given somewhat less attention, inasmuch as even in the recent past defense did not enjoy popularity among military leaders.

And before the First World War hardly a single army in the world considered the defense to be a necessary combat method. Thus, in the French Army on the eve of the First World War, the well-known French military leader Lucas wrote, "The word 'defense' sounded . . . so heinous that we did not dare make it a subject of exercises in plans, let alone on the ground." French Army military theorist Grandmaison even more definitively announced, "Let that mediocrity who recommends a defensive method of operation be damned." In the Russian Army the catch-word "vile" defense was extensively used for a long time. This was also roughly the attitude toward defense in the German Army.

Soviet military specialists, while giving preference to the offense as the primary and decisive combat form, considered it unavoidable and necessary to master all types of defensive battle and operations. The principal theorists who developed the Soviet theory of operation and tactical defense were N. Ya. Kapustin, D. M. Karbyshev, A. Ye. Gutor, A. I. Gotovtsev, V. D. Grendal', F. P. Sudakov, and others.[15]

"Under modern conditions the defender should be ready to meet an advancing enemy attacking with a mass of tanks to the entire depth of the defense" – thus read the *Instructions for Deep Battle*. The 1936–39 field regulations stressed that defense should be, above all, antitank and deep. As a whole, it was assessed as an operational method used to win time, economize, hold especially important regions, and alter a disadvantageous correlation of forces. Defense was not an end in itself, but only a method for operational support and preparation of an offensive.

Two types of defense were permitted: positional (tenacious) and maneuver (mobile). The theory for organizing a positional defense was the most thought-out and developed; this was to oppose successfully mass attacks by the attacker's tanks and aviation and artillery fire, and to strengthen resistance in case of enemy penetration. The army defensive region was to consist of four zones: forward, tactical, operational and rear, each of which included one or two belts. The overall depth of an army defensive zone amounted to 100–150 kilometers.

Such were the characteristics of the content of the theory of the deep operation, or the theory of deep forms of armed combat developed by Soviet military thought by the end of the 1930s. Its currency was provided by the materiel-technical base being created by the Soviet Union's rapidly developing industry.

Technical reconstruction of the army achieved great success. This is attested to by the following indicators included in a report by the People's Commissar for Defense at the fourth session of the USSR Supreme Soviet in 1939: the number of tanks rose 43 times from 1930; the number of airplanes – 6.5 times; the quantity of heavy, medium, and light artillery – 7 times; the quantity of antitank and tank artillery – 70 times; the number of machine guns – 5.5 times. If 3.7 horsepower was necessary per fighting man in 1930, then in 1939 this increased to 13 horsepower per fighting man, despite the fact that during this time overall army strength grew 3.5 times.

At the same time, Armed Forces development was reexamined. They shifted from a mixed system to a unified cadre basis. By 1936, cadre army strength amounted to 1.3 million men, and by 1 January 1939 this had grown to 1.9 million men.[16] A large proportion of the draftees were of workers and collective farmers [*kolkhoznik*] who had obtained a general education and were acquainted with industrial and agricultural machinery.

Thus, Soviet military theory, reflecting the practical side of Armed Forces development, was the theory of a mass army equipped with the newest technological combat means.

The theory of deep forms of armed combat occupied an obvious position in the scientific preparation of command cadres. The Frunze Military Academy's Operations Department (and subsequently that of the General Staff Academy) and the Combat Training Directorate systematized and verified this theory's fundamental tenets, based on various exercises and maneuvers. These were the most effective form for verifying theoretical tenets, which, in turn, enriched the practical side of Armed Forces development and force and commander training.

Thus, combat arms forces and more than 1,000 tanks participated in maneuvers in the Kiev Military District. They worked out the following problems: penetration of a fortified defensive belt by a rifle corps reinforced by tank battalions and *RGK* (Reserves of the High Command) artillery; development of the penetration by a cavalry corps; use of a large air assault; and maneuver by a mechanized corp and cavalry division to encircle and annihilate a penetrating enemy grouping.

In autumn 1936, the summer force training was verified in exercises in the Belorussian Military District. Large formations of mechanized troops and aviation, artillery, rifle and cavalry formations, and parachute units participated.

Later, valuable theoretical and practical conclusions, which played a large role in the subsequent development of our Armed Forces, were reached regarding force maneuver actions. Apropos of this, Chief of the General Staff, Marshal of the Soviet Union A. I. Yegorov noted in his observations that "on the basis of summations and results of the maneuver, a number of valuable tactical and operational conclusions can be drawn, especially in the use of mechanized formations and cavalry."[17]

The General Staff found answers to numerous questions concerning theory and practice (connected, in particular, with the commencement of future war) in operational and strategic command-staff war games. Although the plans used in these games and our notions about possible force operations were shattered by the situation at the beginning of the war, they played a positive role nonetheless.

Problems of the initial period of war were always at the center of the General Staff's attention. Strategic planning, mobilizational deployment, and training and effectiveness of employing armed forces during an entire war depend on the successful and correct resolution of these problems in their theoretical and practical aspects. Therefore, from the moment of its formation the General Staff continually (although inadequately) verified them, based on military-strategic war games and large-scale command-staff exercises conducted in the second half of the 1930s.

The military-strategic war game on operational training, conducted by the General Staff with border district commanders on 19–25 April 1936, was demonstrative in this respect.[18]

As documents attest, this crucial game was worked out in the General Staff over an extended period and with particular care. Several suggestions made during the game, especially with respect to possible forms and methods of repelling an enemy attack and calculating forces and means of the opposing sides, were basically confirmed by the events of 1941. However, a number of principles worked out in the game relied on outdated First World War experience. The correlation of forces of both sides was equal; the main "Red" forces were already deployed on the border; possible enemy preemption in concentrating forces and commencing military operations was not taken into account. The course of the game led both sides to a *frontal* meeting engagement (reminiscent in form of the 1914 border engagements), whose outcome was not decisive. The factor of surprise (as is generally known, the Germans attached exceptional significance to this) was not adequately reflected in the game. Thus, in the game they did not succeed in thoroughly verifying our operational capabilities or working out optimal variants for combat against the German-Fascist Army. However, the game provided great impetus to district and General Staff leaders, and forced them to re-examine many outmoded concepts.

Many issues not properly resolved in 1936 were taken into account in the next game, conducted on the theme "The Army Offensive Operation in the Initial Period of War" in 1937 at the Military Academy of the General Staff (I participated in working out the game mission).

Thus, military theory and practice, mutually enriching one another, were constantly the focus of attention of the General Staff and served as a foundation, on whose basis the Staff drew up its operational calculations and proposals and prepared the armed forces to protect the country against encroachments of imperialist aggressors.

Soviet theory of deep battle and the operation, developed in the mid-1930s and reflected in our regulations, was enriched by new principles, with regard for scientific and technological achievements.

It can be said without exaggeration that in no army in the world was there such a deep and thoroughly developed military theory as in our Armed Forces.

In recent years, opinions have been encountered in print regarding who was, so to speak, the pioneer or founder of the theory of forms of armed combat. It seems to me that the search for concrete authors of this theory is fruitless. The theory of the deep operation and deep battle, founded on Marxist-Leninist methodology and the richest experience of the Civil War and other wars, and relying on the socialist state's new materiel-technical base and military doctrine emerging from Communist Party policies, was suggested by life itself. And a large collective of scholars, practitioners of military affairs, and Red Army leaders, including the *RKKA* Staff and the General Staff, participated in its scientific substantiation and verification of its principles.

Priority in developing this theory unquestionably belongs to Soviet military science. Until 1936 there was not even mention of the operation and deep battle tactics in the works and official manuals of the German and other armies (except for Eimansberger's book *Tank War*, which recommended lightning forms of tank strikes). It is true that in 1935 the German journal *Militaer Wochenblatt*, in the article "A Modern Genghis Khan," pointed out the novelty of ideas expresed in G. S. Isserson's book, *Evolyutsiya operativnogo iskusstva* [The evolution of operational art], which summarized questions concerning the deep operation. Only after 1936, in works published by German generals, does one see how German military thought distortedly interpreted Soviet ideas of new armed combat forms.[19] In this respect, the book *Attention, Tanks!* by Inspector of Tank Troops of the German-Fascist Army General Guderian, published in 1938, is representative. This theorist, brutally defeated more than once during the Great Patriotic War, considered tanks to be the single means capable of penetrating a defense and developing the attack. He treated infantry as an auxiliary combat arm which could "only consolidate success." Guderian rejected close cooperation between tanks with infantry, calling this "suicide." He assigned the same insignificant role to artillery and other ground combat arms, which were to act exclusively in the interests of tanks. Only aviation was acknowledged as a means capable of protecting tanks from the air and destroying enemy reserves. Guderian proposed to use tanks in the offensive in four echelons in roughly the same formation Soviet military specialists had already envisioned in 1933–34. Believing in this far from perfected plan, which we had rejected, Guderian and all German general officers devised nothing different before the end of the Second World War. In this connection, General Manstein's statements that during the last war the Soviet command borrowed expedient tank organizations (the creation of tank and mechanized corps) from the Germans and adopted their method of deep penetration completely contradict historical truth.

The Great Patriotic War confirmed the correctness of the basic principles of the theory of the deep operation (especially in using echelons for the development of success), especially in 1942, when Soviet force offensives began with the penetration of the enemy defense, into which mobile troops (tank armies, tank and mechanized corps) were subsequently committed to exploit operational success into strategic success.

The theory of deep operation has not lost its significance today. It can serve as a basis for creative use by command cadres in resolving many-sided and complex modern problems. Lenin pointed out that "Marxism demands the unconditional historical reexamination of the question of forms of struggle. To pose this question in a non-historical, concrete situation means lack of understanding of the alphabet of dialectical materialism."[20]

NOTES

1 M. Zakharov, "O teorii glubokoy operatsii," *Voyenno-istoricheskiy zhurnal* [Military-historical journal], 10 (October 1970), pp. 10–20. The article was prepared from the manuscript of Zakharov's book *General'nyy shtab v predvoyennyye gody* [The General Staff in the prewar years], published by Voyennoye Izdatel'stvo.

2 See M. V. Frunze, *Izbrannyye proizvedeniya* [Selected works], Vol. II (Moscow: Voyenizdat, 1957), pp. 133, 134.

3 M. N. Tukhachevsky, N. Ye. Varfolomeyev, Ye. A. Shilovsky, *Armeyskaya operatsiya* [The army operation] (Leningrad: 1926); A. K. Kolenkovsky, *O nastupatel'noy operatsii armii vkhodyashchey v sostav fronta* [On the offensive operation of an army as part of a front] (Moscow: 1929); V. K. Triandafillov, *Kharakter operatsiy sovremennykh armiy* [The nature of operations of modern armies] (Moscow: 1929); and others.

4 Central State Archives of the Soviet Army, *fond* 37977, *opis'* 3, yed. *khr.* 368, *listy* 963–1021.

5 Ibid., *listy* 963, 977.

6 Ibid., *listy* 845–87.

7 Ibid., *yed. khr.* 366, *listy* 548.

8 Ibid., *yed. khr.* 365, *listy* 246.

9 Ibid.

10 Archives of the Ministry of Defense, *fond* 112a., *opis'* 796 *delo* 59, *listy* 402.

11 Ibid., *delo* 65, *listy* 486.

12 Ibid., *listy* 14.

13 Ibid., *delo* 59, *listy* 16.

14 In the Great Patriotic War, the echelon for developing the penetration included mobile troops – tank armies, tank mechanized formations and cavalry formations.

15 N. Ya. Kapustin, *Operativnoye iskusstvo v positsionnoy voyne* [Operational art in a positional war] (Moscow: 1927); D. M. Karbyshev, *Inzhenernoye obespecheniye oboronitel'nykh operatsiy* [Engineer support of defensive operations] (Moscow: 1938); D. M. Karbyshev, *Inzhenernoye obespecheniye boyevykh deystviy strelkovykh soyedineniy* [Engineer support of combat operations of rifle formations] (Moscow: 1939); A. Ye. Gutor, *Oborona korpusa na shirokom fronte* [Corps defense on a wide front] (Moscow: 1939); A. I. Gotovsky, *Oboronitel'nyye deystviya strelkovykh diviziy* [Defensive operations of rifle divisions] (Moscow: 1926); V. D. Grendal', *Artileriya v osnovnykh vidakh boya* [Artillery in basic types of battle] (Moscow: 1940); F. P. Sudakov, *Armeyskaya oboronitel'naya operatsiya* [The army defensive operation] (Moscow: 1940).

16 Archives of the Ministry of Defense, *fond* 15a, *opis'* 1842, *delo* 1, *listy* 24–32, 113; *opis'* 2154, *delo* 4, *listy* 27.

17 Central State Archives of the Soviet Army, *fond* 33987, *opis'* 3, *delo* 838, *listy* 152.

18 Ibid., *fond* 37977, *opis'* 4, *dela* 2, 3, and 10.

19 *Voyennyy zarubezhnik* [Military foreigner], 1939, No. 8.

20 V. I. Lenin, *Polnoye sobraniye sochineniy* [Complete collection of works], Vol. XIV, pp. 2, 3.

CHAPTER SEVEN

The Heyday of Operational Art, 1970–86

Soviet preoccupation with nuclear war and the importance of strategy and the resulting eclipse of operational art had entirely eroded by 1970, as Soviet attention to operational art and operational techniques intensified. Enhanced concern for operational art, paralleled by Soviet restructuring of the armed forces to improve their operational capabilities, elevated the importance of that field from its relative positions of neglect in the early 1960s to a major area of concern in the 1970s. The Soviets agreed that the introduction of nuclear weapons had altered the development of operational art and changed the nature of operations. Consequently, they reinvestigated the key subject of the initial period of war, redefined traditional aspects of mass and concentration, and focused on the conduct of maneuver (both operational and tactical) designed to lessen the likelihood of nuclear weapons being used in future war and, if they were used, to lessen the effects of these weapons (particularly tactical nuclear weapons). Throughout the 1970s, Soviet study of maneuver focused on anti-nuclear [*protivoyadernyy*] maneuver and culminated in development of the twin concepts of the theater-strategic offensive and operational maneuver by operational maneuver groups (OMGs). Against this backdrop, Soviet writings on all aspects of operational art and operational maneuver broadened and intensified.

The 1970 article by Major General M. Cherednichenko identified contemporary characteristics of operational art, including careful distinction between nuclear and conventional war, the issue of local war, the concept of theater-strategic offensives, and new technological requirements for war, such as mathematical solution of problems of military art.

Twin 1971 articles by Lieutenant General I. Zav'yalov and Colonel V. Chervonobab sketched out the context, parameters, and nature of operational art and set the tone for subsequent writings in the 1970s. The former returned to the nuclear theme, analyzed the effects of nuclear warfare on traditional relationships between strategy, operational art, and tactics and sketched out the possible impact of nuclear war on specific aspects of operational art. The latter assessed the impact of potential nuclear war on the laws of war and principles of military art.

The first volume of the new *Soviet Military Encyclopedia* [*Sovetskaya voyennaya entsiklopediya*], published in 1976, included a key and substantial article by Colonel General N. V. Ogarkov on the deep operation. The fact that Ogarkov was then First Deputy Minister of Defense lent a certain credence to the subject.

In his 1978 article, Colonel L. I. Voloshin returned to the theme of the deep operation, relating its development and applying it to contemporary and future operations. He concluded,

> Although the term "deep operations (battle)" has not been used in official documents since the 1960s, the overall principles of that theory have not lost their meaning and on the contemporary materiel base of armed struggle they continue to perfect themselves.[1]

Without directly saying so, he articulated the necessary context for development and employment of modern operational maneuver groups.

The same year N. N. Fomin reevaluated the periodization of operational art, underscoring the increasing scope and complexity of modern offensive operations. Subsequent articles intensified the study of operational art and closely analyzed new operational forms. Major General V. F. Mozolev and Colonel General M. N. Bezkhrebtyy focused on the combined [*sovmestnaya*] operation and its role on the complex modern battlefield, emphasizing the necessity for better command and control, use of mathematical modeling, and the growing significance of long-range fires and deep rapid maneuver. Meanwhile, Colonel R. Savushkin surveyed the evolution of the term "operation" during the pre-1930s period and appealed for more intense study of the topic in the future.

Although Soviet fixation on operational art and the combat utility of operational maneuver continued into the 1980s, technological developments and the manner in which foreign armies exploited them generated renewed concern and reaction from Soviet military theorists, particularly in the tactical and operational realms.

By the early 1980s, Soviet theorists were forced by circumstances to address a series of new combat problems, first and foremost of a technical nature as related to new weaponry.

The first problem was the appearance on the battlefield of longer-range high-precision weapons [*vysokotochnoye oruzhiye*], more lethal and sophisticated descendants of older antitank guided missiles (ATGMs) of the 1970s. Compounding the adverse effects this technological revolution had on traditional offensive concepts was Western development of new maneuver and combat concepts. The U.S. concept of airland battle and NATO concept of follow-on-force attack (FOFA) sought to capitalize on the new weaponry by conducting deep battle to strike enemy forces to the depths of their formation. These concepts placed second echelons, OMGs, and rear area facilities in increased jeopardy. In short, the new weaponry and Western operational concepts forced the Soviets to abandon, or at least seriously alter, traditional concepts of echelonment.

By the late 1970s and early 1980s, under threat of tactical and theater nuclear weapons, Soviet military theorists had recommended use of shallower strategic and operational echelonment, in essence, a single echelon of *fronts*, each with the preponderance of its armies also formed in single echelon. The OMG concept represented a solution to the problem by replacing cumbersome second echelons with more dynamic, flexible, and rapidly moving exploitation forces, which could impart a non-linear nature to combat at the operational level of war.

The Soviet solution to the dilemma of countering high-precision weaponry of the 1980s would soon involve their wholesale abandonment of linear concepts of warfare. By 1984 Soviet theorists had defined the problems facing operational art. The solutions they developed to these new problems would usher in a new, more complex period of military development in 1985, made even more complex by ensuing political, economic, and social problems, which shook the foundation of the Soviet empire and state and compounded the difficulties already encountered in mastering the subject of future war.

Western armies' development and fielding of high-precision weaponry and more sophisticated cybernetic systems for command and control and information processing and dissemination posed an immense challenge to Soviet theorists, whose own scientific establishment simply could not compete with their counterparts in the West. What was clear was that basic operational and tactical techniques, as well as force structures, would have to change to meet the new demands of what was increasingly becoming a fragmented, non-linear battlefield.

Several trends were notable as theorists struggled with these new problems. First and foremost, they placed even heavier emphasis than before on maneuver at both the operational and the tactical levels. Second, traditional concepts of concentration and echelonment had to evolve to meet new requirements. Much of this discussion took place within the well-established framework of debate over the historical evolution of operational art.

In the early 1980s, Soviet theorists intensified their study of successive offensive operations as the key to combat success in a prospective theater-strategic operation. Colonel R. A. Savushkin, writing in *VIZh*, surveyed the root of successive offensive operations during the interwar years, and Colonel General M. I. Bezkhrebtyy, writing in *Military Thought*, did likewise for the wartime and postwar years. These articles on the nature of the deep operation laid the groundwork for a more productive debate of contemporary issues.

A 1985 article by Colonel P. G. Skachko typified that debate. In it he examined modern requirements for deep operations, incorporating in his analysis important new means of long-range fire (high-precision weapons) and the growing role of air mobility as a virtual air echelon.

NOTE

1. L. I. Voloshin, "Teoriya glubokoy operatsii i tendentsii ee razvitiya" [The theory of deep operations and tendencies in its development], *Voyennaya mysl'* [Military thought], No. 8 (August 1978), p. 26.

Some Features of Modern Military Art

MAJOR GENERAL M. CHEREDNICHENKO,
CANDIDATE OF MILITARY SCIENCES[1]

As is generally known, military art is a concrete category. Scientific analysis of its principal features is impossible without considering the nature, types, and varieties of wars of the modern era. Recently a series of articles published in *Military Thought* investigated these issues.[2] Therefore, it is not necessary to linger on them in detail. I would only like to emphasize once again that conditions for war to arise against socialist countries have become varied, and can be reduced to the following for the period being reviewed: *direct military attack by imperialists against individual socialist countries or the entire socialist commonwealth; military interference by imperialist states in the internal affairs of individual countries of the socialist commonwealth; unleashing of war by imperialists against developing countries which are friendly with us; and attempts by means of military intervention to pressure progressive popular movements in individual countries which affect the vital interests of the socialist commonwealth.*

The main danger is a world war, which would be a decisive, acutely class-based armed encounter between two opposing social systems: capitalism and socialism. Such a war would inevitably acquire the character of a general nuclear war. Even now the danger of this occurring remains, inasmuch as the nature of imperialism has not changed. However, with every year it is becoming more and more difficult for imperialists to unleash a general nuclear war. This is explained, at the very least, by the following reasons:

- *first*: the sharp change in the global correlation of forces in favor of socialism;
- *second*: the Soviet Union's achievement of superiority over the US in decisive means for waging war;
- *third*: the loss of the former invulnerability of US territory;
- *and finally*: the accumulation of enormous rocket-nuclear potentials on the part of the world's largest countries.

One also cannot fail to take into account the survivability and combat capability of strategic nuclear forces and control and warning systems, which make a retaliatory strike inevitable in any situation. Therefore, aggressive imperialist forces, while continuing to count on a massed nuclear attack, have recently attempted, as one can conclude from foreign press materials, somehow to substantiate the possibility of conducting limited nuclear war or conventional non-nuclear wars (according to the terminology of Western theorists).

In the West, limited nuclear war is understood as war with the use of operational-tactical nuclear weapons in a restricted area and with limited military-political aims. Most of all, the United States is interested in such a war, counting on avoiding an annihilating retaliatory nuclear strike by strategic forces against its own territory.

Bourgeois military theorists think that limited nuclear war will most often result from escalation of a conventional war, when the necessity arises to employ nuclear weapons on the battlefield against military objectives. Such a war, however, will inevitably lead to great destruction and losses among civilians, especially in such a densely populated region as Europe. In addition, it is very difficult to separate operational-tactical from strategic nuclear weapons, and in wartime it is hardly possible, in practice, to control the prohibition of employing strategic nuclear weapons or delivering strikes against specific categories of objectives. There is no guarantee that an aggressor who is unsuccessful will not resort to more powerful assets – strategic nuclear weapons. Thus, limited nuclear war can rapidly develop into general nuclear war.

Western military theorists understand conventional non-nuclear war as war using conventional, non-nuclear means. This is the classical type of war, in which military operations are basically reduced to mutually defeating theater armed forces groupings, and capturing and holding territory. Recently, such wars have arisen many times because of imperialism, predominantly on the periphery. Recent trends, however, have been noted toward widening the regions of military operations and increasing their scope. The escalation of the war in South Vietnam, the bombing of the Democratic Republic of Vietnam, the invasion of Laotian territory by American forces, and Israeli aggression simultaneously against several Arab states in the Middle East can serve as examples. Conventional war is also a great danger to the fate of the world, especially if nuclear powers are drawn into it.

Thus, the danger of a world war is now tied up not only with the possibility of a surprise nuclear attack by imperialists against socialist countries, but also with their unleashing of unlimited nuclear or conventional wars. The interests of ensuring its country's security and that of the entire socialist commonwealth force the Soviet Union to maintain a high level of combat readiness for its strategic nuclear forces – strategic rocket forces, atomic rocket submarines, long-range aviation – and all other conventional means of destruction for the decisive defeat of any aggressor.

As before, an acute problem of military art is *determining methods by which an aggressor can unleash modern wars.* Today, two principal methods which can be used to unleash war are examined: surprise attack and escalation. The surprise attack is the principal and most dangerous method for unleashing war. It can be achieved by an unrestricted nuclear attack, an attack using operational-tactical nuclear weapons, and strikes by aviation, the navy, and ground forces using conventional means.

Western military theorists are widely discussing the following forms of surprise, unrestricted nuclear attack: *delivering a mass nuclear strike at the beginning of or during a non-nuclear conventional war; delivering a mass nuclear strike after individual, provocative nuclear strikes; and delivery of a strike by on-call nuclear forces after a brief, covert preparation, or by the principal nuclear forces after a comparatively prolonged, covert preparation.*

Recently, Pentagon strategists have been focusing increasingly greater attention on the possibilities of escalating a nuclear war. Various scenarios for the development of events are being worked out and researched, which can be reduced to the following: exacerbation of the situation; local conflicts, provocations, and local wars; demonstration of nuclear strength (resumption of nuclear weapons testing in all spheres, provocative nuclear blasts), successive destruction of separate objectives, and strikes with pauses against a limited number of objectives; local nuclear war employing operational-tactical nuclear weapons; and surprise employment of strategic nuclear forces.[3]

On the basis of similar scenarios, plans for the gradual (in stages) development of a world nuclear war were worked out:

- first stage: conflict in a limited region, war using conventional weapons (conventional war);
- second stage: use of tactical nuclear weapons (limited nuclear war);
- third stage: use of strategic nuclear weapons (general nuclear war);
- fourth (concluding) stage: conduct of military operations by armed forces if both sides maintain the capability of continuing them.[4]

The theory of nuclear war escalation has been subject to sharp criticism by individual bourgeois military theorists and politicians. Nevertheless, it would be mistaken to ignore such theories, no matter how improbable they may be.

If one examines conventional wars, then at present the following primary methods of their being unleashed can be noted: *unleashing of military actions under conditions of an undeclared war, as the US did in Vietnam and Laos (use of local reactionary forces, "military advisors," armed forces of an aggressor and its satellites, etc.); and a surprise air attack and invasion of a territory subject to aggression by mobile groups (the strategy of the fait accompli, as in Israel's methods in the Middle East).*

Of course, the above-mentioned scenarios far from exhaust the variety of methods for unleashing wars in an actual situation. The aggressor will always attempt to use the most perfidious devices to catch unawares the country against which it is using armed force. The task of military art consists of continuously generalizing and analyzing methods for unleashing any kind of war by aggressive forces, uncovering actual plans of probable enemies, determining effective methods for preventing perfidious procedures which initiate aggression, and ensuring constant readiness of the armed forces.

The main content of military art is the development of mobile methods for waging war and means for armed struggle. Each war has inherent features characteristic for it alone. *Methods for waging war are understood as the totality of procedures for conducting military operations, and methods for coordinating the use of armed forces to carry out the military-political, strategic, operational, and tactical missions of a given war. Military operations are conducted in a concrete form, limited by missions, space, time, forces, and means.*

The form of military operations is a very important category having organizing power. Modern military art distinguishes strategic, operational, and tactical forms. The first can include operations of strategic nuclear forces and strategic operations in continental and maritime theaters; the second includes various types of joint and independent operations by armed forces services using rocket-nuclear weapons; the third includes various types of battles, using both nuclear weapons and conventional weapons.

Now there is no doubt that a general global nuclear war, should it arise, will, in principle, be conducted differently from past wars. Military-political and strategic aims of such a war can be achieved by annihilating strategic nuclear means, destroying the war economy, disorganizing the system of control, and repelling enemy nuclear strikes while simultaneously routing his armed forces in the shortest time possible. The use of strategic nuclear forces, capable of executing the principal war missions, is acquiring decisive significance.

Modern strategic nuclear forces consist of strategic rockets (in the US they are part of the Strategic Air Command, while we have designated them as an independent armed forces service – strategic rocket forces), atomic submarines with ballistic rockets, and strategic aviation.

In the view of the American command, the basic form of their combat employment will be the conduct of nuclear air-space [cosmic] operations, which will be the totality of simultaneous or successive nuclear strikes, mutually coordinated with respect to aim, location, and time. A nuclear air-space operation is comprised of operations by strategic rockets, strategic aviation, and atomic rocket submarines. During their course, strategic rockets will deliver the first strike by a salvo, and subsequent strikes by either salvos or a successive launch, depending on the readiness of launchers to carry out their missions. Atomic rocket submarines, brought to their firing position region, are prepared to deliver group strikes from underwater positions, coordinated with strategic rocket strikes with respect to time and objectives. Strategic aviation can operate following the first rocket strike to hit ground and maritime objectives with nuclear strikes. It is ready to fly to strike objectives in small groups of airplanes, maneuvering on routes with respect to altitude and direction, and employing various procedures for delivering rocket and bomb strikes, taking into account the enemy air defense situation and the radioactive condition of the air.

Presently, the problem of the further development of strategic nuclear forces is being widely discussed in the foreign press. Principal attention is being focused on improving arms. The main problem for strategic rockets is overcoming enemy air defenses. In the US this is being resolved by outfitting rockets with detachable warheads, creating maneuvering warheads, outfitting warheads with dummy targets and means for passive and active jamming, etc. Important significance is attached to the improvement of the range and precision of firing, automation of preparation processes, and combat use of rockets. Intercontinental rockets can be employed on atomic submarines, and increasing their number on submarines has not been ruled out. Work is being done on the further development of strategic aviation. For example, the FB-111 mid-range bomber with variable wing geometry may soon appear in the US. The development of the B-1A heavy bomber, which earlier had the designation AMSA, is being pushed ahead.[5] It can be assumed that the developmental process will continue.

In this connection, new issues for the further development of methods for the combat employment of strategic nuclear forces are on the agenda. In particular, it is considered that the adoption of more improved rocket systems, especially detachable warheads, will increase many times the combat capabilities of strategic nuclear forces, which may result in a change in methods of selecting nuclear strike objectives and hitting them.

Strategic defense force operations, designated to repel nuclear strikes against objectives on one's territory, will have important significance for the achievement of general nuclear war aims. Western theorists identify with this forces and means of antiaircraft, anti-rocket, and anti-space defense, whose combat capabilities are continuously increasing.

Judging by statements by American specialists, major attention in the further development of strategic defense assets will focus on improving the effectiveness of anti-rocket defense means, among which the US includes the "Spartan" and "Sprint" anti-rockets, and radar stations for detecting and accompanying targets and guiding anti-rockets to them. Operational methods for future strategic defense can, apparently, be reduced to interception of targets, launching of active assets, automatic guidance to targets, and destruction. These forces' combat operations will be distinguished by a high degree of activity, dynamism, and continuity.

In the view of bourgeois military theorists, combat operations in ground and maritime theaters may acquire great scope in a general nuclear war.

Strategic operations will unfold in *ground theaters of military operations* with participation of strategic nuclear forces, ground forces, aviation, air defense, and navies. Here, strategic nuclear forces will resolve the main missions. Ground forces and tactical aviation are assigned to conduct offensive operations following nuclear strikes by strategic nuclear forces, during which they will rout enemy force groupings and aviation using operational-tactical nuclear means and capture territory. Overcoming wide zones of radioactive terrain and regions of fires, floods, and destruction, formed as a result of massive nuclear strikes, will characterize their operations.

Combat capabilities of forces and means assigned to resolve missions in ground theaters following strikes by strategic nuclear forces have grown considerably. This is conditioned by the great shock power found in operational-tactical rockets for ground forces, multi-tube rocket artillery, modern tanks, combat vehicles, helicopters, air defense means, assault forces, reconnaissance, and control. Tactical aviation is outfitted with combat aircraft – fighter-bombers, bombers, fighters with powerful weapons, and reconnaissance and other types of aircraft. Aviation's role in resolving ground theater missions is growing continuously.

All these forces and means will continue to develop intensively. It is stated in the foreign press that soon one can expect the appearance of more improved operational-tactical rockets, combat aircraft with accelerated take-off and landing or with vertical take-off and landing, operational-tactical anti-rocket means, ATGMs, all-terrain combat and transport vehicles, new helicopters and other flying apparatus, etc.[6]

This is introducing substantive improvements in the methods of conducting military operations in ground theaters. *Combat operations are acquiring the nature of a fire strike with both sides using nuclear strikes, following which ground forces and air-assault operations develop after completing the rout of armed forces groupings.* The offensive can unfold simultaneously along many axes at high tempos. Highly mobile operations at great depth, with the absence of continuous fronts, will obviously predominate on the battlefield.

Naval fleet operations will develop in oceanic and maritime theaters. The adoption of atomic submarines with long-range ballistic rockets, atomic submarines with torpedoes and rocket-torpedoes, rocket-carrier aviation with long-range rockets, surface ships with rockets, and other new means, as well as the presence of naval infantry outfitted with modern combat means and assault ships, is increasing many times the navy's role in resolving strategic missions of a general nuclear war. Its operations are carried out on the wide expanse of the oceans.

Naval forces and means will continue to develop intensively. Foreign military specialists think that anti-submarine submarines, armed with torpedoes and rockets, will develop in the direction of increasing underwater speed, depth of submersion, and power of weapons, and automating control. Atomic anti-submarine submarines will apparently remain as a weapon. Surface ships will be further developed, especially helicopter carriers and antisubmarine ships. The US is continuing to build atomic strike aviation carriers. Surface ships on air pillows may appear, and means for reconnaissance, detection, target indication, control, and navigation, especially space, will be developed intensively.[7] *Operations in oceanic and maritime theaters will acquire the nature of highly mobile operations implemented by underwater and surface forces and naval aviation, with delivery of rocket and torpedo nuclear strikes for the destruction of naval forces and the resolution of other missions.*

Military operations in a general nuclear war can, on the whole, proceed in the form of coordinated operations of all armed forces services, with the deciding role belonging to strategic nuclear forces.

Because of its terrible consequences, a general nuclear war is a great danger for the entire world. The struggle to prevent it is a matter for all the nations of the world. The 1969 Moscow Conference of Representatives of Communist and Workers' Parties expressed confidence that, by the combined efforts of socialist countries, the international workers' movement, all peace-loving states, social organizations, and mass movements, a world war can be averted. However, it is necessary to deal with the circumstance that there are aggressive forces in the world, capable of unleashing a general nuclear war. Therefore, it is necessary not to weaken vigilance, and to develop and master the art of conducting a nuclear war.

As was indicated earlier, theorists from the Pentagon *allow for the possibility of conducting a limited nuclear war* in some region, viewing this as a step in the escalation to general nuclear war. What features are included in the methods for conducting a limited nuclear war?

In the opinion of Western military theorists, such a war can be waged in a restricted region. Under these conditions, its principal content could be the rout of an enemy armed forces grouping in the given region and the capture of its territory. The main strike means will be operational-tactical nuclear weapons – rockets, aviation, naval forces, and low- and mid-yield nuclear charges (Western military theorists think that the yield should not exceed 0.6 megatons). An important role is reserved for ground forces, tactical aviation, and naval strike forces.

Recently, imperialist countries, especially the US, have been expending great efforts to develop operational-tactical nuclear forces. The US plans to replace the "Pershing" rocket with a more improved rocket, and the "Little John" and "Honest John" tactical rockets with the new "Lance" rocket with liquid ampulized fuel. Detachable warheads may appear for operational-tactical rockets. The operational-tactical rocket "Pluton" is being developed in France. Artillery is being used increasingly more broadly as a nuclear weapons carrier.

Tactical aviation, used as nuclear weapons carrier, is developing as intensively as before. The new US fighter-bomber is the F-111A, a two-seater, multipurpose airplane with variable wing geometry, armed with bombs and rockets. The F-111D, with improved electronic equipment, and the F-15 tactical fighter are in development. There are plans to use the "Phantom" fighter as a nuclear weapons carrier. Similar aircraft are being developed in France, Great Britain, the Federal Republic of Germany, and other imperialist countries.

It is assumed that in a limited nuclear war nuclear weapons will be used to the depth of the operational formation of forces in the theater (300–500 kilometers). Objects of nuclear strikes may be the following: nuclear means, *front* force groupings, the military control system, communications junctions, crossings, and rear areas. It is accepted that nuclear forces can deliver individual, group, and mass nuclear strikes. Forces will operate following nuclear strikes to complete the rout of the enemy and occupy his territory.

Some foreign apologists of limited nuclear war are attempting to prove that in such a war nuclear weapons will be used only against military objectives and will not affect the population; therefore, such a war can be legitimate even for a densely populated region such as Central Europe. However, this does not correspond to reality. A special war game was conducted in England, in which a limited nuclear war was played out on the territory of one of the Western European countries. The game demonstrated that countries with a small territory and large concentration of industry and population will inevitably suffer enormous losses in men and materiel, not to mention moral trauma. The entire territory of military operations would be covered with radioactive fallout; fires would rage everywhere; populated areas would be destroyed and in flames. The existence of several countries would be in doubt.[8]

Western military strategists are returning increasingly more often to the idea of *the possibility of conducting a non-nuclear war, even in Europe.* Results of Israel's aggression against Arab countries are used as a foundation for this. What, in their opinion, are the features of the methods of conducting a conventional war?

It is said that, with respect to the methods of its conduct, a conventional war will not be a repetition of past wars, inasmuch as classical means of fighting have moved very far forward in their development. Tactical aviation has changed. The air element in armies has appeared, basically comprising helicopters – a powerful mobile combat and transport means. Modern tanks are distinguished by their high combat characteristics and improved armor protection, and are armed with rifled and smoothbore cannons with stabilization in two planes. Armored infantry vehicles have appeared, on which sub-units can fight without dismounting. Artillery has basically become self-propelled and more mobile, despite the increase in caliber, with more powerful shells. Great weight in artillery is given to smoothbore rocket systems. The appearance of smoothbore antitank guns, especially ATGMs, has sharply increased the effectiveness of antitank means. The same can be said for air defense means in connection with arming forces with various types of antiaircraft guided missiles. Small arms have developed considerably in the direction of decreasing their weight and dimensions, automating fire, increasing lethality, and increasing the number of rounds per man. Much attention is being focused on the rapid development of assets for control, reconnaissance, target indication, and support to improve the effectiveness of conventional weapons.

According to foreign military theorists, in the near future conventional weapons and military equipment will develop especially intensively. High-precision rockets with high-explosive fragmentation charges may appear. Future tanks will, apparently, acquire guided rocket shells shot from a tube. All-terrain combat vehicles (especially on air pillows) will appear. Artillery effectiveness will sharply improve, thanks to improvements in systems and employment of new shells (rocket, BL, swept-back, etc.). Swept-back bullets for small arms may appear. The appearance of laser weapons is completely probable. Among ground forces armaments, the importance of helicopters armed with ATGMs, automatic cannons, machine guns, and rocket shells will increase. The creation of army air-defense means is possible. The development of all these and other conventional weapons systems is not only being widely discussed in the foreign press, but is also being incorporated into programs for outfitting the armed forces of many countries.[9]

Therefore, it is thought that methods for waging conventional war under modern conditions will differ greatly from the past. In addition, the threat of sudden use of nuclear weapons will constantly hang over a conventional war. Now there will no longer be the former concentration of forces and means in a restricted region, for, in connection with the threat of a nuclear strike, this is dangerous; moreover, the necessity for a large concentration of forces will no longer arise, since the effectiveness of conventional means of destruction has increased considerably.

The principal events in a conventional war will occur in theaters of military operations (ground and maritime, and in the air). The main strike objective will be armed forces. Strikes are also possible against rear objectives. There may not be a continuous front of combat operations: they will unfold along the most important axes, with a high degree of maneuver. Losses in personnel and combat equipment will inevitably increase, as will expenditures of combat and materiel assets.

Air operations to rout enemy aviation and gain air supremacy will occupy an important place in resolving combat missions. Aviation will deliver massive strikes against airfields, control posts, and ammunition and fuel depots for this purpose. Air defense forces will experience great pressure in repelling air raids.

The primary missions of a conventional war will be resolved by conducting offensive operations of various scales; the offensive of large formations and formations will be conducted in wide sectors along axes, with a small density of forces and means (as compared with the past) and high mobility, predominantly on tanks, combat vehicles, and helicopters. Forms of maneuver such as the shallow and deeper envelopment, flank and rear attacks, and use of air assaults will be widely employed. Destruction and suppression of fire means, without which no offensive is possible, is becoming an acute problem. During the last war this problem was resolved by creating high artillery densities in penetration sectors, which is very dangerous now because of the presence of nuclear weapons. As in the past, before the attack it is necessary to destroy or suppress antitank means, artillery and mortars, tanks, and small-arms fire points. This mission can be resolved successfully by using concentrated artillery fire, especially rockets, and mortars, and by massive bomb strikes and ground attack aviation.

Combat helicopters play a special role in the resolution of this mission. Having great fire power and a high degree of maneuverability, they are capable of suddenly appearing on the battlefield and striking fire means and tanks with rockets and machine-gun fire, thereby paving the way for tanks and motorized infantry. The combat employment of helicopters is introducing substantive improvements into the tactics of force actions on the battlefield. In addition to fire destruction of the enemy, they can be employed to land subunits and units as assault forces in his rear; to transport forces, artillery, mortars, ammunition, fuel, and crossing assets; and to ensure that water obstacles are swiftly overcome.

No less acute a problem for the attacker will be protecting his forces and means against strikes by fire means, which will be an important objective in a conventional war as well. Skillful use of the terrain's protective properties, dispersal, *maskirovka*, maneuver, and other measures will make it possible to protect forces and means during an offensive.

Judging from numerous military exercises which the NATO command has recently conducted, a significant place in conducting non-nuclear military operations is being allotted to *defensive operations and battles*. Increasing the effectiveness of fire means, especially antitank and air defense means, and the expanded capabilities for mechanizing engineer work are making it possible to create a stable defense in a short time. Forces will occupy the most important regions, key positions, road junctions, etc. A significant part of the forces may be located in the depth, and can be used for maneuver operations. Fire strikes against an enemy who is preparing for an attack (counterpreparation), counterattacks and counterstrokes, and concentration of forces and means on threatened axes will acquire great significance in defensive battles.

Methods of air defense forces operations in a conventional war will also have their own features. It can be assumed that the principal efforts of air defense forces in repelling air raids will be concentrated in the theater of military operations. Attempts by aviation to deliver massive aviation strikes against rear objectives (military and non-military) also cannot be excluded, as recent local war experience demonstrates. Strikes against rear objectives by high-precision rockets outfitted with conventional charges having increased power are completely possible (intensive research is being conducted in large capitalist countries to increase the effectiveness of conventional explosives). In this connection, missions for thwarting strikes not only by enemy aviation but also, possibly, rockets against the country's vitally important objectives confront air defense forces.

As the foreign press attests, atomic and diesel-electronic submarines with rocket and torpedo weapons having conventional shells; naval aviation armed with rockets, torpedoes, and bombs; and various classes of surface ships will be widely employed *in maritime theaters*. The sinking of the Israeli destroyer *Eylat* during the 1967 war between Israel and the Arab countries attests to the effectiveness of naval rocket armaments. Before this, there were very few instances in the history of naval warfare where a rather large combat ship was sunk by a single shot. Naval operations will be conducted to rout naval forces, disrupt maritime communications, and assist ground forces in conducting operations on coastal axes. The maneuver use of submarines and aviation, and the ability to concentrate forces rapidly to strike and to restructure them for subsequent operations is acquiring decisive significance in maritime theaters.

The foreign press notes that it is difficult to determine the scale, intensity, and duration of a conventional war under modern conditions. It will hardly acquire a universal character as happened during the Second World War; however, it can become drawn out, as the experience of a number of postwar local conflicts demonstrates, although there are also examples of short-term warfare of this type.

Such are the most characteristic features of military art, which can be seen today when analyzing foreign sources, and which, to some degree or other, are objectively determined by the modern level of development of armaments and military equipment, and by the prospects for their further development.

In conclusion, I would like to emphasize that military art in our time is developing at increasingly rapid tempos, and fundamental revolutionary changes in its basic principles are occurring more and more often. At the basis of this lies ever accelerating scientific-technical progress, which daily confronts Soviet military art with new and increasingly more complex problems. To resolve them successfully, scientific forecasting is necessary for a sizable period, taking into consideration the development of the global military-political situation, armaments, military equipment, and military art. In light of the above, a most important task of Soviet military science is to work out further *problems of military strategy*, as the main component of military art. At the same time, it is necessary to ensure the progressive development of operational art and tactics, inasmuch as they determine the more concrete forms and methods of using armed forces in war.

Tactics, conditioned by the rapid development of armaments and increased danger of the outbreak of a general nuclear war, *is acquiring special significance at this stage*. The mission consists of developing and continuously improving methods for using new armaments and military equipment, that is, the tactics of teams, crews, subunits, units, and formations.

The introduction of mathematical methods for working out problems of military art is acquiring increasingly important significance. It can be confidently stated that in the near future mathematical modeling of military operations will occupy an important place in the process of planning them. For this it is necessary to bring into a strict scientific system the categories of military art, such as types of wars and types, forms, and methods of military operations, and to provide a precise classification of various scales of operations, without which it will be difficult to work on introducing mathematical methods of planning and analyzing military operations. Another such pressing task is the development of a system of mathematical models for conducting bilateral military operations, compiling algorithms, testing models, and introducing them into practice. The resolution of this mission will require great efforts on the part of scholars and military specialists. Working out these problems will ensure the progressive development of Soviet military art.

NOTES

1. M. Cherednichenko, "Nekotoryye cherty sovremennogo voyennogo iskusstva," *Voyennaya mysl'* [Military thought], 2 (1970), pp. 40–50.
2. *Voyennaya mysl'* [Military thought], 2, 5, and 7 (1968).
2. These issues are examined in detail in the works of RAND Corporation and the Hudson Institute (US), the bourgeois theorist Herman Kahn, and those of other Western military figures.
2. May 1969 meeting of the NATO Nuclear Planning Committee. See the article by Yu. Zhukov in *Pravda*, 30 June 1969; the article by General N. Posti in the NATO Military Journal, 1 (1968); the article by Lieutenant Colonel D. P. Hughes in *U.S. Naval Institute*

Proceedings from November 1968; and "Kahn's Nuclear Strategy" in *Der Spiegel*, 15 (1967).

5. See the article by General G. G. Nazaro in the March–April 1968 issue of *Ordnance*.
6. G. Tompkins, *Oruzhiye tret'yey mirovoy voyne* [Weapons of the third world war] (Voyenizdat, 1969).
7. See articles by R. E. Waters in the November 1966 *RUSI Journal*; in *Der Spiegel*, 7 (1967); in *Wehr und Wirtschaft*, 11 (1967); by M. Haply in *U.S. Naval Institute Proceedings*, November (1966); and others.
8. The results of the calculations for this game were published in a speech by the UN General Secretary (A/6858) on the consequences of the possible use of nuclear weapons (New York: 1967).
9. See Tompkins.

The Evolution in the Correlation of Strategy, Operational Art, and Tactics

LIEUTENANT GENERAL I. ZAV'YALOV,
CANDIDATE OF MILITARY SCIENCES[1]

The statement and correct resolution of the question of the correlation of strategy, operational art, and tactics, as it corresponds to reality, have important significance for the theory and practice of military affairs. From the theoretical point of view, an investigation into this correlation makes it possible to follow more thoroughly the action of objective laws of war in battles, operations, and in war as a whole; to clarify the dialectical interconnection among various methods and means for conducting war, and among objective and subjective factors; and to determine that main link which has played or will subsequently play a decisive role in achieving war aims. This makes it possible for military science to foresee possible developmental paths of military affairs and develop practical recommendations for the most expedient resolution of questions of armed forces development and their preparation to repel aggression.

The practical significance of a correct understanding of the correlation of strategy, operational art, and tactics rests in the fact that it makes it possible for command cadres to assess more thoroughly and see more clearly the role of each level of the complex military organism, of each unit, formation, and large formation in the multifaceted process of military operations, in the execution of their assigned combat missions, and in the achievement of the overall war aims; to make decisions purposefully regarding battles or operations; and to plan the combat use of forces and means with greater confidence.

Thus, in what correlation do strategy, operational art, and tactics find themselves? How has this correlation changed in the process of their historical development?

For this question, Soviet military science proceeds from the fact that strategy, operational art, and tactics are three indivisible components of the theory and practice of military affairs. One cannot exist without the other, and they cannot help but affect one another. Among them there exists a close dialectical interdependence, such as among the separate parts of a single whole – military art. Strategy, operational art, and tactics cannot develop or advance without reliance on the development of military art as a whole, just as the latter cannot be manifested or develop outside of each of its components. This means that any significant change whatsoever in any one of the components of military art, resulting, for example, from the appearance of new weapons or other military equipment, will receive the necessary development only when it will make possible the progressive forward movement of its other components, and military art as a whole.

Let us focus on such an example. Increased tactical mobility and maneuverability of Soviet Army units and formations in the second and, especially, third periods of the Great Patriotic War, as a result of an increase in its motorization and mechanization, began to have its greatest effect and most positive influence on the course of combat operations only when these factors, together with tactics, began to be considered and used properly in operational art and strategy, that is, when they acquired the significance of the most important factors of military art as a whole, and began to appear in battles, operations, and in strategic-scale actions.

All this made it possible, on the one hand, to intensify further tactical force mobility and maneuverability, and, on the other hand, to increase offensive tempos and the depth of offensive operations, reduce their duration, and achieve the assigned aims. In other words, as a result of the correct use of increased force mobility and maneuverability, military art took a new giant step in its development.

Here is another example. The use by Soviet forces of a fragmented defense at the beginning of the Great Patriotic War as a compulsory method of action was not developed further, inasmuch as it did not gain a foothold in either operational art or strategy. Nor was such a defense appropriate for the requirements of military art as a whole. With an increase in the Soviet Army's technical outfitting and fire power, this defense became obsolete and was discontinued.

Strategy, operational art, and tactics, as component parts of military art, have their own peculiarities and the ability to develop independently; at the same time, several general traits, characteristic of military art as a whole, are inherent to them.

Among such general traits is, for example, the dependence of strategy, operational art, and tactics on political factors, armed forces combat capabilities, their quantitative and qualitative composition, the developmental level of weapons and military equipment, and the moral-combat qualities of personnel. This dependence can be observed, to varying degrees, in all three components, and in military art as a whole. For example, let us take the dependence of military art on weapons and military equipment. The development of weapons which, with respect to their combat properties, are capable of executing tactical, operational, and strategic missions respectively is characteristic of each component. For example, tactics require weapons which are necessary to conduct battle at a relatively shallow depth, while operational art needs weapons which have greater range and are more powerful. If we take strategy, then the range and power of weapons for it practically have no boundaries. Each weapon, however, develops not in isolation, but dependent on the combat capabilities of all its other forms, in close cooperation with them, and in such a direction that the weaknesses of one are compensated by the strengths of another. Methods of combat operations also change accordingly.

But the correlation of strategy, operational art, and tactics is determined not only by the fact that they have their own and common features and developmental characteristics. A definite interdependence is also inherent to them, ensuing from the predominant or subordinate position of one component with respect to another. This interconnection proceeds from the top down and from the bottom up. From the top down it is expressed in the fact that methods of waging war, strategic objectives, and actions are determined by the political war aims and armed forces' combat capabilities. From here ensue operational objectives, missions, and methods of action of *fronts*, armies, and navies, in accordance with which the missions of formations and units and the methods of tactical actions of troops, forces, and combat means are planned, the distribution of armed forces in theaters of military operations and strategic and operational axes is implemented, and a specific influence on the decision of subordinates and on the nature of force actions is rendered.

Until the appearance of operations, strategy interacted directly with tactics and had a definite influence on tactical force actions. With the emergence of operational art, the direct influence of strategy on tactics diminished. Operational art began to play an intermediate role between strategy and tactics.

Strategy was unable to achieve assigned war aims by means of one or two engagements. In the imperialist era, in connection with increased economic potentials of the warring sides, to achieve victory it was necessary not only to rout the enemy's armed forces, but also to capture his important economic regions and deprive him of the ability to regenerate his routed armies. No single army was capable of resolving this mission by a single blow. It was necessary to resolve a series of intermediate strategic missions on the way to achieving the overall war aim; this is the prerogative of operational art. Thus, the influence of strategy on tactics moves via operational art. Tactics was directly dependent on operational art. Now it is no longer the strategic command, but the operational command that determines missions for units and formations, means for their reinforcement, and methods for conducting combat actions and organizing cooperation. Of course, in resolving these issues the operational command, in turn, proceeds from the aims and capabilities of strategy.

The interdependence of strategy, operational art, and tactics from the bottom up proceeds along the line of executing combat missions and achieving assigned aims. Before the emergence of operational art, strategic success was achieved by executing tactical missions and routing the enemy on the battlefield. With the emergence of operational art, interdependence from the bottom up also became more sophisticated. Tactical success on the battlefield, as a rule, began to determine operational success, and the execution of strategic missions and achievement of the aims of a war or its separate stages depended on operational success.

In essence, the conduct of, for example, an offensive operation to great depth is comprised of the conduct of various types of continuous battles for several days. Here we have the attack on the forward edge of the enemy defense, repulsion of his counterattack, surmounting of occupied lines, dismounted and from the march, forcing of water obstacles, pursuit and the meeting battle, shift from offense to defense, and vice versa. In other words, all the riches of operational art, where each partial success is subordinate to the overall aim and leads to its achievement, are used when conducting an operation. Therefore, it is natural that the principles of tactics cannot help but correspond to the aims of operational art, which, in turn, ensue from the aims of strategy.

The two lines of interdependence which have been examined among the separate components of military art, from the top down and from the bottom up, are not divided by an insurmountable wall. There are no sharply defined borders between them. Both operate simultaneously in various respects. The role of this first line increases as the scope of military operations increases. The direct influence of higher command levels on subordinate chains of command have acquired increasingly greater significance. However, strategic and operational command capabilities for this were limited by the relatively low combat properties of the weapons at their disposal. Therefore, all their efforts were directed mainly toward the achievement of tactical successes by forces directly on the battlefield.

How is the influence of strategy on operational art and the latter on tactics expressed, and how is this influence concretely manifested? First of all, it must be said that the influence is not determined by accidental factors. It ensues from principles of military science concerning the dependence of means of military operations on weapons and military equipment. Whatever means higher commands have at their disposal, such will be the influence on the course of combat operations.

In recent wars, the strategic command created large force groupings with the obligatory inclusion of tank armies in their composition to achieve important strategic aims and conduct corresponding operations. However, it had, in fact, nothing except long-range aviation to pressure directly enemy objectives at a great depth. And this was inadequate, since, with respect to its relatively low combat properties, aviation was unable to resolve strategic missions. It is true that the strategic command had at its disposal various types of reserves, but the range of their weapons also did not extend beyond the bounds of the tactical zone. Therefore, they also could affect the course of combat operations only after their introduction onto the battlefield, subordinated to operational or tactical command.

The operational command was in more or less the same position. It had at its disposal tactical or frontal aviation, long-range artillery, tank armies and divisions, second echelons, combined-arms and special reserves, and antitank and air defense means, and could employ air-assault forces and, on coastal axes, amphibious assaults.

However, the range of the operational command's weapons, except for aviation, also did not extend beyond the bounds of the tactical zone. Fire means, as a rule, were used for direct support and reinforcement of forces on the battlefield, that is, in the interests of tactics, transferred to the disposition of formation and unit commanders or used by commanders of large operational formations to execute tactical missions according to the principle of cooperation.

Thus, the range and strike capabilities of strategic and operational commands' weapons, except for aviation, did not extend beyond the bounds of tactical space, and efforts were, naturally, directed toward ensuring tactical success and, through the execution of an entire set of tactical missions, achieving operational and strategic aims.

It is true that in the operations of the second and, especially, third period of the Great Patriotic War, mobile groups (tank armies) were employed to develop tactical success into operational success. However, being, according to their designation, an asset of a strategic or operational command and operating in the depth, they, all the same, carried out their assigned operational missions by their subunits', units', and formations' tactical actions. There were no weapons at this time, except for bomber aviation, which would have had combat capabilities for directly executing operational and strategic missions. And even aviation, as a rule, operated in the tactical zone, and only in individual cases struck objectives in the operational depth. Results of these strikes almost never achieved strategic scale, and only in individual cases did they acquire operational significance.

All this, of course, in no way belittles the role and significance of operational and strategic reserves in executing operational and strategic missions. It is necessary to take into account that fresh forces capable of resolving tactical missions in the depth are necessary to develop tactical success into operational success. Therefore, no operations would be possible without operational and strategic reserves. Moreover, the use of operational and strategic command assets on the battlefield had a decisive effect on the methods of tactical force actions and their execution of combat missions. In particular, this made it possible to increase the depth of the combat formation of units and formations and heighten their offensive shock force and defensive stability, freed tactical reserves from carrying out some missions, and created conditions for their wider maneuver. This accelerated and ensured the successful execution of tactical and, through this, operational and strategic missions.

The absence of effective long-range means of destruction in the hands of operational and strategic commands is explained by the special keenness of the problem of fighting against enemy reserves. Making use of the relative invulnerability of the operational depth, both sides were able to maintain their second echelons and reserves in a combat-capable state and, at a critical moment in a battle or operation, use them to reinforce forward-operating formations and units to increase defensive stability or exploit offensive success.

The single means capable of delivering strikes directly against these reserves was bomber aviation. Even with relatively limited combat capabilities, its strikes made it difficult for enemy reserves to maneuver, and made it impossible for the enemy to intensify forces and means promptly on the most dangerous axes or those which were most advantageous for him. This provided the tactical command with the ability to concentrate principal force efforts on the battlefield to resolve tactical missions, by which were created favorable conditions to surmount rapidly the enemy defense's entire tactical depth, repel his strikes in the defense, and thwart his offensive.

On the other hand, a successful force offensive in the enemy defense's tactical zone made it possible to maintain and re-establish operational and even strategic reserves, and use them to resolve more important missions in the operational depth. It was this very circumstance that ensured development of a tactical penetration into operational penetration, increase in the overall offensive depth, and achievement of operational aims.

This was also confirmed by recent war experience. Effective use of tank armies and aviation, and of second echelons and operational reserves was one of the conditions for our forces' successful operations in the tactical zone and their deep penetration of the enemy defense in offensive operations of the second and third periods of the Great Patriotic War, and of the high defensive stability.

The quantity of forces and means at the disposal of the strategic and, especially, operational command has a great effect on tactical force actions. Tactical force densities, combat formations of units and formations, the depth of their missions, methods of action, and organization of cooperation, control, and combat and materiel-technical support depend on this. Suffice to say that the absence of necessary forces and means at the disposal of the strategic and operational command at the beginning of the Great Patriotic War compelled our forces to structure a fragmented defense system along axes; therefore, the enemy often penetrated it without special efforts. This was one of the reasons that the offensive of units and formations in this period was characterized by a shallow depth and incomplete execution of assigned missions.

Only as armed forces were deployed and their technical outfitting increased, and as armies and *fronts* were reinforced were conditions created to allocate to the operational command a sufficient quantity of tanks, aviation, artillery, air defense assets, and various types of reserves. This had a definite influence on unit and formation tactical actions. Their dynamism and decisiveness increased in executing their assigned missions, and offensive depth and defensive stability increased as well.

However, all this in no way affected the dependence of operational success on the results of tactical force actions, or the achievement of strategic aims on the execution of operational missions. In the final analysis, tactics – gaining victory on the battlefield – played a major role in resolving operational and strategic missions in past wars. The main efforts of the operational and strategic command were directed toward ensuring these victories, inasmuch as there were no weapons at their disposal which could directly carry out missions inherent to these commands, that is, destroy or demolish operational and strategic objectives in the depth.

The fundamental principles examined above concerning the relationship of strategy, operational art, and tactics were characteristic for past wars. But to what degree are they applicable under modern conditions?

To answer this question it is necessary to keep in mind that

> in a future world war, if it is unleashed by imperialists, rocket-nuclear weapons will be the decisive means of armed struggle. Together with this, conventional weapons will also be employed, and, under specific circumstances, units and subunits will be able to conduct combat actions only using conventional weapons.[2]

This, naturally, cannot fail to affect the correlation of strategy, operational art, and tactics.

In tactics, we are accustomed to viewing the combination of fire and movement as its basis. The appearance of nuclear weapons on the battlefield, or, more correctly, their introduction into tactical space, has violated this principle. The combat might of weapons, which has increased a thousand-fold, and the instantaneousness of their actions over hundreds of kilometers come into conflict with the almost unchanged speed of troop movement on the battlefield. This contradiction is exacerbated even more by the fact that, with the appearance of nuclear weapons, the parameters of the zone of destruction have increased many times, while protection of forces against fire and strikes remains almost at its previous level. Thus, the combat potentials of nuclear weapons are still not grasped in classical tactics. The changed combat properties and capabilities of new weapons negate the old methods of combat actions, and are engendering new ones which correspond to the new weapons. This is an objective law of war and a manifestation of its actions under new conditions.

Such a situation is also characteristic for the other components of military art. For nuclear weapons, tactics, operational art, and strategy have extended far beyond the bounds of representations which are normal for us. Concepts such as offense and defense, front and rear, operation and battle have lost their conventional significance. Together with new weapons, new military art, new tactics, new operational art, and new strategy are emerging, which do not resemble anything that was created in past wars. Their further development is a most important task for today. Here, special significance applies to taking into account the principle that "war can begin with the employment of either nuclear weapons or conventional means of destruction," and "different variants for using all types of weapons which the enemy has are possible."[3]

The creation and dissemination of rocket-nuclear weapons in the armed forces introduced specific changes into the nature of the interdependence among the components of military art. The transfer of nuclear weapons to the disposal of strategic, operational, and tactical commands accords each of them great independence, and allows them to choose means and methods of actions themselves in their zones of responsibility, within the limits of the rights given them. Now nuclear weapons not only can support tactical force actions, but also can directly carry out various strategic, operational, and tactical missions. The ability to influence the strategic leadership for the successful conduct of operations, and the operational leadership for success in tactical force actions has especially increased. Moreover, in a nuclear war, the employment of strategic nuclear weapons can decisively influence the nature of tactical actions. Their enormous destructive properties, range, and high level of combat readiness make it possible for the strategic command to introduce them into actions and attempt to execute strategic missions earlier than operational and even tactical nuclear weapons could be introduced into action. This will inevitably have decisive influence not only on methods of tactical and operational actions, but also on the achievement of overall success.

The interconnection from the top down of strategy, operational art, and tactics is now expressed not only by the determination of the aims of combat actions and assignment of missions to lower levels, but also by the direct influence of the higher command, using its means, on the course of combat actions, by a more precise distribution of missions to be carried out by the strategic, operational, and tactical commands, and by a decrease of the dependence of executing operational and strategic missions on tactical force actions.

Thus, nuclear weapons have changed the traditional, tiered interdependence among strategy, operational art, and tactics, and have granted them greater independence. In actions without the employment of nuclear weapons, the general principles of interconnection among the components of military art are maintained, even under modern conditions. Only their concrete content changes. It has become broader, richer, and more complex, in light of the increase in combat potentials of conventional means of destruction, scope, and dynamism of combat actions.

The interdependence among strategy, operational art, and tactics is also seen in concepts of military art, which lie at the basis of armed forces development and preparation for war. Strategy defines and adopts these concepts or fundamental principles, although their emergence and formation begins in tactics, when new weapons and military equipment appear, and are then transferred to strategy via operational art.

Let us take as an example the tenet known to all on the concentration of force efforts at the decisive moment on the decisive axis. It was engendered in tactics, developed together with them, and shifted to strategy in a changed form. With the appearance of the operation, this tenet became an important requirement of operational art. However, it was not the tactical, but the strategic command which raised this tenet to a principle and entered it into the appropriate regulations and instructions.

The requirement to achieve victory by the joint efforts of all armed force services emerged on the battlefield, and it was also raised to a principle by the strategic leadership and entered into the regulations. Thus, weapons and their combat properties objectively influence the development of principles of military art. These latter ensue from laws of warfare and are consciously consolidated in appropriate regulations and instructions.

We have examined one aspect of the interdependence of strategy, operational art, and tactics. It is basically an objective aspect. It reflects conditions, trends, and factors which determine this interdependence. In warfare phenomena, however, as in all other social phenomena, objective factors do not operate in and of themselves, but in a process of human social actions, with their employment by men. Behind each type of weapon and combat equipment stands a man – the soldier and the commander. One way or another, men determine the methods of employment of weapons and, consequently, methods of combat actions. The effectiveness of using military equipment, success in battles and operations, and victory in war depend on their knowledge, capabilities, skills, and moral-combat qualities. This is already a subjective factor, which cannot help but be taken into consideration when examining questions on the correlation of strategy, operational art, and tactics.

In light of subjective factors, the interdependence of these three components of military art are sharply manifested in commanders' decisions.

After all, making any decision essentially consists of thoroughly assessing, considering and fully using the advantageous aspects of objective conditions to execute assigned combat missions. A decision must be considered ideal if it achieves the most complete correlation of objective and subjective factors, conditions of combat actions, and force capabilities on the one hand, and planned methods for executing combat missions, that is, methods of conducting battles and operations, on the other hand.

If we speak about a decision by the strategic leadership, then this, by determining missions and forces and means for large operational formations, also affects, to a certain degree, the methods of their actions. Thus, the operational command affects the decision of subordinate commanders and, consequently, the methods of formation and unit tactical actions. This influence can be both positive and negative, depending on how fully and correctly the commander assesses and considers objective factors and their influence on force actions in his decision. Here, it is especially important to assess correctly the enemy's and one's own combat capabilities; correlation of forces; the probable nature of enemy actions; the combat capabilities of the forces and means of the strategic and operational commands, which may be used in the interests of strategy, operational art, and tactics; and the influence on troop combat actions of the terrain and time at the disposal of forces to prepare for the execution of assigned missions.

Conclusions from an assessment of these objective factors are expressed in the plan and decisions of appropriate commanders, the distribution of reinforcement assets, designation of sector widths, assignment of combat missions, and organization of cooperation. By introducing corresponding changes into these and other elements of its decision, the higher command dynamically influences the decision of subordinate commanders.

Such influence proceeds along two lines. The first is bringing the combat capabilities of forces and means at the disposal of subordinate command levels into accordance with assigned missions. This is achieved by either reinforcing forces with assets from the operational and strategic command; or reducing sector widths and the depth and the complexity of the missions, and designating appropriate axes for conducting military operations; or allocating additional forces and means at the beginning of and during combat actions, taking into account the importance of assigned missions; or, finally, using reserves, with their missions assigned by the operational or strategic command, in the interests of a battle or operation, respectively.

The second line is fighting using the means of the higher command against enemy reserves, aviation, and artillery which are deployed outside the range of tactical or operational means. By making use of these means, the higher command influences the decision of subordinate commanders in the necessary direction.

In turn, unit, formation, and large formation commanders must, in order to ensure the execution of assigned missions and, thereby, achieve the aims of a battle and operation, understand and assimilate in all specificity the senior chief's plan and the role of their unit, formation, or large formation in implementing this plan, and know of what the assistance from the higher command will consist. A decision is made and the methods of conducting battle and operations are determined, taking this into consideration.

Thus, in light of subjective factors, the interdependence of strategy, operational art, and tactics is expressed in the fact that the strategic leadership dynamically influences correct decision-making by the operational command, and the execution of operational missions. The operational command plays the same role with respect to the tactical command. In turn, the tactical command, making use of existing conditions, strives to execute combat missions using units and formations, thereby ensuring the achievement of operational aims; through them, the strategic war aims are achieved. This interdependence has a character determined by natural law, and neither the strategic, operational, nor tactical commands can fail to take this into consideration.

Under conditions of nuclear war, the role of the subjective factor grows immeasurably. The strategic and operational commands themselves can fully assume the execution not only of strategic and operational missions, but also of tactical missions, leaving for units and formations only missions to consolidate achieved success in various forms.

Such are several principal tenets on the relationship of strategy, operational art, and tactics. This relationship is not permanent. It changes, depending on the role which each component of military art plays in the process of their historical development, changes in means and methods of conducting military operations, and concrete conditions of a given war. In accordance with this, command cadres should precisely envision the place and role of the tactical, operational, and strategic levels of the armed forces in achieving aims in a nuclear war and in conducting combat actions using conventional weapons. In the first case, the ability to consolidate firmly the success achieved by strategic and operational-tactical nuclear means is required; in the second case, it is necessary to ensure the reliable execution of operational and strategic missions by successful force actions on the battlefield.

NOTES

1. I. Zav'yalov, "Evolyutsiya v sootnoshenii strategii, operativnogo iskusstva i taktiki," *Voyennaya mysl'* [Military thought], 11 (1971), pp. 25–33.
2. A. A. Grechko, *Na strazhe mira i stroitel'stva kommunizma* [On guard for peace and the building of communism] (Voyenizdat: 1971), p. 55.
3. Ibid.

Principles of Military Art and their Development

COLONEL V. CHERVONOBAB,
CANDIDATE OF MILITARY SCIENCES[1]

The continuous development of society and, above all, its productive forces has introduced substantive changes in military art and in methods of preparing and conducting military operations. Its developmental tempos were not identical: they accelerated increasingly in accordance with the developmental tempos of productive forces and scientific and technological progress. During the feudal era, military art developed extremely slowly, remaining almost unchanged in the intervals between large-scale wars, which made it possible for enemy states to prepare for a new war by using their preceding experience, and to begin the war using essentially the same methods and means employed at the last stage of the previous one.

During the capitalist era, accompanied by rapid development of productive forces and socio-economic changes, each large-scale war, beginning with the Franco-Prussian War, signified a new step in the improvement of military art. The Franco-Prussian War and the First and Second World Wars were waged using various means and methods, and each was an important landmark in the development of military art.

It should be noted that, in connection with the rapid growth of economics, science, and technology, the development of military art continued during the intervals between these wars as well. For example, the development of the theory for employing large numbers of tanks, aviation and air-assault forces, and the development of the theory of deep battle and operations took place between the First and Second World Wars, and led to the Second World War being waged using different methods in comparison with the First World War. Military art during the Second World War resolved the problem of penetrating a deeply echeloned, prepared defense; exploiting tactical success into operational success; and achieving highly maneuverable operations, which military art was unable to do during the First World War.

After the Second World War, in connection with the enormous development of productive forces and unprecedented scientific and technological progress (a scientific-technical revolution) and, in particular, with the appearance of rocket-nuclear weapons and computers, the technical outfitting of the armed forces, that is, the materiel base of battle, operations, and war on the whole, changed. New weapons also require new forms and methods of force actions; consequently, principles of military art change as well.

Principles of military art are the basic guiding principles for organizing and conducting battle, operations, and war as a whole. These give expression to recognized, objectively operating laws of war. They are not thought up by individuals, but are the result of scientific generalization of practical experience and the revelation of objective, repeated, and necessary associations.

Engels wrote:

> Principles are not the starting point of research, but its conclusive result; these principles are not applied to nature or to human history, but are abstracted from them; it is not nature and mankind which conform to principles, but, on the contrary, principles which are valid only inasmuch as they correspond to nature and history.[2]

The principles of military art ensue from laws of warfare, but are fundamentally different. If the laws of warfare have an objective nature and exist outside men's consciousness in the very phenomena of war, then the principles of military art are ideas which emerge on an objective basis and remain in the sphere of consciousness. They have a dual nature: on the one hand, they are focused on a necessity determined by the actions of the laws of warfare; on the other hand, they express the relative freedom of military leaders' creative activity.

Laws operate independently of the will and desire of man, independent of whether or not they are necessary for a military leader, and whether or not he likes the actions of these laws. He cannot choose for himself one or another of these laws, but must take them all into consideration. On the other hand, principles are consciously employed by a military leader, depending on concrete conditions. They successfully combine both the necessary nature of the actions of the laws of warfare and the relative freedom of men's conscious activity within the framework of this necessity.

The laws of warfare do not point out how one must proceed to achieve victory. Principles, based on laws, include recommendations of the most expedient actions, that is, they recommend what is necessary to do for victory over an enemy, and how it is necessary to operate. However, these recommendations are given irrespective of the concrete situation. Therefore, in a theory which examines principles outside of situations, they are all recognized as identically important; however, in practice their significance changes: in one situation one principle may have predominant importance, while in another situation, another principle may be more significant. *The successful application of principles of military art is directly dependent on*

*the creative activity of the military leader, and his skill in controlling troops,
analyzing the situation, and making correct conclusions from this analysis.*

With a change in conditions and the nature of war, principles of military
art change, with respect to both content and form. Some of them, which
emerged under former conditions, lose their importance, while new ones
replace them. And although the form of some principles do not undergo any
changes for a long time, they themselves, nevertheless, acquire new content.

Soviet science recognized and recognizes principles as general guiding
tenets. They are developed on the basis of generalizing experience of the
employment of armed forces services in past wars, and during operational
and combat preparation, and analysis of the capabilities of modern combat
means; they emerge from practical experience, serve it, and find their confirmation in it.

Let us examine the fundamental principles of military art and some of
their developmental trends.

The most ancient principle of military art, discovered by the Theban
military leader Epaminondas at the Battle of Leuctra in 371 BC, is the
principle of *massing forces and means on decisive axes.*

In researching the military history of the ancient Greeks, Engels wrote:

> Epaminondas was the first to discover the great tactical principle
> which, right up through our time, determines the outcome of almost all
> decisive engagements: unequal distribution of forces along the front to
> concentrate forces for the main attack on the decisive axis.[3]

The essence of this principle is that to achieve victory over an enemy, one
cannot distribute one's forces and means equally along the entire front; their
overwhelming majority must be concentrated on a selected axis (or in a
region) at the necessary time, to create here a decisive superiority over the
enemy. One limits oneself to minimum forces on secondary axes and sectors,
conscious of the specific risk here. An attempt to be equally strong everywhere leads to a dissipation of forces and means along the front and, in the
final analysis, to defeat.

This principle was widely employed by prominent military leaders in all
past wars. And as productive forces developed, new means appeared, and the
size of armies increased, the principle was manifested in different ways. If in
wars of the feudal period only infantry, cavalry, and then artillery had to
be massed on decisive axes, then during the First World War, with the
appearance of tanks and aviation on the battlefield, there already had arisen
the necessity of mass employment of these forces and means. Mass employment of tanks at Cambrai in 1917 made it possible to achieve a tactical
penetration of the defense, demonstrating the necessity of employing large
numbers of tanks on the battlefield.

This principle was used especially widely by the Soviet command during the Civil War and Great Patriotic War. Thus, during the Civil War (1918–20), when the young Soviet state was forced to fight on four fronts (against Kolchak, Denikin, the White Poles, and Wrangel), it successively massed its limited available forces, first against Kolchak, then against Denikin, the White Poles, and Wrangel.

The principle of massing forces and means on the main axis was observed by *fronts* as well. In April 1919, up to the commencement of the counter-offensive against Kolchak, two-thirds of the forces of Eastern Front's Southern Group were concentrated on the main attack axis in a 200-kilo-meter sector, while on the remaining 700-kilometer front there remained only one-third.[4] In July 1920, Western Front, developing the offensive against the White Poles on a 450-kilometer front, concentrated 500 guns, 1,200 machine guns, and 60,000 swords and sabers on the main attack axis in a 120-kilometer sector, while in a 330-kilometer sector there remained only 35,000.[5]

For a penetration during the Great Patriotic War, a multifold superiority was created over the enemy as a result of decisive concentration of forces and basic means in selected front sectors. For example, 1st Ukrainian Front forces during the Vistula-Oder operation, which had an overall front of 250 kilometers, penetrated the enemy defense in a 39-kilometer sector, com-prising 16 per cent of the overall width of the *front* offensive sector. In the penetration sector was concentrated 77 per cent of the rifle divisions, up to 89 per cent of artillery, 100 per cent of tanks and self-propelled artillery, and 100 per cent of aviation, which made it possible to create an operational density of 223–296 guns and mortars and around 80 tanks per kilometer of penetration sector, and to achieve a 9.6:1 superiority in infantry, 9.7:1 in artillery, and 10.2:1 in tanks.[6]

An analogous concentration of principal forces and means on decisive axes was also implemented in defensive operations. In the Battle of Kursk, 28 per cent of the rifle divisions and more than 50 per cent of the *front*'s artillery and tanks were concentrated in the defensive sector of Central Front's 13th Army, comprising around 10 per cent of the width of the *front* sector.[7] In the Balaton defensive operation, 4th Guards, 26th and 27th Armies, 23d and 18th Tank Corps, and 1st Guards Mechanized Corps were used to defend the sector north of Lake Balaton, with a width of 83 kilo-meters, while only Soviet 57th and Bulgarian 1st Armies were allocated to defend south of Lake Balaton on a front of more than 200 kilometers.[8]

The principle of mass employment of forces and means on decisive axes maintains its significance even today, although it is implemented differently than in the past.

During combat actions employing nuclear weapons, there is no need to concentrate large forces and combat means in limited terrain sectors, since superiority over the enemy under these conditions is achieved, above all, by mass employment of nuclear weapons on decisive axes to defeat the main enemy groupings and his most important objectives. By exploiting the results of this action, forces complete the rout of the enemy, operating not in compact, but in dispersed combat formations.

For this reason, the following, for example, is written in the *US Army Field Regulations*: "The use of nuclear weapons is favorable for actions of small, highly mobile units. . . ." Further on, the following is recommended:

> If during an offensive it is necessary to concentrate one's forces, then this is done only at the decisive place, in the immediate vicinity of the enemy, and for a short time. Under conditions when nuclear weapons are not used, a considerable concentration of mobile forces on decisive axes is permitted.[9]

Similar opinions are expressed in West German and American military publications.[10]

During an operation, superiority over the enemy must be constantly maintained on the main axis by skillful maneuver of forces and means from other front sectors and from the depth.

Another important principle of military art, that is, *dispersal*, is closely associated with the principle of massing forces and means on decisive axes.

The increase in the rapid fire capabilities, range, and power of fire means in nineteenth century wars required dispersal of forces to reduce their losses from enemy fire. Thus, the appearance of rifled weapons in the Franco-Prussian War (1871) required a dispersed formation, as Engels wrote, even despite the commanders' will. Subsequently, with the appearance of machine guns and the increase in rifle and machine-gun fire power, gaps between soldiers in ranks continued to increase. If at the beginning of the Russo-Japanese War (1904–05) this gap was 1–1.5 paces, at the end of this same war it had increased to 4–6 paces, and by the end of the First World War, 8–10 paces. With increased artillery fire power and range, division and regimental columns, when approaching the enemy, began to break up into battalion columns at first, and then into company and platoon columns.

Mass employment of aviation during the Second World War, and increased fire power of artillery, especially with the appearance of rocket mortars, required dispersal of formations and units not only on the battlefield, but also when approaching it; this also required that reserves and second echelons be deployed more deeply: army second echelons deployed, as a rule, no closer than 12–15 kilometers and tank corps 20–25 kilometers from the forward edge.

Under modern conditions, in connection with the spatial nature of the strike action of nuclear weapons, dispersal of forces acquired other content, and its significance sharply increased. It is becoming one of the most important principles of military art, and will be executed in all types of military force actions, consisting of the breakdown of units and subunits along the front and into the depth at intervals and distances which will ensure the successful execution of the combat mission and maximum reduction of troop losses from nuclear weapons, air strikes, and fire from conventional means of destruction. Force dispersal will be the normal situation, not only in the zone of combat actions, but also far beyond its borders. It has now become dangerous to be deployed on the terrain and to move in large, compact masses, regardless of the distance from the enemy.

The degree of troop dispersal is established, depending on the nature of the mission being carried out, the degree of force protection, protective properties of the terrain, and probable force of a nuclear strike the enemy can deliver.

Force dispersal does not exclude the necessity of their concentration in the indicated area and at the indicated time to deliver powerful attacks. Now, however, the concentration should be executed from the march, covertly, swiftly, from various directions and from the depth, and precisely at the moment of the attack. After the attack, forces once again swiftly disperse to avoid becoming a target for enemy nuclear weapons. The military leader's skill and degree of force preparation for mobile actions are manifested in the ability to resolve this mission under concrete conditions of the combat situation.

The principle of achieving victory by the joint efforts of all basic combat arms and armed forces services, with their continuous close cooperation, should also be numbered among the general principles of military art.

This principle has also been known for a long time. However, its content has sharply changed from war to war. Thus, if in wars prior to the twentieth century it was necessary to coordinate efforts mainly among infantry, artillery, and cavalry, then by the end of the First World War it was already necessary to coordinate efforts of the above-mentioned combat arms with tanks and sometimes aviation to achieve success. In the Second World War, in connection with the appearance of new armed forces services and combat arms, to achieve success in battles and operations it was necessary to co-ordinate carefully the efforts of infantry and direct infantry support tanks with one another, as well as with supporting artillery and aviation; anti-aircraft means (air defense forces); tank, mechanized, or cavalry-mechanized groups (formations and large formations); air-assault forces landed in the depth; and amphibious assault forces and naval forces on coastal axes.

There is no need to prove that the content of cooperation became increasingly more complex as armies were outfitted with different combat equipment and armaments. The general tendency, however, consisted and consists of using the best possible strengths of each combat arm in the interests of the most rapid and effective execution of the assigned mission.

Cooperation is implemented and maintained during the entire period of military operations, for even its brief disruption disorganizes force actions, reduces the power of a blow against the enemy, and leads to unwarranted losses.

Capable coordination of actions of all battle means, combat arms, and special forces requires thorough knowledge of their combat properties, capabilities, and employment methods under different conditions. Cooperation can be effective only if the commander of each military element firmly knows and correctly understands the aim of the actions, the overall and individual combat assignments, and the methods of their execution, knows with whom, when, how, and why he is cooperating, promptly informs the senior chief about the situation, and exhibits creative initiative directed toward maintaining continuous cooperation.

The principle of surprise also occupies an important place in military art. It has also been known for a long time, and has been employed successfully by prominent military leaders. Historical experience demonstrates that he who made use of surprise in battle always acquired superiority over the enemy. As a rule, the side subjected to an unexpected attack and unable to adapt swiftly to the existing situation was defeated. The prominent Russian military leader A. V. Suvorov used this principle especially widely in the Battles of Izmail, Rymnik, and others.

Lenin spoke many times about the great role of surprise, saying that it was necessary to strike an enemy "where and when an attack was least expected." In the period of preparation for the armed uprising in October 1917, Lenin wrote, ". . . it is necessary to attack to catch the enemy unawares and seize the moment while his forces are dispersed."[11]

Achieving surprise and routing an enemy who has been caught unawares, with one's own losses and expenditure of forces and means at a minimum, was considered and is considered one of the most important indicators of a high degree of military skill for a military leader, the entire command, and army personnel.

Surprise stupefies the enemy, introduces disorganization and indecisiveness into his actions, and forces him to make new decisions which are not often appropriate for the situation.

During the Great Patriotic War, the *Stavka* of the Supreme High Command and prominent Soviet military leaders widely employed this principle. An example is the surprise of our command's conduct of all operations for encirclement, in particular the Stalingrad operation. The statement made after the war (18 June 1945) by the former Chief of Staff of the Operational Directorate in the Headquarters of the German Armed Forces Supreme High Command, Colonel General Jodl, is characteristic of this. Speaking about mistakes of German intelligence, he stated:

The greatest [mistake] was the lack of success in November 1942, when we had fully examined the concentration of large Russian forces on 6th Army's flanks (on the Don). *We had absolutely no idea of the strength of Russian forces in this region. Earlier, nothing was here, and suddenly* a blow of great force was delivered, having decisive significance; after this mistake, the Fuhrer's attitude toward Ground Forces General Staff intelligence data was one of great mistrust.[12]

Surprise can be achieved in combat actions of various scales: in war as a whole, in operations, and battles, and it can have varied significance in achieving success. Depending on the assigned missions and obtained results, surprise is *strategic, operational, or tactical.*

Strategic surprise is one of the most important factors, creating favorable conditions for achieving strategic war aims, especially at its beginning. A surprise commencement of war, as demonstrated by the experience of the attack by Germany's Fascist forces against Poland in September 1939 and against France in May 1940, and by Japan against Pearl Harbor in December 1941, makes it possible to inflict serious losses on the enemy, gain time, seize the initiative, and achieve a number of other advantages, which sometimes decisively influence the outcome of the war as a whole.

Strategic surprise can be achieved not only at the beginning of, but also during a war. Thus, the achievement of strategic surprise by Soviet forces in the Moscow and Stalingrad counteroffensives was, in great measure, responsible for their successful conduct.

Operational surprise is understood as the use of means of destruction and force groupings in operations, for which the enemy, who has not expected such a use, is unable to prepare the necessary countermeasures, and is, therefore, forced to conduct combat operations under unfavorable conditions.

In operations of the Great Patriotic War, Soviet forces extensively employed various methods to achieve operational surprise. An interesting example of achieving large-scale operational results by delivering a surprise attack is the Memel' operation (October 1944), when 1st Baltic Front forces conducted a large operational regrouping to shift the *front's* main attack swiftly from the Riga axis to the Memel' axis.

Five combined-arms and one tank army with large reinforcements moved laterally from the right to the left flank of the front, a distance of more than 100 kilometers, in less than ten days. Concentration of such a large force was executed in the operational zone directly adjacent to the front; thanks to skillful *maskirovka* and disinformation measures, the German-Fascist command was unable to detect the regrouping or establish that a large offensive operation was being prepared on a new axis. As a result of the surprise attack, the entire enemy Baltic grouping was encircled.

Tactical surprise is one of the principal conditions for achieving success in battle, and is employed in the interests of subunits, units, and formations to catch the enemy unawares, achieve surprise actions, and ensure more favorable conditions for one's own forces to fight a battle.

Under modern conditions, the role of surprise in battle has increased significantly. With the surprise employment of new combat means, especially nuclear weapons, there exists the possibility, even in the presence of equal, and sometimes fewer, forces, to inflict upon the enemy irreparable losses in a short time, sharply change the correlation of forces to one's advantage, introduce confusion, disarray, and disorganization, and disrupt control, thereby creating favorable conditions for a decisive rout of his forces. An enemy caught unawares is forced to change hastily his intentions and restructure plans so that they are applicable to the new, unexpected conditions. Countermeasures against the surprise attack must be sought hastily, and, consequently, may often have little effect.

Surprise does not usually arise by chance, in and of itself. It can be achieved only by fervent creative activity on the part of commanders and staffs, and by skillful actions on the part of all forces.

Surprise is incompatible with stereotypical patterning. Such patterning contradicts the very essence of surprise. If the enemy is successfully deceived once, then he will not allow himself to be deceived by the same device a second time. Therefore, it is constantly necessary to seek increasingly newer devices and methods for achieving surprise.

A *sine qua non* for achieving success is *covertness*. An enemy constantly expects an attack, and takes measures to prevent its suddenness. Surprise, even as the result of great success, is achieved only in those operations and battles in which covertness of preparation is ensured. Further improvement of technical reconnaissance means makes it possible to acquire data on forces at a great depth in their deployment, in a shorter time and less dependent on weather conditions, time of day or year, and nature of the terrain than, for example, during the Second World War. Air reconnaissance has especially great capabilities. Modern reconnaissance aircraft, equipped with various reconnaissance instruments, can conduct reconnaissance while located a considerable distance from the object, often even without flying across the front line. All this makes it difficult to achieve surprise, and requires, together with measures for countering reconnaissance, constant improvement of methods and means of *maskirovka* and disinformation, and observation of the strictest *maskirovka* discipline by all personnel.

Dynamic actions and steadfastness in achieving the assigned aim is one of the general principles of military art. Past war experience demonstrates that, all else being equal, he who operates more dynamically and decisively, struggles for the initiative, imposes his will on the enemy, and forestalls him in actions will achieve success.

In a number of his works, Lenin indicated that in armed struggle it is necessary to operate with the greatest dynamism and decisiveness.

Decisiveness and impact comprise three-quarters of success, and "each detachment must remember that, if it lets pass today a convenient occasion which has arisen for such an operation, then it, this detachment, is guilty of an unforgivable lack of action and passivity, and such action is the greatest of crimes."[13]

Force dynamism is reflected concretely in constantly pressuring the enemy, promptly using all favorable conditions and capabilities for delivering blows against him, depriving him of the ability to select favorable situations, time, location, axis, and nature of actions, and paralyzing his will and actions.

Dynamism is closely associated with initiative, expressed in bold and judicious tenacity, the attempt to find the best methods for executing the assigned mission, and readiness to take responsibility for a bold decision. The Great Patriotic War is rich in examples of high dynamism and judicious initiative of Soviet commanders at all levels. A clear example of such dynamism and initiative was the proposal of Marshal of the Soviet Union K. K. Rokossovsky, during the preparation for the Bobruisk operation, to penetrate the enemy defense in two sectors, when the *Stavka* had planned at first a penetration in a single sector.

An instructive example of exhibiting dynamism and initiative in the interests of executing the senior chief's plan were the actions of General A. G. Kravchenko, commander of 2d Ukrainian Front's 6th Guards Army, in the Budapest operation. Arriving on 21 December 1944 at the line of the Gron River, the 6th Guards Tank Army commander, having correctly assessed the situation (7th Guards Army had fallen behind), used part of his forces to cover from the north and northwest, while the army's main forces turned south and struck along the Gron River. Then, cooperating with 7th Guards Army, 6th Guards Tank Army formations destroyed the enemy between the Ippel' and Gron Rivers, and by 26 December had reached the northern banks of the Danube, where they linked up with 3d Ukrainian Front's mobile forces, completing the encirclement of the German-Fascist Budapest grouping.[14]

Thus, an assigned objective can be achieved by various methods, but it is important that the resolution of each intermediate task brings the ultimate objective closer. During combat actions, the situation constantly changes, and unexpected obstacles and different instances arise, which make it necessary to deviate from the original decision. Nevertheless, however complicated the situation may become, one must never forget the main objective. The principal force efforts, and the military leader's ideas and energy must be directed towards its achievement.

Such principles of military art as continuity of military operations are associated with the principle of dynamism. The essence of this principle is that combat actions which have commenced should be conducted dynamically and without interruption at any time of the year or day, in any weather, until the enemy is completely defeated. Here, attacks should be delivered with unabating force.

Our forces served as a brilliant model of continuity in conducting combat actions under complex conditions in a number of operations during the Great Patriotic War. For example, one can cite the Battle of the Dnepr and operations for liberating the Right Bank of the Ukraine [*Pravoberezhnaya Ukraina*]. In the latter, force combat operations developed on a front of 1,400 kilometers and, despite unfavorable weather conditions and the lack of roads in the spring months, it continued uninterruptedly to a depth of 450 kilometers. Here, troops forced a large number of rivers, including the Dnepr, Ingulets, Southern Bug, Dnestr, and Prut. The forcing was done, as a rule, under conditions of spring floods and ice floes, requiring enormous efforts and self-sacrifice from the troops.[15]

Continuous operations ensure the achievement of the objective quickly with the least expenditure of forces and means, and deprive the enemy of the time and ability to bring his forces into order, maneuver reserves, regroup and deliver an attack, bring up materiel supplies, or organize resistance on new lines. Continuous conduct of combat operations at high tempos creates unfavorable conditions for the enemy to employ weapons of mass destruction, since he cannot accurately specify targets to be struck; in addition, he is often forced to shift his nuclear attack means.

Under modern conditions, a halt during combat operations, even for an inconsequential time, means a loss of advantage for attacking forces; in addition, they risk being subjected to enemy nuclear strikes. In that time, the enemy can transfer reserves located at a great distance and create a defense capable of stopping the offensive or slowing its tempo. This is, to a considerable degree, the result of an increase in air and ground mobility of ground forces, as foreign authors emphasize.[16]

The continuous struggle against enemy nuclear attack means is a very important, qualitatively new element of this principle.

In the past, before the appearance of nuclear weapons, the capabilities of individual fire means were comparatively limited, and the results of their action could not decisively effect a change in troop combat capability and the correlation of forces. Enemy artillery batteries which appeared during preparation of the battle did not have to be destroyed immediately upon detection, but could be fixed by subsequently reckoning their hits, for example, during the artillery preparation.

The situation has radically changed. Each nuclear strike, depending on its power and precision, quickly affects force combat capability. Therefore, each enemy artillery piece capable of employing nuclear warheads, and each enemy rocket launcher must be destroyed immediately following their detection. Nuclear warheads at positions, bases, and during their transport must also be destroyed when detected.

The ever-increasing size of modern armies and their outfitting with sophisticated combat equipment and weapons requiring special means for delivery are advancing principles of military art, such as *all-round support of combat operations*, ever more to the forefront. The essence of this principle consists of the organization and steadfast implementation of all measures for supporting combat operations. It points to the dependence of their success on careful, all-round support.

Lenin taught that "any engagement includes the abstract potential for striking, and there are no better means for reducing this potential than organized preparation of an engagement."[17]

All-round support is a most important part of preparation and conduct of each operation. It should be noted that, with the appearance of new types of weapons and combat means, it is becoming increasingly more complex. If in the recent past support of combat operations included only reconnaissance, security, air defense, *maskirovka*, and engineer and rear support, then today new forms have appeared, such as protection against weapons of mass destruction, and others. Here, the content of each type has become immeasurably more complex.

Under modern conditions, all-round support of combat operations, and all the types and measures associated with it are acquiring especially important significance. Without timely and reliable data from reconnaissance of the enemy, terrain, and the radiation and chemical situation, one cannot make a correct decision or effectively employ available forces and means. Without guaranteeing fuel and ammunition for the forces, the most perfected combat equipment will become dead weight.

It should be noted that under modern conditions, in connection with highly mobile combat operations and possible sharp changes in the situation on great expanses (especially under conditions of employing nuclear weapons), all-round support in an operation requires such organization so that each formation and unit, when conducting combat operations, can be, within specific limitations, independent. They themselves are required to conduct reconnaissance and protect against weapons of mass destruction, and carry out *maskirovka*, and engineer and chemical support. As for rear support, formations and units must have everything necessary to conduct combat operations independently for several days, while, at the same time, maintaining high maneuverability.

This does not mean, however, that now the role of higher commanders and staffs in directly providing their subordinate formations and units with means for actions has somehow diminished. On the contrary, it is namely on them that the resolution of the most cardinal missions (for example, air reconnaissance or air defense) relies. They are obliged to inform subordinates systematically about changes in the enemy grouping, radioactivity and other situations, as well as about destruction, floods, and fires on their axes of action and most often at a greater depth than previously. It seems to us that, during the development of an operation, even units operating on independent axes should be continually oriented about the situation at a depth of two or three days' actions. Data of air, radio, radio-electronic, chemical, and engineer reconnaissance of senior staffs should be reported quickly and auto- matically to interested units. In view of the entire set of measures for support being organized in this way, the successful execution of combat missions and achievement of the operational aim may be extremely difficult.

However, the main thing in battle is personnel. Therefore, with all-round support and preparation of combat operations in an operational-tactical, materiel, technical, combat, and engineer respect, it is necessary to be con- cerned with the preparation of personnel. The decisive and intense nature of modern combat operations and the employment in them of weapons with unprecedented destructive force have led to a sharp increase in the signifi- cance of troop morale and, consequently, in the responsibility of comman- ders, political organs, and staffs at all levels for the moral and psychological preparation of personnel for battle. At the basis of this lie loyalty to the socialist Motherland and readiness to give all one's strength and, if necessary, one's life to protect it. Each soldier must be deeply aware of the righteousness of the aims of our struggle, the marauding nature of war on the part of the enemy, and his personal responsibility for the defense of his homeland. Lenin taught that consciousness of the reasons for a war and its aims, and conviction of its righteousness raises the soldier's spirit and ensures victory.

We have examined only the primary and most general principles of mili- tary art. Knowledge of them and their general trend of development will help the military leader (commander) in a given concrete situation to select the most appropriate principles or their successive combination to rout an opposing grouping.

NOTES

1. V. Chervonobab, "Printsipy voyennogo iskusstva i ikh razvitiye," *Voyennaya mysl'* [Military thought], 11 (1971), pp. 34–44.
2. K. Marx and F. Engels, *Works*, Vol. 20, p. 34.
3. Ibid., Vol. 14, p. 355.
4. *Istoriya voyennogo iskusstva. Kurs lektsiy* [History of military art. Course of lectures]. Vol. IV (Voyennaya akademiya im. M. V. Frunze, 1960), pp. 84–5.
5. Ibid., pp. 181–2.
6. Ibid., 1956, Vol. VIII, pp. 91, 92, 96, 123–4.
7. Ibid., Vol. VI, pp. 147–8.
8. Ibid., 1961, Vol. III, pp. 362–4.
9. *US Army Field Regulations. Conduct of Military Actions* (FM 100–5), 1964, pp. 119–20.
10. *Wehrkunde*, January (1968), pp. 3–15; and *Military Review*, March (1969), pp. 3–9.

11. V. I. Lenin, *Polnoye sobraniye sochineniya* [Complete works], Vol. 6, p. 176, and Vol. 34, p. 383.
12. *Voyenno-istoricheskiy zhurnal* [Military historical journal], 4 (1961), p. 89. Translator's note: the emphasis was added by Chervonobab in the original.
13. Lenin, Vol. 11, p. 342.
14. Ministry of Defense Archives, f. 339, op. 13252, d. 2, l. 19; *History of Military Art*, 1961, Vol. III, pp. 250–2.
15. *History of Military Art* (1961), Vol. III, pp. 98–103.
16. Lieutenant Colonel P. Dillon sets forth several principles of conducting combat actions under conditions of mass employment of tactical nuclear weapons in "Nuclear Saturation," *Military Review*, February (1970), pp. 10–18.
17. Lenin, Vol. 6, p. 137.

The Theory of the Deep Operation and its Developmental Trends

COLONEL L. I. VOLOSHIN,
CANDIDATE OF MILITARY SCIENCES[1]

At all stages of the development of the Soviet Armed Forces, our party has devoted tireless attention to the development of military science as one of the most important factors for improving their combat might.

During the Civil War, and especially during the building of peace, life posed a number of demanding problems associated with creating an expedient system for forming an army and navy, reorganizing military leadership organs, and developing new forms and methods for conducting operations, necessary to interpret in a new way and elaborate theoretically.

Military science confronted especially complex tasks in the 1930s, when the threat of a new world war sharply increased with the appearance of attempts on the part of world reactionary forces of Fascist Germany and militaristic Japan to unleash aggression against the Soviet Union.

The nature of the Civil War, which was distinguished by decisive aims, employment of dynamic combat forms, and high maneuverability of combat, decisively influenced the development of Soviet military science. The scientific works of M. V. Frunze, *Yedinaya voyennaya doktrina i Krasnaya Armiya* [Uniform military doctrine and the Red Army] and *Front i tyl v voyne budushchego* [Front and rear in future war] played a great role in the formation of military-theoretical thought. These works developed and theoretically substantiated Lenin's principles on the nature of future war and the most important problems of preparing the country for defense and forming an army and navy.

Frunze, without rejecting the possibility of lightning blows, proposed that war would most probably be protracted. It would combine high force maneuverability when conducting operations with positional forms of battle in separate sectors.

The principles stated by Frunze had an enormous influence on the development of Soviet military science. They were reflected in official documents such as the 1925 *Field Regulations*, the *Higher Command* manual, and combat regulations for infantry and other combat arms. These documents, to a considerable degree, made the establishment of uniform views possible for many issues concerning the preparation and conduct of battles and operations.

At the end of the 1920s, a general theory of operations was developed, including questions of the operational employment of all types of ground forces and aviation existing at that time. The most important achievement of Soviet military-theoretical thought in the interwar period was the development of the *theory of the deep operation.*

Soviet military science, taking into consideration achievements in the development of weaponry and combat equipment of the armies of the principal capitalist countries, and prospects for rearming the Red Army, provided a model, in the form of the theory of the deep operation, for resolving problems concerning the swift and decisive development of the offensive into the operational depth.

This was a principally new theory for conducting an offensive operation, which made it possible to reject methods for slowly and gradually overcoming the enemy's defensive positions, and to shift to more decisive and mobile forms of armed struggle.

The problem of swift and deep development of operations was resolved not in isolation, but in close cooperation with the development of such urgent problems as the organizational structure of forces, their technical outfitting and preparation, and the determination of the nature of future war, operations, and battles.

In resolving these problems, which were important to strengthen the country's defensive capability, prewar five-year plans played a great role. Their successful implementation turned our country from an economically backward land into a progressive and mighty industrial power, which made it possible to increase its military power immeasurably. New branches of industry possessing great productive power – aviation, tank, and automobile – were created.

By the end of the second five-year plan, the Red Army already had at its disposal a solid materiel-technical base. The Soviet Union's industry was able to produce all modern means for armed struggle, which, with respect to their technical and combat features, not only were not second to those found in the armies of capitalist countries, but even surpassed them. Rapidly outfitting the army and navy with new types of weapons and combat equipment sharply increased the fire power and maneuver potential of all military organisms. Under the influence of scientific-technical achievements, the organizational structure of formations and units were improved, and air-assault forces were created and successfully developed. All this created favorable conditions for broad military-theoretical research into the problematic issues of war.

Soviet military science pictured future war as an armed struggle between enormous armies, in which the opposing sides would pursue decisive aims – the complete defeat of the enemy. It was considered that war was acquiring broad spatial scope and would be characterized by great intensity of efforts. It would be protracted and consist of an entire system of strategically significant operations.

The appearance of new types of weaponry and combat equipment, and the creation of massive and well-prepared armies considerably increased defensive capabilities. By combining powerful means for struggle with natural lines, fortified structures, and engineer obstacles, forces could create a continuous defensive front and not only hold occupied lines and regions, but also inflict considerable losses on the enemy. Under these conditions, it was necessary for the attacker to resolve correctly problems of penetrating the enemy defense and developing the offensive into the depth.

The 1920s theory of successive offensive operations, based on the experience of the First World War, became outmoded and was not appropriate for the requirements of future war and new force capabilities. It was necessary to develop a principally new theory of offensive operation and find new forms and methods of armed struggle, which would make it possible to penetrate successfully a prepared defense and develop the offensive at high tempos into the depth to achieve strategic success.

Soviet military science considered that to resolve such complex missions it was necessary to envision delivering attacks of enormous penetrative force against the entire depth of the enemy's defensive operational formation. This could be carried out only by deeply echeloned forces closely cooperating with one another, combining their actions with artillery and aviation strikes against enemy objectives in the depth of the defense, and landing assault forces. This form of combat actions was known as the *deep operation.*

The emergence and development of the theory of the deep operation is associated with the development of the theory of deep battle, whose basis was set forth at the end of the 1920s in the works of such Soviet military theorists as M. N. Tukhachevsky, V. K. Triandafillov, A. I. Yegorov, G. S. Isserson, and others.

Above all, development of powerful and mobile combat means, and improvement (taking into account the introduction of new types of weapons and combat equipment into the forces) of the organizational structure of formations and large operational formations, which acquired the capability not only of suppressing and penetrating the enemy defense to its entire tactical depth and pressuring his immediate reserves, but also of exploiting tactical success into operational success, served as the basis for developing this theory.

The deep operation, the crowning step of whose theory was the publication of the new 1936 *Field Regulations*, included several stages: penetrating the tactical defense, exploiting tactical success into operational success, and exploiting operational success.

The main feature of penetration in a deep operation, as distinct from linear forms of battle, which envisioned gradually driving the enemy out, consisted of deep pressure on him, simultaneous suppression, destruction, paralysis, encirclement, and complete routing of his main grouping. It was implemented by cooperating infantry, artillery, tanks, and aviation, simultaneously hitting the entire depth of the enemy's combat formations. By means of a sudden, deep, and powerful attack, forces penetrated the defense and swiftly made their way through breaches formed in it to reach the operational depth. Here, cooperation among forces was organized and maintained in the interests of infantry.

For the subsequent exploitation of offensive success and increasing the maneuverability of combat actions, mobile forces were introduced and tactical air assaults landed. To accomplish this, it was envisioned to have motor-mechanized or cavalry-mechanized formations as so-called force mobile groups in the composition of army and *front* second echelons. Mobile groups were considered one of the most important elements in army and *front* force formations, and a decisive means conditioning the great depth and scope of an operation, as well as the high tempo of its conduct.

The deep operation also required a deep army and *front* force formation. A shock grouping's operational formation included a *penetration echelon*, an *echelon for developing the penetration (mobile forces)*, an *aviation group*, and an *air assault group*. Shock armies, well-outfitted with combat equipment, transport, and communications means, were to be used on the main axis.

Other important conditions for achieving success in a deep operation were gaining air supremacy, isolating the region of combat actions from the approach of enemy reserves, and preventing supplies of materiel reaching his defending forces.

A special role in executing these missions was played by aviation. Delivering strikes against a withdrawing enemy, bridges and crossings, defensive structures on intermediate lines, and reserves advancing from the depth and in regions of concentration, aviation made it possible to achieve high offensive tempos, while preventing the enemy breaking away from pursuing formations; it also disorganized his lines and isolated the zone of combat actions from the approach of fresh forces, which, in the final analysis, predetermined his piecemeal defeat.

The theory of the deep offensive operation advanced a new mode of combat actions, whose essence consisted of combining the efforts of the penetration echelon, the echelon for developing the penetration, shock groups, holding forces, and other groups, none of which were tactically connected to one another, into a single shock mechanism which ensured hitting and routing the enemy to the entire operational depth of his position.

Taking into account the maneuver nature of offensive operations, appropriate *forms of maneuver* were also determined: frontal attack and attack along converging axes; combined attack (a number of splintering attacks of varied force on a wide front); envelopment; and encirclement.

While according priority to the offensive, the theory also focused definite attention on the development of tactical and operational forms of defense. Defense was regarded as an operational mode of action employed to economize forces, gain time, and change the correlation of forces and means to one's favor. It played the role of an instrument in operational support and offensive preparation.

Such preeminent Soviet military leaders as M. N. Tukhachevsky, A. I. Yegorov, I. P. Uborevich, I. E. Yakir, and Ya. I. Alksnis devoted considerable attention to further development of this theory and all-round practical verification of its principles in war games, exercises, and military maneuvers. It was reflected not only in field regulations, but also in numerous works, periodical literature, and presentations by our army's leadership personnel.

Thus, development of the *foundations of the theory of the deep operation*, which envisioned the simultaneous suppression of the enemy defense and the delivery of deep, annihilating blows against all elements of his forces' operational formation (thanks to which, conditions were created to develop the offensive swiftly to a great depth and transform tactical success into operational success), was a qualitatively new stage in the development of Soviet military art, and one of its great achievements. For the first time a trend was observed to augment the scope of future operations and increase force mobility.

On the whole, theoretical development of the most important problems of preparing and conducting operations in the prewar period made it possible to arm our cadres with progressive military knowledge and begin the purposeful preparation of the army and the navy to repel aggression.

The main principles of the theory of the deep operation and battle found practical application and further development in operations during the Great Patriotic War.

Development of the art of penetration proceeded under conditions of continuous improvement in the enemy's defense. Beginning in summer 1943 and until the end of the war, his defense was characterized by high force stability and stubbornness, dynamism, and maneuver operations. Penetration of such a defense required a high level of skill on the part of the Soviet command and forces. Under these conditions, the *selection of the most effective methods for penetrating the defense and forms of operational maneuver* had great significance.

Depending on the operational concept, the following could be executed: a frontal attack to penetrate the defense deeply and dismember an opposing grouping; frontal attacks with subsequent shallow and deeper envelopment of enemy groups to encircle him independently or in cooperation with neighboring units; frontal attacks to splinter a grouping and destroy it piecemeal.

At the same time, the defender was subjected to powerful fire pressure and air strikes to the entire depth of his formation. The enemy was suppressed with the greatest density in the first defensive belt. After an artillery and air preparation, rifle units and formations launched the offensive. Direct infantry support tanks and self-propelled artillery launchers advanced in the combat formations of rifle subunits.

The offensive was continuously supported by artillery fire and air strikes. Aviation and long-range artillery struck enemy reserves in the tactical and operational depth, paralyzed their maneuver, and disorganized their actions. As a result of close combination of fire and attack, the defense was rapidly penetrated.

> The primary directions for improving the art of penetrating the defense at this time were, first, reducing the number of penetration sectors and their width: a *front* most often penetrated an enemy defense in one or two, and more rarely three sectors. Second, decisively massing forces and means in penetration sectors by weakening other axes, which made it possible to create the necessary (two to three times and more) superiority with an inconsiderable, overall superiority, and sometimes with equal forces. Third, improving the art of structuring shock groupings to take maximum advantage of their combat potential.[2]

More than 50 per cent of rifle formations, as much as 60–80 per cent of artillery and mortars, and 80–100 per cent of tanks and aviation were concentrated in penetration sectors.

Army and *front* mobile groups (tank armies; tank, mechanized, and cavalry corps; cavalry-mechanized groups) were introduced to exploit success, and combat actions shifted into the operational depth. Achieving swift penetration of the defense at high offensive tempos was ensured by delivering powerful attacks in narrow front sectors, with subsequent widening of the penetration in the direction of flanks and continuous advance into the depth.

Increased ground force fire power, maneuverability, and shock force predetermined the successful penetration of a prepared defense at comparatively high tempos and at a great depth.

To maintain superiority over the enemy and intensify efforts during operations, the *operational formation of forces* was continually improved. Thus, for example, during the first period of war *fronts* often had a single-echelon operational formation, weak reserves, and an inadequate quantity of aviation. By mid-1943, stronger first and second echelons, powerful echelons for exploiting success (army and *front* mobile groups) and large reserves of all combat arms had begun to be created in *fronts*.

Constant increase in the quantity and improvement in the quality of combat equipment for the forces, and improvement of the methods for its employment contributed to a deep operational formation of forces and, consequently, the development of an operation to great depth and at high tempos.

Despite remaining difficulties, by mid-1942 a well-organized and rapidly growing war economy was already created in the country by the entire nation's heroic efforts, led by the Communist Party. Restructured in a military manner, it supplied the front with everything necessary.

During the war, the Soviet Union produced twice the amount of weapons and combat equipment, and of better quality, than Fascist Germany. From 1 July 1941 to 1 September 1945 Soviet industry produced 134,100 airplanes, 102,800 tanks and self-propelled artillery, and 825,200 guns and mortars.[3] And this, in turn, ensured an increase in offensive tempos and depths of the combat missions of units, formations, and large formations.

For example, if during the first period of war the depth of an army offensive operation amounted only to 50–90 kilometers, in later periods it increased to 100–150 and more kilometers. At the same time, tactical densities per kilometer of penetration sector increased: infantry – up to 7.6 battalions; guns and mortars – 180 (not including rocket artillery); tanks and self-propelled artillery – more than 20.[4]

Artillery was the principal means for fire suppression of the enemy. The growth in its role was inseparably connected with skillful massing on selected axes, and development of the theory and practice of the *artillery offensive* ensued from the theory of the deep operation. Reliable suppression of the defense during this period of the artillery preparation to a great depth, continuous artillery support of the attack, and artillery accompaniment of attacking forces into the depth turned the offensive into a single process of forward movement by attacking forces under constant cover of artillery fire.

The *aviation offensive* was also a further development of the tenets of the theory of the deep operation. It went from episodic strikes by small groups of airplanes to continuous, echeloned actions by large aviation forces in close cooperation with ground forces.

Naturally, under modern conditions the volume of missions in offensive operations has sharply grown, and methods for artillery and aviation to fulfill them have become complex. However, the experience, obtained during the war, of organizing and conducting the artillery and aviation offensive maintains its significance to a great degree, especially in combat operations where nuclear weapons are not employed.

The achievement of operational aims was determined, to a significant degree, by the timely intensification of our forces' efforts, especially those of tank formations and large formations. One of the most important problems in resolving this mission was determining the time and method of committing tank armies, which comprised the *fronts'* main shock force.

It was considered expedient to commit them after the penetration of the tactical defensive zone. However, experience demonstrated that combined-arms armies of a *front's* first echelon could not, in a number of cases, independently resolve the problem of penetration at high tempos. Therefore, to deprive the enemy of the ability to bring up reserves and occupy prepared lines in the depth, thereby substantively affecting the course of a *front* operation, tank army first echelons were introduced to complete the penetration of the tactical defensive zone. In operations from the second half of 1944 (Belorussian, Iassy–Kishinev, Vistula–Oder), tank armies, as a rule, were introduced after the penetration of the enemy's tactical defensive zone.

This was conditioned, above all, by the increase in shock force of combined-arms armies – the *front's* first echelon. They were reinforced by a large quantity of artillery, direct infantry support tanks, and separate tank and mechanized corps, which made it possible to penetrate the enemy defense successfully. Under these conditions, the commitment of tank armies was carried out in the operational depth, which ensured favorable conditions for developing the offensive at high tempos and achieving the ultimate operational aims.

If we take into account that in a number of operations tank armies were successfully used in the composition of the first echelon to penetrate the defense on independent axes, then it can be said that during the Great Patriotic War a completely new problem of operational art – preparation and conduct of an offensive operation by a tank army – was resolved by the Soviet command.

Experience in organizing and conducting such operations was invaluable for the operational training of tank and combined-arms formations and their staffs under modern conditions.

As a result of rapid penetration of the enemy defense, favorable conditions were created to overcome it rapidly, employing decisive forms of maneuver in the operational depth to rout operational reserves, overcome intermediate lines and force water obstacles from the march, cut withdrawal routes, and encircle large enemy groupings.

Encirclement and annihilation of large groupings became the principal form for our forces to conduct offensive operations. The theory of the deep operation was enriched by the practice of encircling and annihilating the enemy using forces of one or several *fronts*. An encirclement was carried out in the tactical, immediate operational, and greater operational depth.

Soviet operational art was also enriched by the practice of *organizing and conducting successive front and army offensive operations (with respect to depth)*. In the majority of cases, the completion of one offensive operation created conditions for conducting the next operation without pause. Solid and continuous troop control during the entire operation made this possible, to a considerable degree. It was precisely under conditions of a rapidly changing situation and the sharply expressed maneuver nature of force combat actions, especially mobile ones, that timely acquisition and processing of data on changes in the situation by staffs at all levels made it possible for the *front* (army) command to make expedient decisions and implement them.

The most important indicator of the growth in the art of preparing and conducting *front* and army offensive operations during the war was the continuous increase in their scope.

During the third period of the war, *front* operations were conducted to a depth of 400–600 kilometers at an average daily tempo of up to 25–30 and more kilometers; army operations were to a depth of 100–180 kilometers. These indicators exceeded considerably the norms worked out on the basis of the prewar theory of the deep operation. The increase in the scope of operations was a result of increases in the quantity of combat equipment taking part in operations, continuous growth in fire power, mass employment of armored and mechanized forces, continued improvement in the combat expertise of forces and staffs, and their skill in conducting maneuver operations.

Soviet operational art during the Great Patriotic War showed itself to be the most progressive art of that time. It surpassed the German Fascist command's art of preparing and conducting operations. The theory of the deep operation, developed by Soviet military science in the prewar years, was employed in many of the Soviet Armed Forces' operations.

Among the number of most important achievements of Soviet military art, one can cite with complete justification the development and successful practical implementation of a new form of strategic offensive – operations by groups of *fronts* conducted in the interests of achieving a specific strategic aim by the coordinated efforts of several *fronts*, together with large formations and formations of other Armed Forces services.

This was a completely new phenomenon in military art.

The Great Patriotic War introduced major corrections into the theory of the deep operation, retaining the overall idea, but fundamentally changing the content of creating shock groupings and an operational formation of forces, organizing the penetration of the enemy defense, and developing the offensive.

In the postwar period, all combat means rapidly improved and were supplied to the forces in required quantities.

The theory of offensive battle and operations in the initial postwar years developed on a new technological base, taking into account acquired experience. Although it basically retained the same characteristic offensive features, more improved methods for its conduct appeared.

Soviet military theory considered that a *front* (army) offensive operation could begin under the following conditions: penetration of a prepared defense, penetration of fortified regions, penetration of a hastily occupied defense; and a meeting encounter.

Offensive operations involving penetration of a prepared defense were recognized as the most typical form of operations and the most complex type of offensive action. They consisted of creating a breach in the enemy defense by destroying his personnel and combat equipment, as well as capturing fortifications to the entire tactical depth, with a simultaneous widening of the penetration in the direction of the flanks and its further development into the depth. Only after penetration of the enemy's tactical defense and rout of the immediate operational reserves did forces acquire sufficient freedom of action to exploit success and incapacitate and encircle his groupings.

Independent of initial conditions in an offensive operation, the idea of an encirclement of the enemy, with his simultaneous destruction, lay at its foundation. Only a decisive offensive with encirclement of large enemy groupings leads to his destruction and capture, and creates conditions for the rapid capture of strategic or operational objectives and lines.

Mass use of all types of combat equipment, in the first order artillery and tanks, along selected axes and a simultaneous attack on the entire depth of the enemy's operational formation are necessary for the successful implementation of a penetration.

It was considered that quantitative indicators of forces and means employed during the last war to conduct large-scale offensive operations did not lose their significance. It was necessary that created shock groupings possess power capable of overcoming any enemy resistance and ensuring the rout of his approaching reserves and successful advance of forces to the entire operational depth. Hence, the average tactical density of forces and means in a penetration sector per kilometer of front was specified as follows: infantry – 3–4 battalions; guns and mortars (not including antitank artillery) for the period of artillery preparation – 180–220; direct infantry support tanks and self-propelled artillery – 25–30 (for first-echelon formations); combat engineer companies – 4–6.

Decisiveness of aims; operational participation of large masses of ground forces equipped with varied combat equipment, large aviation forces, air-assault forces, and naval forces on coastal axes; large spatial scope; intensity and continuity of combat actions; and a high degree of maneuverability were all considered characteristic features of an offensive operation.

On the whole, after the war Soviet military-theoretical thought correctly defined the nature of the offensive in combat operations with employment of nuclear weapons. The offensive was viewed in the classical form as penetration of a prepared defense, when one or the other side had already created a strategic front, and when all or part of the armed forces had already deployed and could be used to conduct operations. Subsequently, when nuclear weapons were adopted as armaments, this situation was refined.

Nuclear weapons were viewed as the main means for destroying the enemy (his nuclear means, force groupings, aviation and naval forces, and other important objectives). Ground forces were tasked with completing the rout of enemy groupings.

An attempt to take into consideration the experience of the Great Patriotic War as applicable to conditions of nuclear war dominated in the theory of the offensive operation.

Later, extensive equipping of armed forces with rocket-nuclear weapons led to a change in their role.

During this period, principal attention was focused on problems of preparing and conducting offensive operations under conditions of employing nuclear weapons. General tenets of the theory of the deep operation which concerned the nature of offensive operations, their aims and spatial scope, methods of preparation, conduct, and support, and issues of using forces and means in the offensive were developed further.

Employment of nuclear weapons and the considerable increase in force mobility and combat power accorded offensive operations an even greater maneuver, dynamic, and decisive nature, increasing their spatial scope and decreasing their duration. In the armies of capitalist countries, it was felt that the offensive, because of the absence of continuous fronts, would be conducted along separate axes, with a considerable separation of the most combat-capable groupings – above all, tank groupings – from the main forces.

Massing nuclear strikes, maneuver of forces and means along the front and into the depth, and swift force actions following nuclear strikes acquired decisive significance. Offensive operations would be distinguished by an intense struggle to seize and maintain the initiative, and by the variety of methods used to rout the enemy; they would be conducted under conditions of strong radiation contamination, floods, and destruction.

In addition, it was noted that, despite the decisive role of nuclear weapons in operations, success could be achieved only by combining the efforts of all types of ground forces and units and subunits of other armed forces services cooperating with them. The resolution of the problem of delivering deep strikes received new development. The increase in depth of the enemy defensive operational formation, and the location of the most important objectives a great distance from the line of contact of both sides conditioned the necessity of increasing the depth of blows of attacking forces. Increased fire power and the great range of means of destruction, and their high degree of mobility and shock force made it possible to support the conduct of an offensive at great depth and high tempos. The capability appeared for simultaneously hitting all enemy objectives in the operational depth with nuclear weapons and having ground forces and air-assault forces exploit the results.

It was considered that an offensive operation should be the totality of engagements and battles coordinated with respect to aim, place, and time, and conducted on the specific territory by ground forces and aviation in cooperation with the forces of other armed forces services. All force actions should be executed according to a single plan and directed toward the swiftest rout of opposing groupings.

The offensive operation could include the first and subsequent operations by first-echelon forces, combat actions of aviation, and combat actions of units and forces of combat arms and special forces, as well as reserves. The most important component of this operation under conditions of employing nuclear weapons was the first and subsequent nuclear strikes.

The problem of operational formation of forces in an offensive operation was developed further. It began to include not only first and second echelons, but also groupings of combat arms and armed forces services, as well as all types of reserves.

It was envisioned to have a strong first echelon, with the greater part of the forces and means included in its composition, to rout opposing groupings quickly and arrive swiftly in the operational depth.

The second echelon was designated to intensify force efforts and exploit first-echelon success on the main axis; to replace some first-echelon units and formations which had suffered heavy losses; to deliver attacks on new axes; to rout enemy reserves and repel counterstrokes (counterattacks); to complete the rout of the enemy remaining on the flanks and in the rear of attacking forces; and to carry out a series of other missions.

Depending on the existing situation, the operational formation could include a second echelon or reserves, or both simultaneously.

It was recognized that a combination of nuclear strikes and a swift troop offensive must lie at the basis of any *method of offensive operation*. In the armies of capitalist countries, it was considered that the enemy's decisive defeat could be achieved as a result of the delivery of nuclear strikes and a decisive troop offensive along the shortest axes, which would make it possible to incapacitate and splinter defending groupings and destroy them piecemeal.

The question of selecting the main attack axis also received fuller substantiation. Under conditions of nuclear war, this could be delivered not only against weak defences, but also strong defenses. The selected axis had to ensure favorable conditions for committing one's forces, effective employment of means of destruction, rapid destruction of the enemy defense and the stability of his primary groupings, and timely execution of assigned missions.

The following principles lay at the foundation of planning, organizing, and conducting an offensive operation: creation of superiority over the enemy on the main axis; forestalling him in delivering strikes and deploying forces; ensuring a reliable defeat of the entire defensive grouping; swiftly advancing into the depth and widening the penetration in the direction of the flanks; continuously intensifying efforts on the most important axes; widely maneuvering forces and means; and incapacitating enemy forces and destroying them piecemeal.

It was considered that the absence of a continuous front and the potential which arose for creating breaches in the enemy's operational formation could permit the attacker to advance in march columns at high tempos at the very beginning of an operation. Above all, it was necessary to employ tank forces from the first-echelon composition and groupings from the second echelon to advance swiftly into the operational depth.

Much attention was focused on the issue of increasing offensive tempos.

It was assumed that, under nuclear war conditions, a series of operational-tactical measures were necessary to achieve high offensive tempos. Among these were delivery of a decisive strike against the enemy using nuclear weapons, timely and effective exploitation of this strike, selection of the most expedient forms of employing forces and means for resolving operational-tactical missions, achievement of superiority in mobility of forces during an operation, and skillful organization of all types of support.

Extensive use of forward detachments, air assaults, strong tank groupings, bold maneuver, and timely intensification of efforts were envisioned to increase offensive tempos. Here, a special role was given to the element of surprising and forestalling the enemy in delivering strikes.

The question of combating antitank means and ensuring continuity of control was further developed in the theory of the offensive operation. A new problem was reflected in it: the struggle against air-mobile forces.

It was assumed that the problem of combating enemy antitank means could be resolved in the following way. Above all, it was necessary to begin to hit antitank means with fire from all types of weapons at the disposal of attacking forces, and to thwart control of ATGMs. In addition, it was essential to increase the survivability of one's own tanks and other armored objects by both improving the tactics of their employment and introducing additional structures to increase their invulnerability.

The most expedient methods of ensuring continuity of control were improvement of troop leadership organization, command post systems, and communications; improvement of commander and staff work methods; planning and implementation of measures for protecting command posts against weapons of mass destruction; ensuring unfailing operation of radio-electronic means under conditions of strong interference; and development of measures in advance for re-establishing disrupted control.

Resolving the problem of combating enemy air-mobile forces is one of the most urgent issues in the theory of the offensive operation. The fight against air-mobile forces should be conducted at the tactical level, since air defense means capable of firing against low-altitude targets are concentrated here. In the fight against air-mobile forces, it is possible to enlist antitank and rifle-cannon armaments mounted on armored objects. However, the primary means for combating them are antiaircraft rockets and short-range, conventional artillery complexes.

Other questions concerning the offensive operation have been developed recently: the rout of enemy operational reserves and repulsion of his counterstrokes; force actions in contaminated and demolished regions; forcing of water obstacles; employment of tactical and operational air assaults, etc.

Taking into account the preparation for nuclear war by imperialism and the Peking leadership, Soviet military doctrine proceeds from the fact that a possible war will be nuclear. Therefore, all problems of the offensive operation are examined as applicable to nuclear war.

During a war where nuclear weapons are employed, however, combat actions may be conducted using only conventional means on separate axes. In this connection, much attention is also devoted to offensive operations without employment of nuclear weapons.

In this plan, problems are resolved concerning the selection of the main attack axis; creation of a decisive superiority in forces and means, especially fire, on selected axes; determination of the operational formation of forces; methods of conducting offensive operations; planning of operations, organization and support of continuous cooperation and control, etc.

It was noted that the principal condition for a successful offensive without employment of nuclear weapons is the creation of superiority over the enemy in tanks, artillery, and aviation on the main attack axes.

The selection of the main attack axis should ensure that the tactical defensive zone is successfully overcome and that forces quickly reach disposition regions of the most important enemy objectives (nuclear attack means, command posts, airfields for basing aviation, etc.), at the flank and in the rear of the main grouping to rout it.

It was emphasized that the operational formation of forces could include the same elements as in an offensive with employment of nuclear weapons, but it was necessary to create a stronger first echelon; second echelons and reserves could be somewhat closer to the first echelon, ensuring their more rapid commitment and reducing the depth of the operational formation.

Various methods for conducting offensive operations under these conditions were also examined. They could include successive mass strikes by aviation and artillery to the entire depth of the enemy defense, in combination with a swift troop offensive. It was noted that at the very beginning of the operation it was necessary to put the enemy's nuclear attack means and aviation out of action, suppress his reserves, disrupt control, and, during the offensive, intensify strikes continuously, above all by committing second echelons and reserves.

Thus, as the scientific-technical revolution became more profound, the technical outfitting of the Armed Forces, organizational force structure, and methods for conducting combat actions improved.

With the introduction of rocket-nuclear weapons, views on the nature of conducting military actions and the organization of operations changed radically. When preparing and training forces, it was taken into consideration that new weapons had broadened considerably the framework of operations and raised the importance of troop moral-political and psychological qualities.

The principal mission of the ground forces, outfitted with rocket-nuclear weapons of operational-tactical and tactical designation, was to destroy the enemy's nuclear attack means and other objectives, and to rout his remaining groupings. Full exploitation of results of nuclear strikes to execute assigned missions rapidly became something fundamentally new in their actions. The main role in achieving operational aims was given to operational-tactical rocket forces, aviation, and tank, motorized rifle, and air-assault forces.

Personnel training was structured on the basis of the fact that in modern operations the offensive would be characterized by the absence of both continuous fronts and linearity of force actions. Combat actions could develop simultaneously on large expanses along the front and in the depth.

Forces were trained to conduct an offensive along a number of separate axes to splinter an opposing enemy grouping and destroy it piecemeal. In all cases, however, the attacker's main efforts were concentrated on the principal axes, where mass rocket-nuclear strikes were delivered. Offensive force sectors became considerably wider than previously, which made it possible to execute extensive maneuver of forces and means.

Much attention was focused on the conduct of maneuver combat actions. This was caused by the mass outfitting of forces with tanks, BMPs, armored transports, and other highly mobile equipment. During an operation, important significance was attached to the employment of tactical and operational air assaults, *frontal* aviation, air defense forces and means, special forces, the conduct of measures to protect against weapons of mass destruction, etc.

In connection with the radical change in the nature of battles and operations, sharp and rapid changes in the situation were inevitable, which increased the significance of unit and formation independence and commanders' initiative at all levels. This also required troop actions that were bold to the point of audacity, swift penetrations into the depth, and wide employment of deep and shallow envelopments.

Although the term "deep operation (battle)" has not been employed in official documents since the 1960s, the general principles of this theory have not lost their significance, and continue to be improved on the modern materiel base of armed struggle.

NOTES

1. L. I. Voloshin, "Teoriya glubokoy operatsii i tendentsii yeye razvitiya," *Voyennaya mysl'* [Military thought], 8 (1978), pp. 14–26.
2. A. M. Mayorov, "Proryv oborony: teoriya i praktika mirovykh voyn," [The penetration of the defense: theory and practice of the world wars], *Voyennaya mysl'* [Military thought], 5 (1978), p. 84.
3. See *Sovetskaya voyennaya entsiklopediya* [Soviet military encyclopedia] (Voyenizdat, 1977), p. 68.
4. *Armeyskiye operatsii* [Army operations] (Voyenizdat, 1977), pp. 10–54.

Soviet Operational Art: Birth and Primary Stages of Development

COLONEL N. N. FOMIN[1]

Soviet operational art covered a complex path of formation and creative development. Having begun to unfold during the Civil War and foreign military intervention (1918–20) on the basis of experience in preparing and conducting *front* and army operations, it has presently become multi-faceted, encompassing the theory and practice of preparing and conducting joint and independent operations (combat actions) by operational-strategic, operational, and operational-tactical large formations and formations of the Armed Forces.

Accordingly, the following are distinguishing aspects in the structure of Soviet operational art: its general foundations, ensuing from principles of military art and fundamental for all Armed Forces services; and the operational art of each Armed Forces service, taking into consideration the specifics of the organization and technical outfitting of its formations and units, the sphere of action, combat capabilities and employment methods.

Soviet operational art, like the military art of the world's first socialist state, arose during the Civil War and foreign military intervention as a natural event in the development of Marxist military-theoretical thought.

It is generally known that Marx and Engels had already put forward and substantiated many of the initial tenets of a working class military theory, considering it to be an objectively necessary product of new social relationships and a powerful weapon of the proletariat in the struggle against the bourgeoisie.[2] More than once they emphasized that new methods of conducting military operations, resembling nothing before, had to be intrinsic to revolutionary wars. Here, Engels pointed out that the victorious proletariat was obliged to work out such methods.

Lenin, creatively developing Marxist teachings under new historical conditions, enriched Marx's military theory with new content. The crown of Lenin's original imaginative thought in this area is the *study on the defense of the socialist Fatherland*. Plans of the most important operations to rout the enemy, worked out under Lenin's leadership during the Civil War, his instructions and directives to *fronts* and armies on the most important issues of preparing and conducting operations, presentations and lectures at party congresses and meetings of the Republic Revolutionary Military Council, and telegrams and letters concerning regulation of military operations on *fronts* were a very rich foundation for the formulation and development of Soviet operational art.

The fact that, in implementing centralized control of combat operations on all Civil War strategic axes, the military-political leadership, headed by Lenin, provided *front* and army commands with great independence in planning and executing operations, objectively promoted the birth of this new field of military art. Thus, life itself pointed to the necessity of distinguishing an intermediate level of military leadership, whose function was to resolve missions associated with the direct preparation and conduct of concrete operations.[3]

In addition, the very nature of the Civil War, which was, in principle, distinguished from all wars of the imperialist era, had substantial influence on the process of formulating operational art. Inasmuch as it bore a just, progressive character on behalf of the revolutionary proletariat, the Red Army's military actions, including methods of preparing and conducting operations, were distinguished by inexhaustible creativity, boldness, decisiveness, and a high degree of dynamism.

As a rule, the defeat of an enemy was accomplished by conducting a series of successive offensive operations using the forces of one or two *fronts*, usually without significant pauses and with the employment of different forms of maneuver. At that time this was a new phenomenon in operational art. Armies resolved operational missions within the framework of a *front* offensive operation. Their actions were coordinated with respect to aim, place, and time by *front* directives. Thus, the foundations were laid for operational cooperation among large formations.

The approach to planning and conducting *front* and army offensive operations was also distinguished by considerable innovation. Considerable attention was devoted to careful selection of the main attack axis, and the principle of concentrating superior forces on decisive axes by creating shock groupings and purposeful use of reserves was expressed more concretely. This was especially clearly exhibited during the counteroffensive and then the general offensive of Southern Front forces (October 1919–January 1920), in which First Cavalry Army with attached rifle formations acted as the *front* shock group. In generalizing this experience, Southern Front's Revolutionary Military Council required of army commanders that they "not scatter their forces, but fight on selected axes of concentration like a fist in a narrow front, swiftly and decisively."[4]

The art of penetrating a positional defense and the exploitation of tactical success into operational success were raised to a higher level. Cavalry corps and cavalry armies, whose employment made it possible to increase considerably the depth of attacks and offensive tempos and attach a maneuver and decisive character to operations, played an important role in this. Thus, if during the First World War the offensive depth of large operational formations was 10–14 kilometers, and very rarely 80–150 kilometers (Southwestern Front operations in June–September 1916), then during the Civil War this reached 200–300 kilometers for Red Army *front* operations, and up to 100–150 kilometers for army operations.[5] The offensive was conducted at a tempo of 10–12 kilometers and more per day, while pursuit reached up to 20–25 kilometers per day.

The art of preparing and conducting defensive operations developed. In the defense, as in the offense, maneuver methods of action predominated. In separate cases, when holding important objectives and regions (Tsarytsyn, Petrograd, Orenburg, Astrakhan', the Kakhov bridgehead, etc.), the defense was structured deeply, bore a positional character, and had a well-organized fire and engineer obstacle system and a higher density of forces and means.

During the Civil War, the operational art of the Soviet Navy was created as well. In its early stages it was manifested in the form of joint actions with ground forces on coastal axes and along large rivers. In a number of cases, the navy also conducted independent actions, especially in the defense and capture of important naval bases and other objectives on the coast.

Purposeful Red Army party-political work played an enormous role at this time. It made it possible to strengthen the troops' political-moral condition and indoctrinate soldiers and commanders in ideological conviction, steadfastness in battle, and offensive spirit.

Thus, during the Civil War rich experience was accumulated for scientifically based conclusions on the most important questions concerning preparing and conducting *front* and army operations. This experience, which had absorbed the best from past military art, demonstrated clearly that the former division of military art into only strategy and tactics was no longer appropriate for conditions of armed struggle or the forms and methods of conducting it. This subdivision did not yet encompass questions concerning preparing and conducting operations by large *front* and army formations. The natural necessity arose to allocate to military art, together with strategy and tactics, a new, intermediate level – *operational art.*

Civil War experience also made possible the formulation of such important principles of Soviet operational art as dynamism and decisiveness of force actions in operations; conduct of combat actions by the combined efforts of all combat arms, above all infantry, cavalry, and artillery; concentration of force efforts on the most important axes; bold maneuver by troops, forces, and means; surprise in delivering attacks against the enemy; all-round support of force combat actions; and centralized control of forces, both in the preparation of operations and during them.

With the country's transition to peaceful socialist development, problems of operational art were considered among the main issues in the theory and practice of military art. The presence of capitalist encirclement and the constant threat of a new war required the further strengthening of the country's defense capability and an increase in the Soviet Armed Forces' combat might. It was necessary to reorganize the army in a short time, give it a well-coordinated organizational structure, improve its technological outfitting, and improve the training and combat readiness of troops and naval forces. In the field of military art, it was necessary to provide a thorough theoretical foundation of the possible nature of future war, and develop a scientifically substantiated theory for preparation and conduct of operations.

Military-theoretical discussions were held on many of these issues, which made it possible to find a way to resolve existing problems.

An exceptionally great role in the correct understanding of the problems of military development and operational art was played by Lenin's works, in which he warned about the unacceptability of ignoring past war experience, above all that of the Civil War. Also of no little importance were the military-theoretical works and presentations of such prominent military leaders as M. V. Frunze, M. N. Tukhachevsky, A. I. Yegorov, I. P. Uborevich, I. E. Yakir, V. K. Blyukher, R. P. Eydeman, *et al.*

In sum, a single Soviet military doctrine was worked out, and methods were determined for resolving fundamental problems of the organizational development of the Soviet Armed Forces, for training and indoctrinating them, and for conducting operations. Thus, the principle for formulating the scientific bases of the theory of Soviet operational art was laid out. Enormous work was done during this period on preparing army and navy command cadres, and arming them with scientific methods for operational-tactical calculations and the ability to work out decisions and plans for preparing and conducting operations on the basis of calculating actual force combat capabilities.

The ultimate division of Soviet military art into three components – strategy, operational art, and tactics – occurred in the second half of the 1920s. In accordance with this classification, the theory of each of these components began to be developed.

The basic tenets of the theory of operational art were reflected in new regulations such as *Vyssheye komandovaniye* [Higher Command] (1924), *Vremennyy polevoy ustav 1925 goda* [Provisional Field Regulations of 1925], and later *Polevoy ustav RKKA 1929 goda* [Field Regulations of the Workers' and Peasants' Red Army/PU-29], combat regulations for infantry, artillery, and air forces, etc.

The theory of Soviet operational art was given even greater all-round development in the 1930s. The successful completion of the first five-year plan made it possible to create a new, more solid materiel-technical base for strengthening the country's defense and technically rebuilding the army and navy. The formation of units, and subsequently large formations of the most up-and-coming combat arms and forces commenced. Tank units were created in armored forces to reinforce infantry and cavalry, and, in autumn 1932 (significantly earlier than in foreign armies), mechanized corps designated for resolving operational missions were created. Bomber and fighter aviation brigades were formed in the air forces, and, in 1933, air corps were founded. During this same period the creation of units and formations of air-assault forces to resolve operational missions began.

New large operational formations appeared as part of the navy: in 1933 the Northern Flotilla, transformed later into the Northern Fleet, and in 1935, the Pacific Ocean Fleet. Fleets were equipped with new surface ships, submarines, and aviation. Their basing system was improved.

At the beginning of the 1930s, Soviet military science developed the theory of the deep operation, based on the idea of using most fully force fire and shock potentials for simultaneous action against the enemy to the entire depth of his operational formation, and for the defeat of his main grouping. This theory was a great achievement for Soviet operational art. It reflected the most progressive system of views on conducting operations by mass, highly mobile, and technically well-equipped armies. The problem of penetrating the enemy defense and developing the offensive into the operational depth was resolved in a fundamentally new way, marking a decisive shift from positional methods of conducting military operations to more effective and dynamic methods.[6]

In the 1930s, attention was also focused on the development of principles of operational defense. For the first time the requirement was advanced that such a defense be, above all, antitank, antiartillery, and antiaircraft, that it have a deeply-echeloned formation, and that it have the ability to intensify resistance in the depth. In addition to a tactical defensive zone with a depth of 15–20 kilometers, it was envisioned to create an operational zone with a depth of 20–30 kilometers. Army reserves, reinforced by antitank means of the Reserve of the Supreme High Command, were deployed here, designated mainly for delivering strong counterstrokes.

The theory of Soviet operational art was developed further in the second half of the 1930s. By this time, thanks to the successful completion of the second five-year plan and the beginning of the third, a more powerful materiel base was created for the technical reorganization of the army and navy. Taking this into account, the most important tenets of the theory of the deep operation were refined and made more concrete; they were reflected in *Vremmennyy polevoy ustav RKKA* [Provisional Field Regulations of the Workers' and Peasants' Red Army/PU-36].

Much attention was devoted to formulating operational art for the air forces and navy. Objective prerequisites emerged to give birth to a National

Air Defense Forces operational art. Theoretical foundations for the operational rear, the structure of *front* and army control organs, and principles for their functioning were developed.

The theory of the deep operation required further concretization of the most important principles of operational art. Exceptionally great significance was attached, above all, to the conduct of combat actions by joint forces of combined-arms, motor-mechanized and cavalry formations, armies, and air-assault forces; to questions of organizing and implementing operational cooperation of aviation and air-assault forces with formations of the echelon for developing the penetration under conditions of actions in the operational depth; to concentration of force efforts and means on selected axes; to operational dynamism and decisiveness, both at the beginning of an operation and during it; and to execution of bold maneuver of forces (and means), especially of highly mobile formations which could burst forward and operate at some distance from remaining *front* (army) forces. Such principles as surprise; all-round support of troop combat actions, especially highly mobile formations when being introduced into a penetration, and carrying out operations in the operational depth; and centralization of troop control received new content.

The Great Patriotic War of 1941-45 was a severe and all-round test of operational art. In the fierce and prolonged struggle against a strong and technically equipped enemy, it not only withstood all trials with honor, but was also raised to a higher level, having been enriched with new tenets and conclusions.

Strategic aims and missions at a particular stage of war, quantitative and qualitative growth of armaments, improvement of the organizational force structure and command cadre leadership expertise, and changes in the enemy's technical outfitting and methods for conducting combat actions influenced the development of the theory and practice of operational art.

In the first period of the war, Soviet operational art had to resolve a number of problems concerning the preparation and conduct of *front* and army defensive operations.

In addition, from the very beginning of the war the Soviet Army attached primary significance to the further development of the theory of dynamic offensive operations. Thanks to the inexhaustible activity of the Communist Party and the Soviet Government, and the people's self-sacrificing labor, the country's military-economic base widened and the technical outfitting and our Armed Forces' combat might increased. Soviet operational art sought more effective methods of preparing and conducting *front* and army offensive operations on this basis. Efforts were directed, above all, toward more precisely specifying the role and place of *fronts* and armies in resolving concrete operational and strategic missions, selecting the main attack axes, creating shock groupings and boldly maneuvering forces and means on decisive axes, using combat arms and forces more effectively in operations, and organizing their cooperation and control.

As is generally known, according to prewar views the major role in resolving strategic missions was reserved for *fronts*. However, the unprecedented scope and intensity of combat actions as the war developed required the enlistment of not one, but several *fronts* for this purpose. In this connection, the *front* began to be viewed as a higher large operational ground forces formation, designated mainly to resolve operational missions. Strategic aims were usually achieved by the combined efforts of several *fronts*. As a rule, a combined-arms army executed missions within the framework of a *front* offensive operation.

Refining the role of *fronts* and armies in resolving strategic and operational missions made it possible to plan precisely the functions of operational-level leadership; to approach with greater substantiation the specification of missions for large operational formations, their combat composition, and the means of reinforcement and materiel support; and to develop and improve different methods for preparing and conducting operations of various scales.

In the majority of cases, *fronts* delivered the main attack against the weakest area in the enemy defense, with subsequent arrival in the defending grouping's rear to encircle and then destroy them (the counteroffensive at Stalingrad, the Ostrogozh–Rossosh, Voronezh–Kastornoye, and Bryansk offensive operations, and others). In a number of instances, when it was necessary to incapacitate the enemy grouping as quickly as possible and arrive by the shortest path at regions whose capture made it possible to achieve most rapidly the operational aim, the main attack was purposely delivered on an axis where the enemy defense was stronger (Orel, Belgorod–Khar'kov operations, and others). For some operations in the third period of the war, when *fronts* had at their disposal a sufficient quantity of forces and means, *front* delivery of not one but two attacks was characteristic.

A significant step forward was made in the development and practical implementation of the most effective methods for massing forces and means on main attack axes. In some operations the width of *front* penetration sectors amounted to 7–12 per cent of the overall width of the offensive sector. Up to 50–80 per cent of combined-arms formations, up to 70–80 per cent of artillery, 80–90 per cent of tanks and self-propelled artillery, and up to 90–100 per cent of all *front* aviation were concentrated in these sectors (Iassy–Kishinev operation of 2d Ukrainian Front, Vistula–Oder operation of 1st Ukrainian Front, and others).

Massing of forces and means in armies was achieved by reducing the width of their offensive sectors (up to 9–13 kilometers on the *front* main attack axis) and penetration sectors. During the first period of war the width of an army penetration sector was usually 30–40 per cent of the overall width of its offensive sector; subsequently it did not exceed 12–18 per cent.

Increased skill in massing forces and means made it possible to create high force densities on main attack axes. In the majority of offensive operations during the second and third periods of the war, in penetration sectors these amounted to the following: one rifle division per 1.2–3.5 kilometers; 130–218 guns and mortars and 18–70 (and in sectors for commitment of mobile groups, up to 115–130) tanks and self-propelled artillery per kilometer of front. This ensured the achievement of significant superiority over the enemy on main attack axes, which reached on the average three- to five-fold in personnel, six- to eight-fold in artillery and tanks, and three- to five-fold in aviation.

In the final analysis, all this made it possible to increase the scope and decisiveness of *front* and army offensive operations. Their depth and force offensive tempos increased especially sharply. Thus, if in 1942 the depth of *front* offensive operations amounted to 100–140 kilometers and army operations to 50–80 kilometers, then during the concluding stage of the war *front* operations were conducted to a depth of 300–350 kilometers, and army operations to 100–150 and more kilometers. During the first period of the war, offensive tempos did not exceed 6–10 kilometers per day, while subsequently they reached 15–20, and in tank armies 40–50 kilometers and more per day, which ensured that the enemy defense was quickly shattered and his large groupings were swiftly routed.

Soviet operational art also successfully resolved the problem of developing tactical success into operational success, which was achieved by creating echelons for exploiting success (mobile groups) at first in combined-arms armies, and then in *fronts*, as well as by boldly using second echelons and reserves of all types and main aviation forces.

Imaginative employment of the most effective forms of operational maneuver made it possible to rout the enemy successfully in offensive operations. In those cases, when it was necessary to defeat the enemy and quickly capture an important objective or line in the depth of his defense, it was recommended to deliver a powerful cleaving attack along one axis. In some operations, several frontal attacks were delivered to splinter enemy groupings and destroy them piecemeal.

The highest achievement of Soviet operational art was the conduct of operations to encircle large enemy groupings. Starting with the second period of the war, these operations became the usual form of *front* and armies operations.

An important place in the theory and practice of preparing and conducting offensive operations was given to improving forms and methods for the combat employment of artillery and aviation. A new major achievement in this regard was the transition from artillery and aviation preparation to the artillery and aviation offensive respectively, carried out to the entire depth required by operational missions.

In addition, more effective methods were also sought for the timely intensification of force efforts during an operation to maintain constant superiority over the enemy, quickly create operational groupings, organize and conduct meeting engagements, implement high tempo operational pursuit, and force large water obstacles from the march.

During the Great Patriotic War, the theory and practice of preparing and conducting defensive operations were developed further. The main requirement confronting an operational defense was to do all to increase its stability. This problem was resolved, above all, by increasing its overall depth. If in winter 1941 the depth of the *front* defense at Moscow was 90–100 kilometers, in summer 1943 at Kursk it reached 160–180 kilometers (six to seven belts). Great significance was also attached to boldly massing forces and means on the most important axes. For example, in the Battle of Kursk, Central Front concentrated up to 30 per cent of rifle divisions, 50 per cent of artillery, and up to 87 per cent of tanks and self-propelled artillery in a sector comprising 11 per cent of the overall width of the defense sector.

Engineer preparation of the defense was also continuously improved. By the end of 1941 this had already begun to be a multi-belted structure with a system of continuous trenches, cut-off positions, communications trenches, and strongpoints. All artillery, aviation, especially ground attack, artillery antitank reserves, and mobile obstacle detachments were enlisted to resolve this problem.

At the same time, methods for conducting defensive operations also developed. Fire power against an attacking enemy, and counterattacks and counterstrokes using army and *front* assets were planned and implemented more precisely. A new phenomenon in the operational defense was the conduct of the artillery and aviation counterpreparation.

Armed Forces services' operational art made a significant step forward. It was enriched by many new tenets and conclusions regarding the organization of independent operations of varied designation. In the air forces' operational art, views were conclusively developed on the preparation and conduct of air operations, executed to gain air superiority, rout large enemy groupings, destroy and pressure his operational reserves, and demolish large military-industrial targets, administrative-political centers, centers of communication, naval bases, etc. Methods for employing *front* and long-range aviation to support tank armies during their commitment into battle and their operations in the operational depth, and to assist forces in the liquidation of encircled enemy groupings and repulsion of enemy counterstrokes received practical realization.

The National Air Defense forces' operational art was enriched by methods for conducting combat actions by large formations and formations of the National Air Defense, both independently and in cooperation with *front* and army Air Defense forces and the navy. During the third period of the war, a number of features were clearly manifested, characterizing the origin of the air defense operation: combat use of air defense forces and means according to a single plan, their employment of broad operational maneuver within the confines of air defense *fronts* and between them, establishment of operational and tactical cooperation between air defense *fronts* and combined-arms *fronts* in the frontal sector, etc.

In naval operational art, methods were further developed for cooperating with large ground forces formations when conducting joint offensive and defensive operations, as were principles for using naval forces and means in defensive operations for their own naval bases and maritime communications, disrupting enemy maritime communications, and delivering strikes from the sea against his naval bases and other targets.

A significant step forward was made in the theory and practice of combat and special support of operations (reconnaissance, operational *maskirovka*, anti-chemical defense, air defense of forces, etc.) of the operational rear, and of control of forces and means. Means and methods for resolving these problems matched the increased scale and dynamism of combat operations.

Great dynamism and imaginative variety characterized party-political work, which played a significant role in achieving operational success.

On the whole, Soviet operational art during the war, thanks to its creative nature, flexibility, and purposefulness, successfully resolved complex problems of preparing and conducting joint and independent operations. All its most important principles were further developed and replenished with new content. Its multi-facetedness, and the differentiation and integration of the operational art of the Armed Forces services began to be examined more precisely.

The development of Soviet operational art in the first postwar years continued under the direct influence of the experience of the Great Patriotic War, taking into account changes in force technical outfitting and organizational structure of the forces, and in the probable enemy's views on the nature and methods of conducting armed struggle.

The Communist Party and Soviet Government, under conditions of the "Cold War" and the existing arms race, took all measures to strengthen further the country's defense capabilities and increase Armed Forces combat readiness. Soviet economic development on the basis of new scientific and technological achievements made it possible to create necessary prerequisites for fundamentally re-equipping the forces. New, more effective types of weapons and combat equipment became part of all the Armed Forces services. Complete motorization and mechanization of the army was implemented, force organization was improved, their combat capabilities increased considerably, and operational and combat training of commanders, staffs, and troops was raised to a high level.

Basic principles for conducting offensive operations were more precisely formulated in the theory and practice of operational art. The most important of these were gaining air superiority, skillfully selecting the main attack axis, creating decisive superiority over the enemy in forces and means on selected axes and maintaining it during the entire operation, implementing continuous cooperation among formations and large formations, organizing continuous combat and materiel-technical support, and implementing firm and continuous troop control.

Norms for the scope of *front* and army operations were reexamined, taking into account increased combat capabilities of large operational formations.

Methods for organizing and conducting meeting engagements, operational pursuit, forcing of water obstacles from the march, and highly mobile night operations were given thorough scientific substantiation; the theory of the air-assault operation was developed. The increased significance of the factor of surprise raised the importance of the question of operations during the initial period of war in the theory of operational art.

The theory of preparing and conducting defensive operations under various conditions was thoroughly developed.

A significant step forward was made in the sphere of Air Force, National Air Defense Force, and naval operational art, especially concerning the theory and practice of preparing and conducting joint and independent operations.

With the second half of the 1950s, a qualitatively new shift occurred in the development of Soviet operational art on the basis of outfitting the Soviet Armed Forces with nuclear weapons, introduction of electronic means and atomic energy installations, complete force motorization and mechanization, and improvement of conventional weapons. All this produced fundamental changes in the organizational structure and technical outfitting of Armed Forces services, and required that new forms and methods be found for conducting combat operations on land, in the air, and at sea. This also required a reexamination of the basic principles of both the general theory of operational art and the operational art of Armed Forces services.

The content of operations as forms for employing large operational formations changed considerably. In addition to engagements and battles, it now began to include nuclear strikes, which play the main role in achieving assigned missions.

The most important principles of Soviet operational art are being developed further, and are acquiring qualitatively new content. Possible enemy surprise employment of nuclear weapons, which possess enormous destructive power and are fast-acting, is increasing as never before the significance of the principle of constantly maintaining forces at high combat readiness.

Sharp growth in the scope of offensive operations, high dynamism, and the constant struggle to seize the initiative required a principally new approach to the resolution of such issues as intensification of efforts during an operation, increase in the survivability of shock groupings, all-round troop support, replenishment of materiel expenditures, increase in the physical endurance and moral-psychological preparation of personnel, etc.

Constant detection and timely destruction of enemy nuclear attack means, and organization of defense against weapons of mass destruction, radio-electronic warfare, and other types of combat and special support of operations have acquired important significance. Requirements for control of troops, forces, and means have grown significantly.

Together with the all-round development of the general theory of Soviet operational art, the operational art of the Armed Forces services is improving. Here, qualitative changes in their technical outfitting and organizational structure are being considered.

In the system of comprehensive research of current problems in Soviet operational art, the development of methods for party-political work, the main task of which is to indoctrinate personnel with high ideological-political conviction and moral-psychological stability, occupies an important place.

Thus, Soviet operational art continues to develop, and is continuously being enriched with new tenets. The continuous increase in the level of technical outfitting of the forces, changes in their organizational structure, and sophistication of methods for conducting armed struggle are directly affecting this process.

NOTES

1. N. N. Fomin, "Sovetskoye operativnoye iskusstvo: zarozhdeniye i osnovnyye etapy razvitiya," *Voyennaya mysl'* [Military thought], 12 (1978), pp. 16–25.
2. See K. Marx and F. Engels, *Works*, Vol. 7, p. 510.
3. See *Voyennaya mysl'* [Military thought], 1 (1973), p. 47.
4. Directives of Red Army *Front* Commanders (1917–22). *Sbornik dokumentov v 4-kh tomakh* [Collection of documents in 4 volumes], Vol. 2 (Voyenizdat, 1972), p. 361.
5. *Iz istorii grazhdanskoy voyny i interventsii. Sbornik statey* [From the history of the Civil War and intervention. Collection of articles] (Moscow: Nauka, 1974).
6. For a more detailed treatment of the essence of deep operation and its development, see *Voyennaya mysl'* [Military thought], 8 (1978), pp. 14–26. [Translator's note: this is the article by L. I. Voloshin, "The Theory of Deep Operation and Its Developmental Trends," which has been translated for this volume].

The Deep Operation (Battle)

N. V. OGARKOV[1]

The deep operation (battle) is a form of combat action of operational large formations (formations, units). The theory of the deep operation was developed by Soviet military science in the 1930s. Its essence consists of simultaneous suppression of the enemy defense by striking its entire depth, and of penetration of its tactical zone along a selected axis with a subsequent rapid exploitation of tactical success into operational success by introducing into the engagement an echelon for developing success (tanks, motorized infantry, cavalry) and landing an air assault for the most rapid achievement of the established aim. The theory of the deep operation pointed the way out of the positional deadlock created in military art during the First World War. It was principally a new theory of conducting offensive operations by using massive, technically equipped armies. This was a qualitative leap in the development of military art. It clearly revealed the dependence of the forms and methods for conducting combat actions on combat means. Its development was conditioned by the USSR's socio-economic development, the progressive nature of Soviet military science, the technical outfitting and reorganization of the Soviet Army, and the accumulation of combat experience.

The origin and development of the theory of the deep operation is connected with the development of the theory of deep battle, whose foundations were stated at the end of the 1920s in the works of Soviet military theorists M. N. Tukhachevsky, V. K. Triandafillov, A. I. Yegorov, and others. Foreign regulations at this time still did not examine the possibilities of simultaneously affecting the entire depth of the enemy defense for the purpose of penetrating it.

The theory of deep battle was developed in the USSR on the basis of new materiel-technological outfitting of forces (long-range artillery, tanks and armored vehicles, combat aircraft), and also in connection with the appearance of new combat arms (tank, mechanized, air-assault), which made it possible to reject former combat methods, whose essence was the slow and gradual overcoming of each enemy defensive position, and to shift to more effective maneuver forms of combat actions. The most complex stage of deep battle was considered to be penetration of the defense. To effect it, deep force combat formations were required. The tenets of the theory of deep battle, developed in the beginning of the 1930s, were subjected to careful verification in numerous experimental, troop, and command-staff exercises in the Volga, Kiev, Belorussian, and other military districts. The result of this long and painstaking work was first put forth in *Instruktsiya po glubokomu boyu* [Instructions on Deep Battle]; subsequently it found fuller reflection in the combat and field regulations. The *Temporary Field Regulations Of The RKKA Of 1936 (PU-36)*, which expressed the basic principles of deep battle, envisioned the creation of shock and holding forces, reserves, and fire (artillery) groups in the combat formation of formations [*soyedineniye*] and units (Sketch 1). The shock group was designated to advance on the main attack axis. Its recommended composition was no fewer than two-thirds of all unit or formation forces and means. When significant superiority over the enemy in forces and means existed, there was an advantageous situation for encirclement of enemy forces. The creation of two shock groups operating on converging axes was permitted. The holding group was designated for actions on the secondary attack axis and had the mission of attracting the enemy's attention and supporting the advance of the shock group. The reserve (up to one-ninth of the forces and means) was designated to resolve missions which suddenly arose during battle. Penetration of the tactical zone of defense was considered complete when forces reached a depth of 10–12 kilometers. For deep penetration into the enemy defense and an increased rate of advance, a special place was assigned to tanks, divided into three groups: direct infantry support [NPP], long-range infantry support [DPP], and long-range action [DD]. This issue was developed in V. K. Triandafillov's works, and made concrete in K. B. Kalinovsky's works. For more effective combat utilization of artillery, improvement of its cooperation with infantry and tanks, and improvement of control, infantry support artillery groups [DD] were created in divisions according to the number of rifle regiments; in corps, long-range groups were created according to the number of first echelon divisions; and in individual cases artillery destruction groups [AR] were created. Organic and attached antiaircraft artillery of formations were joined under the command of the senior chief in executing overall missions.

In 1940–41 Soviet regulations established the understanding of deep battle as "combined arms battle," whose success was determined by surprise and decisiveness of force actions; skillful use of movement, all types of fire, and maneuver; and solid and continuous cooperation of all combat arms and special troops participating in a battle or executing missions to support it. By this time several theoretical tenets of deep battle and tactical norms had been reexamined and refined. Together with the creation of shock and holding forces, the structuring of division combat formations into two echelons and that of regiments into three echelons was envisioned. According to the draft *1941 Field Regulations (PU-41)*, the combat formations of combined-arms

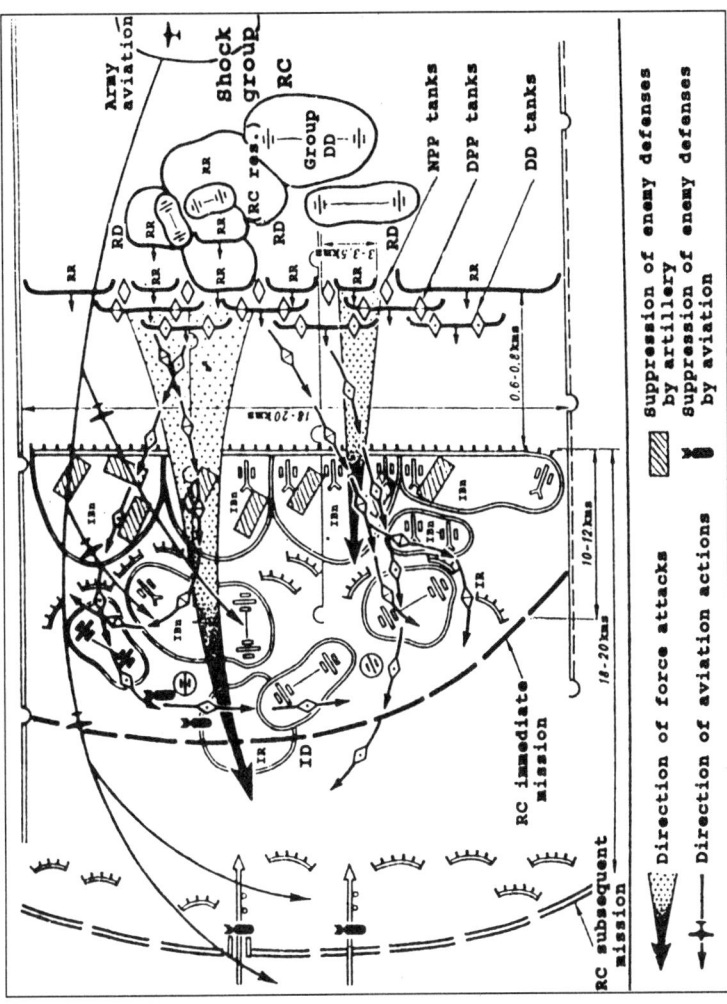

Sketch 1.
Offensive of a rifle corps and division according to the 1936 *Field Regulations*

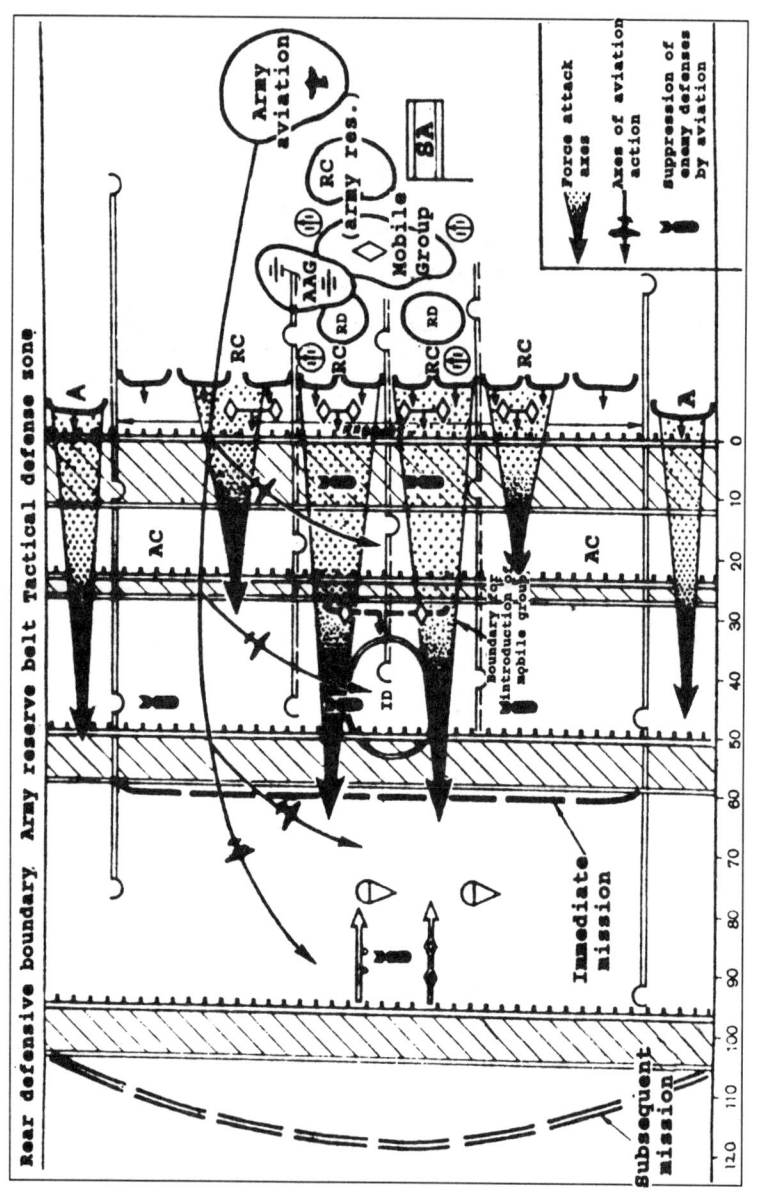

Sketch 2.

Offensive operation of a shock army according to prewar views (principal scheme)

formations and units in offensive battle consisted of combat echelons, artillery groups, tank support groups, and reserves (general, tank, and anti-tank). In addition to existing artillery groups (PP, DD, and AP), artillery anti-tank [APTG] and antiaircraft [ZAG] groups were recommended. Such a combat formation structure facilitated troop cooperation and control.

The theory of deep battle touched on a number of cardinal problems of Soviet operational art and permitted the development of the theory of the deep operation. In the 1930s, as the international situation intensified, the theory of the deep operation had already gained increasingly important significance and became more and more current. Such well-known Soviet military leaders as M. N. Tukhachevsky, A. I. Yegorov, I. P. Uborevich, I. E. Yakir, Ya. I. Alksnis, and others focused much attention on the further development of this theory and the thorough practical verification of its tenets in military games, exercises, and force maneuvers. In the mid-1930s the theory of the deep operation was basically worked out. In Soviet military works the deep operation was thought of as an operation conducted by a *shock army* operating on the main attack axis (Sketch 2). To inflict a power-ful first attack against the enemy and rapidly develop success, a deeply echeloned operational formation of forces, including an attack echelon [AE], echelon for developing the penetration [ERP], reserves, aviation, and air-assault forces, was envisioned. The attack echelon, whose composition envisioned rifle corps reinforced by tanks and artillery, was designated to penetrate the tactical defense. The echelon for developing the penetration (a mobile group made up of several mechanized and cavalry corps) served to develop tactical success into operational success. The introduction of the echelon for developing the penetration was considered most expedient after penetrating the tactical depth of the enemy defense. When the enemy's defense was inadequately developed and lacked large reserves, and when fortified sectors having permanent structures (permanent fire positions, earth-and-timber fire positions) had been penetrated, the echelon for developing the penetration could be used to complete the penetration of the tactical zone, together with the attacking echelon. However, this variant was considered less expedient. Operational methods were worked out for the echelon for developing the penetration in the operational depth using deci-sive maneuver of forces and means. All this increased the capability for successfully penetrating the enemy defense and developing the offensive at high tempos to great depth, and made it possible to transfer the tenets of the theory of the deep operation to *front* offensive operations. In this connection, opinions changed concerning the role of *front* and army large formations.

Not long after the Great Patriotic War started, the conclusion was reached that deep operations could be conducted not only by a single *front*, but also by several cooperating *front* large formations with the participation of large aviation forces and, on coastal axes, those of the navy. The *front* was now viewed as an operational-strategic large formation. Army large formations were designated mainly for actions within the *front* composition. The independent conduct of a deep operation by an army was acknowledged as possible only on separate operational axes or under special conditions (in mountains, deserts, etc.). To conduct a deep operation, it was considered expedient to have three–four shock armies and one–two conventional armies, one–two mechanized, tank, or cavalry corps, and from 15 to 30 aviation divisions in the *front* composition. It was suggested that with such composition a *front* could conduct an offensive in a sector of up to 300–400 kilometers and to a depth of up to 200–300 kilometers, inflicting the main attack in a sector of 60–100 kilometers where the following density was created: one division per 2–2.5 kilometers, 50–100 guns, and 50–100 tanks per kilometer of front (Sketch 3). The duration of the operation could, according to contemporary opinions, reach 15–20 days with an average daily rate of advance of 10–15 kilometers for infantry and 40–50 kilometers for mobile forces. The *front* was envisioned to create a strong operational first echelon (of combined-arms armies), a mobile group (of tank, mechanized, and cavalry formations), and an aviation group and reserves. An army advancing on the *front's* (shock army) main attack axis could consist of four–five rifle corps, one–two mechanized corps or cavalry corps, seven–nine artillery regiments, and seven–eight antiaircraft artillery battalions, and its actions supported by two–three aviation divisions. With such a composition the army was considered capable of penetrating the enemy defense in a 20–30-kilometer sector and advancing in a sector with a width of 50–80 kilometers to a depth of 70–100 kilometers. The army mobile group could be employed to complete the penetration of the enemy's tactical defense zone or be committed into battle after the penetration of the second defense zone to exploit success. The theory of the deep operation attached great significance to the organization of Air Defense, carried out by fighter aviation and antiaircraft forces.

The theory of the deep operation (battle), developed by Soviet military science, was rapidly accepted and disseminated in Soviet military academies, forces, and staffs. The correctness of its basic tenets was confirmed in maneuvers of troops of the Kiev (1935), Belorussian, Moscow, Odessa (1936) and other military district forces, as well as in combat operations at Lake Khasan (1938), at Khalkhin-Gol (1939), and during the Soviet–Finnish military conflict (1939–40). The necessity was demonstrated for mass utilization of forces and means on decisive axes, the expediency of creating echelons for the development of success, the importance of close cooperation of all combat arms, and the increasing role of artillery, tanks, and aviation.

The development of the theory of the deep operation (battle) on the eve of the Second World War was very useful and necessary for the Soviet Army. The viability of its basic tenets was clearly manifested in offensive operations and battles during the Great Patriotic War. During the war this theory

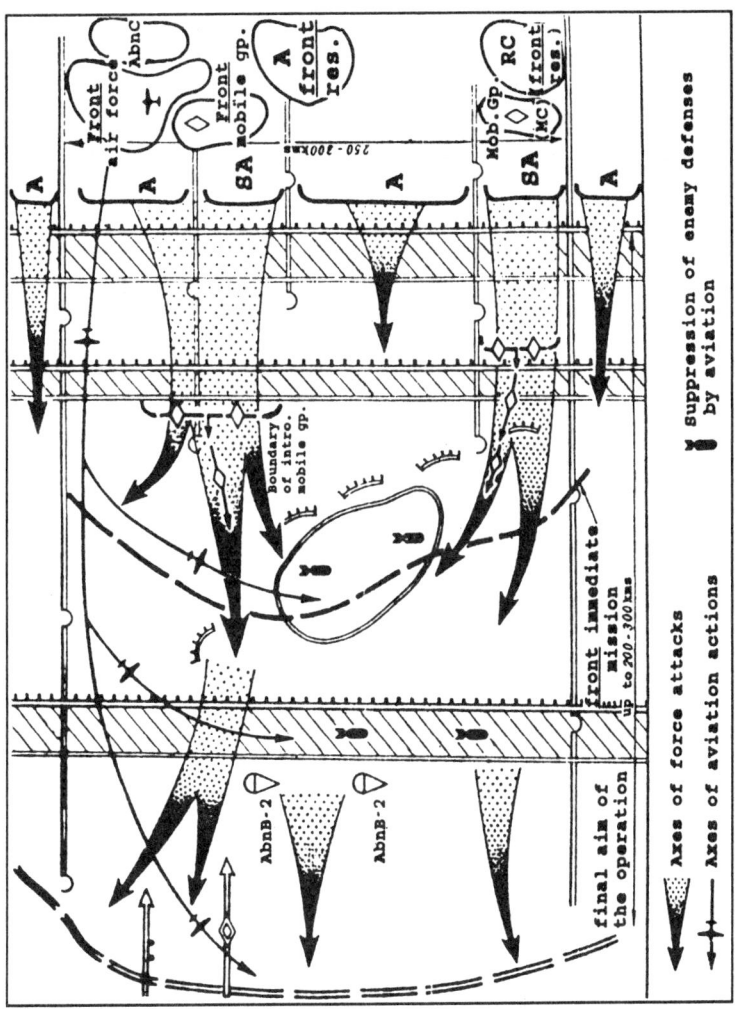

Sketch 3.

Offensive operation of a *front* according to prewar views (principal scheme)

was continuously improved in accordance with the outfitting of Soviet forces with increasingly more effective equipment and armaments and changes in their organizational structure and the nature of the enemy defense. Problems of penetrating a powerful, deeply echeloned enemy defense were resolved successfully. The penetration was executed by a *front* in one or several sectors, with its subsequent development into the depth or on the flanks, as well as along converging axes to encircle and destroy large enemy groupings. The tempo of the penetration sharply increased. In a number of operations (Iassy–Kishinev, Vistula–Oder, and others) this amounted to 20–30 kilometers and more per day. By the end of the war, the depth of an offensive operation had significantly increased and reached 100–180 kilometers in army operations, and 400–600 kilometers in *front* operations. Here, in narrow penetration sectors, comprising 7–12 per cent of the width of the *front* and army offensive sector, often up to 70–80 per cent of artillery and up to 100 per cent of the tanks and self-propelled artillery pieces were concentrated. Operational force formations and combat formations changed, depending on conditions. Thus, in 1942, when the enemy was still not employing a deeply echeloned defense, single-echelon combat formations were introduced at all levels – from rifle platoon to rifle division (Order No. 306 of the People's Commissariat for Defense). Such a structure of combat formations provided for inflicting a strong preliminary attack and was expedient in penetrating a shallow defense. When the enemy shifted to the formation of a deeply echeloned positional defense (1943), a decision was made to shift to a more deeply echeloned combat formation of rifle corps, divisions, and regiments. In the artillery the regimental [RAG], divisional [DAG], and corps [KAG] artillery groups – in the army, army artillery groups [AAG] – were finally approved. Artillery actions during the penetration of an enemy defense included conducting a powerful artillery preparation, support of the attack, and accompaniment during battle in the depth. The density of artillery increased, and beginning in 1943 in separate operations it reached 200–250, and sometimes even 320 guns and mortars per kilometer of front in penetration sectors. The density of tanks and self-propelled artillery pieces in 1944–45 offensive operations was 75–80 and more per kilometer. Combat methods for employing aviation also changed significantly. Consequently, the destruction of the enemy at a significant depth and continuous fire support for the advancing troops were achieved. Second echelons, strong mobile groups, and reserves from all combat arms were created in *fronts* and armies to exploit success. Mobile groups were designated to develop offensive operations to a great depth at a high tempo. In *fronts* they consisted of one–two tank armies and in armies, one–two tank or mechanized corps. Cavalry-mechanized and cavalry-tank groups consisting, as a rule, of a mechanized (tank) corps and a cavalry corps under single command were also used for these same purposes. When there were insufficient direct infantry support tanks [NPP], they were sometimes committed (especially army mobile groups) to complete the penetration of the enemy's tactical defense. In conducting operations, great success was achieved in the art of encircling large enemy groupings by the forces of one or several cooperating *fronts*. The art of liquidating encircled groupings by cutting them up into units already during the encirclement and subsequently annihilating them (Vitebsk–Orsha, Bobryusk, East Prussia offensive operations, and others) were developed further.

In the postwar period, the developmental principles of the theory of the deep operation (battle) continued to evolve on a higher technical basis. Fundamentally new types of military equipment and weapons with great destructive force were created. Together with nuclear weapons, the Armed Forces were outfitted with the most modern types of conventional means of destruction. Ground forces formations and large formations were completely mechanized and motorized, and their mobility, shock force, and fire power increased. A qualitative jump occurred in the development of all Armed Forces services. All this significantly increased the capability for simultaneously striking the entire depth of the enemy formation, penetrating his defense at high tempos, and swiftly exploiting success. In comparison with the Great Patriotic War period, methods for organizing and conducting an operation and battle changed substantially. The term "the deep operation (battle)" has not been used since the 1960s in official documents; however, the general principles of this theory have not lost their significance even today.

NOTE

1. N. V. Ogarkov, *Sovetskaya voyennaya entsiklopediya* [Soviet military encyclopedia], sv "Glubokaya operatsiya (boy)," Volume 2, 1976, pp. 574–8.

On the General Fundamentals of the Theory of Soviet Operational Art

MAJOR GENERAL V. F. MOZOLEV, CANDIDATE OF MILITARY SCIENCES[1]

Soviet operational art, as is generally known, encompasses the theory and practice of preparing and conducting joint and independent operations (combat actions) by large Armed Forces formations.

At present, the theory of operational art is a well-formed and scientifically substantiated system of knowledge concerning operational-scale combat actions on land, in the air, and at sea. It consists of general principles and theories of Strategic Rocket Force, Ground Force, National Air Defense Force, Air Force, and Naval operational art, and the theory of the operational rear. Dialectically interconnected, all components of the theory of operational art resolve a complex set of problems.

The basis and core of the entire system of the theory of operational art are its general fundamentals. Among these are general theoretical theses defining the essence, place, and role of operational art in military art, its subject and structure; the content of the most important categories; classification and characteristic features of modern operations and principles for their preparation and conduct; the role, place, and missions of Armed Forces formations and large formations and methods for their coordinated employment in joint operations, as well as the basis for control of different forces and means during their preparation and conduct.[2]

In this article, an attempt is made to describe the basic content of the general fundamentals of Soviet operational art theory.

The place and role of operational art in the overall system of military art is determined by the scope and nature of missions resolved by large Armed Forces services formations. Forms of operational-scale military actions are components of strategic operations, whose aims are achieved by the totality of efforts of Armed Forces large formations and formations participating in these operations. The degree to which each operational mission is resolved is, in turn, determined by the results of tactical-scale combat actions, that is, formation and unit battles which are part of the given large formation.

Therefore, operational art occupies an intermediate position between strategy and tactics, and plays a connecting role between them. It flows directly out of strategy, which specifies its missions and the direction of development. Operational art occupies a dominating position with respect to tactics and specifies its missions. However, a reverse relationship also exists.

When determining the aims, missions, and methods of conducting strategic operations, in addition to other factors it is necessary to take into account actual capabilities of large operational formations and basic principles in the theory of operational art. In exactly the same way, when preparing and conducting operations, formation and unit combat capabilities and their methods of combat employment are considered. And this is completely natural, since the course and outcome of tactical combat actions directly affect operational results, while the latter influence the achievement of both intermediate and ultimate strategic aims.

The subject of the theory of operational art is combat actions on an operational scale. It investigates the regularities, content, and nature of modern operations, methods for preparing and conducting them, and the role, place, and basis for the employment of formations and units of Armed Forces services and combat arms. Great significance is attached to the development of methods and means for organizing and maintaining continuous co-operation, all-round support of participating forces and means, and control. In addition, the theory of operational art specifies requirements for organizing and arming Armed Forces services and combat arms, and the content and methods for operational training of officer personnel and control organs, and generates recommendations for operationally outfitting a theater of military operations. The theory of operational art also analyzes and considers the probable enemy's views on the conduct of operational-scale combat actions.

It is completely understandable that no theory exists in isolation, but rather is given life by the practical experience with which it is inseparably linked. *The theory of operational art illuminates the practical path by resolving current problems of preparing and conducting operations under various conditions.* Marshal of the Soviet Union D. F. Ustinov, member of the CPSU Central Committee Politburo and USSR Minister of Defense, points out that

> Strengthening and improving the Army and Navy is a complex, all-encompassing, creative process, in which there is no place and cannot be a place for stagnation. That which was new yesterday has today become a stage of the past. In this is the essence of the dialectics of military affairs.[3]

On the basis of rapid scientific-technological progress, since the 1950s serious qualitative shifts have taken place in military affairs. The outfitting of the Armed Forces with nuclear weapons, qualitative development of conventional weapons, automation of troop and weapons control, and other factors prompted a fundamental reexamination of many tenets in all areas of military art, advanced a multitude of urgent problems for Soviet military theory, and necessitated fresh resolution of force organization problems, and improvement of combat employment methods and forms and methods of training and indoctrinating personnel. The most characteristic feature of the modern stage of development of the army and navy materiel base is the steady reduction in replacement time of one generation of weapons with another. This continuing trend of rapid combat means renovation is inevitably accompanied by serious changes in views on preparing and conducting operations.

Chief of the Armed Forces General Staff and USSR First Deputy Minister of Defense, Marshal of the Soviet Union N. V. Ogarkov noted:

> Under modern conditions, the rapid development of the economy, science, and technology are making it possible to create comparatively rapidly the latest models of weapons and combat equipment, which, entering into the forces, is objectively resulting in the necessity to change and develop existing forms and methods of armed struggle. . .[4]

Here, it is necessary to emphasize that, as a result of the ever increasing qualitative gap between combat means in the Second World War and contemporary means, scientific foresight and forecasting of developmental trends for military affairs, in particular the theory of operational art, are now acquiring primary significance.

The structure of the theory of operational art and its content are continuously evolving on the basis of developing combat means, organizational force structures and methods for their combat employment. Outfitting the Armed Forces with rocket-nuclear weapons and other modern types of weapons and combat equipment has led to the creation of new types of forces and combat arms, and to serious changes in existing organizational structures: Strategic Rocket Forces were created, and new formations and units appeared in the Armed Forces services, which have sharply increased the combat capabilities of combat arms. All this has fundamentally changed the structure of the theory of operational art. Thus, for example, the theory of Strategic Rocket Force operational art was created and developed; new areas and divisions appeared in theories of other Armed Forces services' operational art, associated with employment of rocket-nuclear weapons, antiaircraft rocket and radio-technical forces, new types of aviation, strategic rocket submarines, navy submarines, and other operational forces and means.

The operational rear's outfitting and organizational structure have been continuously improving. Its complete motorization and the development of railroad, automobile, road, and pipeline forces and air and other types of transport have prompted the further improvement of existing subdivisions and creation of new subdivisions in the theory of the operational rear, as well as the appearance of new types of rear support.

In addition to the increasing multi-facetedness of operational art as a whole and for each individual Armed Forces service, the trend in their increasingly greater interconnection is continuously strengthening. This is conditioned by the fact that under modern conditions successful resolution of the most important operational tasks is, as a rule, associated with skillful use of various forces in an operation, that is, large formations and formations of different Armed Forces services. Joint operations have become the principal form not only of strategic, but also operational-scale combat actions.

Essentially all Armed Forces services can participate in *front* and army operations. In addition to the navy, air forces, *front* forces and means operating on a coastal axis, and others will participate in naval operations.

Thus, *joint resolution of operational missions by heterogeneous forces in all spheres of an armed struggle is the most characteristic feature of operational-scale combat actions.* Consequently, research in and development of problems of preparing and conducting joint operations is the most voluminous and important task of the theory of operational art and, above all, its general principles. In this connection, the importance of thorough development of problems of cooperation of forces and means participating in such operations is growing immeasurably. Finally, the increased significance of the theory and practice of preparing joint operations poses in a new way the problem of further improvements in operational training of military cadres and control organs. *Above all, we are speaking about considerably broadening the professional knowledge of military cadres and of their ability to resolve in a highly qualified way the problems of effectively using not only subordinate, but also cooperating forces in modern operations.* All these problems, which have emerged on the basis of the specific significance of joint operations in the matter of achieving success in combat actions, have made the theory of operational art's general fundamentals, whose conclusions and recommendations must guide all other elements of this theory, its most important component. The theory of operational art's general fundamentals occupy a leading position with respect to the theory's other components, because they arm military cadres with knowledge of the laws of armed struggle and principles of operational art arising from them; this makes it possible to resolve complex problems of modern military affairs from scientific positions.

As is generally known, the *principles of military art* are the fundamental ideas and most important tenets and recommendations for the preparation and successful conduct of combat actions on any scale. However, despite a definite universality, their concrete employment within the framework of strategy, operational art, and tactics has many specific peculiarities. Therefore, the detailed development of these principles as they apply to the preparation and conduct of operations by Armed Forces services and their successful use are one of the important tasks of the theory and practice of operational art.

The theory of Soviet military art, relying on the Marxist dialectic method, considers that principles of military art continuously develop, influenced by changes in the materiel base of armed struggle. Some principles acquire primary significance, while others change their content, and still others emerge once again.

Thus, on the basis of all generalized historical war experience and the development of the theory of military art in the initial postwar period, the following principles were consolidated in the leading documents of the Soviet Armed Forces:

- massing forces and means and creating superiority over the enemy at the decisive place and time;
- exhibiting a high degree of dynamism and initiative, and seizing and holding it during the operation;
- boldly maneuvering forces;
- maintaining their combat capability;
- promptly regenerating second echelons and reserves;
- thoroughly supporting operations; and
- implementing firm and continuous control.

Further development of the theory of military art, and deeper penetration into the active mechanism of the laws of armed struggle under conditions of employing both nuclear and conventional weapons led to a reexamination and refinement of the content of earlier formulated principles. On the basis of generalizing past war experience and operational force training over the last decade, as well as results of completed research, Soviet military art worked out a scientifically substantiated system of contemporary principles of operational art.

This system includes the following:

- a constant high level of force combat readiness to conduct combat actions both with and without the employment of nuclear weapons;
- dynamism and decisiveness of actions, and a constant attempt to seize and hold the initiative;
- close cooperation of all troops, forces, and means participating in the operation;
- decisive concentration of efforts on the most important axes (regions) at the decisive moment for executing principal missions;
- simultaneous attack of the enemy to the entire depth of his operational formation;
- continuity in conducting combat actions;

- bold maneuver of troops, forces, and means;
- timely creation, use, and regeneration of reserves;
- surprise actions;
- consideration and full use of troop moral-political capabilities in the interests of accomplishing operational missions;
- all-round support of operations (combat actions);
- maintenance and rapid regeneration of force combat capabilities; and
- firm and continuous troop (force) control.

All these principles of operational art, when embodied in the practice of preparing and conducting operations (combat actions), decisively influence their course and outcome. They are inseparably and dialectically unified and closely interconnected.

Thorough understanding and skillful and imaginative implementation of the principles of operational art, taking into account the concrete situation and excluding any stereotypical patterning in actions, are very important conditions for successful achievement of the aims of operations (combat actions). An operation is not only a combat and moral-psychological contest between two sides. It is also a struggle of intellects, talents, creativity in military art, and the will and experience of commanders and their staffs who are controlling the combat actions of opposing operational force groupings. He who can seize the initiative in preparing an operation and firmly hold it in subsequent combat actions will be victorious. The correct employment of these principles is directly dependent on the creative and organizational capabilities of commanders and staffs, and their knowledge and understanding of the content and nature of the most important categories of operational art and their place and role in armed struggle.

Among the most important categories of operational art are, above all, forms of combat actions inherent to operational-strategic, operational, and operational-tactical large formations when they are executing their missions. These are the operation, engagement, systematic combat actions, and the strike.

Of all forms of large formation combat actions, the most complex and voluminous is *the operation*. The tendency for its spatial indicators to increase, both along the front and in the depth, has been most clearly exhibited in its historical development. Foreign military specialists note that in the last decade there has also been an increasing tendency toward completely equipping armed forces services with various types of aviation and a large quantity of air defense means. Therefore, combat actions in modern operations will be conducted by ground-air and air-naval force groupings of both sides, more clearly expressed than in the Second World War. As a result, the spatial framework of operations by large formations of armed forces services will be characterized, with respect to their scope, not only along the front and in the depth, but also in the vertical dimension. *Hence, modern operations will consist of a system of nuclear and fire strikes, engagements, and combat actions on land, in the air, and at sea, conducted simultaneously and successively on a broad front and into the entire depth of the operational formation of the enemy's opposing groupings.* Extensive maneuver of forces and means in all spatial spheres will be executed during operations.

Each operation has its own aim, that is, the ultimate expected result of force actions, which fundamentally changes the operational situation on a given axis (in a given region) and resolves one of the intermediate strategic or operational missions in a given theater of military operations. Its concrete content depends on the designation and sphere of actions of large formations, and the composition of forces and means on both sides. Operations are also distinguished from one another with respect to employed means of destruction, and the time, scale, and methods of conducting combat actions. Correct consideration of these factors makes it possible to substantiate completely the classification of operations according to specific types.

With respect to times of conduct, joint and independent operations can be initial and subsequent. Initial operations are those conducted at the beginning of war and combat actions during the initiation of the next strategic operation. With respect to scale of operation, they are divided into operational-strategic, operational, and operational-tactical.

Depending on force composition and means being used, to whom they belong, and the spheres of their actions, operations are divided into *front* (army), air defense, air, and naval. With respect to type of combat actions, some are divided into offensive and defensive.

In accordance with employed means of destruction, operations can be conducted with the use of nuclear weapons or with only conventional means of destruction.

The cited classification of modern operations is not exhaustive. The appearance of new types of weapons and the further development of organizational force structures and means by which they resolve operational missions may lead to the emergence of still other types of operations.

In the system of operations being examined, *joint operations* occupy a leading place. Operational aims in joint operations are achieved by co-ordinated efforts of several Armed Forces services' large formations and formations, each of which resolves particular operational missions within its framework, employing forms and methods of combat actions inherent only to it. Therefore, each Armed Forces service's theory of operational art cannot encompass the entire range of preparing and conducting a joint operation. The theory of the general fundamentals of operational art resolves this task.

As the experience of the Second World War, above all the Great Patriotic

War, and local wars show, among joint operations are, as a rule, operations not only by *fronts*, but also fleets; there are also air, air defense, air-assault, amphibious-assault, and anti-assault operations. Ground force, air force, air defense force, and naval large formations and formations usually participate, as do the operational rear's formations, units, and installations.

This is most clearly apparent using the example of a *front* operation conducted on a coastal axis. Thus, during 3d Belorussian Front's conduct of the Koenigsberg offensive operation (6–9 April 1945), six combined-arms armies operated in its composition. Two *front* air armies, one aviation corps each from Leningrad and 2d Belorussian Fronts' air armies, aviation from the Red Banner Baltic Fleet, and a long-range aviation air army – in all, 2,500 aircraft – were enlisted for air support. Red Banner Baltic Fleet forces supported *front* forces from the sea. *Front* and naval force groupings were reliably covered during the operation against enemy air strikes by sufficiently powerful air defense forces and means.

Within the framework of this *front* offensive operation, ground force, air force, air defense force, and naval large formations and formations resolved their particular missions according to the overall concept and plan in the interests of achieving the operational-strategic aim. Thus, combined-arms armies, which played the main role in the *front* operation, conducted army operations, during which the enemy's main force groupings were routed. Long-range and frontal aviation large formations and formations conducted air operations to demolish military targets in the fortress and town of Koenigsberg, and also supported the offensive of the large ground force formations. Red Banner Baltic Fleet forces protected the *front* forces' maritime flank against enemy fire strikes from the sea and enemy assault landings, supported the force offensive by ship and shore artillery fire, landed amphibious assaults in the rear of the German-Fascist forces, and thwarted their evacuation by sea.[5]

In generalizing past war experience and operational training of our forces and foreign armies in the postwar period, the complete essence of the modern joint operation can be formulated specifically. *It is the totality of operations, engagements, battles, and strikes, coordinated with respect to aim, time, and place, and conducted on a specific strategic or several operational axes (regions, zones) of a given theater of military operations by large formations and formations of different Armed Forces services, with one of them playing a decisive role.* A joint operation is conducted according to a single concept and plan to rout opposing enemy groupings and achieve operational-strategic or operational results.

With respect to its content, the modern joint operation is a very complex form of combat action. Thus, for example, an offensive operation of *front* forces may include the following:

- initial and subsequent offensive (and sometimes defensive) operations of first-echelon large formations;
- commitment to battle of operations and their conduct by second-echelon large formations;
- air combat actions, air operations, and air engagements;
- air-assault operations; and
- amphibious-assault operations, combat actions of rocket forces, artillery, air defense forces, special forces and reserves. In a nuclear war, the most important component of a joint operation will be initial and subsequent mass nuclear strikes.

The role of large formations and formations of the Armed Forces services taking part in different types of joint operations is varied. Thus, in *front* operations the ground forces play the decisive role, while in air, air defense, and naval operations this role belongs to the air forces, air defense forces and naval large formations or formations respectively. Questions concerning organizing cooperation and control of troops, forces, and means in a particular joint operation are resolved accordingly.

For example, in a *front* (army) operation, cooperation is organized in the interests of ground force large formations or formations executing the main operational missions. The principal organizer is the commander of *front* (army) forces participating in the operation. In a joint naval operation, cooperation of all forces and means, including participating ground forces, is organized in the interests of naval forces resolving the main operational missions. The organization of air-assault, naval, and anti-assault operations have certain peculiarities. If they are conducted within the framework of a *front* operation, their principal organizer is the commander of *front* forces, while if they are a component of a naval operation, then these functions are carried out by the fleet commander.

When organizing cooperation of troops, forces, and means in the interests of achieving operational aims, the following are coordinated:

- missions of units and formations of the different Armed Forces services, combat arms, and special forces, and the methods and sequence of their execution;
- procedure for employing means of destruction;
- methods and means of mutual identification among forces, and transfer of information on the situation on land, at sea, and in the air;
- actions of all air defense forces and means; and
- joint measures for all types of support and organization of control.

Here, it is very important to have uniform systems of reconnaissance, identification, notification, and control. The successful conduct of joint operations will still depend, to a great degree, on the continuous maintenance of precise cooperation among all forces and means. Undervaluing the increased role of cooperation in joint operations can result in the most serious consequences. Thus, during the 1973 Arab–Israeli War, the absence of constant cooperation between Egyptian Army air forces and air defense forces led to heavy aircraft losses due to actions of their own air defense forces and means.

When conducting a joint operation, it is very important to specify promptly the procedure for joint combat employment of different forces, taking into account the existing situation, and to use maximally their combat capabilities, compensating for weak areas of one service or combat arm with strong aspects of others.

The aim of joint operations is achieved by conducting coordinated and interconnected engagements, battles, and strikes.

An engagement [*srazheniye*] is a component of an operation, during which one of the important intermediate operational missions is resolved. Thus, according to the experience of the Great Patriotic War, engagements were conducted in a *front* operation to rout the main forces of the enemy's first echelon, his counterstriking grouping, or his operational reserves. In addition, *front* air armies conducted air engagements to destroy enemy tactical aviation main forces and to gain air superiority, as happened in the Kuban' and at the Kursk salient in 1943.

Under modern conditions, as before, each such engagement will ensue during a specific time period and in a limited expanse, within whose confines the opposing groupings are operating. Here, the rout of the enemy in an engagement will be executed by simultaneously or successively delivering nuclear and fire strikes, and conducting battles using forces and means of formations and units of a given large formation, whose actions are coordinated by an overall operational concept for executing a specific operational mission.

Engagements can be combined arms, air defense, air, and naval, depending on the nature of the medium in which combat actions are taking place and the composition of the force groupings conducting them.

Together with engagements conducted on main axes (in regions, zones), operational aims will be achieved as well by conducting *systematic combat actions*. In operational art, this category is viewed as a form of using Armed Forces services' large formations to resolve limited-scale missions. Their results will definitely effect a change in the operational situation along a given axis (in a region). For example, air defense forces and means can conduct systematic combat actions to repel strikes of separate enemy groups and individual enemy airplanes on various operational axes. Systematic *front* aviation combat actions are the totality of nuclear and fire strikes and battles conducted simultaneously and successively to destroy and suppress the ground and air enemy in different regions while supporting and covering ground forces and supporting the combat actions of formations of other types of aviation.

Another category of operational art is the *strike*. This is a special form of combat action, consisting of hitting enemy force groupings and ground, air, and maritime targets by a powerful, short-term action against them using nuclear or conventional weapons for destruction or suppression.

Under modern conditions, as a result of the increase in range and power of nuclear and other types of weapons, a trend has been seen in battles and engagements to increase the strike range of both sides. Because of this, nuclear and fire strikes are acquiring ever increasing independence, making it possible to deliver a decisive strike against an enemy grouping, destroy his targets, and resolve operational missions at great distances.

The role of strikes in operations of Armed Forces services is varied. Thus, for example, massed and concentrated nuclear and fire strikes delivered by artillery and aviation are an important component of the operation, and one of the methods for achieving its aims. At the same time, for rocket forces, for example, the rocket-nuclear (fire) strike is the sole method for executing combat missions and sole form of their combat actions. Consequently, the strike is acquiring increasingly greater independence and is making it possible to resolve assigned missions by single actions of groupings of forces and means.

Such categories as *operational maneuver* are acquiring increasingly greater significance for successfully conducting modern operations. It is executed by moving large formations and formations to a new axis (line, region) or retargeting strikes by aviation, operational-tactical rockets, and artillery against more important enemy objectives, as well as redistributing materiel-technical means in the interests of successfully executing assigned missions.

As troop mobility and the range of means of destruction increase, maneuver begins to acquire new qualities, the most important of which is a considerable reduction in the overall time of its conduct. This is achieved basically by increasing troop movement speed and reducing movement distance, and by increasing the share of maneuver by nuclear and fire strikes. This makes it possible not only to reduce the time for executing it, but also to deliver strikes against the enemy without significant regrouping of forces and means, or even without resorting to this at all.

The complex nature of modern operations, especially joint operations, presents a very high level of requirements for troop control of large formations during their preparation and conduct. Therefore, it is completely natural that a component part of the theory of operational art's general fundamentals is research and development on basic issues of troop control in joint operations. Among these are tenets reflecting the essence, content, principles, structure, and methods of troop control, as well as features of its organization when preparing and conducting joint operations.

The organization of troop control is understood as a set of measures conducted by a commander and staff directed toward creating a stable system of control and achieving its constant functioning when preparing and conducting an operation. The troop control system of a large formation is a set of functionally associated control organs and command posts, a communications system, and a system and means for automated troop control.

As war experience has demonstrated, in a joint operation, constant troop control is ensured only when the systems of command posts and communications of participating Armed Forces services formations are reliably interconnected, deployed, and moved, and operate in coordination. Responsible representatives (operational groups) from staffs of attached, supporting, and cooperating Armed Forces services formations (with necessary means and documentation for communications with their command) are sent to the command post which is playing the main role in the given joint operation.

The experience of the Great Patriotic War demonstrated that only when leadership over all troops, forces, and means participating in a joint operation is completely centralized, and when commanders of cooperating and subordinate large formations exhibit reasonable initiative is the fullest achievement of operational aims ensured.

The tenet of the necessity of a strictly scientific, optimal distribution of functional responsibilities among operational control organs at different levels is also acquiring primary significance. In his speech to the XXV Party Congress, General Secretary of the CPSU Central Committee, Chairman of the USSR Supreme Soviet Presidium, Comrade L. I. Brezhnev, said that

> The essence of organizational issues, to put it simply, is that everyone who has the necessary authorization for this and who bears within his bounds complete responsibility must deal with his own affairs. This vital, elementary rule is, at the same time, the basis for the foundations of the science and practice of control.

Under conditions of a constant struggle to reduce time in the control cycle and develop a trend toward increasing the number of objects of control in each large formation and formation, it is necessary that each control organ resolve missions only within the framework of its duties and competency.

The theory of operational art, and military art as a whole, is constantly developing. This process of improving the theory of preparing and conducting joint operations is not implemented spontaneously. It is the fruit of enormous creative efforts by military cadres. And the more fully the combat capabilities of new weapons and combat equipment are studied and effective methods for resolving operational missions are developed on this basis, the more qualitatively and effectively practical tasks for the strengthening of combat readiness of troops and naval forces will be resolved by commanders, staffs, and political organs.

NOTES

1. V. F. Mozolev, "Ob obshchikh osnovakh teorii sovetskogo operativnogo iskusstva," *Voyennaya mysl'* [Military thought], 3 (1979), pp. 13–22.
2. *Sovetskaya voyennaya entsiklopediya* [Soviet military encyclopedia], Vol. 6 (Voyenizdat, 1978), p. 53.
3. *60 let Vooruzhennykh Sil SSSR. Dokumenty i materialy* [60 years of the Armed Forces of the USSR. Documents and materials] (Moscow: Politizdat, 1978), p. 34.
4. *Pravda*, 19 February 1978.
5. *Operatsii Sovetskikh Vooruzhennykh Sil v Velikoy Otechestvennoy voyny 1941–1945* [Soviet Armed Forces operations in the Great Patriotic War, 1941–1945], Vol. 4 (Voyenizdat, 1959), pp. 81–2, 87.

On the Issue of the Origin and Development of the Operation

COLONEL R. SAVUSHKIN, DOCENT, CANDIDATE OF
HISTORICAL SCIENCES[1]

One of the unresolved questions of the history of military art is when did the operation emerge as a form of armed combat? Until now it has been dated from various historical epochs. This is so because the operation as a form of military action, before reaching its modern level, experienced a long and complex developmental path, so that to determine the moment of its origin more or less precisely is a rather difficult matter.

In this article an attempt is made to examine the question of the evolution of both the concept of the operation itself and its content.

The word "operation" is of Latin origin. It means action (*operatio*). In military science and in military history the combination "military operation" was most often used. This term began to be used in seventeenth century works to indicate a system of military actions. Thus, the Austrian General Montecucculi in the fourth chapter of his book *Notes of Raimond Count Montecucculi, or Primary Rules of Military Science*, published in 1664, wrote about "military operations" and conditions necessary for their successful conduct. Among the basic "military operations" which require good organization and support, the author included the march and force deployment for rest,[2] that is, two systems of purposeful actions.

In 1784 in London a book appeared by the bourgeois military theorist Henry Lloyd, *Military and Political Memoirs of General Lloyd*, which expressed the exceptionally correct idea (as it turned out) about the logical integrity of force actions within the framework of an operation and the homogeneity of the term "operation." In analyzing the practical experience of military actions in the Seven Years War, Lloyd focused attention on the achievement of the ultimate war aim, as a rule, arising from force actions directed toward resolution of a series of intermediate missions (aims). Here, the achievement of the indicated aims was the totality of repeated military actions – relatively uniform in nature and sequence of military actions (concentration of forces, march-maneuver, battle, or threat to communications) – whose beginning and end are limited by two points on the terrain: the "base" (magazine)[3] and some indicated point on one's own or foreign territory. Lloyd called all this the operation.

Completing the foundation of the operation's logical integrity, Lloyd mentally joined the base and end point of the operation by a single line, along which the army was to proceed, and called this the "operational line."

From this moment the operation began to be considered not as any totality of military actions, but only that which was encompassed by a geometric model: "base" – "operational line" – "end point" (see Sketch 1). Thanks to this discovery, as Lloyd considered it, the time arrived when "one can calculate all operations with geometric precision."[4]

Sketch 1

Lloyd's geometrism was adopted and thoroughly developed by the military theorist G. Bulow in his book *The Spirit of the Newest Military System* (1799). Bulow unreservedly ordered that "each military operation be based on three points: the *subject* or foundation of the operation, the *operational line*, and the *object*."[5]

In developing Lloyd's theory, Bulow demonstrated that the operation having at its disposal only one magazine is poorly supported. Therefore, in his opinion, it must operate on a system of magazines forming a line – a base. In such a case, its geometric form will have a slightly different look (Sketch 2).

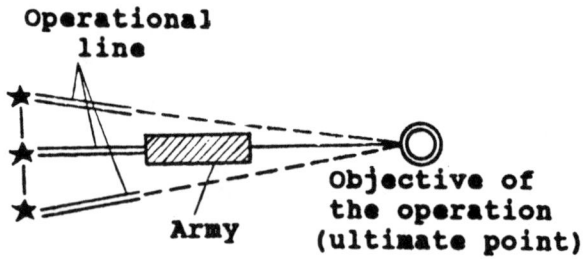

Sketch 2

In addition to these problems, Bulow developed an entire series of new ones related to the initial problems. He attached especially important significance to the question of operational aims. In his opinion these could be defeat of the enemy, siege of a fortress, and threat of engagement (demonstration), but most often – in the epoch of cordon-maneuver strategy – disruption of the enemy's supply system.

Achievement of the operational aim was always associated with movement (march) and occupation of a specific geographic point, that is, the objective of the operation. However, this was not always accompanied by battle.

Bulow was the first to attempt to divide all military art into strategy and tactics. He proposed the term "strategy" itself, which meant (according to Bulow) the field of military art which has the objective of preparing for and conducting war. He wrote, "Strategy is the science of movement in which the enemy is the aim but not the objective."[6] Bulow explained the content of strategy and tactics by means of a graphic example: "where there is an exchange of blows, this is tactics; where there is no battle, this is strategy."[7]

Bulow's ideas elicited a broad response among military theorists of all European countries. For example, Archduke Karl of Austria wrote:

> *Each operation relies on a base, has as its aim the achievement of the operational objective, and is conducted along operational lines which join the base and the objective.* The operation encompasses either the flow of the entire war or that of the entirety of a single campaign; or it attempts only to occupy some strategic point and achieve advantages connected with it.[8]

The outstanding authority in the field of military theory, A. Jomini, General of the French and then the Russian Armies, took much from Bulow. He was a theorist of the French Revolutionary and Napoleonic Wars, that is, of the time when mass bourgeois armies were created, the mixed requisition-magazine supply system was introduced, and "shock strategy" was formed to counterbalance the cordon-maneuver strategy of the period of the Seven Years War. Therefore, according to Jomini's theoretical scheme, the operational objective was considered to be not a "geographic point," but rather the enemy army; the basic principle of his theory became the concentration of forces for a decisive engagement to annihilate the enemy. For Jomini, "military art consists of introducing as great a force as possible into battle at the decisive point in the theater of operations. . ."[9] And if rivers of sweat from soldiers exhausted by long, often purposeless marches are seen through the geometrism of Bulow's system, then a sea of blood of general engagements is perceptible through the practicality and bourgeois efficiency of Jomini's system.

Like his predecessors, Jomini related questions concerning preparing for and conducting war to the field of strategy, whose content he enriched with the new concepts of "operational zone," "operational front," and others.[10]

Thanks to the rather broad dissemination of work of the above-mentioned authors at the end of the eighteenth and beginning of the nineteenth century, the new terminology permeated armies and was persistently connected with the practice of armed combat. Thus, in military documents of A. V. Suvorov, M. I. Kutuzov, and other Russian military leaders, we find the terms "operation" and "operational line" everywhere.[11]

In the second half of the nineteenth century, an attempt was made in Russian military literature to provide a scientific definition of the operation and demonstrate its place in the theory of military art. The most precise formulation was given in *Entsiklopediya voyennykh i morskikh nauk* [The encyclopedia of military and naval sciences]:

> Each war consists of one or several campaigns, each campaign of one or several operations, which represent a certain complete period, from the *strategic deployment* of the army at the initial line of the operation until the ultimate resolution of the latter by a *triumphant* battle on the battlefield, if the battle was prefaced by encirclement of the shattered army; in the opposite case – by energetic exploitation of the victory won by means of pursuit on the battlefield and in the theater of military operations [emphasis in the original].[12]

In the same publication it was directly indicated that preparing for and conducting an operation is the prerogative of military strategy. In another place it emphasized that "each operation embraces all of strategy."[13]

G. A. Leer was an undisputed authority in the field of the theory of the operation in Russia and abroad for more than 40 years. His works on strategy, published since the middle of the 1860s, brought him particularly great renown and praise.[14]

We are indebted to him to a significant degree for the fact that large strategic operations in theoretical and historical works came to be known by the name of the populated area, river, or geographic object along which they were being conducted. Thus, in the work *Korennyye voprosy* [Fundamental Issues] he mentioned Napoleon's St. Gondskaya operations (1814), and then analyzed in detail the "Ulm operation" (1805) and many others.[15]

In Leer's wake in the field of the development of military theory appeared N. P. Mikhnevich, who, in working out strategic questions, proceeded from definitions of war and the operation worked out by the Leer school.[16] He went significantly farther than Leer in investigating problems of preparing for and conducting operations during the initial period, and in studying the stages and separate elements of a strategic operation.

A. A. Neznamov worked simultaneously with N. P. Mikhnevich on strategic problems, based, as were Mikhnevich's works, on those of his predecessors. He wrote:

As the entire war breaks down into a complete series of operations, so each operation breaks down into a complete series of particular *immediate missions* in which the preceding one conditions the following one and they all join together into a single operational aim in absolutely the same way as all operations are connected to one another by the *primary, leading idea of the war plan "in aim and direction"* [emphasis in the original].[17]

Neznamov considered the crown of the entire operation to be the general engagement [*srazheniye*]. "The general engagement," he emphasized, "is what any operation is inclined towards, it is its logical end."[18]

Principally new in Neznamov's strategic views was posing the problem of conducting strategic operations not by separate armies, but by groups of armies, that is, by recently formed operational large formations (*operativnoye ob"yedineniye*). According to Neznamov's concept, within the framework of an operation were groups of armies, each carrying out its own army operation. This already was a qualitatively new stage in the development of the theory of the operation. However, the armed forces still did not have sufficient combat experience to investigate this problem thoroughly.

The fundamental tenets of military thought of the seventeenth through nineteenth centuries which have been examined concerning the operation make it possible to conclude that the military theorists of this period made a significant contribution to the development of the theory of the strategic operation. Above all, they successfully revealed the essence of this phenomenon and correctly evaluated its role in military art. However, in the opinions and concepts of all the authors of that time there were serious shortcomings and thoroughly erroneous statements. Thus, Lloyd's works suffered from extreme mechanism. Bulow was extremely carried away by geometrism and overlooked the onset of a new epoch in military affairs. Jomini (on the basis of the experience of the Napoleonic Wars) declared it absolute that the operation behaved according to internal operational axes (lines). For a long time several Russian military theorists remained followers of erroneous Leerian positions on the "timelessness and immutability" of the principles of military art, etc. The main reason for this was the idealistic metaphysical method of cognition by which bourgeois science was guided.

In examining questions concerning the *time of origin* of the operation, one cannot fail to take into consideration several tenets of Marxist classics, in particular Engels' statements on military campaigns in the period of slave-owning and feudal societies. Engels thought that the *military campaigns* of ancient and medieval armies did not differ from *the operation*. Thus, in characterizing the features of military art in the period from the sixth through twelfth centuries, he noted that feudal particularism made it "impossible to have any kind of large operations." Therefore, they were extremely rare. "Over this entire period," Engels pointed out, "the only significant *operations were the campaigns* of the German emperors into Italy, and the crusades."[19]

In describing the military-historical events of slave-owning and feudal society, Engels attempted as much as possible to single out three principal elements in each operation (campaign): the operational base, operational line, and operational objective. This is especially characteristic of the work *On the History of the Ancient Germans*, where he writes about the town of Mainz, an operational base in southern Germany, on the most convenient operational line for Roman main forces, and an operational objective.[20]

Further development of the theory of preparing for and conducting operations occurred under the influence of material factors engendered by the imperialist era. The appearance at the beginning of the twentieth century of million-man armies and the commencement of arming troops with rapid-fire small arms and artillery, which forced the rejection of a dense infantry formation, led to an expansion of the strategic deployment front and, especially important to emphasize, an expansion of armed combat forms.

Thus, if during the engagement at Gravelotte in the Franco-Prussian War a total of 430,000 Germans and French conducted military operations on a 12 kilometer front, already by 1904, during the Russo-Japanese War, 380,000 Russians and Japanese fought on a front of up to 100 kilometers along the Shakhe River. The First World War provided even more striking examples. In the Marne engagement (1914), 600,000 Germans and French had a front of around 300 kilometers, and in that same year the front line of the Galician engagement, in which 500,000 Russians and Austrians took part, extended over 400 kilometers.

Railroads and the electric telegraph played a large role in the development of all processes of conducting operations. With their appearance it became possible to deploy forces strategically at higher tempos, provide supplies, and create a dynamic control system for army large formations and corps scattered over the enormous expanses of the theater of military operations.

All this led to significant qualitative changes in armed combat forms. For the most part, its content also changed. The outcome of military confrontation began to be decided not by a single general engagement but by the totality of engagements, battles, and maneuvers conducted on enormous territories according to a unified plan. Not only large ground force formations but also other combat arms now participated. New phenomena required thorough theoretical comprehension and practical mastery.

This task was successfully resolved by Soviet military science. In particular, A. A. Svechin, professor of the RKKA Academy, who approached the resolution of the question from positions of historical analysis, made a significant contribution to working out this problem. He stated that the "recently discovered" phenomenon was nothing more than a new historical step in the development of a long-known form of military action, that is, the operation.

In analyzing the processes of armed combat, Svechin demonstrated that under new conditions within the framework of an army operation, a mutual movement, even a confluence, of the engagement and the march-maneuver occurred. A new amalgam of operational elements occurred. Svechin wrote:

> Quantity is shifting to quality. The engagement formerly had only slightly noticeable fissures which divided it into separate battles. An increase in the expanse of the engagement led to the fact that the engagement has been broken up into separate pieces which are connected only in a whole operation.
>
> If formerly the operation was divided into maneuver and engagement, then now we must establish other boundaries; now they maneuver partly on rail, partly in the very whirlpool of combat events, attempting to group separate battles to achieve the operational aim. Maneuver has partly given way to operational deployment, and is partly sandwiched between separate battles . . .[21]

Proceeding from the above, Svechin provides a new definition of the operation: "We call an operation that act of war during which force efforts are directed without any interruption into a specific region of the theater of military operations to achieve a specific intermediate aim."[22]

Such eminent Soviet military leaders and theorists as M. V. Frunze, A. I. Yegorov, S. S. Kamenev, M. N. Tukhachevsky, I. P. Uborevich, B. M. Shaposhnikov, V. K. Triandafillov, and others also made a great contribution during the 1920s–30s to the development of the theory and practice of preparing for and conducting an operation.

During the further development of military art, especially during the Second World War, the scale, nature, aims, and missions of the operation changed. The modern operation is defined as

> the totality of coordinated engagements, battles, and attacks, mutually connected in aim, location, and time, conducted in a theater of military operations or strategic (operational) axis according to a uniform concept and plan for resolving strategic, operational-strategic, or operational missions.[23]

The short analysis we have presented on the development of military thought from the end of the eighteenth to the beginning of the twentieth century makes it possible to conclude that the theoretical resolution of operational problems had already begun in the eighteenth century. The operation itself, however, as an objective phenomenon of armed combat originated significantly earlier. Its sources must be sought in the remote past. This is also confirmed by the research of several Soviet military historians who devoted a number of their works to the examination of military operations of slave-owning, feudal, and capitalist societies.[24]

Questions concerning the origin and development of the operation, in our opinion, should find suitable reflection in modern works on the history of military art.

NOTES

1. R. Savushkin, "K voprosu o vozniknovenii i razvitii operatsii," *Voyenno-istoricheskiy zhurnal* [Military-historical journal], 5 (May, 1979), pp. 78–82.
2. See Ye. A. Razin, *Istoriya voyennogo iskusstva* [History of military art], Vol. 8 (Voyenizdat, 1961), p. 540.
3. Magazines (storehouses) were created on the eve of or during the war, most often in fortresses. Ammunition, food, forage, and uniforms were concentrated. From here all types of provisions were supplied to the troops by cart trains.
4. *Strategiya v trudakh voyennykh klassikov* [Strategy in the work of military classics], Vol. 1 (Moscow: Vysshiy redaktsionnyy sovet, 1924), p. 21.
5. Ibid., Vol. 2, p. 36.
6. Ibid, p. 57.
7. Ibid.
8. Ibid., pp. 92–3.
9. Ibid., p. 123.
10. A. Jomini, *Essays on Military Art*, Vol. 1 (Voyenizdat, 1939), p. 88.
11. See, for example, A. V. Suvorov, *Dokumenty* [Documents], Vol. 4, Voyenizdat, 1953, pp. 200–2, 293–6, 310–11; M. I. Kutuzov, *Sbornik dokumentov* [Collection of documents], Vol. 4, part 1, Voyenizdat, 1954, pp. 85, 112, 115, 266, 268–9.
12. *Entsiklopediya voyennykh i morskikh nauk*/Encyclopedia of military and naval sciences, Vol. 5, (SPb, 1891), pp. 456–7.
13. Ibid., p. 457.
14. For more details about Leer's work see G. P. Mesheryakov, *Russkaya voyennaya mysl' v XIX veke* [Russian military thought in the nineteenth century] (Moscow: Nauka, 1973).
15. *Strategy in the Works of Military Classics*, Vol. 2, pp. 277, 280.
16. *Strategiya* [Strategy], book 1. Compiled by General of Infantry N. P. Mikhnevich (SPb, 1911), p. 152.
17. *Russkaya voyenno-teoreticheskaya mysl' XIX i nachala XX vekov* [Russian military-theoretical thought of the nineteenth and beginning of the twentieth century] (Voyenizdat, 1960), p. 557.
18. Ibid., p. 612.
19. K. Marx and F. Engels, *Works*, Vol. 14, p. 26.
20. Ibid., Vol. 19, pp. 456, 457, 458, 459, 463.
21. A. A. Svechin, *Voprosy strategii i operativnogo iskusstva v sovetskikh voyennykh trudakh (1917–1940)* [Problems of strategy and operational art in Soviet military works (1917–1940)] (Voyenizdat: 1965), p. 241.
22. Ibid., p. 219.
23. *Sovetskaya voyennaya entsiklopediya* [Soviet military encyclopedia], Vol. 6 (Voyenizdat, 1978), p. 64.
24. A. A. Svechin, *Evolyutsiya voyennogo iskusstva* [The evolution of military art], Vol. 1 (Moscow–Leningrad: 1927). On operations of the slave-owning society, see pp. 44, 79; that of the feudal society – pp. 210, 213; that of the capitalist society – pp. 337, 353, 358, 361. *Voprosy strategii i operativnogo iskusstva v sovetskikh voyennykh trudakh* [Problems of

strategy and operational art in Soviet military works], pp. 222–8, 238–41. N. A. Levitsky, *Polkovodcheskoye iskusstvo Napoleona* [Napoleon's art of military leadership], (Voyenizdat, 1938), pp. 100, 110, 140, 186. G. Isserson, *Voyennoye iskusstvo epokhi natsional'nykh voyn vtoroy poloviny XIX veka* [Military art of the epoch of national wars in the second half of the nineteenth century] (Moscow: Izdatel'stvo VAF, 1933), pp. 11–111.

The Joint Operation – The Main Form of Modern Combat Actions: An Analysis of Historical Experience and Contemporaneity

COLONEL GENERAL M. I. BEZKHREBTYY[1]

Objective conditions for the birth of the joint operation as a form of combat actions for resolving strategic and operational missions using various forces arose at the end of the eighteenth and beginning of the nineteenth century. Combat actions in the *Russo-Japanese War* can serve as a prototype for such large-scale operations. They were characterized by large spatial scope, participation of all combat arms and naval forces according to a single plan, a variety of forms and methods for routing the enemy, and unity of command.

Contours of the joint operation on a strategic and operational scale appeared, however, in greatest relief *during the First World War*. As many as 8–11 field armies, several thousand guns and mortars, up to 1,000 airplanes, and several hundred tanks participated simultaneously in such operations, which were an entire complex of engagements conducted simultaneously and successively. They developed on a front of 400–700 kilometers and lasted from 8–16 days to three or more months. Combat actions began to be conducted not only on land, but also in the air, and ground forces actions on coastal axes were supported by naval forces.

Participation of large masses of infantry, tanks, artillery, aviation, and naval forces in First World War operations distinctly framed the problem of precisely coordinating efforts of various large formations and formations on the basis of a single concept and plan of combat actions, and creating commands of large groupings of different forces.

As a result, for the first time in the history of military affairs there appeared such operational-strategic large formations as the *front* (Russia), and the army group (Germany, Austro-Hungary, France). These large formations were used during the preparation and conduct of strategic and operational joint operations. Large naval force combat actions were conducted in the form of naval operations.[2]

With respect to the quantity and types of employed combat means, they were all, in fact, joint. Their most characteristic feature was that infantry and artillery combat actions played a major role in resolving strategic and operational-tactical missions. The relative weight of missions executed by other combat arms and armed forces services was quite small.

For example, aviation provided air reconnaissance and struck separate targets directly on the battlefield. On the whole, it still could not have any significant effect on the outcome of the operation. Because of their low numbers, inadequate fire power and armored protection, and low speeds and cross-country mobility, tanks were employed only for direct infantry support during penetration of the enemy's positional defense.

Questions of cooperation and support of combat actions were resolved only in the most general terms during conducted operations. Commanders and staffs of various armed forces services and combat arms were not particularly familiar with the combat capabilities of cooperating troops, forces, or means, which reflected negatively on the results of joint actions of different forces. Nevertheless, the principle of coordinated use of different large formations, formations, and units in operations to resolve combat missions on land, in the air, and at sea during this period of development turned into one of the principal factors in achieving victory in battle and operations.

During the Civil War (1918-20) forms and methods for conducting joint operations were developed further. The Eastern, Turkestan, Southeastern, Caucasus, Southern, Southwestern, Western, and Northern Fronts were formed during different periods of the struggle against internal counter-revolution and foreign intervention. They were deployed and conducted operations jointly with aviation and, on coastal axes, with naval forces. River flotillas and part of the naval forces (during actions on coastal axes) were, as a rule, operationally subordinate to a *front* or army.

During Civil War operations, rich experience was acquired in joint operations of combined-arms large formations and formations with large masses of cavalry. The use of cavalry armies jointly with aviation in the enemy's operational depth was a prototype for *front* and army mobile group operations during the Great Patriotic War.

After the Civil War, the nature of our army changed because of the enormous achievements of the socialist economy. It was outfitted with the latest models of weapons and combat equipment. The theory and practice of preparing and conducting joint *front* and army operations continued to develop on this basis, and the final division of Soviet military art into strategy, operational art, and tactics occurred.

During this period, *the development of the theory of deep battle and operation* was of great merit for Soviet military science. This was essentially a theory for preparing and conducting joint operations on a new armed forces materiel base.[3]

In accordance with prewar views, *front* and army operations were to be conducted with obligatory participation of large aviation forces (naval forces on coastal axes). It was recommended to have three–four shock armies and one–two combined-arms armies, one–two tank, mechanized, or cavalry corps, 15–30 aviation divisions, and air defense formations and units in *front* composition.

On the basis of the general theory of the deep operation, theories on the operational employment of air-assault forces, air forces, air defense forces, and naval forces were further developed.

The correctness of the basic tenets of the theory of the deep operation was confirmed by the Soviet Army's successful conduct of a large number of *joint operations on various scales during the Great Patriotic War*. During these operations, trends for increasing the composition and role of forces and means of various combat arms and Armed Forces services participating in operations by armies, *fronts* and groups of *fronts* were closely examined.

As a result of the growing scale of combat actions and sophistication of forms for conducting them, strategic missions, as a rule, began to be resolved by a group of *fronts* as early as the first period of the war. Each participating *front*, proceeding from the content of the assigned missions and the significance of the axes, consisted of three–six armies made up of 20–40 rifle, one–three tank, and two–four cavalry divisions, two–six mixed air divisions (300–400 airplanes), up to 600 tanks, and 1,500–3,000 guns and mortars.

The success of such *front* combat actions completely depended on how well the commander succeeded in organizing and implementing coordinated use of each combat arm and Armed Forces service, maximally using their combat capabilities on the basis of a single plan.

In joint operations, ground forces formed the basis for shock groupings. It was they who resolved the most important missions in the defense and offense.

Analysis of the most important Great Patriotic War operations attests that the crushing defeat of German-Fascist forces would have been unthinkable without joint, strictly coordinated actions of different forces and means according to a single concept and plan and on the basis of centralized command in preparing and conducting joint combat actions.

With each year of the war and with each new joint operation, the integration of efforts and the composition and scope of missions for large formations and formations of all participating Armed Forces services and combat arms steadily increased.

Principal aviation efforts were directed toward assisting combined-arms large formations and *front* and army mobile groups in routing the opposing enemy. For example, air armies participated in almost all *front* offensive operations, using more than 46 per cent of their sorties (and long-range aviation more than 43 per cent) for the destruction of enemy forces and equipment directly on the battlefield. Other very important missions for aviation were gaining air superiority, reconnoitering the enemy, routing his immediate operational reserves, etc.

During the first period of the war, *front* aviation had at its disposal an insignificant quantity of forces and means; therefore, its actions were limited to preparation for the attack and episodic support of advancing forces.

The significant quantitative and qualitative growth of the air forces by summer 1942 made it possible to broaden the volume of aviation missions in *front* offensive operations.

Air force actions in joint operations during the second and third periods of the war were executed in the form of the air offensive, whose basis consisted of aviation preparation for the attack, support of the infantry and tank attack, and accompaniment of advancing forces into the depth of the enemy defense.

Thus, the term "aviation offensive" essentially encompassed all aviation missions in joint offensive operations. The resolution of these missions was assigned to *front* air armies and air corps of the reserve of the Supreme High Command, while the organizer of these actions was the *front* commander.

Success in the aviation offensive was achieved by the presence of a sufficient quantity of forces and means, their maximum intensity, and the expertise of flight personnel. Precise planning of the combat employment of aviation, continuous control, and close cooperation with combined-arms large formations and formations had important significance.

To create conditions for flexible and timely airfield maneuver in the operational depth, *front* and army mobile groups received missions to capture and hold enemy airfields, and ground forces engineer units and subunits were used to restore and construct airfields. This experience has not lost its significance even under modern conditions.

National Air Defense forces were used in ever increasing scales and for resolving the most varied missions in joint actions with combined-arms large formations.

Thus, from the beginning of September 1941 to the end of March 1942, aircraft of Moscow Air Defense's 6th Fighter Aviation Corps completed 26,000 sorties to cover ground forces and deliver strikes against enemy groupings. From November–December 1941, Air Defense antiaircraft artillery repelled enemy tank and infantry attacks in the regions of Solnechnogorsk, Istra, Dmitrov, near Tula, and in other areas, and near Voronezh and Stalingrad in summer and autumn 1942. In subsequent operations, air defense forces fought against enemy aviation and covered forces during the conduct of large-scale strategic and operational regroupings, *front* lines of communication, railroad junctions, crossings, and the most important rear objectives in *front* sectors during their offensive. In a number of instances, National Air Defense forces and means, in cooperation with *front* and naval aviation and antiaircraft means, carried out missions supporting the defense of naval bases (Sevastopol', Leningrad), covering naval convoys, and accompanying bombers (aviation corps of the reserve of the Supreme High Command).

The *Navy's main efforts in joint strategic operations* were directed toward assisting ground forces in resolving defensive and offensive missions; therefore, part or all of the forces of a particular navy were placed in full operational subordination to the *front* commander.

During the first period of the Great Patriotic War, the most important mission of the Northern, Red Banner Baltic, and Black Sea Fleets was to cover the flanks of ground formations and large formations, and assist them in conducting defensive operations. Fleets (especially their aviation and ship and shore artillery) played a large role in the stubborn defense of naval bases and ports (Leningrad, Odessa, Sevastopol', Tallin, Khanko, the islands of the Moonzund Archipelago, and Murmansk). During this period, the Baltic and Black Sea Fleets conducted several operations to evacuate forces from Tallin, Khanko, Odessa, and Sevastopol'. For example, in the 1941 Odessa defensive operation, the Odessa Naval Base (with its attached ships), together with the Coastal Army, comprised the Odessa Defense Region, which was given the mission of creating a solid and dynamic defense of the town. The Black Sea Fleet supported ground forces, ensured delivery of replacements, arms, and supplies to Odessa, and evacuated wounded, civilians, and valuable property from the town.

During subsequent periods of the war, the range of naval force missions sharply broadened. They were used to participate in joint offensive operations on coastal axes, for which formations of surface ships, submarines, aviation, shore defense artillery, and naval infantry were enlisted. The contribution of naval forces in resolving the principal joint operation missions unalterably increased.

Naval and shore artillery and fleet aviation participated in artillery and aviation support of forces during their penetration of the enemy defense. To prevent the landing of enemy assault forces, joint measures were conducted by naval forces and *front* forces to organize an anti-assault defense of the coast on the flanks and in the rear of the advancing forces.

In assisting ground force groupings, the fleet established a blockade, pressing enemy forces to the sea, preventing delivery of replacements and supplies by sea to enemy forces isolated from dry land, and also preventing their evacuation from occupied bridgeheads. The fleet destroyed enemy transport means and personnel at ports for loading and unloading and during their sea crossing, and laid mines on approaches to enemy ports.

The fleet landed amphibious assault forces in the enemy rear to assist attacking forces in encircling and destroying enemy groupings. During the Great Patriotic War, more than 100 operational and tactical assaults were landed. During the first period of the war, landings were executed by a small number of forces (with the exception of the Kerch'–Feodosiia amphibious operation); during the second and especially third periods, these operations were executed on larger scales (Kerch'–Elting, Moonzund operations, and others).

Naval infantry actively participated in joint operations. It acted success-fully during the defense of Murmansk, Lipai, Tallin, Khanko, the Moonzund Islands, Odessa, and Sevastopol'. Naval rifle units heroically fought on the approaches to Leningrad and in defensive battles at Moscow and Stalingrad.

Strategic operations during the third period of the war had an even more pronounced joint character. In a number of cases they were conducted by forces of two to four *fronts*, with the employment of several air armies, long-range aviation formations, air defense forces, and the forces of one fleet and one or two flotillas. These operations were conducted with decisive aims: routing large enemy groupings (usually consisting of 20–60 divisions); capturing economically and politically important regions and the system of naval bases, ports, and shipbuilding centers; driving Fascist Germany's allies out of the war; and liberating occupied territories and enslaved peoples.

The theory and practice of preparing and conducting joint offensive operations developed further in Soviet force operations in the Far East during the rout of the Japanese Kwantung Army, conducted from 9 August through 2 September 1945. In the Manchurian strategic operation, the co-operation of large formations and formations of different Armed Forces services consisted of the following: ground forces of three *fronts* and their air armies resolved the main mission, that is, the rout of the Kwantung Army. At this time the Pacific Fleet was fighting against the enemy navy on the Kwantung Army's and mother country's lines of communication, and cover-ing the ground forces from the sea. Part of the fleet's forces cooperated directly with forces attacking into North Korea. The Red Banner Amur Flotilla was interacting with 2d Far Eastern Front's main grouping during the Sungarian operation. In addition, this *front*, in cooperation with the Pacific Fleet, successfully conducted several assault operations to liberate Southern Sakhalin.

The successful actions of Soviet forces in Manchuria and Sakhalin created a favorable situation for conducting an assault operation to liberate the Kurile Islands.

The conduct of coordinated actions of large formations, formations, and units of all Armed Forces services and combat arms according to a single plan required enormous efforts on the part of the Supreme High Command, the commands of the Armed Forces services, commanders, and staffs. Questions of coordinating actions of combined-arms armies and *front* and army mobile groups, assigning missions to artillery and aviation to be resolved during the artillery and aviation offensive, maintaining firm and continuous cooperation, and controlling operational large formations were especially complex.

The successful resolution of these and other complex problems in preparing and conducting large-scale joint operations was made possible by many measures, those having especially great significance being the strengthening of the practice of personal, practical contacts among commanders of co-operating large formations and formations, exchanges of operational groups (representatives) between staffs, joint development of plans for combat actions and tables of cooperation, co-location of command posts, organization of reliable communications for cooperation, and precise reciprocal information among staffs of the different forces.

Thus, the Great Patriotic War clearly manifested the trend toward continuous growth in the number of joint strategic and *front* operations (especially offensive), conducted with participation of large formations of the Ground Forces, Air Forces, Air Defense Forces, and Naval Forces, and toward a growth in their role in these operations. Each joint operation, because of the variety of operational-strategic situations, was conducted in an original manner, and differed from others in its forms of maneuver, the nature of actions of participating forces, the procedure for employing means of destruction, and conditions of cooperation.

In all cases, however, the achievement of success in joint operations required careful organization of operational cooperation, which, as a rule, was assigned to the *front* commander and staff. The essence of such cooperation was coordination with respect to aim, place, and time of ground forces, *front* aviation, and naval force attacks against enemy ground, maritime, and air groupings, in mutual support of forces conducting combat actions, in the cover of troops and naval forces from the air, and in *front* forces' execution of missions to capture ports, large airfields, and other important objectives in the interests of the navy and aviation.

A large range of questions was subject to coordination during the preparation for landing operational amphibious assaults in the *front* offensive sector. This was explained by the necessity of enlisting a considerable quantity of forces and means to ensure reliable pressure against the enemy's anti-assault and air defense, effective support of actions of the landed assault forces, and the timely arrival of attacking *front* forces in their operating regions.

When organizing cooperation, precise times and procedures were determined for covering amphibious assault forces from the air, delivering strikes by *front* and naval bomber and fighter-bomber aviation in the interests of the execution of missions by assault forces and advancing *front* groupings, and conducting the artillery and aviation preparation to penetrate the anti-amphibious defense. To ensure safe flight of air-assault forces, reliable destruction of enemy air defense means was envisioned. In addition, the procedure and time for delivering long-range aviation strikes against advancing enemy reserves, large centers of communications, command posts, naval bases, and ports were coordinated.

The operational plan determined the sequence of resolving particular missions of *front* forces, air force groupings, air defense forces, and naval forces, and organization of reconnaissance and other types of operational support, and planned measures for control.

In the *postwar period*, the further development of the theory and practice of preparing and conducting joint operations was conditioned by the qualitative growth in the technical outfitting of all combat arms and Armed Forces services.

The principal mission of military art during this period was to generalize the experience of the last war and reveal trends in the development of methods for conducting joint operations, taking into consideration prospects for the complete army and navy mechanization and motorization, as well as the creation of new means for armed struggle.

We understand joint operations as combat actions of operational and strategic force groupings on land, in the air, and at sea, in which the main missions are carried out according to an overall plan and under a single command by the joint efforts of all Armed Forces services, with the leading role given to one of them, depending on the operational sphere. Here, the nature of modern operations, in comparison with those of the last war, predetermine closer coordination of efforts of various forces during their preparation and conduct, with respect to missions, place, and time. The actions of these forces knit together and intertwine, as it were, and are becoming an inseparable part of each operation.

Today, joint operations have become the primary form of combat actions in all spheres, and their preparation and conduct are a leading trend in the development of the theory and practice of military art.

This trend is a result of those objective factors associated with revolutionary progress in the development of means for armed struggle and methods of resolving operational-strategic missions. Today, no single armed forces service is capable of successfully resolving its own specific missions without participation of other services.

Take, for example, operations in continental theaters of military operations. The depth of the probable enemy grouping's defensive formation in *front* operating sectors have increased considerably in comparison with the last war and, according to foreign opinions, may reach 150–200 kilometers, while in the tactical sector the number of armored and antitank means has sharply increased; strong second echelons and reserves are being created in field armies and army groups, whose make-up includes highly mobile, mainly armor and mechanized, formations, which will be committed into an engagement with the support of large aviation forces capable of strongly influencing the course and outcome of combat actions.

Penetration of such a defense and development of the offensive at high tempos is now impossible without mass use of aviation in the tactical and operational depth; without gaining air superiority and reliable cover of ground forces against enemy strikes from the air and sea; without simultaneous pressure on the entire depth of the enemy's formation, using all types of aviation, and amphibious and air assaults; and without naval force combat actions to thwart enemy strikes from a coastal axis.

The same can also be said about operations at sea and in the air. For example, to conduct modern air operations successfully, it is necessary to enlist naval aviation, primary air defense forces and means to fight against enemy aviation, and part of combined-arms large formation forces to penetrate the enemy's air defense system, etc.

In operations in ocean (maritime) theaters of military operations, the efforts of not only naval forces, but also air forces, forces and means of combined-arms large formations, rocket forces, and air defense forces are required.

During the postwar period, trends toward integrating the efforts of all armed forces services in land, air, and sea operations are being examined in the development of military art of the aggressive NATO bloc armies.

This bloc's bourgeois military theorists are assessing the combined power of large ground force, aviation, and naval force groupings with their nuclear weapons directed against the Soviet Union and other socialist states as the main means for achieving war aims. In their opinion, the primary forms of conducting military actions are large-scale operations on continental theaters of military operations conducted with decisive aims and with the support of tactical and strategic aviation (and naval forces on coastal axes), which is confirmed by exercises.

It is noted in the foreign military press that, with the appearance of nuclear weapons aircraft carriers, naval rocket-carrier aviation, submarines with atomic engines and rocket-nuclear weapons, fast-moving surface ships with rocket-artillery weapons, air defense and radio-electronic warfare means, and new assault force means, naval force and aviation potentials have sharply increased for conducting joint combat actions with ground force groupings.

Thus, at the contemporary stage of development of military art, joint operations on a strategic and operational scale have become the main form of combat actions.

In comparison with operations of the last war, they will be characterized by enormous scales; participation of practically all armed forces services, equipped with fundamentally new, very complex weapons systems and combat equipment; and speed and maneuverability of combat actions.

These characteristic features of modern operations present increased demands on the theory and practice of their preparation and conduct, for professional expertise of military cadres, for operational training of generals, admirals, and officers, and for organs of control of formations and units of all Armed Forces services.

Therefore, comprehensive research into the problems of modern joint operations is an important task for Soviet military science. Here, the research of such issues as ensuring strictly coordinated use of different forces, taking into account their combat capabilities and the specifics of their combat employment, achieving close cooperation among them, and organizing reliable troop control during operations has particular significance.

NOTES

1. M. I. Bezkhrebtyy, "Sovmestnaya operatsiya – glavnaya forma sovremennykh boyevykh deystviy (Analiz istoricheskogo opyta i sovremennost')," *Voyennaya mysl'* [Military thought], 7 (1979), pp. 27–34.
2. For greater detail, see *Voyennaya mysl'*, 12 (1978) and 3 (1979). [Translator's note: both these articles have been translated for this volume. See N. N. Fomin, "Soviet Operational Art: Birth and Primary Stages of Development"; and V. F. Mozolev, "On General Fundamentals of the Theory of Soviet Operational Art."]
3. For more detail on the essence of deep operation, see *Voyennaya mysl'*, 8 (1978), pp. 14–26. [Translator's note: this article has been translated for this volume. See "The Theory of Deep Operation and Its Developmental Trends," by L. I. Voloshin.]

The Preparation of Successive Offensive Operations: History and Contemporaneity

COLONEL GENERAL M. I. BEZKHREBTYY,
CANDIDATE OF MILITARY SCIENCES, DOCENT[1]

Successive offensive operations are understood as operations conducted by a *front* (army) after completing previous operational missions. During the Great Patriotic War, all successive *front* offensive operations were components of strategic operations, while successive army offensive operations were components of *front* operations; they were conducted in accordance with their plan and, as a rule, with or without short operational pauses.

The necessity for *fronts* (armies) to conduct several offensive operations successively with respect to depth within the framework of a single strategic (*front*) operation was conditioned by the existence of large enemy force groupings deployed not only in the operational, but also in the strategic depth, and designated for maneuver; this was also conditioned by the impossibility of using a quantity of forces and means in the *front* (army) composition to ensure the rout of opposing groupings by conducting only a single operation. In addition, while completing the initial operations, *fronts* were often unable immediately to bring the composition of their shock groupings and operational formation into accord with the sharply changed operational situation, or to provide forces with materiel sufficient for conducting combat actions to the entire depth of the strategic operation.

Classical models of successive *front* and army offensive operations conducted to rout deeply echeloned enemy groupings decisively without operational pauses or with very brief intervals between operations during the Great Patriotic War are Voronezh Front's Ostrogozhsk–Rossosh' operation (13–27 January 1943), Voronezh and Bryansk Front's Voronezh–Kastornoye operation (24 January–17 February 1943), and almost all *front* operations conducted within the framework of the Belorussian strategic offensive operation, whose preparation and execution confirmed the high level of Soviet military art. For example, during the Belorussian strategic offensive operation (23 June–29 August 1944), two *fronts* – 1st Baltic and 2d Belorussian – successively conducted two *front* offensive operations each, 1st Belorussian conducted three, and 3d Belorussian conducted four, each at a depth of 140–160 kilometers.

During the Belorussian operation, of 109 enemy divisions and seven brigades, 17 divisions and three brigades were completely destroyed, and 50 divisions lost more than half of their personnel. *Front* forces advanced up to 550–600 kilometers westward, purged the Belorussian SSR and part of the Lithuanian and Latvian SSRs of the enemy, entered Polish territory, and reach the borders of East Prussia.

In the Vistula–Oder strategic offensive operation, 1st Belorussian and 1st Ukrainian Fronts were to conduct one operation each at a depth of 300 and 350 kilometers respectively. In fact, they each conducted two operations, an initial and a successive one, during which they advanced to a depth of up to 570 kilometers. During the operation, in a short time the *fronts* routed and destroyed 60 German-Fascist divisions, liberated a considerable portion of Poland, and shifted combat actions to Fascist German territory.

Analysis of the experience of preparing and conducting these and other successive *front* offensive operations demonstrates that there were very important inherent features whose contents are of great interest for modern conditions as well. These are *decisiveness of aims and great spatial scope of operations; high maneuverability and dynamism of combat actions; conduct of the offensive at high tempos along axes with extremely disproportionate advance of formations and large formations and great separation of highly mobile groupings from remaining front forces; and sharp changes in the operational situation, especially by the commencement of the successive operations.*

Front (army) commanders and staffs prepared almost all successive operations while executing subsequent missions of preceding operations in a complex operational situation. Conditions characterizing their preparation are as follows:

1. When making decisions about successive offensive operations, *front* commanders did not have situational data at their disposal, an analysis of which would have made it possible to formulate their plan immediately and conclusively, since initial operations were still developing. In addition, it was difficult to determine the combat composition, level of combat capability, operational situation, and nature of actions of both one's own forces and those of the enemy in the *front* (army) sector by the time the new operation commenced. This required careful prognosis and specific skills for forecasting the development of the operational situation.

2. To conduct successive offensive operations, *fronts* (armies) did not, as a rule, have either prepared shock groups or a sufficient quantity of combat-capable formations in reserve which could have been designated for these purposes without having been used earlier. Therefore, force groupings on *front* (army) attack axes were created while completing the preceding

operation, to a considerable degree by maneuvering and regrouping first-echelon formations and large formations.

3. As a result of the disproportionate advance of first-echelon armies and their arrival at different times at the final line of the preceding operation, as well as the difference in their combat composition and manning, the aims, missions, and scope of successive army offensive operations were varied, and the commencement of the transition to resolving missions in the new, successive operation was not always simultaneous.

4. The uncertainty of the situation in which preparation of the successive operation took place necessitated refinement or complete change of the *front* main attack and other axes by the time the operation began. This also required foresight in the operational plan to permit conduct of appropriate maneuver of forces and materiel.

The experience of the Great Patriotic War demonstrated that the most effective successive operations were those executed after or without a brief operational pause. This was conditioned by the fact that continuous conduct of two *front* operations at a great depth, one ensuing from the other, deprives the enemy of the ability to regroup forces to oppose attacking *front* forces, introduce reserves into the engagement in an organized manner, or create a stable defensive front along new lines.

Conduct of successive operations without operational pauses was most typical of army offensive operations. *Front* offensive operations required a pause to carry out necessary force regroupings to new axes, bring up army and *front* rear services, re-establish communications, deliver a large quantity of materiel, and conduct other measures to prepare for a new operation.

Analysis of Great Patriotic War experience showed that successive *front* and army offensive operations conducted without careful advance preparation during an ongoing operation could turn into an indiscriminate advance fraught with possible frustration in the execution of assigned missions. This is clearly confirmed by the course of Southwestern and Voronezh Front combat actions during offensive operations in the concluding stage of the 1942–43 winter campaign. By the commencement of successive operations, these *fronts'* forces had suffered heavy losses, were very exhausted, and had deficiencies in weapons, ammunition, and fuel; rear areas were stretched out 250–300 kilometers. They were separated from airfield centers for basing *front* aviation and did not have necessary aviation support and cover. Because of these and a number of other reasons, instead of developing the offensive operation to great depth, forces were compelled to conduct exacting defensive engagements and then withdraw under attacks by German-Fascist groupings, which had gone over to a counteroffensive.

These facts confirmed the correctness and vitality of Lenin's instructions that "any engagement includes the abstract possibility of defeat, and there is no better way to reduce this possibility than organized preparation of the engagement."[2] Therefore, to ensure success in a successive operation, it is necessary when concluding the current operation to implement a set of organizational measures for its all-round support. *This preparation should be implemented, taking into account that the commencement of the new operation should be a direct continuation of the preceding one.*

Based on Great Patriotic War experience, we think that command and staff work methods in preparing a successive operation, and the content of measures to be undertaken will be greatly influenced not only by the operational situation, degree of main force combat capability, and nature of the enemy's actions, but also mainly by the presence and condition of engaged reserves, the manning (personnel and combat equipment) of formations and large formations used to execute the successive *front* operation, and the condition and situation of the operational rear and lines of communication in the the offensive sector. The presence of materiel, especially ammunition and fuel, has great significance.

During preparation of successive *front* offensive operations in, for example, the Belorussian, Vistula–Oder, and East Prussian strategic operations, the operational situation and condition of *front* large formations at their commencement were most varied.

In all these operations, the list of measures undertaken while preparing successive operations was almost identical. However, their volume and content depended, to a great extent, on the operational situation of the forces: indeed, this determined the scale of regroupings undertaken to achieve superiority in forces and means on the main and other attack axes (such measures included their commencement time; conditions for delivering materiel; the necessity of eliminating gaps between the first-echelon operational formation, rear units, and army and *front* installations; particulars for evacuation of wounded and damaged equipment, etc.).

Under modern conditions, the influence of the operational formation of forces, their degree of support, and the condition of the rear on the volume and content of measures for preparing successive operations has increased greatly because of increased mobility and maneuverability of both one's own and the enemy's forces. The period for executing necessary measures, however, must be reduced considerably. At the same time, it is necessary to take into account the high level of dynamism in the development of the preceding operation, the disproportion of the troop advance, especially during the concluding stage, and their varied materiel expenditures.

The greatest difficulties in preparing successive operations arose in those instances where, by the time the successive operation commenced, all *front* large formations were in the first echelon, resulting in their formations suffering heavy losses, there were limited materiel reserves, and some formations needed personnel and equipment replenishments and a full or partial regeneration of combat capability. All this will be typical in contemporary war, and will determine the characteristics of preparing successive operations. Moreover, the combat situation may be complicated by significant growth in the degree of enemy pressure against our forces using aviation and rocket strikes, both nuclear and conventional. This is confirmed by the fact that, as noted in the foreign military press, in combat actions being conducted with employment of only conventional weapons, an effective means for destroying enemy forces deployed in the depth or maneuvering will be guided ballistic and cruise missiles with warheads having cluster bombs with antitank, anti-personnel, and incendiary bombs and shells.[3]

The time allotted for their conduct has considerable influence on work methods and the content of preparing operational measures. Experience demonstrates that the *front* commander and staff began to prepare an operation, so as to ensure that the secrecy of its plan and covertness of preparation were undisclosed, and a sufficient quantity of time was allotted to armies to prepare their operations, and to divisions, regiments, and battalions to organize combat actions. Here, decision-making, planning of combat actions, and the entire set of fundamental organizational measures were conducted, as a rule, with small intervals of time at the operational and tactical levels of control.

Indeed, this method of preparing successive operations made it possible to reduce or completely eliminate pauses before their conduct. As already emphasized, all *fronts* participating in the Belorussian and Vistula–Oder strategic offensive operations each conducted a number of *front* offensive operations successively, without pauses. During their preparation, *front* commanders spent up to a day in decision-making; the remaining time – from two to 12 days, and more in some cases – was allotted to armies and divisions (they also used this time to complete the subsequent missions of preceding operations). When preparing successive operations, decisions were made, combat actions were planned and organized, forces were replenished with personnel and equipment, materiel was delivered to support the new operations, and forces were regrouped.

In specifying formation combat missions, it must be taken into consideration that during Great Patriotic War operations a considerable part of the rifle divisions conducted combat actions to the entire depth of the army operations. Thus, for example, in the East Prussia operation, 130th Rifle Division of 3d Belorussian Front's 28th Army attacked continuously in the first echelon, day and night, for ten days (13 through 22 January 1945), while this army's 6th Rifle Division fought for nine days. Here, as in many other cases, divisions maintained their combat capability, thanks to skillful alternation of the location of combat units in the first and second echelons and reserve.

Under modern conditions, the reality of conducting an offensive without pauses between operations is conditioned by the incomparably greater potentials than in the last war for formations to conduct continuous combat actions. However, short interruptions are also possible in their development of dynamic offensive actions, especially by groupings operating on independent axes.

The order and contents of *planning successive offensive operations* is of great interest. This was usually done beforehand, simultaneously with making the operational decision, that is, during the preceding operation; this ensured timely and more expedient use of forces, means, and materiel for resolving missions assigned to the *front* and achieving the aim.

The operational plan was a set of documents, whose basis was the general operational portion. It always expressed precisely the aim, missions, and concept of the operation, methods for routing the enemy, the sequence for completing combat missions (immediate and subsequent), composition of groupings, and their operational formation, distributed force strength and materiel means to execute each mission, and established procedures for force cooperation and the organization of political work, all-round support, and control. Planning successive offensive operations was done more carefully and promptly when a special group was created, under direct supervision of the *front* chief of staff, which developed necessary operational documents, together with guidance for troop combat actions, according to the current operational plan. In these instances, full and centralized resolution of all organizational problems associated with preparing a successive operation was achieved during the preceding one.

A feature of planning successive operations was that missions and force actions in the future operational plan were shown as tentative, based on suggested variants of enemy opposition and taking into account newly created front force groupings; it was then completed as the situation became clearer and the time neared for conducting the successive operation. As a rule, the plan reflected preceding force operations and missions, and the time for their completion. A larger-scale map was often prepared for executing the immediate *front* (and especially army) mission upon receiving more concrete situational data. There were instances when, before initiation of the successive operation, a decision had to be fundamentally refined or made anew, in connection with a sharply changed situation. Sometimes the *front* staff, because of insufficient time, did not work out the entire set of documents, but was limited to a detailed formulated decision.

In addition, to ensure continuity in conducting combat actions, the new operational plan envisioned alternation of combat actions with the rest of formations and their probable offensive axes at night, in accordance with the expected nature of enemy opposition. If necessary, methods were specified for increasing army combat capability by the time the execution of the successive operation commenced.

The content of planning a *fire strike* against the enemy in the last war was closely coordinated with the nature of force actions in the preceding operation and initial conditions of the successive operation, as well as with the selected method for executing the mission. Thus, if a new operation began with the penetration of an intermediate enemy defensive line, then its fire strike was planned in detail in large formations and formations, taking into account aviation resources allotted to them and strikes being delivered against objectives by *front* means.

Inasmuch as large formation commanders and staffs will not, as a rule, have at their disposal timely and reliable information on the condition of the opposing enemy grouping and his intentions by the commencement of the operation, the quantity of one's own forces and means necessary to commit to action on attack axes upon its commencement will be determined on the basis of forecasting.

Under modern conditions, in view of the great dynamism of the developing situation, the earlier the decision is made, the less will be the forecasting reliability. Here a dialectical contradiction arises, leading to the conclusion that completion of planning long before the commencement of an operation will not result in considerable gains in time for working at army, division, and regimental level, since subsequently it will be necessary to refine the developed plan and introduce appropriate additions and corrections to it.

It is also impossible to exclude the possibility of a radical change in the grouping of one's own forces created for the subsequent operation, because at its commencement formation positions may not be as speculated, as a result of unforeseen enemy actions. After new situational data arrive, the plan will be refined, and its degree of detailing will increase as the time for conducting the operation approaches.

Consequently, the specifics of work on planning a successive operation rest in the fact that it will continue uninterruptedly until its very commencement. Obviously, it is also necessary to consider the possibility that the operation will not begin simultaneously for all *front* forces, since when completing the preceding operation individual armies will be conducting combat actions at different depths and terminating different combat missions. However, commanders and staffs must always strive to eliminate such undesirable occurrences and ensure a powerful and simultaneous attack against the enemy at least on all of the most important axes.

Force cooperation in a successive offensive operation is organized according to the same principles as the preceding one, that is, to the entire depth, with respect to axes, lines, time, and methods for its execution, with the greatest detail given to the entire depth of the immediate mission. Previously coordinated force actions can be maintained and used during the conduct of the new operation, especially when it is a direct continuation of the former.

Despite the limited time allotted to preparing a successive operation and the necessity of shifting forces to fulfill its mission without pauses, careful organization of cooperation at all levels to the depth of the immediate mission – most detailed in the interests of the shock groups and fulfillment of one of the first intermediate missions of the successive operation – should be implemented under any conditions. In the interests of fulfilling the subsequent mission, general coordinating instructions are necessary, which should be detailed and refined during the operation.

Commander and staff work methods in organizing cooperation will be determined, to a great degree, by the characteristics of the situation existing during the execution of the subsequent mission of the preceding operation, available time, the selected method for routing the enemy, conditions of the transition to resolving missions in the successive operation, time of arrival of reserves in the *front's* operational sector, number of reserves, and the operational situation of its main forces.

According to war experience, the *front* commander specified the basis for cooperation when making his decision, and then reported it to subordinates when assigning missions. Questions of cooperation were usually worked out in detail after force missions were assigned and decisions were made by commanders of armies and combat arms and chiefs of special forces and services in a sequence which was determined by the operational situation and assignment of each army.

In a situation where it was possible for a *front* to use two armies in the composition of the grouping delivering its main attack, including a second-echelon army with its formations moving up from the depth, cooperation between them and their supporting forces and means was organized simultaneously on a terrain mock-up or on maps. The *front* commander gave instructions on the procedure and times for all forces and means participating in the operation to execute their missions, coordinated the procedure for using allotted forces and means, and played through the most important individual episodes with army commanders. Under conditions where the successive operation was prepared in an extremely short time and in a complex situation, the *front* commander coordinated force actions only with those army commanders whose forces were participating in the delivery of the main attack. Sometimes, at the same time he assigned missions, he personally gave instructions on basic questions of cooperation.

With a successful transition of *front* forces to a successive operation and continuing development of the offensive by each army in its sector, when they were advancing along separate, sometimes isolated axes the *front* commander limited himself to instructions on cooperation transmitted by technical means of communication. To assure that army commanders and others correctly understood these instructions, deputy commanders, commanders of combat arms, and chiefs of services, directorates, and departments of the *front* field directorate came directly to the troops.

In all instances, the *front* commander pointed out to army and formation commanders questions which required careful coordination to execute the missions, specified the methods and procedure for actions of cooperating forces and means in resolving particular missions in the successive offensive operation, and briefed them concerning other possible actions and maneuver in case of sharp changes in the operational situation.

In addition, when preparing a successive offensive operation on a coastal axis, issues of joint repulsion of enemy air raids, destruction of his coastal groupings, capture of ports, bases, and important coastal sectors, and prevention of the transfer of enemy reserves and materiel by sea were coordinated between the *front* and fleet. The *front* was also informed about other missions being executed by the fleet in naval operations, which were taken into consideration when resolving *front* missions on a coastal axis.

Special attention was focused on organizing cooperation among forces operating at junctions with neighboring *fronts*. The basis of their operational plan was always reported to the *front* commanders; they knew the missions of flank force groupings and coordinated the actions of their own forces and means with them to deliver a fire strike against the enemy and rout his grouping by joint efforts. The possibility of exploiting the success of a neighboring *front's* offensive operation by maneuvering one's own forces and means across his sector to deliver attacks against the enemy's flank and rear was envisioned. Issues of control of forces maneuvering in a neighboring sector, air cover, and intensification of fire support for their actions were coordinated beforehand to accomplish this.

The fact that, when organizing cooperation under any conditions, independent of the degree of detail of coordination for particular problems, *front* (army) commanders strived so that subordinate commanders solidly mastered the content of their assigned combat missions and the methods by which both their own and cooperating forces and means were to execute them merits attention. A strict procedure was established for exchanging information between headquarters concerning the situation and to warn forces concerning enemy aviation; a uniform system of coordinating signal, target indication, and warning, and uniform numeration of targets and objectives in the offensive sector were created.

Thus, the principal aim of organizing cooperation should be consolidation of the efforts of all available forces and means to achieve successfully the aim of a successive operation. Continuous maintenance of cooperation was ensured by a correct understanding of the operational aim and combat missions by all responsible persons, continuous troop control, sensible use of their combat capabilities, constant operation of communications, and timely and complete information exchange.

The creation of a main and other front shock groups will be required to conduct a successive operation on attack axes.

Analysis of the experience of the most important operations of the last war – Belorussian, L'vov–Sandomierz, Iassy–Kishinev, and Vistula–Oder – makes it possible to formulate requirements for their creation under contemporary conditions. The principal ones are as follows: *complete accord of the quantitative and qualitative composition of groups with the operational concept and plan; superiority over the enemy on attack axes, especially on the main axis; and the potential for delivering a powerful preliminary strike and swift development of the offensive into the depth and in the direction of the flanks.* In addition, it is important to ensure the execution of rapid maneuver of formations within the shock groups and between them, and the dispersion of forces in the operational formation to maintain their combat capabilities in case of enemy employment of nuclear weapons. When creating the principal groups, replacement of weakened formations operating on selected axes by combat-capable forces should be envisioned.

One of the most important factors contributing to the fulfillment of these requirements and, on the whole, the successful conduct of successive operations is the maintenance or creation of strong second echelons and reserves in large formations by the time the current operation is being completed. This will permit the creation of a new shock group or reinforcement of the first echelon on the necessary axis in a short time without complex regroupings during combat operations and without long operational pauses between the first and successive operations. Experience demonstrates that such favorable conditions may not always occur. During the preceding operation, the larger part of initially created second echelons and reserves may be engaged, and formations committed instead will have to be brought up to strength and will need their combat capabilities regenerated.

All this will necessitate the conduct of a set of timely measures to create shock groups to conduct the successive operation. Such measures may be regroupings of formations and units in army sectors and within a *front* while completing the preceding operation; redistribution of forces and means among army formations and *front* armies; and replenishment of losses in personnel, combat equipment, and materiel. Resubordination of some combined-arms formations from armies whose advance is planned on secondary axes to armies designated for operations on the main axis is not excluded, nor is the redirection of *front* aviation.

Relying on Great Patriotic War experience, it should be emphasized that, under contemporary conditions, regroupings of forces and means to conduct a new operation will be a fundamental measure to ensure the creation of necessary groupings on all attack axes. Indeed, the high art of conducting large-scale, intra-*frontal* regroupings in a short time in the last war, especially during its concluding stage, made it possible to execute a number of successive *front* operations without operational pauses. Thus, for example, 1st Ukrainian Front, after completing the Vistula–Oder operation, conducted a large-scale force regrouping from the left flank to the right to conduct the

Lower Silesian offensive operation; after its completion, the regrouping was once again to the left flank to conduct the Upper Silesian operation without a pause. Immediately after the destruction of German-Fascist forces in the Berlin operation, a considerable part of 1st Ukrainian Front was regrouped in a few days to the Prague axis. Skillful regrouping of forces and means deprived the enemy of the ability to organize a stable defense and reinforce his forces by maneuvering reserves.

Analysis of probable developmental conditions of modern operations shows that to create shock groups it is expedient to regenerate second echelons several days before completion of the current operation and commencement of the new one by withdrawing the necessary number of forces from the first echelon, to bring them up to strength beforehand, to replenish them materielly, and to prepare to conduct the successive operation on the most important axes in the first echelon. In a number of instances, an army which has been introduced into battle from the second echelon, and which has retained a high degree of combat capability in the preceding operation, may be used on the axis of the *front's* main attack. However, to create the necessary density of forces and means in the most important sectors, if possible it is necessary to reinforce the army with several divisions from the reserve or armies operating on secondary axes. Sometimes one or two combat-capable first-echelon armies in a more favorable operational position may be included in the shock group composition, but they will be in need of reinforcement.

Some features of creating shock groups may be a result of the nature of the actions of one's own forces and enemy resistance when shifting to the successive operation. Thus, for example, under conditions where first-echelon forces have captured the line of the subsequent *front* mission and are continuing successfully to develop the offensive in their sectors without encountering significant enemy resistance, a successive offensive operation will, in fact, be a non-stop continuation of the preceding one, without the necessity of regrouping formations along the front. Even in this case, however, it is necessary to take measures to exploit success, especially in the direction of the main and other attacks, without allowing a slowing of offensive tempos or suppression of the new operation. This can be achieved by introducing several fresh divisions into the composition of the armies delivering the main attack, resubordinating reinforcement means to them, executing multiple air-assault landings in their interests, and also employing aviation.

It is possible that one of the methods for creating groupings of forces and means can be where, on the basis of skillful foresight of the probable course of development of an operation being conducted in its concluding stage, it becomes possible beforehand to shift force efforts to a new, more promising axis by weakening secondary sectors, on which limited forces may be left.

This was achieved in the Great Patriotic War by changing army missions, assigning armies other offensive sectors, resubordinating reinforcements, and allocating more combat-capable forces for their composition, which would have made it possible to shift to dynamic offensive actions in a successive operation along new axes without a pause.

The method of determining the necessary superiority and densities of forces and means on attack axes, which would ensure defeat of the enemy in a successive offensive operation, was the same as in the initial operation; however, their indicators could be, to a considerable degree, less, in that, as war experience demonstrates, during successfully conducted offensive operations (Belorussian, L'vov–Sandomierz, Vistula–Oder, etc.) defending enemy groupings always suffered heavier losses than offensive groupings. Newly formed enemy formations and newly created enemy reserves could be less prepared and coordinated for combat.

The creation of special force groupings, as well as combined-arms and other reserves, will be implemented the same way as in the preparation of the first operation.

Rear support. The enormous scope of the Belorussian and Vistula-Oder operations, in each of which several successive *front* offensive operations were conducted, required an enormous expenditure of materiel. Thus, in the Belorussian operation, the expenditure of ammunition amounted to up to 3.5–5 *front* rounds, while that of POL was up to 15 refuelings. This was delivered by motor vehicle transport because of enormous destruction of railroads and an inadequate quantity of forces and means in *fronts* to repair them, which may be characteristic of contemporary conditions as well.

In preparing a successive operation, the first resolved questions included timely deployment of the rear in accordance with the operational plan along newly selected axes for the main and other attacks; accumulation and correct echeloning of materiel reserves; preparation of a new, uniform transportation system to support forces and materiel reserve regroupings and their rapid delivery to the troops, especially the main groupings; and rendering medical assistance to the wounded and sick. Constant operation of all rear links depended on reliable protection, security, defense, and continuous functioning of the control system, already coordinated and operating during the preceding operation.

Great Patriotic War experience demonstrated that the principal measures for rear support had to be executed before completion of the preceding operation's immediate mission, because this required more time.

In conclusion, we will note that achieving the aims of modern successive offensive operations will depend to an even greater degree than during the Great Patriotic War on completeness and care in conducting beforehand all measures for their preparation. Decisiveness of actions, increased spatial scope of operations, sharp and frequent changes in the situation, and the intense struggle to seize and hold the initiative predetermine the fact that, in preparing successive operations, one cannot count on operational pauses, during which it would be possible, in a relatively calm situation, to plan operations, create shock groups, or organize cooperation, all types of support, and control.

The majority of issues related to preparing successive offensive operations will have to be resolved during preceding ones in a short time and under complex conditions. This will require of commanders and staffs profound knowledge and the ability to foresee thoroughly the development of the operational situation and conduct all necessary measures beforehand for subsequent actions, so as to ensure the continuity of the offensive.

NOTES

1. M. I. Bezkhrebtyy, "Podgotovka posleduyushchikh nastupatel'nykh operatsiy," *Voyennaya mysl'* [Military thought], 7 (1982), pp. 28–38.
2. V. I. Lenin, *Polnoye sobraniye sochineniya* [Complete works], Vol. 6, p. 137.
3. *Voyennyy zarubezhnik* [Military foreigner], 6 (1972).

On the Question of the Origin of the Theory of Successive Offensive Operations (1921–29)[1]

COLONEL R. SAVUSHKIN,
CANDIDATE OF HISTORICAL SCIENCES

In our country, the theory of successive offensive operations began its development in the 1920s on the basis of generalization of experience of the First World War and the Civil War. It is natural that Soviet military theorists focused particular attention on investigating events closest to them, that is, Civil War events. The offensive of Western Front forces against the White Poles, from positions along the Berezina River to the ultimate line along the Vistula River (July–August 1920), as the most typical example of successive operations, developed in the following way (see Sketch 1).

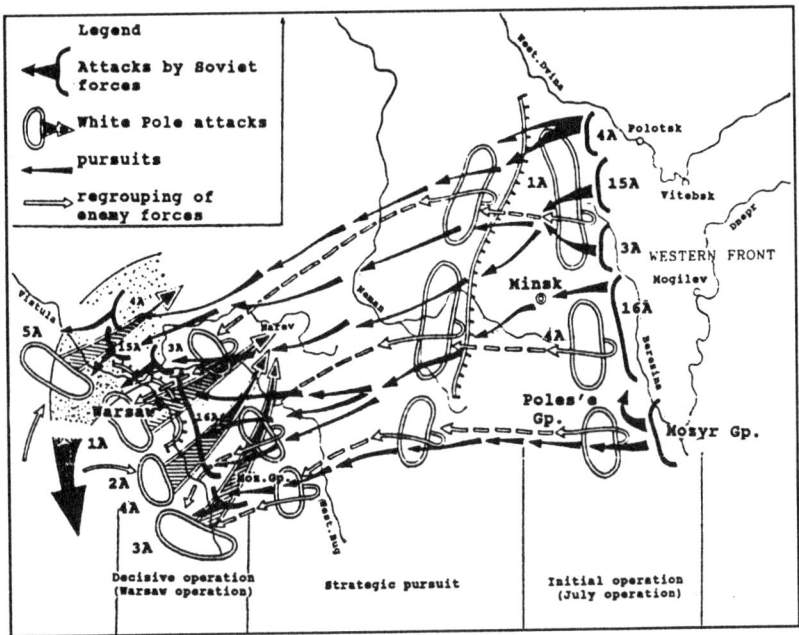

Sketch 1.
Successive operations during the 1920 Soviet–Polish War

From 4–7 July 1920, the Western Front began the July operation and inflicted a serious defeat on the enemy. Under the blows of Soviet forces, the White Poles were compelled to withdraw. Western Front armies undertook pursuit, which continued for around a month. During this, the enemy attempted to delay Soviet forces along two lines (the first – along the Neman and Shara Rivers, the second – along the Narev and Western Bug Rivers), where the attackers had to conduct bitter engagements. Finally, on 9 August Western Front forces reached the Mlava, Sedl'tse, Lyubartuv line, and from here began a "decisive offensive" (Battle on the Vistula). However, the Polish command was able to strengthen its forces and go over to a counter-offensive. Weakened in preceding battles and without reserves, Western Front forces were compelled to withdraw to the Lipsk, Svisloch' line, 15 kilometers east of Brest-Litovsk, where the Polish Army's further advance was halted.[2]

In analyzing these events in his work *Pokhod za Vislu* [Campaign for the Vistula] (1923), M. N. Tukhachevsky concluded that it is impossible to defeat a prepared enemy army "by one blow," and that it is necessary to resolve this task *gradually* by conducting a series of successive offensive operations. He wrote that only "a series of successively conducted offensive operations joined by continuous pursuit can replace that destructive engagement which was the best type of encounter in former armies. . ."[3] These ideas were comprehensively developed in his book, *Voprosy vysshego komandovaniya* [Questions of Higher Command],[4] and in the collective work, *Armeyskaya operatsiya* [The Army Operation].[5]

Subsequently, questions concerning successive operations were elucidated upon in V. K. Triandafillov's work, *Razmakh operatsiy sovremennykh armiy* [The Scope of Operations of Modern Armies].

> The center of gravity of a series of successive operations lies not in their commencement, but in their conclusion. The theory of a series of successive operations envisions a decisive encounter with the entirety of the enemy's main forces (and this is entirely correct) at the end or before the very end of the operation.[6]

Therefore, according to the author, efforts in successive operations should not diminish, but rather increase.

N. N. Movchin made a significant contribution to the theory of successive offensive operations. In his work, *Posledovatel'nyye operatsii po opytu Marny i Visly* [Successive Operations According to the Marne and Vistula Experience], he indicated that military operations of the German armies' right wing at the beginning of the First World War developed not in the form of one gigantic encirclement operation as was planned (Sketch 2), but in a series of successive operations: border engagement (operation); strategic pursuit, during which combat operations were conducted to destroy with-

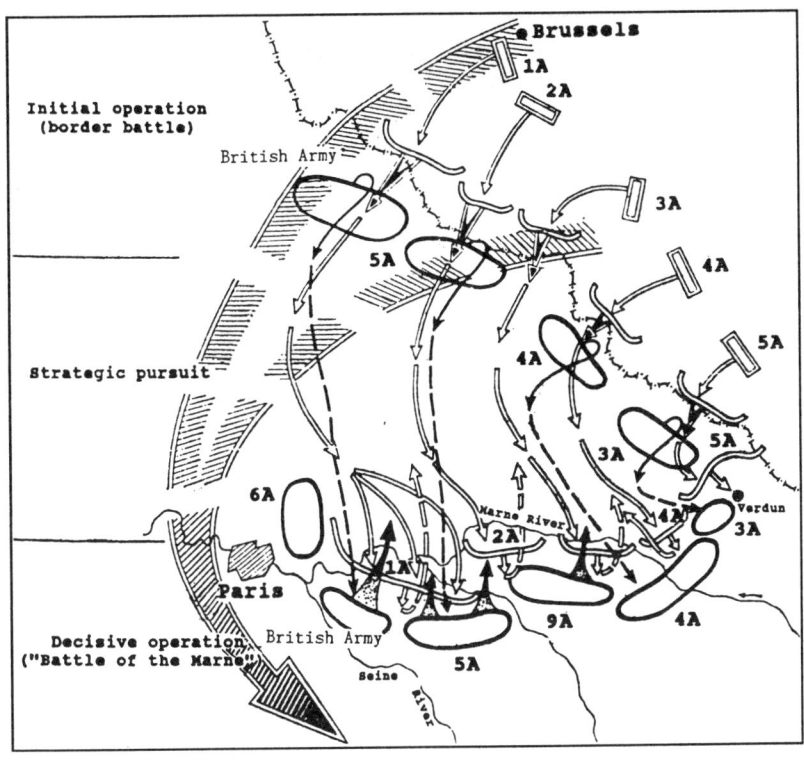

Sketch 2.
Successive offensive operations of the German Army in the Western Theater
during the 1914 campaign

drawing forces on intermediate lines; the Marne engagement (operation), during which the German command's plans were frustrated by the surprise operations of the Anglo-French forces.

On the basis of completed research, N. N. Movchin reached a conclusion concerning "the impossibility under modern conditions of destroying an entire enemy army in one operation."[7] He was the first military theorist to propose the subdivision of successive operations into the *initial operation, pursuit operation, and decisive operation.*[8]

An important role in perfecting the theory of successive operations was played by the work, *Budushchaya voyna* [Future War], by the IV Directorate of the *RKKA* Staff, in whose development M. N. Tukhachevsky, Ya. K. Berzin, A. N. Nikonov, and Ya. M. Zhigur participated. Together with other issues, their work revealed the nature of successive operations, missions resolved during their conduct, and conditions for achieving ultimate aims. The work pointed out that

To destroy enemy forces which, in the presence of sufficient materiel and human resources and a sufficient depth of the theater of military operation, will continually be nourished and replenished from the depth of the country, it is necessary to conduct a series of offensive operations, appropriately assigned with respect to time and space. By means of the combination of operations, it is necessary to force the enemy to exhaust his materiel and human resources or compel the enemy to accept battle for his main mass of troops under conditions unfavorable for him, and then to liquidate them.[9]

The capstone of the development of the theory of successive offensive operations in the 1920s was, in essence, Triandafillov's book, *Kharakter operatsiy sovremennykh armiy* [The Nature of the Operations of Modern Armies] (1929), which had several editions,[10] and A. K. Kolenkovsky's work, *O nastupatel'noy operatsii armii, vkhodyashchey v sostav fronta* [On the Offensive Operation of an Army as Part of a *Front*] (1929). Thus, *the theory of successive offensive operations was the fruit of many Soviet military theorists' collective work.* It was engendered by objective conditions and based on historical experience.

In a series of successive front offensive operations, the initial operation occupies a special place, since everything which follows depends on its success (Sketch 3). During this operation, an attack has to be delivered against the enemy's main grouping, forcing him to abandon the occupied defensive sector and withdraw to rear positions to regroup forces and replenish them with reserves.

The impossibility of completely defeating the enemy grouping in the initial operation was explained, above all, by the attacker's lack of long-range suppression means and by the deep enemy offensive operational formation. According to foreign opinions in the 1920s, first-echelon divisions could occupy a defense four–six kilometers deep. Corps reserves were deployed eight–ten kilometers from the forward edge of the defense. Army reserves were located at 20–35 kilometers, part of the army reserves in vehicles were located at 80–100 kilometers, and army group reserves were even further from the forward edge. Triandafillov wrote:

Simultaneously with engagement in battle, the defender adopts a whole series of measures to reinforce forces being attacked. First the immediate reserves . . . arrive. If the focus of events is located on an axis which is important from the point of view of conducting the war (and the operation), then deeper reserves and even forces taken from other *fronts* (or parts of *fronts*) arrive. If the reserves begin to arrive quickly and in sufficient quantity, then the operation can enter a new phase and last for a very long time.[11]

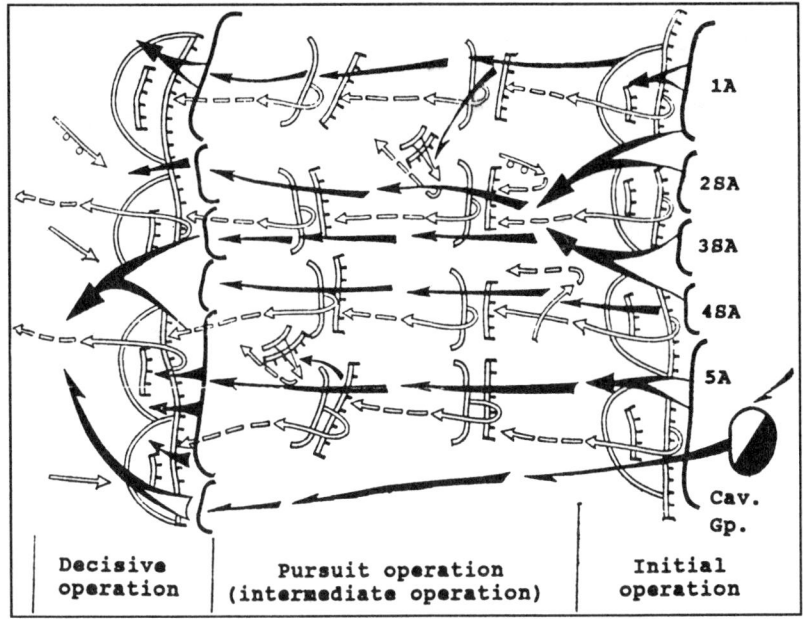

1A

2 SA

3 SA

4 SA

5A

Cav.
Gp.

| Decisive operation | Pursuit operation (intermediate operation) | Initial operation |

Sketch 3.
Successive operations of a *front* according to 1920s' views

Under more favorable conditions, it is considered possible to penetrate the enemy's defensive front and create a threat to his flank and rear. However, lack of means for implementing decisive maneuver at high tempos and the low mobility of advancing forces made it impossible to preempt the enemy from reaching withdrawal routes and prevent him slipping out from under the attack. All this made it necessary to conduct successive operations.

The purpose of pursuit operations was to inflict a subsequent partial attack on the enemy and create conditions which would make it difficult for him to realize his attempts, by means of mobile (maneuver) defense, to gain time, regroup forces, bring up his reserves, and create a new defensive front. For the attacker, the principal essence of these operations was continuous pursuit while simultaneously preparing a decisive operation.

A *decisive operation* occurred, on the one hand, as a result of the withdrawing forces' desire not to lose principal vital centers, thus depriving themselves of the possibility of further combat, and, on the other hand, as a result of the pursuers' attempt to reach the enemy army and, by seizing those centers, deprive him of the capability of continuing the conflict. The purpose and main content of the decisive operation was the completion of the defeat of enemy armed forces on a given axis, the enemy being unsuccessful in regrouping and reinforcing by means of reserves, or being forced to halt the withdrawal because of a lack of available space (sufficient depth of territory).

It was proposed that, in practice, the missions of the so-called "pursuit" could not be resolved in a single operation. After the initial operation there had to follow not one but several "intermediate operations," leading forces to the decisive operation.

The principal indices of *front* successive operations are as follows (compiled on the basis of numerical data in Triandafillov, *Nature of the Operations of Modern Armies*, pp. 148, 157, 171, 184, 185–7, etc.):

Nature of Operation	Depth (km)	Tempo (km/day)	Duration (days)
Initial	30–50	5–6	5–6
Intermediate	150–200	8–10	18–20
Decisive	30–50	6–7	5–6
Average Sum	250	6–7	30

On average, the offensive sector of a *front* consisting of five armies can be up to 400 kilometers at the initial position; the depth of operation is 250 kilometers, the average tempo is six–seven kilometers, and duration is 28–32 days.

The following were considered the most typical means for resolving missions in an initial and decisive *front* operation: penetration with a subsequent avalanche-type offensive by main forces on the side of the denuded flank and rear of the enemy's principal grouping; penetration with subsequent frontal pressure and radial-type offensive, depending on the extent of penetration into enemy dispositions; and a "concentric operation" or encirclement operation.[12] The most effective method was considered the encirclement of the enemy, which, under favorable conditions, could lead to the destruction of a significant portion of his armed forces. However, such a method of combat action, in the opinion of the authors, required a much greater quantity of forces than a frontal offensive. Considering that the Red Army still did not have sufficient forces, the following conclusion was reached:

> Modern means and the organization of our western neighbors' armies, as well Red Army means, do not in any way assure success for such operations. Success for such operations, considering the present state of the armies, can only be haphazard.[13]

In developing operations using a frontal offensive, it was pointed out that they could ensure inflicting destruction on the enemy only under specific conditions. Moreover, Triandafillov stated the following in one of his works:

> Such a ram [that is, a frontal attack], even if it was on a properly

chosen operational axis, could not ensure great results at the tempo of development of combat operations which were characteristic of modern weapons. With such an attack, the enemy's main forces, if they considered battle under these conditions unfavorable, would always be able to evade battle and slip out from under the attack.[14]

Operational success is related to *proper selection of the main attack axis (or two attacks in an encirclement operation), massing of forces and means on the chosen axis, and operational formation of forces.* The main attack and resulting maneuver of attacking forces were to be executed along an axis which would ensure the arrival of sufficiently powerful attacking groupings at an enemy defensive area where an active threat would be created against his entire grouping's operational-strategic flank and rear, and his communications.

Judging by the works of Tukhachevsky and Triandafillov, the *front* operational formation was to consist of one echelon and a reserve. Shock armies and conventional armies were deployed in the first echelon.

Shock armies were to play a leading role in the *front* operation. They were designated to advance on the main attack axis (axes). They resolved problems of massing forces and means on the chosen axis. Therefore, each shock army was organized in such a way that within the framework of the *front* operation it could conduct a series of successive operations with its own forces.

It was anticipated that a shock army's offensive frontage would be around 50 kilometers, including a 25-kilometre main attack frontage.[15] An army operation's depth, according to the concepts at that time, could fluctuate within the limits of 25–30 kilometers up to 50 kilometers, with its duration being five–six days and its offensive tempo five–six kilometers per day.[16]

The theoretical tenets of successive *front* offensive operations were verified in 1928 at a command-staff war game prepared by the *RKKA* Chief of Staff V. K. Triandafillov. During the war game an initial operation was planned and the line of the decisive operation marked. There was no planning for a pursuit operation, because it was considered impossible to anticipate changes in the situation. The *front* executing the successive operations consisted of four armies. Railroad and automobile transport from the depth was given to the troops to strengthen the forces.[17]

The theory of successive offensive operations was a progressive one for its time. However, for its successful realization it was necessary to supply the Red Army with a sufficient quantity of combat and technical means. The authors of *Future War* considered the following among such means:

1. motorized rifle-machine gun units reinforced with fast-moving tanks and motorized artillery;
2. large cavalry units reinforced by armor (armored cars and fast-moving

tanks) and fire means, prepared to conduct dismounted and combined battle;

3. large air-assault units.

It was considered that, without the creation of the enumerated formations with special arms and organization, modern operations would not satisfy the prerequisites for decisive destruction of the enemy.[18]

Successful execution of the first five-year plan, in particular the plan for military development, made it possible to significantly increase the Soviet Armed Forces' military might. The Red Army received the means to suppress an enemy defense and his reserves and to prevent maneuver of forces and means to the penetration area. On this basis a new theory was created in the 1930s (1930–37) – the theory of deep battle and the deep offensive operation, which was the highest achievement of military art during those years.

In the new theory, developed on a higher technological base, three types of operations (initial, pursuit, and decisive) came together into a single offensive operation, whose aim was already not the *gradual* annihilation of a large enemy grouping by several operational efforts, but rather its *complete defeat* during a single operation. In future war, as Triandafillov wrote, "initial and subsequent operations would combine into a single, continuous, prolonged operation,"[19] that is, successive operations extended in time and space, in which only small parts were "bitten off" the enemy grouping and destroyed, formed a new operation-strategic amalgam – a single, destructive operation which pulverized the enemy grouping on a lesser expanse and in a shorter time than was required by a series of successive operations.

Thus, the idea of a complete defeat of a large enemy grouping in a single *front* operation was embodied in the 1930s in the theory of the deep offensive operation. Its primary tenets were realized during offensive operations by *front* and army forces during the Great Patriotic War.

NOTES

1. R. Savushkin, "K voprosu o zarozhdenii teorii posledovatel'nykh nastupatel'nykh operatsiy," *Voyenno-istoricheskiy zhurnal* [Military-historical journal], 5 (May, 1983), pp. 12–20.
2. M. N. Tukhachevsky, *Izbrannyye proizvedeniya* [Selected works], Vol. 1 (Moscow: 1964) p. 167.
3. Ibid., p. 142.
4. Ibid., pp. 185–97.
5. M. N. Tukhachevsky, N. Ye. Varfolomeyev, and Ye. A. Shilovsky, *Armeyskaya operatsiya. Rabota komandovaniya i polevogo upravleniya* [The army operation. Work of command and field control]. Under the editorship of M. N. Tukhachevsky (Voyenizdat, 1926).
6. V. Triandafillov, *Razmakh operatsiy sovremennykh armiy* [The scope of operations of modern armies] (Voyenizdat, 1926), p. 23.

7. N. Movchin, *Posledovatel'nyye operatsii po opytu Marny i Visly* [Successive operations according to the Marne and Vistula experience] (Moscow–Leningrad: Gosizdat, military literature section, 1928), p. 40.

8. Ibid., p. 118.

9. *TsGASA* [Central Archives of the Soviet Army], f. 33988, op. 2, d. 688, pp. 16–17.

10. V. K. Triandafillov perished in the summer of 1931 in an air crash. All subsequent editions of his book were patterned on the 1929 edition.

11. V. Triandafillov, *Kharakter operatsiy sovremennykh armiy* [The nature of the operations of modern armies] (Gosvoyenizdat: 1932, p. 149).

12. Tukhachevsky, Varfolomeyev, Shilovsky, pp. 59, 70.

13. Central Archives of the Soviet Army, f. 33988, op. 2, d. 688, p. 18.

14. Triandafillov, *Nature of the Operations*, p. 205.

15. Ibid., p. 140.

16. Ibid., pp. 147–8, 288.

17. Central Archive of the Soviet Army, f. 37977, op. 3, d. 209, pp. 1–20.

18. Ibid., f. 33988, op. 2, d. 688, pp. 18–19.

19. Triandafillov, *Nature of the Operations*, p. 178.

Simultaneous Action against the Entire Depth of the Enemy's Operational Structure – Leading Trends in the Development of the Theory of Operational Art

MAJOR GENERAL P. G. SKACHKO,
DOCTOR OF MILITARY SCIENCES, PROFESSOR[1]

Analysis of the experience of the Second World War and local wars, and the development of military affairs at present demonstrate that the principle of *simultaneous action against the enemy to the entire depth of his formation and against objectives in the deep rear* is one of the most important in military art. With the appearance of nuclear and other new combat means, its role in achieving success under modern conditions has grown immeasurably.

Before the appearance of nuclear weapons, in strategy a desire to pressure strategic reserves and deep rear objectives by aviation forces was noted on the part of the opposing sides. Available weapons then, however, were imperfect, which sharply reduced the effectiveness of air strikes. This did not improve, even with the creation of V-1 and V-2 rockets, employed by the Wehrmacht command in the Second World War.

Under new conditions, strategic nuclear forces are capable of hitting objects with high precision at practically any depth, which radically changes the nature of armed conflict. The simultaneous action of these means against military and military-economic objectives deployed in the deep rear of the warring sides will, from the very commencement, turn their territory into an arena of dynamic and destructive actions.

This principle is also acquiring decisive significance in operational art and tactics. As long-range nuclear and fire weapons and radio-electronics improve, its role increases even more. It evolved further in the theory of deep operation (battle), developed by Soviet theorists in the 1930s. At the contemporary stage, such operations are called "three dimensional" in our military press, while in the armies of the US and other NATO countries these are called "air-land" and "deep attack."

We will examine the evolution of the content of this principle in operational art and trends in the development of deep attack forces and means. This principle came into being in ancient times. Talented military leaders were then striving to employ mobile forces skillfully to deliver surprise deep attacks against the flank and rear of the enemy's main groupings, pursue his routed forces, and capture crossings, road junctions, and other important objectives on their routes of withdrawal. In wars of the eighteenth and nineteenth centuries, various formations in the form of "flying" (mobile) corps (*corps volants*) or special (forward) detachments, whose basis consisted of cavalry units, were widely used for this purpose. The depth of their combat actions and their separation from the main forces reached 70–100 kilometers and more in the Russian Army.

A general developmental trend of the theory and practice of simultaneous actions against the enemy to great depth during past military campaigns was employing mobile forces as the most effective deep attack means and increasing their mobility, the volume of their assigned combat missions, and their depth of operations.

In the era of mass armies, use of mobile forces acquired even greater significance. During the First World War and the Civil War, cavalry groups were employed successfully as deep attack means. Their composition was varied: in an army, a cavalry division was usually assigned as a mobile group; in a *front*, a cavalry army or corps played this role. Often cavalry formations included newly formed means for deep actions, namely armored detachments. Aviation detachments dynamically operated in the rear. The main tasks of mobile forces usually consisted of conducting decisive raids against enemy rear areas, routing his reserves and headquarters, and capturing crossings, centers of communication, etc.

In the 1930s, in connection with the motorization and mechanization of armies and the appearance of shock aviation and air-assault forces, the principle of simultaneous action against the enemy to the entire depth of his formation and rear objectives were embodied in the Soviet theory of the deep operation. This examined mobile groups, aviation, and air assaults as effective deep attack means, designated to penetrate into the enemy's rear area, disrupt operational stability, and rout opposing groupings. A decisive role was given to tank, mechanized, and cavalry formations and large formations. The creation of echelons for exploiting success in *fronts* and armies – mobile groups [MG], which acquired the name of cavalry-mechanized groups [KMG], and which became integral elements of *front* and army operational formations – were envisioned on this basis. They received the following missions: pursuit of a withdrawing enemy, exploitation of tactical success into operational success, rout of deep reserves, disruption of troop control, and seizure of important lines and objectives, whose capture ensured the most rapid achievement of initial operational aims and creation of favorable conditions to conduct a subsequent operation. During commitment of the mobile group (cavalry-mechanized group) into an engagement, the dropping (landing) of air-assault forces was envisioned, which were to cooperate with them and with aviation, and resolve missions for seizing important operational objectives in the enemy rear (airfields, road junctions, crossings across large water obstacles), and pinning down or destroying enemy reserves. Thus, it was envisioned to penetrate quickly into the enemy's operational depth, using the combined efforts of mobile groups, aviation, and air-assault forces, and to act simultaneously against him from the front and the rear. The mobile group (cavalry-mechanized group) would be introduced into an engagement after first-echelon forces had penetrated the tactical defense zone, or before its penetration with their participation.

During the Great Patriotic War, the Soviet Army acquired the richest experience with simultaneous action throughout the entire operational depth, especially by means of mobile forces. The first mobile groups, formed in some armies during the Moscow counteroffensive, were of mixed composition, and included tank, mechanized, and cavalry formations. In the Battle of Stalingrad, tank, mechanized, and cavalry corps were employed as mobile groups, and, beginning with the 1943 Kursk counteroffensive, tank armies of homogeneous composition were used as *front* mobile groups, and tank and mechanized corps (cavalry-mechanized groups) were employed in armies. The presence of mobile groups in *fronts* and armies operating on important axes increased immeasurably force capabilities to convert tactical success into operational success rapidly. Having entered the engagement, they quickly penetrated into the depth, considerably separated from first-echelon forces; conducting raid actions, they disrupted the enemy defense's operational and strategic stability, which made it possible to achieve operational victory quickly.

Historical experience demonstrates that the might, range, and quantity of deep action means has been steadily growing. During each preceding war means have appeared which were subsequently used on a larger scale. Long-range artillery and cavalry were principal examples of this in the First World War and the Civil War. However, at that time aviation and armored forces had already come into being, as had air-assault forces in the interwar period. During the Second World War, the principal deep attack means were armored forces, aviation, and air-assault forces. Cavalry had lost its former role, having been superseded by tank armies and tank and mechanized corps. The strike force of bomber and ground-attack aviation increased steadily, as did that of air-assault forces. At the same time, during the Second World War, a fundamentally new deep action means began to appear: ballistic rockets (V-1 and V-2). However, their technical characteristics and combat capabilities were inadequate to have a cardinal effect on the results of armed conflict.

In the postwar period, as scientific-technical progress evolved in the most developed NATO countries, the combat capabilities of shock aviation, air-assault forces, and long-range artillery steadily increased. There arose fundamentally new weapons: nuclear weapons and strategic, operational, and tactical rockets. At the same time the process of armoring and mechanizing ground forces took place, and their shock and fire power, maneuverability, and capabilities increased sharply. Air-assault formations and combat helicopters appeared. In addition, the process of creating high-precision weapons, above all reconnaissance-strike (recce-strike) and reconnaissance-fire (recce-fire) complexes, was initiated. Recce-strike and recce-fire complexes, rocket forces, and aviation will be the most important among these.

The development of new combat means, especially high-precision weapons, and the complete outfitting of forces with them have resulted in changes in the views of the military leadership of the US and its NATO allies on the possible nature of modern war. The concept of "operational art" was introduced into US military art. Its basis is the concept of the "air-land operation (battle)," while in the armies of the NATO bloc the "deeply echeloned attack" is its variation. It should be kept in mind that both these concepts are viewed not as a form of combat action but as a method for employing various ground and air force forces and means in corps, army, and army group operations.

The essence of these concepts consists of the simultaneous delivery of massed strikes not only against an opposing grouping's first-echelon forces, but also against the most important rear objectives (second echelons, reserves, rocket force positions, artillery, airfields, command posts, communication centers, large warehouses, lines of communication, etc.) to the entire depth of a large formation's operational formation. Plans are to attack deep objectives using various forces, their actions strictly coordinated with respect to aim, place, and time, in accordance with the combat actions of forces attacking from the front to rout the enemy quickly. Primary attention is given to surprise shifts to the offensive and seizure of the initiative in actions.

Essentially, the ideas of our prewar theory of the deep operation are used fully in the concept of the air-land operation, but they are implemented with the help of contemporary combat means. The depth of a simultaneous strike against objectives can reach 15 kilometers using brigade means, 70 kilometers using division means, 150 kilometers using army corps means, and up to 500 kilometers and more using army and army group means. During the rout of force groupings, special attention is given to fighting against second echelons, reserves, and other forces for exploiting success, and disorganizing troop and weapons control.

According to NATO exercise experience, the army group can employ the following deep action means: in the tactical zone – long-range artillery, rocket systems for salvo fire, and helicopters; in the operational zone –

tactical aviation, rocket forces, air-assault and airborne forces, and rapid deployment forces; in the strategic zone – ground- and naval-based rockets, aviation, and cruise missiles. The principal aim of these deep attack forces is to deliver powerful fire strikes against all the most important elements of the other side's operational formation and swiftly use their results to reinforce success by employing airborne (air-assault) units and the most mobile ground force units. Here, priority is given, above all, to rocket and air echelon forces: aviation, airborne forces, and air-assault formations and units.

We will examine the views of foreign military theorists on the employment of these mobile forces, whose principal movement means will be contemporary and future air vehicles.

Analysis of armored forces employment in deep actions against the enemy during the Second World War demonstrates that, having greater mobility than the primary force mass, advancing at that time in dismounted formation, with appropriate support they quickly distanced themselves from first-echelon formations of combined-arms large formations and conducted daring, bold, and effective raids in the rear, shattering the defense's operational stability.

However, the uniform postwar motorization of a majority of countries' armies eradicated the difference in mobility between armored (tank) forces and motorized infantry. Therefore, according to statements by many foreign military theorists, a certain crisis appeared in the matter of practical implementation of the principle of simultaneous action against the enemy. A gap was formed between the sharply increased capabilities of nuclear and fire strike means and the relatively poor mobility of those forces called upon to consolidate quickly the results of nuclear and fire strikes. The mobility of armored (mechanized) formations and units came into conflict with the sharply increased rapid action, depth, and power of nuclear and fire strike means. In this connection, it was thought that forces designated for deep action against the enemy and the timely exploitation of deep nuclear and fire strike results had to have a fundamentally different technical base for movement in space and an appropriate organizational structure, which would ensure them greater mobility relative to currently existing ground forces formations. Air assets (helicopters, airplanes, flying platforms, and other apparatus using the principle of the air cushion) were recognized as a suitable base for them.

It is considered that such mobile forces could include primarily both air-mobile units and highly mobile formations moving on the ground. Then, as new air transport means are created they will become fully air-mobile and comprise the attacking forces' air echelon. Because the difference in tempos of action of this echelon, in comparison with the ground echelon, will be more substantive, such air-mobile units and formations will be able to deliver simultaneous strikes much faster against the entire depth of the enemy's operational formation. It is assumed that their tempos of advance will exceed the advance of main forces by two or three times and more. Calculations show that if ground forces, according to American regulations, are able to advance during battle only up to 30–40 kilometers a day, air-mobile forces can advance up to 90–120 kilometers and more.

To implement accepted concepts in NATO armies for increasing ground force mobility, especially that of formations designated for actions in the operational depth, army aviation, including various types of helicopters and airplanes, has been created. For example, the US has airborne and air-assault divisions. Mobile forces have been created in NATO, including ground and air force subunits. Organizationally they consist of a headquarters and seven reinforced battalions allocated from the composition of the armies of the US, Britain, the Federal Republic of Germany, Belgium, Italy, Luxembourg, and Canada. Battalions are manned in accordance with accepted TO&Es for mobile forces, and each have three parachute (infantry, mountain-infantry) companies, a support company, and an artillery battery. Some have attached engineer and communications subunits, army aviation, and rear support. In addition, in a number of bloc armies battalions, regiments, and brigades of antitank helicopters and other ground force subunits and units, equipped with various helicopters, have appeared. A clearly expressed trend is manifest here: to have highly mobile forces on a fundamentally new base, that is, flying vehicles.

Analysis of combat capabilities, calculations, and experience demonstrates that air-mobile forces can be employed successfully in all types of combat actions, but most effectively in the offensive. Their advantage over ground forces consists of the fact that, with the help of helicopters, they are able to overcome easily almost any natural obstacles and defensive positions by air or go around the enemy from the flanks and rear. They can begin an offensive from separate, widely scattered regions, join up on the flight route or in the region of the objects of attack, and then disperse before strikes are delivered against them. A characteristic feature of air-mobile units and the basis for their success in battle is their ability to transfer efforts and fire swiftly from one target to another and deliver strikes from the air and on land against enemy fire means, command posts, and rear objectives. It is thought that they will be widely used to conduct deep raids into the rear to disrupt the operational stability of the defense. High mobility and fire power, combined with effective air reconnaissance, are a specific feature of their actions, which makes it possible for them to approach the enemy swiftly, detect and destroy his objectives quickly, and implement extensive air maneuver. The principal factors which determine their success in battle are excellently operating deep reconnaissance (super-receptivity), separation from the ground and movement by air, high speed and maneuverability, and swift attack and impact. Their great fire power and effectiveness are called upon to compensate for the relatively limited number of such groupings.

In the American press the idea has been expressed that it is sufficient to have one corps-type formation per army group to conduct such actions. Transported and supplied by air, this super-mobile element of the operational formation should have the ability to deliver swift and deep attacks against the most important objectives in the depth of the defense in operational co-operation with ground forces.

Foreign military theorists observe that the basis for creating such formations already exists. In their opinion, the task now consists of creating a wider family of flying vehicles. As distinct from airborne forces, air-mobile forces must have secondary mobility. This means that their mobile groupings operating in the enemy's deep rear must have the ability to deliver successive attacks against many objectives, using their organic means for air movement for battlefield maneuver and fire power against the enemy. These can be various types of flying vehicles – for air transport of combat units and their air support, for air cover, and for rear service.

Three variants for delivering personnel to the combat region have been examined in the Western press. The first is to equip each soldier with a flying vehicle; the second is to have from a group (squad) to a platoon of soldiers in one flying vehicle; the third envisions the creation of large flying vehicles which can hold large groups of men, combat equipment, and weapons. Here, preference is given to the second variant. Taking into account the probability of heavy losses of personnel in the third type of vehicle, it is recommended that these be used to transport materiel. It suggests dropping cargoes to regions of troop deployment using parachutes or delivering them in adjustable containers with slow vertical drop, reminiscent of the fall of maple leaves; landings using aircraft with shortened take-off and landing are another method.

Thus, the general trend in the development of air-mobile forces as a deep action means is substantiated not only theoretically. Practical work is being done to create a technical base for them: flying platforms, apparatus using the air cushion principle, and others. Army aviation is being supplemented by the latest types of combat and transport-combat helicopters. Their fire and shock power, radius of action, flight altitude, and cargo capacity are increasing.

As for *tactics of actions*, abroad it is considered, for example, that primarily mobile forces will conduct the offensive in combined fashion: a specific portion of them will begin to move by air on low-flying vehicles, "jumping" across artificial and natural obstacles to deliver sudden attacks, together with their remaining portion (advancing on land), against important objectives; destroy them; and complete the maneuver to the next objectives. With the development of army aviation, all primary combat units, including tank units, will arrive by air, using flying vehicles, at the region of the objectives being attacked.

Thus, simultaneous action against the entire depth of the defense formation is becoming a leading trend in the development of combined-arms battles and operations as well. It will be implemented in operations by all forces and means, above all by air-mobile forces, which have a fundamentally new base of movement. Essentially it is a matter of a new nature of combat actions. Enemy forces are dismembered in the depth, second echelons and reserves are isolated and destroyed, and blows are delivered against other important objectives by precisely coordinated fire strikes of all means and first-echelon formation actions from the front simultaneously with those of air-mobile forces in the enemy rear; this ensures a high tempo for conducting the operation. Closely cooperating with the air forces, air-mobile forces, including airborne (amphibious) forces and other forces and means, can disrupt the enemy's troop and weapons control system, create hotbeds of fighting in his rear, and disrupt the defense's operational stability, thereby in every way assisting first-echelon formations to accomplish their assigned missions successfully.

Analysis of the above demonstrates that the basis for development of deep action means is an increase in their range, fire power, and air mobility. Thus, if during the last war the depth of their actions was up to 20 kilometers for artillery, up to 200–250 kilometers for aviation, and up to 80–100 kilometers for penetration of mobile groups into the enemy defense, then under contemporary conditions the depth will increase considerably and reach up to 30–40 kilometers for artillery, up to 1,000 and more kilometers for aviation, 150–700 kilometers and more for tactical and operational-tactical rockets, up to 500 kilometers for air-based cruise missiles, and 150–200 kilometers and more from the line of combat contact for air-mobile forces.

During the last war, one of the important principles of employing deep action means against the enemy, especially mobile forces, was using them on the main attack axis to the entire depth of the offensive operation. This tenet will undoubtedly be retained in future operations as well. However, under new conditions it will be necessary to resolve a number of problems of their operational, tactical, and rear support. Most urgent are questions of supplying materiel, repairing weapons and combat equipment, and evacuating the sick and wounded.

Maintenance of close cooperation of deep action means among themselves and with forces advancing from the front was one of the decisive factors for achieving success. The significance of its stability in our time is increasing in connection with the dynamic nature of operations, rapid changes in the operational situation, and unevenness in the advance of forces. All this requires more precise organization of cooperation and maintenance of its continuity, especially between forces operating in the enemy's rear and strike means.

One can expect with a great degree of certainty that operations in which all deep action means are widely used will bear a truly three-dimensional character and require the resolution of a whole series of new problems. It is necessary to work on their resolution now.

NOTE

1. P. G. Skachko, "Odnovremennoye vozdeystviye na vsyu glubinu operativnogo postroyeniya protivnika – vedushchaya tendentsiya v razvitii teorii operativnogo iskusstva," *Voyennaya mysl'* [Military thought], 7 (1985), pp. 18–24.

CHAPTER EIGHT

The Debate Over Defensiveness, 1987–91

By the end of 1985, a date which Soviet tactical specialist Lieutenant General V. K. Reznichenko identified as the end of the old and the beginning of a new period of military development, Soviet military theorists were facing a military dilemma which accompanied growing economic problems. The prospective quickening pace of combat, resulting from improved force mobility and the burgeoning lethality and accuracy of weaponry, called into question long-held assumptions regarding the nature of future ground combat. The Soviets still adhered to the general concept of the theater-strategic operation, and Soviet theoretical writings still evidenced an all-abiding faith in the offensive as the best guarantee of victory in future war. Central to that concept were the, by now, traditional aspects of deep battle and deep operations and the vehicle for operational maneuver, the OMG.

Major problems, however, plagued Soviet theorists. The first problem was that of adjusting operational concepts to address the battlefield presence of high-precision weaponry. The second was to counter Western concepts of deep battle. The initial Soviet solution to both problems was their near total abandonment of linear concepts of warfare. Soviet theorists advanced new concepts of non-linear war, identifiable down to the lowest tactical level, which were characterized by the adoption of new echelonment techniques, the formation and employment of tailored combined-arms forces, increased frequency of independent actions by operational and tactical forces, and a proliferation of air-assault forces (an air echelon) at every level of command.

As recently as 1987, the concept of (anti-nuclear) operational maneuver still provided a cornerstone for Soviet operational and tactical techniques designed to preempt, preclude, or inhibit enemy resort to nuclear warfare. At the same time, Soviet analysts had concluded that high-precision weapons essentially posed the same sort of threat to attacking forces as had tactical nuclear weapons, and that even greater emphasis on operational and tactical maneuver was also a partial remedy to countering enemy use of high-precision weaponry. To capitalize fully on the effects of maneuver, the Soviets believed that they had to reduce planning time and execute command and control more precisely. This required increased emphasis on the use of cybernetic tools, including automation of command and expanded reliance on tactical and operational calculations.

The Soviet concept of non-linear [*ochagovyy*] combat was the nucleus of a larger Soviet concept of land-air battle, evolved in 1988 in juxtaposition with the early U.S. concept of airland battle. The concept of non-linear war in no way conflicted with traditional Soviet operational concepts (deep operations) and represented but another stage in a long evolution from the 1930s. The 1988 article by Colonel V. I. Ul'yanov exemplified continued Soviet analysis of deep operations and reaffirmed its contemporary applicability.

Sharp changes, however, soon occurred, halting this evolution in its tracks. In all likelihood, these changes were prompted by the worsening Soviet economic and political situation and not by military necessity. Military-theoretical writings remained remarkably evolutionary and consistently offensive right up to 1987, when the Soviet political and military leadership announced a fundamental shift to a defensive military doctrine. Understandably, the General Staff journal, *Military Thought*, was the first to reflect altered military doctrine. Whereas, prior to 1987 the journal had consistently published two to four times as many articles on offensive themes as on defensive ones, in 1987 the ratio began shifting in the other direction. By 1990 defensive articles in the journal outnumbered offensive ones by a ratio of three to one. Other military journals soon followed suit.

The 1987 article by Colonel R. A. Savushkin commenced a reexamination of Soviet defensive thought in the interwar years, a trend which would culminate the following year in the full rehabilitation of A. Svechin, the predominant, but long-discredited defensive specialist of the 1920s. The January 1988 lead article in *Military Thought*, which appeared as an unsigned editorial, provided the rationale for defensive doctrine and explained its implications for military art. Colonel E. G. Korotchenko's subsequent article carefully knitted the principles of military and operational art into the fabric of defensiveness.

The less than full enthusiasm of most military theorists for this process surfaced from time to time as they attempted to accommodate older offensive and new defensive themes. Representative of this trend was Army General G. I. Salmanov's December 1988 article in *Military Thought*, which gently reminded readers that operational art and the nature of modern war did not change overnight, but that defensive doctrine was essentially a new political approach to the problem of war and global stability. That gentle warning was vividly underscored by Colonel General I. N. Rodionov's 1991 article, which, with other important writings, represented a reserved approach to the wisdom and feasibility of too much defensiveness. Finally, the preeminent Soviet tactician, Lieutenant General V. G. Reznichenko, presented readers with a balanced assessment of both offensive and defensive army operations, and Colonel A. N. Zakharov wrote a net assessment of the impact on recent technological changes on the nature of armed combat.

Beginning in 1991 with Rodionov's article, voices have been raised among the ranks of military analysts which question the wisdom and validity of too great a dependence on defensiveness and express concern that planners err on the side of prudence when attempting to define what future force satisfies the requirements of defensive sufficiency, first in a Soviet, and then in a CIS and Russian context.

The Evolution of Views on Defense in the Interwar Years

COLONEL R. A. SAVUSHKIN,
DOCTOR OF HISTORICAL SCIENCES[1]

During the period between the Civil War and the Great Patriotic War, serious attention was focused on questions concerning organizing and conducting the defense. Already during the 1920s the principle had been formulated that in future wars the necessity would arise on separate axes to go over to the defense and conduct *front* and army defensive operations on a wide front to economize forces for an attack on the decisive axis, gain time necessary to create groupings of forces and means for an offensive, hold space (regions, lines, roads), and disorganize the enemy offensive to transition subsequently to a counteroffensive. Views on defensive aims basically remained unchanged during the entire interwar period. However, under the influence of a number of factors, above all those connected with the Soviet Armed Forces' increased technical outfitting and the development of the probable enemy's military art, views on preparing and conducting the defense underwent significant changes.

In 1921–29, the idea was proposed to contain and exhaust the enemy by holding defensive zones and employing a maneuver defense. Such a defense was characterized by concentration of principal efforts in the first belt and deployment of relatively small reserves (corps, army, *front*) in others; containment and weakening of the attacker in the tactical zone by stubbornly holding positions (lines) and continuously intensifying efforts from the depth; consideration of the limited capabilities of defending forces, their inability to hold the positions being defended for an extended period, and the necessity of maintaining constant readiness to withdraw and slip out from under an enemy attack; extensive use of the principle of successive action of defending forces, echeloned with respect to depth, against attacking shock groups; and employment of a maneuver defense by surrendering space to wear the enemy out and gain time.

Handbooks and guides for command personnel of the Workers' and Peasants' Red Army, and field and combat regulations were aimed at ensuring that the defense would be stubborn and dynamic. Attention was focused on educating personnel in the spirit of a high degree of creativity and revolutionary steadfastness, independence, stability, and an unswerving confidence in the power of their weapons. It was envisioned to echelon the defense in depth, carefully conduct engineer preparation of the terrain, create in an army (*front*), in addition to a security belt, up to three or four defensive belts, and construct a system of fire, taking into account the maneuver nature of forthcoming actions. In a *front* (army) system of defense, each of the defensive belts had its own assignment.

The *security belt* (forward defense area) was designated mainly to force the enemy to deploy prematurely and focus his attack. Thanks to this, his power, intention, and flanks were revealed.[2]

The *first belt* (primary belt or belt of main resistance), in which a large formation's main forces were deployed, had the task of defeating and morally suppressing the attacker on the approaches to the belt of main resistance, and, in case of enemy penetration, of destroying him.[3]

The *second belt* ("rear" belt of the corps reserves) was the area for deployment of reserves and their support when conducting combat actions. *Rear lines*, on which army and *front* reserves were deployed, could be created behind this upon the decision of the higher command. If a troop withdrawal was necessary, they served as the basis for creating a new defense system.

"Intermediate belts" (positions), designated for regrouping during the defense, were to be created between defensive belts.[4]

The principal missions of *front* and army defensive operations were resolved in the tactical defense zone [*TZO*], that is, within bounds of the first and second belts. *Front* and army command operations were directed mainly toward the timely reinforcement of forces defending the tactical defense zone by committing reserves and regrouping from secondary axes. The rest of the time, *front* and army operations were a set of defensive battles of rifle corps. The width of a rifle corps defensive sector was 24–30 kilometers;[5] that of a three-corps army was 80–100 kilometers, and that of a *front* having three–four armies was up to 400 kilometers. Its overall depth, taking into account the deployment of army and *front* reserves, was around 100 kilometers, while the depth of an army defensive region was 20–35 kilometers.

The operational formation of a *front* and army in the defense was single echelon with an allocation of reserves. The *front* reserve consisted of rifle formations, while the army reserve included, in addition, "fire artillery means possessing great mobility in order to attach the necessary artillery density to the most dangerous sectors in a timely fashion."[6] Special attention was focused on the creation of an antitank defense system [*PTO*], which included preparation of antitank ditches, antitank mine fields, and appropriate preparation of river banks and ravines.[7] It was suggested using field artillery as a dynamic means against tanks. In order to make maneuver of reserves and force regroupings safe during a defensive operation, provision was made for protection of communication centers against enemy air raids using antiaircraft artillery and aviation means. As for the formation and functioning of the *front* and army air defense system, this issue had only begun to be worked out.

On the whole, in characterizing views on the preparation and conduct of defensive operations, one cannot fail to note that in the 1920s Soviet military theorists correctly took into consideration the probable force of an attacking enemy and the limited capabilities of our forces in the defense. Under these conditions, the principle of stubbornly holding defensive belts, combined with a maneuver defense, was singularly correct. On the operational and operational-tactical scales, the following issues were well developed: formation of the defense system (deployment and designation of belts, deployment and missions of forces, norms, etc.); preparation of the defensive operation (specification of the method for conducting defensive actions, detection of a dangerous axis, choice of the first defensive line, formation of troop and unit organisms for carrying out combat tasks and the system of fire, planning of counter-artillery preparation, organization of control and cooperation, etc.); and conduct of the defensive operation (use of reserves, organization of counterstrokes, parrying of penetration of the defense by regrouping forces on threatened axes, implementation of a planned withdrawal to rear lines, etc.). Questions of engineer preparation of the terrain were inadequately resolved. Antitank defense and air defense were in the formative stage.

From 1930 to 1938, the development of views on the defense was determined, to a significant extent, by the technical reequipment of the Soviet Army, development of the enemy's military art, the influence of the experience of conducting battles under positional conditions during the First World War and subsequent local wars, and Soviet military theory's development of the deep offensive operation, which made it possible to investigate defensive problems, carried out well ahead with regard to the enemy's development of means for enemy offensive actions.

The primary distinction between defense in the 1930s and defense in the 1920s was the successive implementation of the requirement for its insurmountability: *"The defense must be insurmountable for the enemy, however strong he may be on the given axis."*[8] It was thought that this could be achieved by troop steadfastness, self-sacrifice, and heroism, and by the use of new means and procedures for action against the enemy.

The basic idea of the defense consisted of a harmonious combination of stubborn resistance of forces of the holding [covering] echelon occupying the tactical defense zone with the delivery of powerful blows from the depth by specially created mobile force groupings. For this, according to the draft instructions for directing higher formations of the Workers' and Peasants' Red Army, planned for publication in 1935–36, the defense "must have a powerful shock echelon to attack an enemy weakened by penetration and to re-establish the position. The shock echelon includes cavalry, motor-mechanized forces, and rifle units";[9] aviation was to cooperate in these actions. Thus, the concept of continuous supply of replenishments (reserves) for the tactical defense zone, the basis for defense in the 1920s, was replaced by the idea of maximum exhaustion of the enemy, using available means of the holding (first) echelon and delivery of an annihilating counterstroke against the enemy grouping from the depth.

Implementation of developed views depended, to a great degree, on the ability of the defense to neutralize enemy measures directed at simultaneous suppression of the defense to its entire depth. An appropriate defensive formation, echeloning of forces, and engineer preparation of the terrain were recommended for this purpose.

A *front* (army) defense was divided into three basic zones with respect to depth: tactical, operational, and rear. In the absence of direct contact with the enemy in front of the tactical zone, an obstacle belt was created, defended by forward detachments.[10] On the eve of war this comprised the basis of the forward operational obstacle zone.

It was thought that the tactical defense zone was the most important defensive zone. First-echelon rifle corps, whose forces were to hit enemy infantry and tanks and exhaust his shock group without relying on the continuous arrival of replenishments, were deployed within its bounds.

The third belt – the army defensive line (army rear boundary) – was the basis of the *operational zone*; various army reserves, whose totality formed the shock echelon (group), control organs, materiel reserves, and army rear organs, were deployed here. During a defensive operation, forces and means located in this zone were to attack with such force against the enemy, that the enemy would have to abandon a further offensive.

The rear defensive belt (position), in which part of the army reserves and the main *front* reserves (shock group) were deployed, was prepared in the *rear zone*; behind this zone were heavy aviation airfields, organs of *front* and partial army control, and rear organs.[11]

The creation of "cut-off defensive belts ('cut offs') situated between the main belt and the rear line" was also envisioned.[12] Their task was to dismember the enemy shock group into units, isolate them from one another, attack them, and force them back to their staging area.

In addition to the holding and shock echelons, an aviation group and a rear defense group, designated for fighting against air assaults and mechanized units which had penetrated, were part of an army's operational formation.

The *front* operational formation was envisioned as a single echelon: all armies making up the holding echelon were formed up into a line. In addition, a *front* had small reserves and an aviation group.

The principal requirement in organizing a *front* (army) defense was the creation of strong antitank protection of primary centers to the entire depth. It was assumed that the line of primary fire repulsion against attacking tanks would run along the forward edge, while behind it would be the antitank defense belt, where the principal strike would be delivered against enemy tanks. In the depth would be the army antitank region in case of penetration by mechanized units to the deployment areas of the shock group and reserves.

In 1933 Volga Military District force exercises, the antitank defense of a large formation included actions of various forces and means relying on anti-tank regions, specifically maneuver (motorized) groups of small-caliber artillery and large-caliber machine guns, which implemented a "mobile anti-tank defense"; engineer and chemical subunits, which set up obstacles; and tank, aviation, artillery, and airborne units and formations, which delivered coordinated counterattacks.[13]

In the 1930s the organization of air defense began to receive significantly more attention than in the previous decade. In the projected instructions for directing higher formations of the Workers' and Peasants' Red Army it was allotted a special chapter. The aim assigned to air defense forces and their immediate rear was to protect personnel and combat means against enemy attack and air reconnaissance. Accordingly, the following concrete missions for air defense were also specified: to fight dynamically against enemy aviation, destroying his airplanes; to prevent enemy planes from reaching defended objectives; to thwart enemy execution of combat missions; and others. Among air defense means were antiaircraft and field artillery (adapted for firing against airplanes), fighter aviation, antiaircraft machine guns, barrage balloons, antiaircraft searchlights, sound locators, etc. It was assumed that all air defense means on the scale of an army defense region would be joined in the service of army air defense. National air defense forces protected deeper *front* and national rear objectives.

Tenets of the theory of *front* and army defensive operations were verified in district maneuvers and test exercises. Thus, in Ukrainian Military District maneuvers in 1934, the following were worked out: river defense; defense of a rifle formation under maneuver conditions; defense of a hastily occupied, unprepared portion; and organization of countermeasures, using operational reserve forces against an enemy corps which had penetrated. In the same year, the correctness and prospects for the idea of using a cavalry division in cooperation with artillery, tanks, and aviation as part of a shock group in repelling an enemy penetration of the defensive belt and eliminating the threat from landed enemy air-assault forces was confirmed in test exercises.

In 1939–41, defensive questions were worked out, proceeding from peculiarities in the nature of Fascist German force actions in the offensive. All tenets formulated in the 1930s were adjusted from this point of view. A number of important questions on preparing and conducting the defense were verified during battles on the Khalkhin-Gol River and in the Soviet–Finnish War. As a result, refinements were introduced into the defensive formation.

At a meeting of the higher leadership personnel of the Workers' and Peasants' Red Army, held by order of the Party Central Committee at the end of December 1940, a major fundamental discussion took place concerning basic directions in the development of military theory and on the increase in force combat capabilities. At the meeting it was noted that an army could defend in an 80–100-kilometer sector and have three defensive zones: the forward operational obstacle zone (with a depth of 25–50 kilometers), a tactical defense zone (20–30 kilometers), and an operational defense zone (20–30 kilometers).[14] The main zone of resistance, where *front* and army main forces were concentrated, was tactical, and consisted of three belts, including a security belt, and was defended by army first-echelon rifle corps. The operational zone, consisting of a maneuver zone and a rear army position, was occupied by army reserves and designated to fight against large mechanized forces which had penetrated the tactical zone. *Front* reserves, control organs, and rear organs were deployed in the rear zone.

In connection with the high level of technical outfitting of Fascist Germany's armed forces and the stake the Fascist command put on their stupefying tank and air strikes, much attention was given to increasing defense survivability. In prewar regulations, as well as in documents of the December 1940 meeting of Red Army leadership personnel, it was stressed that the defense had to be *anti-artillery*, capable of protecting personnel and fire means against strikes of massed artillery fire; *antitank*, capable of repelling massed enemy attacks on decisive axes, whose tank density reached as much as 100–150 per kilometer of front; and *antiaircraft*, capable of countering strong bomber and ground attack strikes by enemy aviation. The highest level of stubbornness, dynamism, decisiveness of actions, and a constant attempt by forces not only to repel strikes of an attacking enemy, but also to annihilate him, were considered guarantees of success.

The width of the defensive sectors of formations and large formations had scarcely changed; only its depth increased, as had the level of engineer preparation and materiel outfitting.

Wire obstacles, trenches, escarpments, barriers, antitank minefields, land mines, etc. were the basis of engineer preparation of the forward operational obstacle zone (forward defense area). Engineer preparation of the first zone was to include antitank barriers and engineer structures which protected forces against enemy artillery fire. The main efforts of engineer forces during preparation for a defensive operation and battle were concentrated on antitank preparation of the area between the first and second belts.

The *front* operational formation was envisioned, as in the 1930s, as a single echelon with allotment of various types of reserves; that of an army was a single echelon (rifle corps and separate divisions in line) with army reserves reinforced with antitank means of the Reserve of the Supreme High Command. Artillery-antitank reserves were created from the latter. If possible, tank units or formations were included in the reserve composition. The opinion was expressed that, together with the first echelon, a second echelon (two rifle divisions and one tank division) could be created. Opinions differed at the December 1940 meeting on the question of using motor-mechanized formations. Some thought that such formations should be at the disposal of the army commander; others that they should be in the hands of the *front* commander. It was suggested using cavalry to fight against air-assault forces. A large role was given to aviation groups. Fundamentally new in the operational formation was rejecting the subdivision of forces into holding [covering] and shock groups (echelons), since being assigned to contain the enemy and not destroy him led to psychologically undesirable effects.

The conduct of a strategic defense on the scale of an entire *front* of armed conflict was envisioned only during the initial period of war. It was suggested first repelling the aggressor's blow and then exhausting his shock groups in defensive operations, and only after this to go over to the counteroffensive. The necessity of withdrawing an entire strategic *front* was considered improbable; therefore, it was not worked out in detail.

The Great Patriotic War was a verification of the basic tenets of prewar views concerning preparing and conducting defensive operations. Some of them were not implemented or were subject to refinement and reworking, for example, the width of the defensive sector, the depth of the operational formation, and methods for shifting to the defense. Others (a very large number), such as the operational formation of forces and maneuver of forces and means, were developed further and firmly entered into the practice of armed conflict.

NOTES

1. R. A. Savushkin, "Evolyutsiya vzglyadov na oboronu v mezhvoyennyye gody," *Voyennaya mysl'* [Military thought], 1 (1987), pp. 37–42. This article continues the theme of the development of the defense, begun by Colonel B. P. Frolov in the June 1986 *Military Thought*.

2. *Boyevaya sluzhba pekhoty. Rukovodstvo dlya komandnogo sostava RKKA* [Infantry combat service. Manual for command personnel of the Workers' and Peasants' Red Army] (Moscow: Vyssheye voyennyy redsovet, 1924), pp. 120–1.

3. Ibid., p. 121.

4. A. Syromyatnikov, *Oborona* [The defense] (Moscow–Leningrad: Gosizdat/Otdel voyennoy literatury, 1928), pp. 15–16.

5. *Polevoy ustav RKKA (PU 29)* [Field regulations of the Workers' and Peasants' Red Army (PU 29)] (Moscow–Leningrad: Gosizdat/Otdel voyennoy literatury, 1931), p. 87.

6. N. Kapustin, *Operativnoye iskusstvo v pozitsionnoy voyne* [Operational art in a positional war] (Moscow–Leningrad: Gosizdat, 1927), p. 262.

7. V. K. Triandafillov, *Kharakter operatsiy sovremennykh armiy* [The nature of operations of modern armies], 2d ed. (Moscow: Gosvoyenizdat, 1932), p. 122.

8. *Vremmennyy Polevoy ustav RKKA (PU 36)* [Provisional field regulations of the Workers' and Peasants' Red Army (PU 36)] (Moscow: Gosvoyenizdat, 1937), p. 16.
9. Central State Archives of the Soviet Army, f. 37977, op. 3, d. 606, l. 170.
10. *Instruktsiya po glubokomu boyu. 1935* [Instructions for deep battle. 1935] (Moscow–Leningrad: Otdel izdatel'stva Narodnogo komissariata oborony Soyuza SSR, 1935), p. 29. *PU 36*, p. 134.
11. Central State Archives of the Soviet Army, f. 37977, op. 3, d. 604, l. 102.
12. Ibid., d. 660, l. 542.
13. Central Archives of the Soviet Army, f. 33988, op. 2, d. 702, ll. 63–4.
14. *Istoriya vtoroy mirovoy voyny 1939–1945* [History of the Second World War, 1939–1945], Vol. 3 (Moscow: Voyenizdat, 1974), p. 415.

The Defensive Nature of Soviet Military Doctrine and Troop (Force) Preparation[1]

The Soviet Armed Forces entered the new 1988 training year, the year of its glorious 70th anniversary, notable in many respects.

With respect to domestic policy, this will be the year of the XIX All-Union Conference of the CPSU, further development of *perestroyka* and its new stage, steady implementation of the party policy for accelerating socio-economic development of Soviet society, constructive and practical work in implementing the plan for the third year of the twelfth five-year plan, and execution of strategic missions planned by the XXVII Party Conference.

With respect to foreign policy, 1988 will be a year of even more dynamic struggle to strengthen peace and socialism, defuse international tension and prevent war, and curtail the arms race, with a subsequent reduction in the level of military confrontation. The historic treaty for the elimination of two classes of nuclear rockets, and important agreements adopted on other issues are opening a new period in the development of international relations and creating genuine prerequisites for reducing the level of the military threat.

In the plan for resolving missions directly confronting the Armed Forces, the upcoming year will be a year for practical realization of the tenets of Soviet military doctrine and the uniform military doctrine of the Warsaw Treaty Organization member-states, as well as their defensive orientation; it will be a year of their further qualitative improvement.

Contemporary Soviet military doctrine is a system of officially accepted, fundamental views on preventing war, military development, preparation of the country and the Armed Forces for repelling aggression, and methods of conducting armed struggle in the defense of socialism.

From this definition it ensues that Soviet military doctrine is directed not at preparing for war, but against it, at strengthening the foundations for international security. It originates from the inadmissibility of war and specifies a set of effective political and defensive measures directed toward preventing war and prohibiting an aggressor from unleashing it in the illusory hope of gaining victory through counting on any kind of advantages.

It should be emphasized that the position on preventing war, given in such a direct and unmistakable statement, is included for the first time in our doctrine's definition. Of course, formerly the military activities of the Soviet Union and other socialist countries envisioned a struggle against war. However, now this mission is not only in policy, but also in military doctrine. It advanced to the foreground and became the main, determining factor.

A most important feature of contemporary Soviet military doctrine is its particularly defensive nature. This characteristic has been further developed. It includes the defensive essence of the military-political tasks which the Soviet State has placed before itself in all its practical affairs – internal and foreign policies – and in the nature of military planning, military development, and Armed Forces training.

The defensive orientation of Soviet military doctrine and the military doctrine of all Warsaw Treaty Organization member-states stands out most clearly in the following key principles:

1. The Soviet Union and all Warsaw Treaty Organization member-states threaten no one and will never take the path of aggression. They have no territorial claims on any state, neither in Europe nor beyond its boundaries. They regard no state or nation as an enemy. On the contrary, they are ready to build relations with all countries on the basis of mutual consideration of interests, security, and peaceful coexistence.
2. The USSR and Warsaw Treaty Organization member-states will never, under any circumstances, be the first to initiate military actions against any state or alliance of states if they themselves are not the object of aggression. The Soviet Union will never be the first to employ nuclear weapons.
3. The USSR and Warsaw Treaty Organization member-states are strengthening their defense, conducting military development in strict accordance with the principle of military balance, and attempting to maintain military-strategic parity at the lowest possible level sufficient for defense. They are not striving for superiority, but will also not allow superiority over themselves.

These pivotal principles comprise the basis of our military doctrine. They are finding genuine incarnation in military practice, that is, in concrete Soviet Armed Forces development and training programs.

As is generally known, Soviet military doctrine has two aspects: political and military-technical.

The political aspect is the main one. It specifies the attitude toward problems of war in the nuclear age and the nature of military-political tasks for strengthening the defense of socialist states, ensuing from Lenin's understanding that "any revolution is worth something only if it can be defended."[2]

Its most important principle is the conclusion of the XXVII Party

Congress that, no matter how great the threat to peace created by policies of aggressive imperialistic circles, there is no fatal inevitability of a world war; it can be averted. Here, it is considered that in the age of nuclear weapons it is impossible to prevent war and ensure security only by military-technical means.

Political means are acquiring ever greater significance in resolving the given task. A reliable defense is also necessary against any possible external encroachment. As General Secretary of the Central Committee of the CPSU M. S. Gorbachev noted:

> While the danger of war continues and while social revanchism remains the fulcrum of the West's strategy and military programs, we will henceforth do everything necessary to maintain our defensive might at a level which excludes the military superiority of imperialism over socialism.[3]

The military-technical aspect of doctrine is subordinated to the political. It defines strictly military, organizational-technical, strategic, and military-economic measures for preventing war and repelling possible aggression; reveals the probable nature of war, if an aggressor attempts to unleash it on the USSR and other socialist countries; and establishes what armed forces are necessary for peacetime and for conducting war, how to prepare the country, the army, and the navy to repel aggression, and how to employ them. All this comprises the complex, fundamental issues, and correct response to them has great theoretical and practical significance.

A practical assessment of the nature of military danger and imperialism's military preparations plays an important role in their resolution. It is generally known that US and NATO military-political leadership, although it has been proven that it is impossible to win a nuclear war, nevertheless views the threat of its being unleashed as a practical instrument for achieving their military-political aims. The US does not yet intend to renounce its prospective military programs, and continues to develop and deploy qualitatively new strategic weapons systems. The treaty on mid-range and short-range rockets has still not been ratified, and ways of compensating for them are already being worked out.

Tactical nuclear means and conventional forces are being developed at breakneck speed by re-equipping them with new high-precision weapons systems, developing shock tactical aviation, and qualitatively strengthening naval forces.

A special place in the aggressive military plans of the US has been given to the militarization of space. Implementation of SDI has risen to the level of higher state policy. They are counting, on the one hand, on protecting their territory from a retaliatory strike using a "cosmic shield" – a multi-echeloned anti-rocket defense – and, on the other hand, on deploying space-based shock forces, which, in combination with offensive strategic means, would make it possible for the US to deliver a "disarming" nuclear strike with impunity against the Soviet Union and other Warsaw Treaty Organization states, or at least constantly threaten the use of such a strike.

The aggressive orientation of US and NATO military preparations and their military doctrines can be seen clearly in their basic instructional documents on developing the armed forces, in the strategic concepts of "direct confrontation" and "flexible response," and in the latest American and NATO operational-strategic concepts of "air-land operation (engagement)," "air-sea engagement," and "forward sea lines."

The daily activity of US and NATO armed forces are acquiring a threatening nature. Exercises and maneuvers, conducted annually in Europe, the Atlantic, and other strategically important regions, are becoming difficult to differentiate from real force deployments to conduct war.

From this the necessity follows for increasing the vigilance and readiness of the Soviet Armed Forces, and for constantly improving their training. When resolving this problem it is necessary to keep in mind that, in the presence of the defensive nature of Soviet military doctrine, the USSR Armed Forces proceed from the principle of retaliatory actions, and their development is conducted on the basis of balance and defensive sufficiency.

The composition, quality, and quantity of arms with which they are equipped is strictly commensurate with the level of military threat and are determined by the actual requirements necessary for reliable defense and repulsion of aggression. *It is in this that the main sense of the principle of defensive sufficiency lies.*

However, under conditions of a constant military threat, created by the military preparations of imperialism, defensive sufficiency cannot be treated unilaterally. Moreover, it would be a mistake to understand it as unilateral disarmament. Defensive sufficiency is closely associated with the principle of military balance. Its bounds are limited not by us, but by the practical actions of the US and NATO. To preclude the chance of being caught unawares, it is necessary to further maintain military-strategic parity and keep the Armed Forces manned and in such condition that they would be able to repel reliably any aggression.

The content of defensive sufficiency is precisely defined in the document accepted at the Berlin meeting of the Warsaw Treaty Organization's Political Consultative Committee: "The armed forces of socialist states are maintained in combat readiness sufficient to avoid being caught unawares; in case they are attacked, they will deliver annihilating repulsion to the aggressor."[4]

The defensive nature of Soviet military doctrine presents higher and stricter requirements *to all elements of combat readiness and Armed Forces training*; to the level of combat training of officer cadres, staffs, large formations, formations, and units; and to the organization and high level of discipline of army and navy personnel. This is understood. Ground and naval forces must be ready to repel aggression by conducting retaliatory defensive actions. However, this does not mean that they will only passively repel enemy attacks. If there is aggression against the USSR or its allies, they will immediately deliver annihilating retaliatory blows against the enemy and will act with maximum decisiveness and dynamism. Whatever kind of war an aggressor may unleash – nuclear or conventional – he will not escape retribution. This defines the general orientation of Soviet Armed Forces development and training in 1988.

Their training must be subordinated to the execution of decisions and requirements of the XXVII Congress of the CPSU and the latest Plenums of the party's Central Committee on strengthening defense in all ways, maintaining army and navy combat might and combat readiness at a level which will ensure war prevention and repulsion of imperialist aggression, and maintaining their ability, jointly with allied armies, to defend reliably the state interests and the security of the USSR and countries of the socialist commonwealth and to inflict annihilating repulsion against any aggression under any conditions at the beginning and during conduct of war.

The army and navy entered into the next practical stage of restructuring, during which, while strictly carrying out negotiated international agreements, their accelerated qualitative development and improvement would be carried out, and the requirements of military doctrine and its defensive orientation would be realized in practice.

While executing the tasks of the new training year, all army and navy personnel, especially the leading military cadres, must deeply learn the essence and concrete requirements of Soviet military doctrine and its most important principles, and understand how its implementation affects the resolution of all practical questions concerning the theory and practice of military affairs, military development, and operational, combat, and political training.

In connection with the defensive orientation of military doctrine, the significance of ground and naval force readiness to suppress possible military provocations from imperialism in peacetime, to act in an extreme situation, and to repel a possible enemy attack in various forms, especially with the delivery of a surprise strike, is growing. The resolution of this problem must be viewed in broader scope. Candidate Member of the Politburo of the Central Committee of the CPSU, Minister of Defense of the USSR, General of the Army D. T. Yazov stated:

> Distinct from any other field of activity, in combat readiness there are no secondary missions. There is nothing in it that can be postponed until tomorrow to be executed haphazardly. Any omission, mistake, or

error can turn into a large-scale failure and lead to the failure of a combat mission.[5]

At the center of attention of all commanders, staffs, and political organs must always be issues of intelligence, ensuring a prompt and organized transition of ground and naval forces from a peacetime to a wartime situation, and rapid deployment and preparation for successfully executing combat missions. It is important to improve constantly the combat readiness and preparation of on-call forces and means, constantly smooth out the entire system of carrying out a tour of duty and combat service, and work out methods of action for executing suddenly arising missions. Everyone must learn lessons from the conclusions reached by the Politburo of the Central Committee of the CPSU regarding violation of Soviet air space by a West German airplane.

High Armed Forces combat and mobilization readiness is ensured by their qualitative outfitting, constant technical readiness of weapons and combat equipment, presence and correct composition of necessary materiel reserves, high level of personnel combat training, and their discipline, political tempering, and high moral-psychological qualities. It must always be kept in mind that in the final analysis troop (force) readiness depends namely on men and how well they have mastered combat equipment and weapons.

There is no ultimate limit to the improvement of combat readiness. It cannot bear a provisional or seasonal character. The task consists of constantly intensifying, developing, and maintaining it at a level required under the concrete conditions of the situation.

The result of high combat troop (force) readiness should be the reliable, guaranteed execution of combat missions under any war conditions, including the most complex.

In view of the defensive nature of military doctrine, a new approach is necessary with respect to training forces for actions employing various types of weapons. There is no doubt that it would be premature and inadmissible to weaken our efforts in preparing troops (forces) for actions using nuclear weapons, inasmuch as imperialism not only does not intend to renounce them, but is constantly affirming its readiness to be the first to employ these weapons. Therefore, as before, *a very important task is to maintain constant troop (force) readiness to deliver retaliatory nuclear strikes against an aggressor, with unacceptable damage to him.* In preparing for such actions, we should view this as a method of preventing nuclear war.

At the same time, it is necessary to increase attention paid to preparing ground and naval forces to conduct combat actions in a conventional war with its new, more dangerous and complex forms, including under conditions of mass enemy employment of high-precision weapons, taking into account their possible premeditated destruction of atomic power stations and chemically dangerous enterprises. This too requires a high degree of skill, refined military expertise, and more detailed development of methods for executing each combat mission.

In view of military doctrine's defensive orientation, it is necessary to study all types of operations and combat actions. At the same time, it is necessary to focus great attention, first and foremost, on problems of preparing and conducting defensive battle and defensive operations, and organizing and delivering against the aggressor retaliatory and retaliatory-meeting strikes, which at the beginning of a war will comprise the basis of Soviet Armed Forces actions. It is especially important *to overcome the under-appreciation of the defense* and put an end to the simplified approach of working it out in exercises. It is necessary to assimilate different variants of assuming and conducting a defense and fully resolve tasks concerning the engineer preparation of defensive lines and positions and organization of a system of fire and obstacles.

The modern defense must successfully withstand a powerful enemy offensive, organized according to the principle of the air-land operation, and ensure the repulsion of swift blows delivered to a great depth, envelopment from the air and sea, and dynamic actions by enemy diversionary-reconnaissance forces. The main purpose of the defense is to repel an enemy offensive, hold occupied lines, prevent deep penetration, preclude the loss of a significant part of one's own territory, in a short time hit attacking groupings which have penetrated, throw them back, and create conditions for shifting to a counteroffensive. This aim has always confronted the defense, but now its achievement requires especially great skill, a modern defensive formation, and a guarantee of greater stability against the newest enemy attack means. It must be more dynamic and must envision effective delivery of powerful fire strikes, counterattacks, and counterstrokes against the enemy.

It is important to study the use of populated areas, water obstacles, and other natural barriers in a system of defense. It is bolder to employ maneuver of fire and forces and remote mining means to concentrate efforts swiftly on the most dangerous axes. At the same time, however, it is necessary to prevent stereotypical patterning in executing counterattacks and counterstrokes where they are inexpedient and, practically speaking, impossible. In exercises, counterattacks and counterstrokes, carefully prepared and reliably supported, should be combined with the use of second echelons and reserves to occupy and hold defensive positions, lines, and regions.

Past war experience clearly demonstrates that counterattacks and counterstrokes can succeed only if they are executed suddenly, at an advantageous moment, and if the forces executing them are well covered from the air and supported by a stable defensive front, especially on the flanks. This experience retains its significance even at present. Moreover, now it is also necessary to consider many additional requirements, arising in connection with possible enemy employment of high-precision weapons.

In exercises and classes it is necessary to study the experience of the Battle of Kursk and how shifting to a forced defense, undertaken under unfavorable conditions, with considerable enemy superiority, but with premeditated organization, can provide substantive advantages.

In view of military doctrine's defensive nature, a very important task in force training is the study and practical mastery of methods for shifting from the defense to the counteroffensive. On a strategic scale this is associated with the study of problems of the strategic counteroffensive; on an operational-strategic scale – with a *front* counteroffensive; on an operational-tactical and tactical scale – with improving methods for conducting meeting battles and engagements, shifting to the offensive against an attacking enemy or one who has consolidated, and preparing such an offensive already during the defense. The study of actions which would make it possible to change quickly the course of combat actions, gain air superiority, and seize the operational and tactical initiative has decisive significance.

In shifting to a counteroffensive, it is necessary to master modern, highly mobile methods for its conduct; strive to improve tempos; during the offensive boldly use air envelopment of the enemy; master the delivery of strikes, and decisive dismemberment, envelopment, and rapid destruction of his groupings; and maintain a high focus of attention on forcing water lines and conducting offensive actions under special conditions.

Requirement for careful practical preparation of each operation and battle must be increased in the new training year. The level of decision-making and operational planning and their substantiation must be raised. It is very important to overcome stereotypes and patterning, and to develop creativity and initiative on the part of commanders and staffs in all possible ways. Here much depends on class and exercises leadership, which should highly grade atypical decisions and plans, and decisions which are out of the ordinary and creative, including deep operational thought and military cleverness, which most fully reflect the actual conditions of the situation.

However, special efforts must be concentrated on organizing the execution of adopted decisions. To do this it is necessary to study carefully how to reconnoiter the enemy; correctly plan fire; implement cooperation on maps and directly on the terrain; fully conduct all necessary measures for all types of combat, technical, and rear support; and practically organize control and communications and political work with personnel. Proceeding from new requirements, it is especially important to work out the conduct of reconnaissance, radio-electronic warfare, *maskirovka*, and materiel-technical support. Experience demonstrates that this is not a simple matter. Its success depends on precise organization, a strictly thought-out system of control, and detailed planning and coordination of the work of commanders, staff officers, and political organs in subordinate formations and units.

The 1988 training year should be a turning point in ground and naval force combat training. It is necessary to increase decisively the organization and quality of combat training in all Armed Forces services. Combat training should be placed in the center of all practical activities of commanders, staffs, and political organs, and viewed as the foremost duty, principal factor, and main condition for improving ground and naval combat capability, a decisive means for inculcating personnel and strengthening organizational qualities and discipline. It is necessary to struggle even more steadfastly against all stagnant phenomena in combat training; decisively surmount elements of sham ostentation, connivance, indulgence, and oversimplification; and introduce everywhere into the training process the most advanced achievements in methodology. From the very first days of the new training year, it is necessary to fully include all personnel in combat training, and increase the level of demand for quality in conducting each class and exercise, and the personal responsibility of all command-political cadres and staff officers for the condition and results of combat preparation and the execution of training plans and schedules. It is necessary to improve the training-materiel base in a systematic and purposeful way, and to transfer it to a qualitatively new foundation in all Armed Forces services and combat arms.

Further improvement in the level of field, air, and sea training of ground and naval forces is acquiring special significance. Training must increasingly and more consistently be brought as close as possible to combat reality. The principle of "teach troops what is necessary for war" must be invariably observed. Control organs, formations, units, and ships must be prepared for the actual execution of missions under maximally complex conditions, for fighting against a strong, technically outfitted and perfidious enemy.

Special attention in all Armed Forces services should be focused on further improvement of tactical training. New tactical procedures must be constantly sought, developed, and mastered, and the foremost experience in troop (force) tactical training must be analyzed more thoroughly and disseminated more dynamically. A very important task is the universal improvement of *march training of forces*, that is, improvement of formation and unit readiness and ability to complete in an organized fashion long marches over great distances in a strictly established period of time. In this connection, the significance of preparing commanders and staffs in skillfully organizing and conducting marches, and leading columns over great distances, is increasing.

It is necessary to concentrate attention on *ground and naval force night training*, and on the ability to withstand prolonged combat intensity, conduct continuous combat actions, and resolve combat missions at night and in poor visibility as effectively as during the day.

Other types of training – fire, technical, special – must be planned as well in close combination with tactical training. It is especially important to increase fire effectiveness and the reliability of hitting targets at extreme distances with minimum expenditure of ammunition. In 1988, *the level of personnel drill and physical training* must be increased significantly, and troop (force) drill efficiency must sharply rise. It is necessary to strive for high physical endurance on the part of personnel and an ability to bear high operational stress. The *Manual for Physical Training of the Soviet Army and Navy* (1987) is going into effect. It should be fully mastered.

Soviet military doctrine's defensive nature is having enormous influence on the orientation of operational and combat training of all Armed Forces services, including Air Defense Forces, the Air Force, and the Navy.

A most important task for Air Defense Forces is the further improvement of their readiness to stop decisively possible violations of Soviet air space and repel an enemy air attack where new means are employed.

In the Air Force, it is important to concentrate principal efforts on mastering methods of air actions when repelling a surprise enemy attack or his invasion, and on gaining air superiority to rout aviation and rocket-nuclear groupings and ground forces shock groupings.

Naval formations and ships must be ready for actions under more complex conditions when repelling aggression. This includes working out solutions for combat missions in the presence of a less favorable correlation of forces on maritime theaters when repelling powerful surprise enemy attacks from maritime directions.

A most important condition in improving the level of troop (force) combat training is the fundamental *improvement of officer personnel professional training*. The aim should be that every officer be ideologically tempered; have good organizational capabilities; have firmly mastered the principles of military affairs; know well combat and combined-arms regulations, manuals, training programs, the weapons and equipment with which he has been entrusted, and control means; and be able to resolve his assigned tasks creatively and with initiative, issue orders clearly and strive for their execution, organize the daily life and activities of troops (forces), strengthen discipline, and painstakingly conduct individual educational work with personnel.

No less important a role in training and indoctrinating soldiers belongs to the *sergeants*. Their command skills should be the constant concern of all unit and ship commanders.

The Central Committee of the CPSU and the Soviet State require that the Armed Forces *decisively turn toward science and a knowledge of military affairs* on the basis of the latest achievements in theoretical thought and the experience of the Great Patriotic War. Principal efforts in *scientific work* should be concentrated on thoroughly and scientifically working out emerging fundamental and applied problems, taking into account new requirements of Soviet military doctrine and its defensive orientation. It is necessary to find effective countermeasures to the enemy's military preparations and his new strategic and operational concepts. The coordinated conduct of military-theoretical, military-technical, and military-historical research is acquiring distinctive significance. The effectiveness of activities of Ministry of Defense military academies and scientific-research organizations must be increased. It is necessary to improve the leadership of scientific work and the quality, effectiveness, and practical significance of scientific-research work being conducted, scientific works being published, and dissertations being defended.

An important role in troop (force) training belongs to *military schools,* which should concentrate their main work efforts on fundamentally restructuring the training-indoctrination process and improving troop and unit indoctrination, the military-professional training of students, and the practical orientation of their training. *The principal criteria of the work of higher military schools should be providing students with a thorough knowledge of the fundamental principles of military art, higher military-technical training, solid command skills for controlling ground and naval forces under the complex conditions of modern battle, and development of a high level of personal discipline and executive skills, with self-demand for precise execution of the requirements of Soviet laws and military regulations.*

A very important task for the Armed Forces in 1988 is further intensification of efforts to universally strengthen troop and unit discipline. At the center of attention should be mobilization of personnel to maintain regulation order and training discipline, improvement of everyday life and concern for the men's health, overcoming of shortcomings in officer service activities, and eradication of those negative occurrences which still arise in relations among servicemen. It is necessary to increase the personal responsibility of commanders, political organs, and the party and Komsomol organizations for organizing service and the everyday life of personnel in strict accordance with the requirements of new regulations. The following are also necessary: to achieve complete self-involvement in work to strengthen discipline; to work actively to harmonize the soldier collectives, creating attitudes of friendship and camaraderie; to propagandize the best traditions of the army and navy; and to strengthen the influence of the collective in indoctrinating each serviceman with a high sense of responsibility for executing his duty. It is necessary to carry out in practice a decisive turn of all toward the main strategic task, that is, individual work, which the XXVII Party Congress has specified as the most important form of education.

In the new training year, it is necessary to focus special attention on pro-

foundly restructuring party-political work and increasing its effectiveness.
The basis of party-political work should be a thorough explanation to
personnel of the contemporary requirements of the Communist Party and the
Soviet State for ground and naval force training. It is necessary to form a
Communist world view in servicemen on the basis of required study of the
strategic course and policies of the CPSU and missions assigned to the
Armed Forces by the XVII Party Congress. Servicemen must be aware of
their dynamic position and high personal responsibility for executing
their duty. At present, qualitative shifts in political training of soldiers
are necessary so that the tenets of Marxist-Leninist theory can be more
decisively introduced into practical work.

The issue of *renovating the system of Marxist-Leninist training* of officers
and the political instruction of soldiers, sergeants, and warrant officers is
acquiring particular significance. The main thing here is to turn each class
into a school of creativity and scientific analysis of current problems. It is
necessary to introduce dynamic training forms and methods more steadfastly
into the education process.

Ideological-political indoctrination of personnel, and its content, forms,
and methods should be brought into full accordance with the realities of
domestic and international life. It is necessary to increase soldiers' political
vigilance and class self-awareness, overcome pacifist attitudes, and indoctrinate bourgeois ideology's inacceptability and a readiness to respond fully
armed to any ventures on the part of imperialism's reactionary forces. At the
foundation of ideological-indoctrination work should be a thorough and
creative study of the decisions of the XXVII Party Congress, subsequent
Plenums of the Central Committee of the CPSU, and materials dedicated to
the 70th anniversary of the Great October Revolution and the 70th anniversary of the Soviet Armed Forces. Such study should be closely connected
with the life of the country, the army, and the navy.

The style of activities of political organs, party committees, and bureaus
requires fundamental changes. The main thing in their work is steadfast
affirmation of the revolutionary spirit of *perestroyka*, an atmosphere of
creativity, a sense of principle, and self-criticism; a thoughtful attitude
toward questions of selecting and distributing cadres and toward improving
their sense of responsibility for assigned matters; thorough study of the state
of affairs in units and subunits, timely disclosure and a principled assessment
of shortcomings, and adoption of energetic measures to eliminate them; and
maintenance and dissemination of the foremost experience of *perestroyka*.

At the XXVII Party Congress, the primary party organizations were called
the vanguard of *perestroyka*. In the new training year it is necessary for army
and navy party organizations and the party *aktiv* to be the initiators and
organizers of *perestroyka*, to be an example of new approaches and the unity
of word and deed. It is necessary to focus principal attention on the maxi-

mum activization of Communists so as to bring forth those who have not renounced the old work methods.

Simultaneously, it is necessary to develop more broadly democracy in the life of the army and navy, increase the dynamism and alertness of Party and Komsomol organizations, and widen their real participation in overcoming inadequacies in training and indoctrinating personnel, in improving work with officer cadres, warrant officers, sergeant-majors, and sergeants, and in resolving social issues. At the same time, it is necessary to strengthen everywhere "sole responsibility" [*yedinonachaliye*] on a Party basis and improve the authority of commanders and chiefs.

Perestroyka in the army and navy will be successful and dynamic only when leadership personnel set the tone for it. The main thing in its restructuring activity is mastery of Lenin's style of work with people: renunciation of bureaucratic administration, superfluous regulation and prohibition, petty guardianship over subordinates, and lack of faith in their intelligence, experience, and responsible approach to matters. Leadership personnel must be a model of ideological stability, observance of discipline, fidelity to duty, honor, decency, integrity, modesty, and impatience toward violations to our morale.

Under conditions in which *perestroyka* is being implemented, *the mechanism of socialist competition* also requires renovation. This year it must be directed toward being worthy of the 70th anniversary of the Soviet Armed Forces and the XIX All-Union Party Conference. *It is important that not only these noteworthy dates, but also the entire jubilee year be distinguished by the achievement of high results in combat training and discipline.* In the organization of competition, the main thing must be to overcome formalism, stereotypes, and over-organization; to affirm Lenin's principles of organizing competition; to broaden further democracy and *glasnost'*; and to ensure genuine participation of each soldier, sergeant, and officer in competition. It is necessary to interest people in its results and to develop a desire in them to strive for improving their professional training.

Implementation in soldier collectives of the principle of social justice in assessing results and determining victors is important. Socialist competition and its course should inspire people with a feeling of confidence that it is conducted for the sake of improving matters as a whole, as well as each of its participants and the collective as a whole.

The Soviet Armed Forces is meeting its 70th anniversary at a very important stage of *perestroyka*. The main concern of commanders, political organs, and party and Komsomol organizations is the practical implementation of the decisions of the XXVII Party Congress, subsequent Plenums of the Central Committee of the CPSU, principles of Soviet military doctrine and the uniform military doctrine of the Warsaw Treaty Organization member-states (and these doctrines' defensive nature), and USSR Ministry of Defense requirements for training ground and naval forces. The sacred duty of each Soviet soldier is to make a worthy contribution to the matter of maintaining the Soviet Armed Forces' combat capability and combat readiness.

NOTES

1. "Oboronitel'nyy kharakter sovetskoy voyennoy doktriny i podgotovka voysk (sil)," *Voyennaya mysl'* [Military thought], 1 (1988), pp. 3–13.
2. *Polnoye sobraniye sochineniy* [Complete works], Vol. 37, p. 122.
3. M. S. Gorbachev, *Oktyabr' i perestroyka: revolyutsiya prodolzhayetsya* [October and perestroyka: the revolution continues] (Moscow: Politizdat, 1987), p. 55.
4. *Pravda*, 30 May 1987.
5. D. T. Yazov, *Na strazhe sotsializma i mira* [On guard for socialism and peace] (Moscow: Voyenizdat, 1987), p. 40.

The Development of the Theory of Deep Offensive Battle in the Prewar Years

COLONEL V. I. UL'YANOV[1]

After the Civil War and intervention, the Soviet republic was able to develop peaceful construction. Under Communist Party leadership, our nation created powerful industry and carried out collectivization of agriculture and a cultural revolution. The Party developed a military policy and determined the direction and tasks of military development. Together with improvement in Red Army and Navy organization, their technical rearmament, and command cadre training and education, Soviet military science also developed. Synthesizing the best from past military-theoretical legacies and combat experience from defending the socialist country, and enriched by new theoretical tenets, military science outstripped existing theories of armies of capitalist countries on many questions concerning the conduct of battle. In its development, three instances were considered. *First*, the theory of group tactics, answering the conditions of the 1920s, did not correspond to the requirements of future war. Consequently, the necessity arose to develop a fundamentally new theory of conducting battle and searching for such methods and means of combat operations which would make it possible to surmount successfully the strong curtain of fire of a continuous enemy front, and to inflict a blow against his shock groupings quickly.

Second, technical combat means had increased qualitatively and quantitatively, and mobile formations were being created. Our prewar regulations viewed the infantry as the main combat arm, since it bore the principal weight of battle and was able to provide for seizure and extended retention of terrain. However, other combat arms, including aviation, had to support the infantry. These views were an objective prerequisite for resolving problems of offensive battle in a new way. *Third*, Soviet military science, adhering to defensive doctrine, proceeded from the idea of a retaliatory attack against the enemy. This idea arose from the very essence of the socialist system and from Soviet state policy, vitally interested in maintaining peace and intending to attack no one.

A great achievement of Soviet military science was the theory of the deep operation, in accordance with which the theory of deep offensive battle was developed. Taking into account the development of technical combat means, questions of increasing maneuverability, force shock power, and their combat capabilities provided the base for this theory's tenets. The theory of deep offensive battle arose because battle became combined arms and its aim could be achieved on the basis of cooperation of all combat arms by decisive offensive operations, to be concluded by encirclement and annihilation of the enemy. It also considered the circumstance that rifle units and formations had acquired a large quantity of light machine guns, company, battalion, and regimental mortars, and antitank, antiaircraft, and field artillery guns. For example, the overall number of machine guns in rifle formations increased 5.5 times from 1930–39. At the same time, fire capabilities of rifle divisions tended to grow (see Table 1).

TABLE 1

COMPARATIVE TABLE OF FIRE CAPABILITIES OF A RIFLE DIVISION

According to division equipment table	Number of rifle/ machine gun shots per minute	Weight of one mortar salvo, kilograms	Weight of one artillery salvo, kilograms	Overall weight of one artillery-mortar salvo, kilograms
1923	89,820	–	336.0	336.0
1924	96,430	–	522.0	522.0
1929	128,910	–	578.4	578.4
1931	141,550	–	584.6	584.6
1935	160,910	55.8	1,026.8	1,082.6
1939	200,950	375.3	1,326.0	1,701.3
1940	353,120	433.8	1,388.4	1,822.2

The principal tenets of the theory of deep battle were formulated in *Instruktsiya po glubokomu boyu* [Instructions on Deep Battle], which appeared in 1935, and in the *Temporary Field Regulation for the Workers' and Peasants' Red Army* [*PU-36*]. The essence of the theory of deep offensive battle consisted of simultaneously striking the enemy's combat formation "to the entire depth of his disposition." This was achieved by aviation strikes and artillery fire, swift penetration of long-range action tank groups into the deployment area of enemy artillery and tactical reserves, decisive forward advance of long-range infantry support tanks, continuous advance of infantry with direct support tanks, and dynamic air-assault operations.

The development of the theory of deep offensive battle has its own history.

This idea was first advanced in 1928 by M. N. Tukhachevsky. He pointed out that the army's new materiel-technical base (long-range artillery, tanks, aviation, assaults) made it possible to reject previous exhausting combat forms for each enemy position separately, and achieve new, more effective forms and means of conducting battle.[2] It is proper to note that other Soviet military scholars were occupied with the development of the theory of deep offensive battle. An important role in the development of new tactical principles was played by the works of M. V. Frunze, A. I. Verkhovsky, N. Ye. Kapurin, Ye. K. Smyslovsky, and many others.

The theory of deep battle was continually tested. Its individual tenets were refined on the basis of the experience of exercises and maneuvers conducted in military districts, and of battles in the Lake Khasan area, on the Khalkhin-Gol River, on the Karelian Isthmus, and during the initial period of the Second World War. Thus, V. K. Triandafillov defined concretely the idea of the possibility of simultaneously striking the enemy to the entire tactical depth, having three tank groups (direct infantry support [*NPP*], long-range infantry support [*DPP*], and long-range action [*DD*]) in cooperation with long-range artillery and aviation. K. B. Kalinovsky developed tactics for these groups' actions.

The theory of the deep operation envisioned the resolution of the initial task, that is, penetration of the enemy defense, as being executed by rifle formations reinforced with tanks and artillery operating in the army's first operational echelon. The development of tactical success into operational success was to be achieved by swift mobile and air-assault force operations and aviation strikes. These principles were also included in the theory of deep offensive battle.

At that time, the highest tactical formation was the rifle corps which, depending on the situation, could operate in one of the combat echelons of the army operational formation on the main or secondary axis, or in the *front* reserve. Operating in the first combat echelon, the rifle corps, consisting of three rifle divisions, two artillery regiments, separate antiaircraft, engineer, and communications battalions, had to resolve the principal missions of penetrating the entire enemy tactical defense zone and creating conditions for developing success.

As for the rifle division, from September 1939 through April 1941 its wartime establishment [TO&E] changed three times. A division equipped according to the new establishment was capable of firing 96,500 rifle and machine gun rounds more than a division with the 1939 establishment. This underscores the fact that its armaments to the greatest degree began to respond to missions which it could be assigned in offensive battle. It became the principal tactical formation. In the prewar years rifle divisions existed with a complement of 12,000 and 6,000 men. The difference between them, unsubstantial in truth, existed in armaments, including guns of various calibers. The mountain-rifle divisions existing at that time were significantly smaller than rifle divisions in personnel and armaments (see Table 2). However, according to wartime establishment these and other divisions were organized similarly. According to the 1941 establishment, the division consisted of three rifle and two artillery regiments, one antitank and one antiaircraft artillery battalion, engineer and communications battalions, and support and maintenance subunits.[3]

TABLE 2
COMPARATIVE CHARACTERISTICS OF RIFLE DIVISIONS ACCORDING TO
PEACETIME AND WARTIME EQUIPMENT TABLES

Type of rifle division	Personnel	Motor vehicles	Horses	Armaments					Guns			
				Rifles and carbines	Heavy machine guns	Light machine guns	Automatic weapons	Small-caliber	Medium-caliber	Heavy-caliber	Mortars
12,000 men	10,291	414	1,955	7,818	164	371	1,159	62	70	12	150
6,000 men	5,864	155	905	3,685	163	324	691	52	62	12	108
Mountain-rifle division	8,829	203	3,160	6,960	110	314	788	8	56	–	120
According to peacetime equipment tables	14,483	558	3,039	10,420	166	392	1,204	54	66	12	150

Corps and division offensives were envisioned against an enemy who: prepared in advance a positional defense under field conditions or in fortified regions; had quickly gone over to the defense; or was employing a mobile defense. The offensive commenced either with or without direct contact with the enemy. Methods for carrying out combat missions and the structure of combat formations, for which there were concrete requirements, were determined based on this. In particular, combat formations were to provide for inflicting decisive defeat on the enemy along a selected main attack axis; better use of all combat means and cooperation of all combat arms for achieving the assigned aims; flexibility and control, providing, to the necessary degree, an ability to change the structure of the formation; and the capability of repelling enemy counterattacks.

Proceeding from these requirements, the 1936 *Vremennyy polevoy ustav RKKA* [Temporary Field Regulation of the Workers' and Peasants' Red Army] recommended the creation of offensive combat formations *from shock and holding groups and a reserve.*

A shock group was designated to advance on the main attack axis. It consisted of two-thirds of the forces, whose basis was organic and attached fire means. The main criterion for infantry sufficiency within a group was the ability to annihilate the enemy conclusively to the entire depth of his disposition in cooperation with tanks, artillery, and aviation. Extreme oversaturation with infantry was avoided, since this entailed unjustified losses.

The width of the shock group's front depended on existing forces and means, the nature of the terrain, the degree of enemy engineer defensive preparation, its stability, and also the systems and strengths of enemy fire. Thus, a division shock group consisting of no fewer than two rifle regiments reinforced by tanks and supported by the principal mass of divisional and attached artillery could conduct an offensive in a 3–3.5-kilometer sector.[4]

A holding group was designated for operations on a secondary axis. Its composition included organic forces and means. It was assigned the mission of pinning down the enemy by dynamic actions and preventing him regrouping his forces for operations against the shock group.

However, the experience of the Soviet–Finnish War demonstrated that the creation of holding groups doomed these troops to passive actions. Therefore, on the eve of the Great Patriotic War it was acknowledged as inexpedient to divide combat formations into shock and holding groups. According to the draft 1941 *Field Regulation*, rifle formation and unit offensive combat formations were subdivided into combat echelons, artillery groups, infantry support tank groups [*TPP*], and reserves (general, tank, and antitank).[5]

Prewar recommendations concerning the structure of the combat formation did not, in full measure, reflect the essence of deep offensive battle. In particular, a deeply echeloned structure of formations, units, and even subunits was envisioned. As a result of such echeloning, a significant portion of the division's forces and means did not participate in battle. Subsequently, these views were reexamined, and second echelons began to receive active missions and to support the first echelon with all available fire means.

The rifle regiment combat formation included two echelons (in the shock group, battalion behind battalion) or three (battalion behind battalion); the division shock group included two echelons (regiment behind regiment) or one echelon (regiments on line). The rifle corps offensive combat formation was usually structured in one echelon (divisions on line). Such a formation was explained by the significant depth of division combat formations and convenience of control. Use of operational reserves was envisioned to strengthen the force and increase the depth of the corps attack. In all instances, it was envisioned to support the attacking forces' first echelons by fire means of all subsequent echelons and, above all, by artillery. The chief purpose of the second echelons was not to replace the first, as in the past, but to augment the force of the attack to develop the offensive into the depth.

It is necessary to keep in mind that it was envisioned to divide parts of the force into reserves (combined arms and antitank), independent of the echelonment depth of the division (regimental) combat formation, in case of unexpected events, which could arise during offensive battle, to reinforce the combat formations' antitank means, and to advance swiftly during exploitation of the offensive's success.

Operative prewar regulations and instructions did not define the width of the offensive sector. However, as practical experience demonstrated, a rifle corps advancing in an army's first echelon and on the main attack axis could receive a sector 18–20 kilometers wide. A rifle division reinforced by tanks and artillery advanced in a 5–7-kilometer sector. However, influenced by combat experience at the Khalkhin-Gol River and in Finland in 1940–41, and also as a result of the enemy defense's increasing fire power, the width of offensive sectors decreased to the following: for a rifle corps – 8–12 kilometers; for a division – 3–4 kilometers on the main axis, and 5–6 kilometers on a secondary axis. The depth of corps missions increased from 10–12 to 20 kilometers (see Sketch 1).

To penetrate a prepared and occupied enemy defense to the entire tactical depth, it was necessary to create two- and threefold superiority in forces and shock means on the main axes. Therefore, it was considered that a rifle corps could penetrate a defending enemy infantry division on the main axis, and a rifle division could penetrate an enemy infantry regiment.

A rifle division advancing in a 3-kilometer sector could create the following average tactical densities per kilometer of front: three rifle battalions, 401 machine pistols, 97 light machine guns, 55 heavy machine guns, 22 mortars, eight antitank guns, and 26 artillery guns.

Thus, division capabilities for creating the indicated densities of forces and means, with cooperation of infantry with artillery, tanks, and aviation, provided for penetration of the enemy defense and his simultaneous destruction to the entire tactical depth of the defense.

The combat mission of a rifle corps and division was subdivided into immediate and subsequent. Since a rifle corps structured its combat formation, as a rule, in one echelon, the depth of its combat mission coincided with the depth of the missions of rifle divisions advancing on the main axis. The division's immediate mission was to seize the main enemy defensive belt (six to eight kilometers), while its subsequent mission was to develop success and seize the second defensive belt. For regiments the immediate mission was to capture regimental reserve positions and areas of principal artillery firing positions (three–four kilometers), while the subsequent mission was to seize divisional reserve positions.

According to the theory of deep offensive battle, the immediate mission was to be resolved, as a rule, in the initial structure of the combat formation, the second defensive belt was to be penetrated and captured from the march, and penetration by the corps of the entire tactical depth of the enemy defense was to take place on the first day of the operation, that is, in the course of 10–12 hours of battle. Penetration was considered accomplished when the infantry overcame the entire depth of the enemy's antipersonnel and antitank defenses, captured or at least fully suppressed his artillery, and repelled counterattacks by tactical reserves.

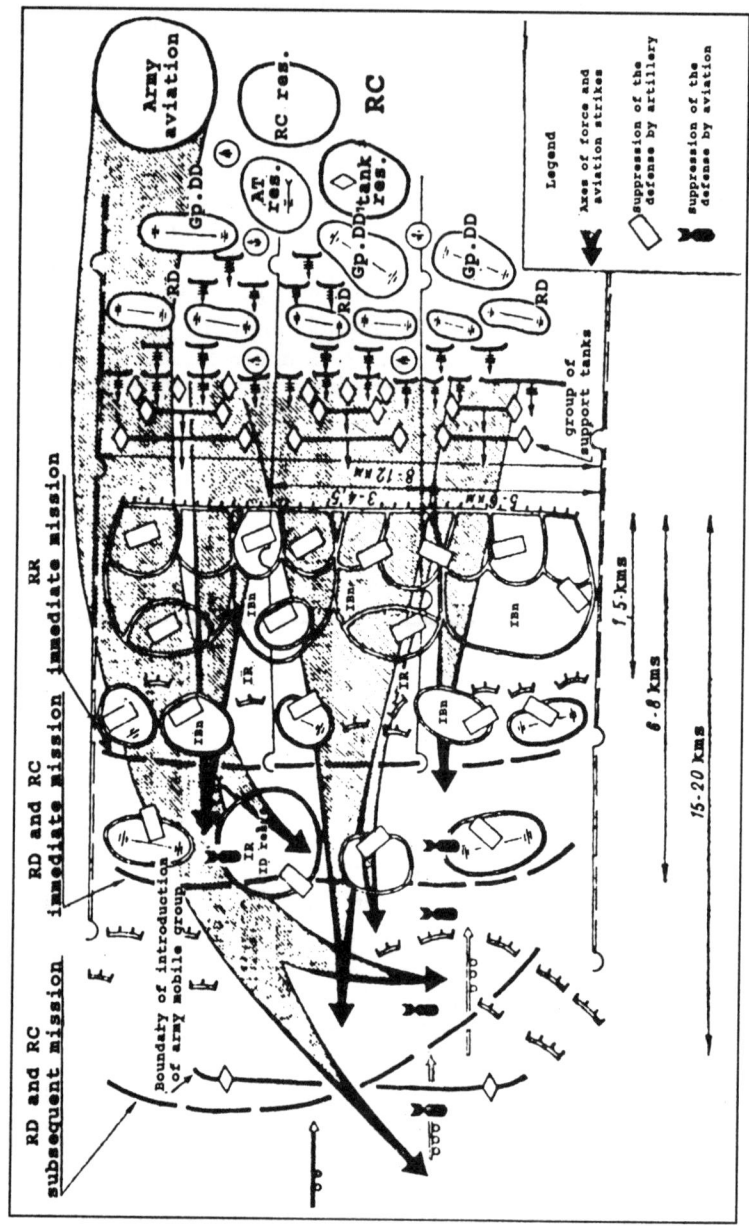

Sketch 1.

Offensive of a rifle corps and division according to prewar views

In selecting main attack axes, terrain conditions and enemy forces, especially that portion of the grouping, whose rout would provide for successful accomplishment of the assigned mission, were taken into account. The main attack was delivered in the specific front sector where the greater portion of forces and means for suppressing corps and divisions were concentrated. Infantry was the foundation of the advancing forces' combat echelons. By decisive operations supported by other combat arms, it was to resolve the outcome of battle. Infantry commenced its advance from an initial line located no more than 300 meters from the forward edge of the enemy defense, and went over to the attack when the first echelon of tanks arrived at the forward edge of the defense, and the artillery shifted fire into the depth. The attack was to commence simultaneously in the entire rifle corps sector, and was to be conducted continuously day and night.[6] For the organization of continuous artillery fire support of infantry and tanks, forward artillery observers were moved into company and battalion combat formations.

The rifle division's first combat echelon was designated to overcome the main defensive belt. The second echelon was committed to strengthen the force of the blow and exploit success. Forward detachments were assigned to pursue a withdrawing enemy.

The draft 1941 *Field Regulations* envisioned penetration of the defense by mechanized formations, whose principal means of action was the tank attack. Behind the tanks advanced motorized infantry, cleaning the penetration sector of enemy remnants, reinforcing captured objectives, widening the penetration, and securing the flanks and rear of the tank formations. Tanks were the shock means for penetrating the defense. Cooperating with artillery and aviation, they destroyed fire means, disrupted the defender's fire system, and cleared a path for the attacking infantry through the entire depth of penetration of the enemy's tactical defense. Special tank support guns, whose mission was to fight against antitank guns, were allotted for support. Two types of tank groups were created: long-range action and infantry support. After a short artillery preparation, the long-range action tank group penetrated into the deployment area of enemy divisional reserves and artillery and annihilated them; then infantry support tanks went over to the attack, leading the infantry behind them.

After exercises and the experience of the Soviet–Finnish War was considered, long-range groups were abolished, and no longer envisioned in the draft 1941 *Field Regulations*. It prescribed the structuring of tank combat formations (infantry support) in three echelons. The first echelon, consisting of heavy tanks, was designated to suppress the antitank defense and destroy artillery. The second echelon consisted of medium tanks. It advanced behind the first echelon, suppressing and destroying heavy machine guns and antitank guns in the depth of the defense. The third echelon, made up of light tanks, led the infantry behind it and suppressed enemy personnel and fire means.

First-echelon tanks attacked the forward edge while the infantry was preparing for a rush and the artillery was shifting fire from the forward edge into the depth. In an offensive against an enemy deployed behind large natural barriers or powerful antitank obstacles, tanks advanced after the penetration of the forward edge of the defense by infantry, artillery, and aviation.

However, these new tenets did not become guiding ones for all command personnel, and in the first year of the war they were principally guided by the provisions of *PU-36* and draft *PU-39*. This was mainly because of weak requirements for command training and incomplete combat training methods. The actual level of our Armed Forces combat training on the eve of the war did not fully correspond with the requirements of the situation.

In the theory of deep battle, artillery was assigned an important role. Possessing great force and firepower, it was designated to suppress and annihilate personnel and equipment and destroy engineer fortifications.

Artillery groups were subdivided into infantry support groups [*PP*], long-range action groups [*DD*], destruction groups [*AR*], and antiaircraft artillery groups [*ZAG*]. The first three prepared and supported the attack and further advance by infantry and tanks to the entire depth of the enemy defense, while the antiaircraft artillery group protected the combat formation against aviation raids. Artillery support of offensive battle was planned to the entire depth of penetration of the main enemy defense sector and included artillery preparation, artillery support of the attack, and artillery accompaniment of battle into the depth.

The artillery preparation's aim was to disrupt the enemy's fire system, suppress his artillery, destroy detected antitank guns, etc. It was not only conducted in daylight, but sometimes at night, when it ended at dawn. The presence of forces and means, the time necessary to complete the mission, and other factors determined its duration. Sometimes a period of destruction before the commencement of the artillery preparation was envisioned to destroy a strongly fortified defense. Its duration was 1.5 hours and more; the period of destruction could begin several days before the offensive. The artillery preparation for the attack was concluded by a fire raid along the forward edge.

Artillery support of the attack pursued the aim of preventing the enemy from reestablishing the disrupted fire system and supporting the rush of infantry and tanks into the attack for seizure of the forward edge and development of the battle into the depth. Artillery support was carried out by a fire barrage or successive fire concentrations against the most important defensive objectives; they were also used in the following way: the fire barrage was used to a depth of 1.5–2 kilometers, while successive fire concentrations were used at greater depths. Working out these methods was an important achievement in the development of artillery tactics.

Aviation operations were planned massively in accordance with the theory of deep battle, and in close cooperation with infantry, tanks, and air-assault forces. Aviation support of a rifle corps and division consisted of an aviation preparation and aviation support of the attack and battle in the depth. The aviation preparation was conducted in the period preceding the artillery preparation. However, if it was conducted simultaneously, then it was co-ordinated with respect to time with the artillery preparation. During the preparation, aviation prevented enemy counterattacks and the approach of reserves, and hindered withdrawal and occupation of the second defensive belt.

One of the most important conditions for achieving success in battle was the organization of cooperation among the combat arms. The principal mission of cooperation was to coordinate efforts and operations of all combat arms, aviation, and special forces with respect to aim, time, and place.

The organization of cooperation was carried out by the combined arms commander, who conducted all basic work on the terrain, enlisting all commanders of subunits, units, and formations operating respectively in rifle corps, division, and regimental sectors. The actions of artillery and aviation were coordinated to support the infantry and tanks in the rush into the attack, seizure of the forward edge, and advance into the depth of the defense. Thus, from the commencement of the attack, artillery was to conduct fire against detected antitank guns and areas of their presumed location. At this time, tanks under cover of artillery fire suppressed enemy machine guns and artillery; the infantry, following behind the tanks, was to attack centers of enemy resistance and by their own fire means assist the tanks. At the same time, aviation, by powerful strikes, suppressed fire means and troop concentrations, accompanying infantry and tanks to the entire depth of the offensive.

Control of battle was implemented by corps and division commanders from command posts located on the main attack axis. A command post consisted of the commander's observation post, when necessary an additional observation post, an operational group, and communications center. For better organization of cooperation, joint location of the command posts of combined arms commanders and commanders of supporting subunits and units was recommended.

Thus, the theory of deep offensive battle was developed on the foundation of the Soviet Armed Forces' military-technological base created in the pre-war years, taking into account the achievements of Soviet military science and experiences of the first period of the Second World War. Conclusions were reached which refined and developed individual issues. However, far from all recommendations developed by Soviet military science succeeded in being carried out, for the Soviet government did not have at its disposal appropriate materiel means to realize its conclusions. The country's economy did not fully provide for outfitting the Armed Forces in that quantity of the newest weapons and combat equipment required in accordance with the conclusions of military theory. There were other reasons, including subjective reasons, connected with the events of 1937–38. On the whole, the theory of deep battle was a fundamentally new theory which reflected qualitative changes which had taken place in the development and technical equipping of the forces. Its principal tenets were progressive and responded to the spirit of the requirements of the approaching war. They guided forces and staffs in combat training, and then in combat practice until 1943. For the most part they have maintained their significance even under modern conditions.

NOTES

1. V. I. Ul'yanov, "Razvitiye teorii glubokogo nastupatel'nogo boya v predvoyennyye gody," *Voyenno-istoricheskiy zhurnal* [Military-historical journal], 3 (March 1988), pp. 26–33.
2. *Taktika* [Tactics] (Moscow: Voyenizdat, 1966), p.18.
3. *Istoriya vtoroy mirovoy voyny 1939–1945* [History of World War II 1939–1945], Vol. 3 (Moscow: Voyenizdat, 1975), p. 419.
4. *Vremennyy Polevoy ustav RKKA 1936 g. (PU–36)* [Temporary field regulation of the Workers' and Peasants' Red Army 1936 (PU-36)] (Moscow: Gosvoyenizdat, 1937), p. 102.
5. *Istoriya voyn i voyennogo iskusstva* [History of wars and military art] (Moscow: Voyenizdat, 1970), pp. 110–11.
6. *Voprosy taktiki v sovetskikh voyennykh trudakh* [Problems of tactics in Soviet military works] (Moscow: Voyenizdat, 1970), p. 94.

On the Evolution of the Principles of Military Art

COLONEL YE. G. KOROTCHENKO,
CANDIDATE OF MILITARY SCIENCES[1]

An investigation of the changes in the content and forms of manifesting the principles of military art is one of the key trends in the development of its theory and practice. In this article the author examines the development of several principles as applicable to operational art, and states his viewpoint on how changes which are taking place may be reflected in practical activities in preparing and conducting modern operations.

The principle of constant high combat readiness is viewed as fundamental for the armed forces of any state. The aims which the military-political leadership of various countries is striving to achieve are, however, far from uniform; they are conditioned, first and foremost, by the state's wartime political and strategic missions.

For example, high combat readiness for the United States Armed Forces assumes the implementation of the strategy of "flexible response," which bears an offensive character. With NATO's 1984 adoption of the "Rogers Plan," its command, in using military force, stressed the delivery of pre-emptive strikes to the entire depth of the Warsaw Treaty Organization countries to deprive them of the ability to conduct successful defensive actions. The American operational-strategic concept of "air-land operation (engagement)" and the NATO operational-strategic concept of "fighting against second echelons (reserves)" pursue this aim. These concepts have not only been declared, but have also been implemented in armed forces development and training. Annually conducted US and NATO army troop (force) exercises in various regions – and their number amounts to 200 – are becoming difficult to distinguish from actual force deployments to wage war. Thus, up to one half of the formations and units deployed in the Central European theater of military operations are brought up (to field regions) for large-scale exercises such as "Autumn Forge."

Considering today's military-political situation and the particularly defensive nature of Soviet military doctrine (at the basis of which lies the principle of retaliatory actions), the necessity arises *to improve the vigilance and combat readiness of the Soviet Armed Forces, and to improve further their training.* The above-mentioned principle in no way presumes passivity when repelling an aggressor's strikes. Retaliatory strikes should be distinguished by extreme decisiveness and dynamism.

Proceeding from this, *priority significance in the content of the principle of constant combat readiness* must be given to such elements as constant readiness and reliability of forces and means carrying out combat duty; timely and organized transition of ground and naval forces from a peacetime to wartime footing, their rapid deployment and preparation to carry out combat missions; a high level of combat training for officer cadres, staffs, and forces; constant technical readiness of weapons and combat equipment, and proper maintenance of the necessary materiel reserves; and high moral-psychological qualities of personnel.

The combat readiness of the armies of the majority of leading imperialist states has a completely different orientation and content. It is noted in the Western military press that the constant high combat readiness of NATO armed forces has primary significance in the implementation of plans for a surprise attack. Counting on surprise is viewed as a decisive condition for achieving ultimate war aims. An attempt to concentrate maximum efforts at the very beginning of combat actions on fast-acting, high-precision means for striking the most important groupings of forces and objectives in the rear of another country is clearly seen in the nature of US and NATO military preparations. It is thought that in a world war, or in armed struggle on the whole, surprise is acquiring global scope and very important significance. Thus, the ability to deliver a surprise strike of enormous destructive force against a probable enemy under modern conditions requires that the problems of the defensive capability of the Soviet state and its allies be examined in a new way.

In this regard, the problem posed by Colonel General V. N. Lobov on the necessity of a deep theoretical comprehension of the principle of surprise, which is new in content, taking into account seeking effective methods of troop actions, is very timely.[2] In our opinion, the suggested focus on the category of "unexpectedness" and on the disclosure (still in a general form) of its content is also completely justified. It is apparent that this will make it possible to reveal more thoroughly its internal mechanism as a phenomenon and sort out the most important problems, whose resolution should be given primary attention.

Continuing Colonel General Lobov's concept that at present a definite imbalance in force capabilities and the level of theoretical resolution of the problem of surprise has arisen, it must be said that such a situation is the result of an established intellectual stereotype. This is manifested in particular in the clearly disparate research into questions about surprise force actions in the defense, the counteroffensive, and the offensive.

Past war experience, especially the Great Patriotic War, attests that surprise in the defense made it possible to compensate for shortcomings in forces and means; it forced the attacker to conduct combat actions in an unfavorable situation, change earlier specified force plans and missions, and execute unanticipated regroupings; and it led to partial or complete enemy loss of initiative, while simultaneously increasing defense stability.

The most effective methods for achieving surprise in the defense are as follows: constant and detailed study of a potential enemy, his capabilities, and his opinions regarding methods for unleashing war and conducting combat actions; the ability to analyze thoroughly the probable course of a modern defensive operation (battle); conduct of effective reconnaissance of the enemy and dynamic struggle against his reconnaissance and diversionary forces; decisive rejection of stereotypical patterning in structuring the defense, creating groupings, and deploying forces and means on the terrain, as well as in methods of force actions; wide employment of military stratagem by undertaking effective measures to ensure covertness and to mislead the enemy with respect to one's plans; massed action, unexpected for the enemy, against his troop and weapons control system, while providing for solid and reliable control of one's own forces and means; maintenance of the concept and plan for forthcoming actions in strict secrecy, etc.

In the foreign military press, it is stressed that, at present, important factors for achieving surprise also include extensive use of raid actions by ground and air-mobile forces and combat helicopters; infiltration and saturation of the enemy rear with highly mobile formations and units, and creation in the rear of a front of dynamic actions with the most decisive aims; and preparation and delivery forces of unexpected strikes by these mobile forces at the most inappropriate time for the other side.

Western military specialists attached special significance to realizing the principle of surprise to *reliably striking enemy groupings at the maximum possible distance from the line of contact of the opposing sides.* Within the framework of the air-land operation, for example, an entire system of mutually coordinated measures was developed for this, which could include the following: concentration of efforts and comprehensive use of forces and means on the most important axes or in specific regions; delivery of pre-emptive, massed fire strikes in combination with remote mining and radio-electronic suppression; wide employment of airborne, air-mobile, and amphibious assaults and diversionary-reconnaissance formations; and location of air intercept lines deep in enemy territory. Finally, part of the battalion tactical groups could operate upon reaching up to ten kilometers and more beyond the front line to disorganize the actions of attacking (counterstriking) groupings. The missions of such groups would be to raid, counterattack, strike the enemy with ambush fire, etc.

Substantive changes in the content of *the principle of dynamism and decisiveness* are predetermined by the high degree of dynamism of combat actions, the decisiveness of the opposing sides' operational (combat) aims, mass employment of highly effective means of destruction, and sharp changes in the situation. Under these conditions, seizing and holding the initiative, and constantly imposing one's will on the enemy to force him to act in a manner not in accordance with his earlier worked-out operational plans will have primary significance.

Seizing and maintaining fire superiority and readiness to resolve new fire destruction missions such as weakening (or, under favorable conditions, thwarting) the initial massed fire strike; striking rocket groupings, high-precision weapons systems, automated reconnaissance systems, and the dispersed computer network of formations and large formations; preventing the advance and deployment of second echelons and reserves; striking enemy groupings in his rear and reinforcement troops in landing regions and during a sea (air) crossing; and thwarting enemy re-establishment of disorganized systems of control, reconnaissance, radio-electronic warfare, and technical support are acquiring extraordinary importance.

The increasing decisiveness of combat actions is leading to sharp differences between types of combat actions being eliminated with definite systematic regularity, and methods of their conduct in the offense and defense are drawing together. Modern operations are increasingly acquiring the nature of fierce offensive-defensive ground-air engagements and battles having the aim not so much of repelling enemy strikes, but more of thwarting his actions and then completely routing him.

As for changes in the content of the principle of continuous conduct of combat actions, here two mutually exclusive trends are manifest. In accordance with one of them, outfitting forces with modern weapons systems increases their ability to conduct continuous combat actions at any time of the year, day or night, in any weather, and on varied terrain. In the Western military press in particular, it is noted that high-precision weapons make it possible to deliver effective fire strikes independent of the time of day, and, very importantly, to implement deep and uninterrupted fire support of forces. After the systematic outfitting (by the mid-1990s) of tactical aviation with more improved navigation systems and high-precision weapons models, it is assumed that the massed air strike at night will be preferable.

On the other hand, sharply increased troop losses, great expenditures and difficulty in replenishing materiel, prolonged actions in zones of radiation and chemical contamination, delays in the advance of second echelons, and psychogenically debilitating factors create the prerequisites for extended operational pauses.

The uniqueness of the content and forms of the manifestation of *the principle of decisive concentration of efforts on the most important axes* at the decisive moment for executing the main missions is widely discussed in our press. To supplement what has already been stated in previous publications, one could mention one more aspect associated with the practical realization of the principle under examination, the necessity of concentrating efforts with respect to results. The essence of this is seen in the following: under any conditions, the resolution of each concrete task requires the use of a precisely calculated quantity of forces and means to ensure the achievement of a specific operational (tactical) result with minimum expenditure of time.

In implementing the principle of concentration of primary efforts when executing many operational (tactical) missions, it will now be necessary to employ a more refined and precise instrument for use of actual combat potential than the creation of the necessary densities and correlation of forces and means, which is practiced at present. For this, in modern operations it will be necessary to isolate in the enemy's operational formation the main groupings, systems, and objectives, against which actions will, to the greatest degree, facilitate the achievement of the established aim; and to determine precisely and concretely (in percentages of inflicted damage, time that they will not be combat capable, etc.) the aim of actions when resolving each operational (important tactical) mission, such as thwarting a fire strike being prepared or the enemy offensive on a specific axis; destroying or suppressing a grouping of his fire means; exhausting an encircled enemy; suppressing his air defense system for a specific time; disrupting or complicating the actions of his reconnaissance forces and means, etc. Then, on the basis of the selected target of actions and multiple variants as calculated on a computer, the necessary quantity of the most effective forces and means to execute each concrete operational (tactical) mission in the existing situation is established.

Such an approach, in our opinion, will introduce great operational purposefulness into the combat employment of large formation forces and means, and make it possible to exclude, to a great degree, mechanical manipulation of combat power by qualitative indicators, while advancing as a foundation the maximum use of the qualitative aspect of available combat potential.

Changes in the content of *the principle of cooperation*, in our opinion, basically concern two trends. *First*: the circle of issues traditionally resolved in operations by coordinated employment of forces and means is becoming complex, and the volume and degree of detail of measures undertaken for this are increasing. *Second*: the necessity is arising to coordinate actions of forces and means when resolving qualitatively new missions, on whose execution the achievement of the ultimate operational aims is dependent to an increasingly greater degree.

In particular, foreign military specialists emphasize that success in modern operations will depend, to a great degree, on the coordinated and complete use of the potentials of long-range means of destruction, airborne and air-mobile forces, and diversionary-reconnaissance formations, that is, those forces and means which make it possible to achieve simultaneously deep and effective action against the enemy. At the same time, it is noted that organization and maintenance of cooperation between them and forces operating on the line of contact of the two sides is one of the most complex issues which must be resolved in the planning of and during operations. This is associated with, first and foremost, the complexity of organizing communications and control; the necessity of not only precise, but also constant coordination and refinement of missions for a large number of varied forces and means in a short time (especially when delivering coordinated strikes by fire assets and formations operating in the enemy rear); the high probability of a change in the decision made at the very beginning of the combat actions; complexity in reporting the missions, etc.

Thus, for example, *the question of cooperation in the interests of protecting troops and forces (especially tank groupings) against the enemy's high-precision weapons and combating his antitank means* requires most careful detailing and precision with respect to time for the efforts to be undertaken. Western military specialists give one of the central places in conducting any type of combat action to antitank stability. The complexity consists, first and foremost, of the density of antitank means in the combat formations of formations being increased three–five times in comparison with the Great Patriotic War, as shown by the following:

QUANTITY OF TANKS AND ANTITANK ASSETS AND THEIR DENSITIES
IN THE DEFENSE

	Fascist Germany		FRG	US
	Infantry Div		Mot Inf Div	Mot Div (Inf Div)
Year	1941	1945	1986	1986
Tanks	–	89	252	290
Antitank assets	156	275	2,185	866[3]
Average density of antitank assets and tanks (units per kilometer of defensive front)	14	33	80	40

There has also been a sharp increase in capabilities for mobility and armor protection, and increased effectiveness of enemy antitank means. Thus, it is necessary to coordinate efforts on a qualitatively new basis for the protection of armored equipment against strikes by high-precision weapons from above, and for fighting against such enemy systems and means as recce-strike and recce-fire complexes, complex robotic antitank systems such as the "Demon" (including the combat control tank and several robots), pilotless strike drones, widespread computer networks (making it possible, according to assessments by foreign specialists, to maintain stable control over the entire set of combat means, even in a nuclear war), etc.

War experience demonstrates that the more dynamic and decisive the combat actions, the greater the role of skillful implementation of the principle of maneuver. *In modern operations, maneuver can often be not only a uniformly effective means for countering the enemy, but also the most reliable method of bringing troops and forces out from under enemy strikes (including those of his high-precision weapons) and re-establishing the operational stability of the troops (forces).* It is important to be ready not only for changes in separate elements of the operational situation, but also for sharp and prompt changes in its entire content. This is why swift reaction to situational changes is now required of command cadres and staffs, while covert preparation, timely execution of assigned missions and reduction to a minimum of the time from when the enemy delivers a fire strike to the time when our forces deliver a retaliatory strike are required of the troops (forces). At the same time, a necessary condition for successful maneuver is the simplicity of its concept, especially in a complex situation.

Execution of maneuver by troops and forces may possibly lead to the weakening of specific axes. A commander's skill will consist of not only concealing the maneuver, but also surreptitiously reducing pressure against the enemy on such axes. Otherwise, the diminishing force of strikes may indicate to the enemy a weakening in our groupings on these axes, and he can deliver strikes here by superior forces or regroup part of them to the threatened front sector.

To achieve success in modern operations, *actions in the air and across air space will acquire special significance.* In realizing tactical and operational air mobility, various types of helicopters will be used more extensively. The contribution of air-assault actions in offensive and defensive operations is increasing. It is characteristic that they will resolve an increasingly greater volume of missions to rout enemy assault forces operating in our forces' rear area. Exercise experiences, in particular, demonstrate that counter-assaults will be widespread to reduce the period of maneuver and deliver strikes against assault forces.

As has been noted in the foreign press, a new element in NATO armies in the content of the principle under examination is *maneuver by deep, high-precision fire strikes.* Concentration of these strikes in a short time increases the degree of destruction of the enemy in selected regions, and the possibility appears for a broad selection of axes and number of penetration sectors, and for the frustration of enemy force maneuver (regrouping). The increased capability of high-precision means with respect to maneuver by trajectory will presumably be used for rapid intensification of mixed minefields and rapid set-up of jammers to disorganize control in threatened sectors. It has been noted that the effectiveness of destruction increases significantly when delivering fire strikes in close combination with remote mining and radio-electronic jamming.

Analysis of the experience of local wars and operational preparation demonstrates that one of the priority tenets in the content of the well-known *principle of maintaining force combat capability and its prompt regeneration* now belongs to ensuring their stability and survivability. Therefore, it is necessary to work out and implement beforehand a set of measures not only for regenerating disrupted force combat capability, but also for increasing their survivability and resistance to the action of any weapons. Implementation of this tenet as applied to large formation second echelons and reserves, elements of air defense and control systems, and air groupings, which are the principal objectives against which the enemy plans to strike, is acquiring special significance.

Modern weapons are suffused with new content and pose complex problems in implementing *the principle of firm and continuous troop (force) control*. It is necessary to keep in mind that, in the opinions of the NATO command, one of the principal missions high-precision weapons are to resolve is to disorganize control and communications systems. Substantive increase in the effectiveness of enemy reconnaissance makes it difficult to achieve covertness of operational preparations. Bloc leadership thinks that now there is the potential for reliably uncovering retaliatory measures being prepared by the opposing side approximately three days before commencement of military actions.

Under such conditions, firm troop control, including covertness of preparation of initial operations, can be achieved only with strict centralization of all work for organizing the repulsion of aggression, with full use of the potentials of automated troop and weapons control systems and computer technology. *At the same time, when using an automated control system, the task of reporting to commanders (chiefs) and staffs only that information necessary for the resolution of the concrete task at the given moment should be resolved purposefully.*

In the matter of improving stability and continuity of control on the basis of using an automated control system, reduction of the system model and improvement of informational and mathematical software are also of no little importance. Thus, in NATO armies it is planned to replace the 300 programming languages currently being used with a single language, "Ada." In realizing the principle of firm and continuous troop and force control, it is necessary to equip staffs with efficient mathematical models, to prepare generals and officers more purposefully to perform calculations for alternative variants for using troops (forces), and to teach them to make thorough conclusions. The necessity for creating means for automated analysis of a situation has also ripened.

Now we are at a turning point in the development of military affairs. Many long-standing principles of military theory are being reassessed, and fundamentally new approaches to resolving basic problems of military art are being worked out. A witness to the profound transformations in military theory is the appearance of a number of scientifically substantiated recommendations for conducting armed conflict under altered conditions. It can be said that some of them are being formulated as new principles of military art. One of them can, in our opinion, be formulated as an undeviating *rapprochement of methods for conducting operations* and the rout of enemy groupings with employment of both nuclear and conventional weapons. The action of this principle is exhibited in the fact that distinctions are disappearing in the majority of elements of the structure of these methods and in missions being resolved by opposing sides in operations using conventional and nuclear means. Thus, in the opinion of foreign specialists, to achieve surprise, to exploit its results fully, and *to rout the primary enemy grouping in the shortest time, the possibility has arisen of delivering very effective fire strikes using conventional weapons not only against weak, but also strong areas in the enemy's operational formation*, creating a so-called "window for action" for one's own shock (counterstroking) grouping. This will have special significance in the first operations of the initial period of a war, since it is namely then that it is proposed to use one's strike potential and achieve the assigned aims by delivery of a powerful fire strike and by practically simultaneous actions by force groupings (especially mobile ground and air-mobile forces) to the entire depth of the defender's operational formation in a short time, without significant regroupings, and with maximum decisiveness. At the same time, our forces are also able not only to parry strikes, but also to thwart (in a nuclear war as well) enemy offensive operations and deliver a decisive strike against him while repelling aggression, using fire power and radio-electronic warfare means. Data cited in the following table demonstrate that the skillful use of the fire power of large formations during the Great Patriotic War made it possible to achieve not only tactical, but also great operational results.

Finally, it is necessary to take into account the following circumstance as well. The NATO leadership, having analyzed the consequences of accidents at atomic power installations, has come to the conclusion that military results can be achieved by delivering strikes against these objectives, as well as against chemical industry installations and hydroelectric dams located on territory occupied by opposing forces. Therefore, in operations conducted with the employment of conventional weapons, it is necessary to organize and implement constantly the entire set of protective measures envisioned for combat actions with the employment of means of mass destruction.

In our opinion, another already formulated principle of military art is *the principle of asymmetric threat*. In essence it consists of the capability and necessity of creating in any situation conditions under which the enemy will be forced to undertake countermeasures requiring the expenditure of considerably large resources against our actions (which will require the minimum necessary forces and means).

EFFECTIVENESS OF ARTILLERY COUNTERPREPARATION DURING THE GREAT PATRIOTIC WAR

Large Formation, Time of Conduct Counterpreparation	Duration (min)	Front of Counterpreparation (km)	Results of Counterpreparation
16th and 19th Armies Western Front, 2 October 1941	10	10	Enemy attack weakened in region of Iartsevo
13th Army, Central Front, 5 July 1943	30	32	Enemy began arty prep 2 hours and offensive 2.5 hours later
6th, 7th Guards Armies, Voronezh Front, 5 July 1943	30	18 and 16	Enemy offensive delayed 3 hours
46th Army, 3d Ukrainian Front, 1 June 1944	30	3	Enemy went over to the offensive 2.5 hours after the counterpreparation

The high effectiveness of implementing the principle of asymmetric threat, created, for example, by subunits in the enemy rear, is confirmed by local war experience. According to the assessment of the Israeli command, in the invasion of Lebanon (1982) the actions of even separate commando groups in carrying out the mission of disorganizing control were often more effective than air strikes.

Analysis of principal trends in armed forces development, directions for improving organic organizational-establishment structure, and methods of troop (force) actions demonstrates the steady appearance of the desire to increase steadily their *combat independence and autonomy*. This tenet is now acquiring the significance of an independent principle of operational art. Thus, in the assessment of the American command, with the implementation of the "Army-90" program, mechanized and armored division brigades will be capable of executing deep fire destruction and conducting highly mobile combat actions under any conditions, including extended separation from the main forces. The latter is especially noted, since it is namely such actions which lie at the foundation of air-land operations. In other NATO armies they are proceeding along the path of creating conditions for independent combat actions not only by brigades, but also battalions. It is acknowledged that combat independence is a most important prerequisite for the successful execution of missions by subunits, units, and formations.

The principle of autonomy is expressed in the creation of force groupings which, because of their composition and support, would be capable of resolving their assigned missions without relying on the senior chief's forces and means under conditions of deep and intense enemy fire power, wide enemy use of assault forces, various types of raid detachments, and diversionary formations over a necessarily extended period of time.

Evolution of the principles of operational art, expressed in changes in their content, forms of manifestation, and appearance of a series of new principles, reflects the main trend in the development of military affairs. Rethinking existing principles of operational art and mastering new ones, and their imaginative use in practice are a necessary condition for improving combat readiness of large formations and formations to resolve missions ensuing from the defensive nature of our military doctrine.

NOTES

1. Ye. G. Korotchenko, "Ob evolyutsii printsipov voyennogo iskusstva," *Voyennaya mysl'* [Military thought], 9 (1988), pp. 22–30.
2. *Voyennaya mysl'*, 3 (1988), p. 3.
3. Taking into account the organic quantity of antitank grenade launchers.
4. *Front* operations in the Great Patriotic War

Soviet Military Doctrine and Some Views on the Nature of War in Defense of Socialism

GENERAL OF THE ARMY G. I. SALMANOV[1]

In assessing the contemporary stage of the development of socialism and the world as a whole, one can conclude that the most acute problems confronting the USSR and countries of the socialist commonwealth are the following: war prevention, especially nuclear war, and the maximum realization in a short time of socialism's previously unexploited potential. Both these problems are in close dialectic association. The general condition for their successful resolution is a reduction of tension in the military-political situation and improvement in relations between the USSR and the US, first and foremost. Only on this basis can the danger of the emergence of a new world war and nuclear catastrophe be reduced, and numerous concrete proposals for disarmament, introduced in recent years by the USSR and the socialist commonwealth countries, be implemented.

Despite a certain stabilization in relations between the USSR and the US, as a result of the implementation of a course of new political thinking, it would be incorrect to suppose that militaristic circles in the US have renounced their imperial ambitions or strivings for military superiority. Up to now, a "position of strength" has remained the cornerstone of the United States of America's foreign and military policy.

All this does not preclude the fact that a certain warming which has begun in relations between the USSR and the US can replace the polar cold. And if at present there are no grounds, then they can be artificially created, and for this we are constantly ready.

In such a situation, the development and presentation to the world community of the foundations of our refined, strictly peace-loving military doctrine, which places war prevention and the strengthening of international security as one of the main aims, are a clear example of the new political thinking of the CPSU and Soviet State, and an important contribution toward improving international stability and creating more favorable conditions for resolving economic and social tasks assigned by the XXVII Congress of the CPSU and the XIX All-Union Party Conference.

Two questions are examined in this article. The first is devoted to the clarification of the essence of Soviet military doctrine and the dialectic of refining its content. The second is devoted to possible changes in the nature of a world war, if it is unleashed by imperialistic militarism.

THE CONCEPT OF "MILITARY DOCTRINE" AND REASONS FOR CHANGES IN ITS CONTENT

Military doctrine is a historical category. Its tenets can be changed and supplemented under the influence of a multitude of factors: political, economic, military, and others.

In the overall plan, military doctrine is understood as a system of official views of a state on the nature of a possible war, and on preparation of the country and armed forces for war. In such an interpretation, war is thought of as a violent instrument for achieving political aims (including expansionist), while the army and the armed forces are considered the main means for such violence. It was this way before the Great October Socialist Revolution. It remains so in capitalist countries.

Already on the day after the victory of the armed uprising in Petrograd, V. I. Lenin, addressing the II All-Russian Congress of Soviets with a speech on peace, denounced war as a means for achieving expansionist political aims, and called on the workers to deliver themselves from the horrors of war. This principle became the cornerstone of the military policy and doctrine of the world's first socialist state.

In addition, foreseeing that the victory of the proletariat in one country would inevitably result in furious opposition from the world's bourgeoisie, Lenin was fully aware of the necessity of defending the victorious revolution: "Any revolution is worth something only if it can be defended."[2]

Taking into account such an approach, Soviet military doctrine was defined as a system of scientifically substantiated views, officially accepted in our country, on the nature of war, which could be imposed on the Soviet Union, and on military development and preparation of the country and the Armed Forces to defend socialist gains and rout the aggressor.

Comparing this definition with the general interpretation of military doctrine, it can be seen that, although the basic elements (nature of war, preparation of the country and the armed forces for it) are still retained structurally in it, each of these elements has qualitatively new content. War is unambiguously viewed as a forced type of action which can be employed only to defend the gains of socialism against possible aggression. The Soviet Armed Forces are also designated for this very purpose. A peace-loving, defensive nature was always an organic trait inherent to Soviet military doctrine.

The new situation unfolding now in the USSR, the socialist commonwealth countries, and in the world, and new thinking concerning issues of foreign and military policy have necessitated the refinement of our military doctrine, to include statements of principles which emphasize the defensive orientation of the military doctrine of the Soviet Union and the other Warsaw Treaty Organization countries.

At present, the military doctrine of the Warsaw Treaty Organization member-states is an officially accepted system of fundamental views on war prevention, military development, preparation of their countries and armed forces to repel aggression, and methods for conducting armed struggle in defense of the gains of socialism.

It is not difficult to observe that a new element – "war prevention" – has appeared in the cited definition. This most important doctrinal tenet conditions a substantive widening of functions and constitutional designation of the Soviet Armed Forces, and advances new requirements for their development.

The Armed Forces of the USSR must be capable not only of "defending the socialist Fatherland and being in constant combat readiness to ensure swift repulsion of any aggressor,"[3] but also of making a substantive contribution to preventing any war which might be unleashed against the USSR and socialist commonwealth countries.

What are the features of the new situation and the reasons which necessitated the refinement of our common military doctrine with our allies?

The logic of modern global socio-political development, the accumulation of enormous nuclear reserves, and the increased destructive properties of so-called conventional weapons confronted humanity extremely acutely with the problem of preventing a new world war, which would bring countless misfortunes to nations.

It was proven that the explosion of even one-tenth of the amassed 60,000 warheads with an overall power of more than 15,000 megatons (in TNT equivalents) would lead to instantaneous death for hundreds of millions of people. Those who remained would experience serious consequences of radiation and irreversible ecological changes. This provides a basis for stating that nuclear war goes beyond the bounds of the well-known formula that "war is an extension of politics by other (violent) means." As M. S. Gorbachev announced at the forum entitled, *For a Nuclear-Free World, For the Survival of Humanity*, "The nuclear maelstrom will sweep away socialists and capitalists, saints and sinners."[4]

The awesome danger of a new world war and real potentials for averting it necessitated new political thinking in approaching the problem of war and peace, and at the same time served as the *first main reason* for refining the content of our military doctrine.

The allied socialist states concluded that to view war, and even more so a world war, as a means for achieving political aims is not only amoral, but also criminal. Conditions have developed in the contemporary world, under which the antagonism between capitalism and socialism can and should continue only in forms of peaceful competition. Contested issues and conflict situations must be resolved politically, at the negotiating table. The principle of force in resolving international problems has been renounced by the majority of the world's countries.

However, the US military-political leadership is intensively expanding the material base for preparing a new war, on which hundreds of billions of dollars are allocated annually, to be spent on an unrestrained arms race, including space weapons. The US maintains an army numbering more than three million (including strategic reserves). Five hundred thousand American servicemen are located at more than 1,500 bases and military objectives, primarily located around the USSR and other socialist countries. In the development of weapons and its armed forces, the US clearly observes the pre-eminence of the offensive. The majority of US and NATO military-strategic concepts are based on surprise and pre-emption. The consolidation of the leading capitalist states on an anti-socialist, anti-Soviet basis is a serious danger.

It is not without interest to analyze the contemporary logic of the US military-political leadership's political thinking.

For the majority of politicians, and for the majority of people with commonsense who are not blinded by anti-Sovietism, it is clear that the US administration does not believe in the "deadly military threat" hanging, so to speak, over America, an idea which is pounded daily into the heads of American citizens. Indeed, the American military-political leadership is very well aware of the real state of affairs; by frightening the American and world community, it is pursuing specific political aims. The main aim is an attempt to achieve military superiority over the USSR and socialist commonwealth countries such as would, in combination with economic and political pressure, force us to our knees, ensure US hegemony in all important regions of the globe, establish an advantageous economic and political order, and increase profits and political influence for what President Eisenhower in his time called "the military-industrial complex."

In the US, including official circles, voices are often heard that if the Soviet Union achieves the aims established by the XXVII Party Congress in the economic and social spheres, this would strengthen its prestige in the international arena, increase the attractiveness of the Soviet system for developing countries, and extend the authority of the CPSU domestically and abroad, thereby (follow the logic here!) increasing the threat to US national security. On this basis, certain circles conclude that failure of the socio-economic policies of *perestroyka*, conducted in the USSR under the leadership of the CPSU and the Soviet government, would serve US national interests. From this ensues the majority of difficulties with which we must contend in the practical implementation of all peaceful initiatives and concrete proposals on disarmament advanced by the USSR and other socialist commonwealth countries. From here also ensue those negative, and sometimes malicious statements directed against us, often heard in the West, including from the "high" tribunals.

In light of the above, a perfidious *political plan* has been clearly sketched out, which lies at the basis of relations between Washington and the Soviet Union, namely, to provide the USSR and countries allied with it with an alternative: to force us to concede in an extremely costly arms race, thereby making it possible for imperialism to achieve military superiority, shatter existing parity, and dictate to us its political will from a position of force; or to force us to be included in an imposed, ruinous arms race, thereby exacerbating our existing economic difficulties, with all the negative consequences emanating from it. In this connection, one of the main tasks before the Soviet State and socialist commonwealth countries, as well as their armed forces, is to smash these alternatives imposed upon us by imperialism by finding a variant for our development by which we would be able to resolve our economic and social problems successfully while implicitly maintaining strategic equilibrium.

The necessity of breaking down the political alternative imposed on us by imperialism was the *second main reason* for refining Soviet military doctrine, and the military doctrine of the Warsaw Treaty Organization member-states as a whole. Carrying out the principles of the refined military doctrines, in addition to preventing war, should also facilitate an improvement in the conditions of our internal development by realizing *the principle of defensive sufficiency*, a principle in accordance with which the development and preparation of the Soviet Armed Forces, as well as the armed forces of our allies, should be implemented without diverting additional resources over and above those necessary for defense.

Realization of the principle of sufficiency "assumes steady reduction of the degree of military confrontation, while observing reciprocity, equality, and uniform security of the sides."[5]

What is the sense in publishing and reporting to the world community the basic refined tenets of Soviet military doctrine? After all, as is known, earlier there was no sense in this.

The fact is that the leaders of imperialism and the powerful and highly professionally trained propaganda apparatus serving them, to justify their militaristic policies before the world community, tirelessly brandish the bugaboo of the Soviet Union's aggressiveness, its, as it were, predominant aggressive might which is directed, first and foremost, at seizing Europe and setting up pro-Communist regimes in the developing world. They frighten Europeans with red arrows penetrating this continent to the Bay of Biscay. As for the American citizen, he is kept in constant fear of a kind of "sword of Damocles" hanging over his head in the form of a Soviet nuclear attack.

All this creates in some parts of the world community an incorrect, false impression of the position of the USSR and its allied socialist countries with respect to the problem of war and peace, and generates tension, thereby increasing the real danger of unleashing a third, devastating world war.

Under these conditions, publication of the basic principles of the military doctrine of the Warsaw Treaty Organization member-states makes it possible to reveal to humanity our true intentions in the military sphere and our love of peace, thereby helping to remove the mutual suspicion and mistrust built up over the years, and to achieve a better understanding of one another. Proposals to NATO member-states to conduct consultations to compare the military doctrines of both sides are also directed toward this.

WHAT IS NEW IN THE CONTENT OF SOVIET MILITARY DOCTRINE AND ITS REFLECTION IN VIEWS ON THE NATURE OF A POSSIBLE WAR IN DEFENSE OF SOCIALISM?

The nature of war is understood as the totality of the most substantive characteristics and indicators which reflect its socio-political and strategic content.

The socio-political content of war and its just or unjust character is deter-mined by the class affiliation of opposing sides and their political aims.

The strategic content of war, which reflects its military-technical essence, should disclose the nature of strategic aims and missions of opposing sides in a war, possible conditions and methods for unleashing it, types of weapons to be used, the scope of participating states and combat actions, methods and forms of its conduct, possible duration, periodization of war and the content of its major periods, peculiarities of military operations, their expected consequences, etc.

A complete representation of the enumerated indicators is a most impor-tant condition for a correct and substantiated approach to all problems of defensive development.

Working out this complex problem is *one of the main missions of Soviet military science.* Soviet military science bases its solution on doctrinal positions, reflecting the most fundamental features in views on the nature of a war which may be imposed upon us by imperialistic militarism. A necessarily more detailed picture of a possible war in defense of socialism is being recreated on the basis of systemic analysis of facts, making it possible to reveal the connection between various indicators of war and factors having the most substantive effect on them: political, economic, military, scientific-technical, geographic, etc. The development of new concepts of military art, and methods and forms of conducting military operations to ensure the most effective employment of all Armed Forces services to repel any military aggression in complete correspondence to the requirements of defensive doctrine are acquiring primary importance in the resolution of this task.

An important question Soviet military doctrine must answer is: who will unleash a war against the USSR and the socialist commonwealth countries, and what kind of war will it be? Materials from the XXVII Party Congress and the XIX All-Union Party Conference provide a precise answer to the first part of the question. In his speech at the XIX All-Union Party Conference, Gorbachev noted:

> imperialism, in fact, created around us and our allies an extreme situation. The Western military bloc, headed by the US, has behaved with open aggression toward socialism. The military threat has become, for us, a constant. Even now it has not been removed.[6]

As for the second part of the question, the doctrine of "direct confrontation," adopted by the US, helps to provide a substantiated response. This doctrine envisions conduct of both universal (world) wars (nuclear and conventional) and wars in theaters in which both nuclear and conventional weapons may be employed. The Soviet Union and socialist commonwealth countries have been declared the main enemy in them. A significant place in the doctrine of "direct confrontation" has been reserved for "low intensity" conflicts. Among these are local wars, as well as the entire spectrum of possible minor military conflicts in which the armed forces of the US and its allies could participate.

It is obvious that the USSR and socialist commonwealth countries must be ready for all the enumerated wars. Main emphasis should be placed, in our opinion, on preparing countries and their armed forces for the most serious variant, that is, *a prolonged world war*, if it should be unleashed by imperialist militarism.

Such a war is capable of acquiring extremely destructive forms; all types of weapons, including nuclear, could be employed, and military operations conducted on enormous expanses under conditions of extreme physical and psychological stress for armed forces personnel and the populace, with serious losses and destruction.

There is justification for assuming that warring sides will attempt to achieve their own strategic and political aims by employing only conventional means of destruction. Even here, however, as a result of strikes against atomic and chemical industrial objectives, an extremely complex situation can arise. In addition, in a conventional war the constant threat of enemy employment of nuclear weapons remains.

All this forces us to conclude now that it is very dangerous to make a cursory assessment of the enemy and the nature of possible war, and exaggerate our abilities to repel aggression. *The enemy is strong enough, and it will not be at all easy to rout him, although there can, naturally, be no other outcome.*

What, then, is new in the content of Soviet military doctrine, and how can it be reflected in the nature of a possible war?

First and foremost, *there is the reinforcement and emphasis of its defensive orientation*, a demonstration of the political will of the USSR to apply all efforts to resolve the fundamental task of mankind – to prevent war, both nuclear and conventional, and to reject war as a premeditated means for achieving political aims.

In the fundamental tenets of the Warsaw Treaty Organization member-states' military doctrine, published at the end of May 1987, it is stated that the USSR and countries allied with it will under no circumstances be the first to begin military operations against any state or alliance of states whatsoever; that they will never be the first to employ nuclear weapons; that they have no territorial claims; and that they regard no one state as their enemy.

At the same time, it was announced that if the USSR or other Warsaw Treaty Organization countries are, nevertheless, attacked, then they will crushingly repel the aggressor.

In accordance with the military doctrine's strictly defensive orientation, views on the *correlation of the offense and defense* (in the military-technical aspect), and on methods and forms of conducting military operations have undergone changes.

Under modern conditions, with the commencement of a war, priority is given to retaliatory actions, that is, to defense and conduct of defensive operations. Readiness for this must be ensured to the maximum possible degree in peacetime.

Defense in the initial period of war is now viewed not only as a means, with whose help it is possible with comparatively fewer forces to exhaust the aggressor, stop him as quickly as possible, and create the necessary conditions for dynamic counteroffensive operations; but also as a means (and this is very important) to force the enemy to think it over many times before deciding to attack. The defense can also be employed in separate theaters of military operations to hold the enemy for a prolonged time on previously prepared lines with comparatively few forces.

Currently, one necessarily encounters statements that, with approximate equality of forces on both sides in a theater of military operations and with improvement in modern intelligence, the unleashing of a war by an aggressor in, for example, Europe is a chimera. Insisting on this opinion, they state that an aggressor can decide to attack only under the condition that, as a result of his first strategic operation, he achieves important strategic aims (that he can reach the border of the USSR, for example).

To achieve such an aim, an aggressor must have a three- to fourfold superiority in forces on the main attack axes (and one cannot fail to agree with this). It is obvious that it is not possible to create such superiority covertly before the beginning of a war.

All this is actually so, if one does not take into account the completely new quality in the enemy's fire capabilities, the sharply increased mobility of his shock groups, and his admitted main method of unleashing war – a surprise attack.

Even with an approximately equivalent correlation of forces before the commencement of military operations, an enemy who has suddenly unleashed war will attempt to change this correlation to his advantage on separate axes. It is obvious that such a situation can be achieved during an air-land operation by the action of powerful fire strikes in punching corridors through our combat formations and rapidly introducing into them strong groupings of mobile infantry units, large assault forces, army aviation, specially trained diversionary-reconnaissance detachments (groups), etc. The actions of these groups will apparently develop covered on their flanks by continuous fire. Our reserves' approach will be blocked by deep fire strikes delivered by aviation and long-range, high-precision weapons.

Many may regard this variant for the development of events as fantastic. However, if we are not thoroughly prepared for it, then this fantasy can turn into an awesome reality.

Thus, the new doctrinal approach to the correlation of the offense and defense, and the extreme importance of effective preparation to conduct the first defensive operations of the initial period of war urgently dictate that, *first*, the main efforts in preparing the Armed Forces must be concentrated, first and foremost, on their organizational deployment and successful execution of missions to repel aggression during the initial period of a war, employing both conventional and nuclear weapons. Special attention must be focused on timely detection and prevention of an aggressor's intended surprise attack. In resolving this task, well-organized reconnaissance [intelligence] must play the main role. It must under any conditions provide timely data concerning the enemy's immediate preparation for an attack and an approximate time for its commencement.

Second, it is also important to have our defensive grouping prepared beforehand, in well defended defensive groupings, and in the necessary composition, with a guarantee of the ability to increase its combat readiness adequately as the enemy intensifies his readiness for a possible attack. Our peacetime grouping, especially the first operational echelon, should, in case of an aggressor's attack, be able to conduct the first defensive operations independently and without reinforcement, preventing the enemy from reaching the depth of the territory and creating conditions for successful conduct of subsequent actions to rout him.

Third, we should be able to create promptly a system of fire, in whose presence the enemy, in response to his commencement of aggression, would receive a swift and annihilating massed retaliatory fire strike capable of sharply weakening his offensive potential even before the moment of commitment of his second-echelon shock groups into the engagement. From here it follows that when planning the formation of Ground Forces, Air Forces, and Air Defense Forces, special attention must be focused on their ability to gain fire and air superiority from the very commencement of war.

The development of means and methods for countering new weapons which the enemy plans to introduce into his armed forces in the next 10–15 years is acquiring particular urgency. It is extremely important to find answers promptly, which will ensure the reduction of effectiveness in the enemy's use of high-precision, land-, air-, and sea-based weapons; low-powered laser weapons, designed to blind personnel and put surveillance and targeting instruments out of commission; and radio-absorption coverings, which can substantially reduce the capabilities of our air defense in fighting tactical aviation.

Fourth, in our opinion it is necessary to focus particular attention on ensuring reliable cover of second echelons, reserves, and rear objectives against strikes by enemy aviation and high-precision weapons during his conduct of an air-land operation.

Under these conditions, the defense will not only be a means capable of repelling enemy incursions, but will also create prerequisites for recapturing the initiative and conducting effective successive operations to rout him.

In case of an attack by an aggressor, it is very important to prevent the loss of a considerable portion of one's territory. For this, it is necessary to take all measures to improve its *stability*. In any case, the defense must be dynamic.

A complex requirement now confronting the defense is maximum exploitation of its advantages, with all-round economization of forces and means. Implementation of this is a most important condition for the rout of an aggressor.

All this can be actually achieved by the self-sacrificing daily work of commanders and staffs, high level of combat training and moral-psychological preparation of soldiers and officers, excellent knowledge of the enemy and deep foresight of events; and, finally, by the conduct of a broad set of measures for the all-round preparation of the defense beforehand (in peacetime). The logic of military-political thought is such that the enemy, knowing about our preparation and constant readiness to repel aggression swiftly, and the stability, dynamism, and power of our defense, will ponder many times over the well-known truth that "war is easier to start than to stop."

The intensive development and improvement of weapons and combat equipment has an enormous effect on the nature of a possible war and the methods and forms of its conduct. Engels' thesis that

> success of equipment, even if it has just become applicable and, in fact, barely employed in military affairs, immediately – almost violently, often against the will of the military command – causes changes and even revolutions in the method of waging war[7]

has manifested itself especially powerfully under modern conditions.

The sharply increased destructive features (range and precision) of conventional weapons continue to impart a new quality to them: in their massed employment, they approach weapons of mass destruction. Now the potential has arisen for conventional weapons to destroy swiftly not only separate subunits and units, but also whole elements of the combat formation and operational formation. Centers and extended communications sectors, landing strips at airfields, deep reserves, etc. can be put out of action quickly. All this will complicate maneuver of forces and reduce the effectiveness of employing aviation and other armed forces services.

The possibility for simultaneous destruction of force groupings to the entire depth of their operational formation will obviously become one of the principal methods of combat actions in conventional war. Under these conditions, the role of the moral-psychological factor sharply increases, as does the requirement for protection of troops and the population. Gaining fire superiority is acquiring enormous significance.

The constantly increasing maneuver potentials of ground forces make it possible to regroup in a short time (while observing secrecy) along the front and in the depth. The rapid growth of army aviation – first and foremost, helicopters – is resulting in battles and operations taking on an increasingly three-dimensional form.

Increasing capabilities of air-assault forces and the widespread employment of helicopters for infantry assault landing conditions the fragmented nature of the battle and engagement. In addition to dynamic actions on the principal front, it is necessary to undertake considerable efforts to combat assault forces in the depth of the defense, and to take measures beforehand to protect rear objectives.

The destructive nature of a possible war, and steadily increasing fire power, together with the sharp increase in the effectiveness of radio-electronic warfare with respect to disrupting the troop control system, can result in a significant part of the formations and units, as well as separate subunits, being forced to operate in isolation, without control from above and without support from neighboring units.

We think that it is already necessary now to focus serious attention on preparing forces (first and foremost, ground forces) for autonomous actions in a complex situation. Under these conditions, initiative, bravery, and boldness of ideas and actions, the success of which will depend, to a great degree, on the reliability and stability of rear and other types of support, will acquire a special role.

The continuously increasing complexity of weapons has already very distinctly posed the question concerning the realization of the combat potentials placed in them. Its resolution depends on the quality of personnel. An inadequately trained serviceman is unable to ensure the effective employment of a new weapon or piece of combat equipment. Moreover, as a result of inadequately intelligent actions, he may quickly put them out of action. All this compels us to seek *new methods for manning the Armed Forces and preparing reserves.*

Mass introduction of radio-electronics into the armed forces of both sides, and the trend to equip thoroughly elements of the troop and weapons control system with radio-electronic installations sharply increases the significance of radio-electronic warfare. It is completely possible that in the near future radio-electronic warfare will turn into an independent type of struggle with its own forms of action. Success in battle and operations will directly depend on the effectiveness of such a struggle.

It is necessary to be ready for the fact that, in case war is unleashed by an imperialist aggressor, massed employment of radio-electronic means will precede powerful enemy fire strikes. This can substantially complicate the organization of defensive actions and facilitate the ability to impose one's will on the other side.

In light of the NATO concept of "fighting against second echelons," the advance of our second echelons and reserves from the depth may become a serious problem. Very serious attention must be focused on organizing their reliable cover.

The NATO command attaches enormous significance to tactical aviation, viewing it as the main means for delivering deep fire strikes. The augmentation of the role of tactical aviation is conditioned by the sharp increase in its combat capabilities through the adoption into the armed forces of effective, high-precision aviation weapons – such as guided rockets and bombs – and long-range cruise missiles with self-guidance to the final sector of the trajectory, which are especially dangerous. As is generally known, such rockets can be launched before the appearance of an airplane in our air defense's zone of effective action.

All this compels us to seek intensively new methods for fighting against enemy tactical aviation, keeping in mind that methods of radar concealment being developed by the "Stealth" program will presumably be shifted to this aviation's aircraft.

Intensive development of military-space means and implementation of Reagan's strategic defense initiative program (SDI) will have an increasingly substantial influence on the nature of modern wars. Waging war is not now considered by US and NATO military circles without the broad employment of space systems, both support and combat.

Under conditions of continuous US use of various space reconnaissance means, equipped with optical-electronic, photographic, infrared, radar, radio-technical, and other reconnaissance apparatus, even in peacetime it is necessary for all commanders and staffs to remember that we are in full view, and our measures, attended by unmasking signs visible from the air or from space, are being effectively detected by US space reconnaissance. This must be remembered, and all necessary measures taken.

In the currently ongoing development of military-space means in the US, the trend of turning them into effective combat means can be clearly seen. They are counting on creating space weapons to conduct military operations in space and deliver strikes from space against objectives on the earth's surface. The overall plan for the creation and employment of combat military-space means is to gain superiority in space and shatter existing strategic parity. This is dangerous, but, unfortunately, completely real. Therefore, it is necessary to continue intensive research on neutralizing the threat arising from space, and to find effective and economically justifiable answers.

Military doctrine, which reflects the main essence of policies in the field of our country's defense and security, is the most important instrument in a uniform, purposeful scientific approach to resolving complex problems. In this connection, it is appropriate to speak of the necessity of increasing the role of military science and the military problem-solving of other sciences in working out future trends for the development of military art, and the development and training of the Armed Forces. It is necessary to concentrate principal efforts on a thorough analysis of the characteristic features of armed conflict, operations, and combat actions during the initial period of war, and to work out scientifically the practical tasks of improving combat readiness, taking into account the requirements of defensive military doctrine. *Broadening the content of Soviet military doctrine and, as a whole, the military doctrine of the Warsaw Treaty Organization countries is the result of the new political thinking of the CPSU in its approach to the problem of war and peace, and to issues of strengthening international stability.*

Realization of new doctrinal tenets requires definite restructuring and new approaches to our defensive development. Therefore, in training the army and navy, *the main efforts must necessarily be concentrated on carrying out the resolutions of the XXVII Party Congress, the XIX All-Union Party Conference, and subsequent Plenums of the Central Committee of the CPSU on ensuring the reliable defense of the USSR and allied socialist countries, shifting to qualitative parameters in military development and the development of military science and military art, and maintaining Soviet Armed Forces combat readiness and combat capability at a level which will ensure war prevention and the successful repulsion of aggression under any conditions in which it might be unleashed.* Today, as never before, an important role in the resolution of these complex problems belongs to Soviet military science.

NOTES

1. G. I. Salmanov, "Sovetskaya voyennaya doktrina i nekotoryye vzglyady na kharakter voyny v zashchitu sotsializma," *Voyennaya mysl'* [Military thought], 12 (1988), pp. 3–13.
2. V. I. Lenin, *Polnoye sobraniye sochineniy* [Complete works], Vol. 37, p. 122.
3. *Konstitutsiya (Osnovnoy Zakon)* [The constitution. The fundamental law] (Moscow: Yuridicheskaya literatura, 1987), p. 31.
4. M. S. Gorbachev, *Izbrannyye rechi i stat'i* [Selected speeches and articles], Vol. 4 (Moscow: Politizdat, 1987), p. 380.
5. D. T. Yazov, "Kachestvennyye parametry oboronnogo stroitel'stva," [Qualitative parameters of defensive development], *Krasnaya zvezda* [Red Star], 9 August 1988.
6. *Pravda*, 29 June 1988.
7. K. Marx and F. Engels, *Works*, Vol. 20, p. 176.

Preparation and Conduct of Army Operations: Historical Experience and Contemporaneity

LIEUTENANT GENERAL (RET.) V. G. REZNICHENKO[1]

This article examines problems of preparing and conducting a number of army operations during the Great Patriotic War, and basic trends in the development of operational art which have maintained their significance under modern conditions as well.

DEFENSIVE OPERATIONS

The USSR's military doctrine emphasizes that the Soviet Armed Forces' principal operational method at the beginning of the war, with respect to repelling aggression, is defense. This promotes more than a few new problems for military art: for example, when and how to prepare and occupy the defense so as to prevent a surprise enemy attack while not provoking him to unleash a war; and when and how to shift to counteroffensive operations to complete the rout of an aggressor. The experience of the Great Patriotic War has great importance for successfully resolving these problems, but it is necessary to exploit this while taking into account today's requirements.

In the prewar years, combined-arms armies deployed in the border zone had the mission of stubbornly defending sectors outfitted with fortifications and permanent structures, preventing an enemy incursion, and supporting force mobilization, concentration, and deployment. *The composition of armies was not uniform.* It depended, first and foremost, on the importance of the axis being covered and the numerical strength of the opposing enemy grouping. Thus, Kiev Special Military District's 5th Army, covering the shortest axis to the Ukrainian capital, consisted of 15th and 27th Rifle and 22d and 9th Mechanized Corps, with 14th Mixed and 62d Bomber Aviation Divisions in operational subordination. With the commencement of combat operations, 1st Antitank Artillery Brigade, a howitzer artillery regiment, three antiaircraft artillery battalions, units of three fortified regions, and two border detachments were subordinated to the army commander. In all, the army totaled 102,500 men, 682 tanks, 1,521 guns and mortars, 490 antitank and 111 antiaircraft guns, and 265 airplanes. As a result, the densities of forces and means in the defended sector (176 kilometers) were 1.5–2 times lower than anticipated by prewar views.[2] A rifle division covered an average of 44 kilometers, with 87th Rifle Division covering 54 kilometers.

Against 5th Army the enemy concentrated a grouping comprising 12 infantry, five tank, and three motorized divisions and a motorized brigade. It was two-three times superior to Soviet forces (three-five times on the main attack axis). The average operational density of enemy forces in the main attack sector was one division every five kilometers of front. However, the correlation of opposing forces and means is only one of the factors in preparing and conducting defensive operations. *Also important is how well planned and organized is their practical use, especially the conduct of defensive measures on the whole.*

Experience demonstrates that defensive decisions by army commanders were formulated as covering plans, which originated from the presence of a "threatening" period: even first-echelon army formations had to be brought up to strength. For example, 5th Army rifle divisions were manned in personnel at 65–68 per cent; motor vehicles at 62 per cent; artillery at 85–100 per cent; and antiaircraft guns at 75 per cent. It was planned to form the majority of army communications units upon the announcement of mobilization.[3] The army operational formation was basically a single echelon with rifle corps in the first echelon and mechanized corps in the reserve. *Rifle corps*, together with fortified regions and border detachments, received the mission of defending the state border in 80–100-kilometer sectors. Thus, 5th Army's 15th Rifle Corps was to cover the state border in an 84-kilometer sector, while 27th Rifle Corps with the Vladimir-Volynsk Fortified Region, the first and second defense centers of the Strumilov Fortified Region, and 90th Border Detachment was to cover a 92-kilometer sector. Rifle corps combat formations were usually structured in a single echelon. *Mechanized corps* (22d and 9th) comprised the army reserve, designated, first and foremost, to deliver counterstrokes. As a rule, *rifle divisions*, defending on probable enemy attack axes, structured their combat formations in two echelons. The depth of a division's defensive sector (in practice, the depth of the tactical defense zone) did not exceed 10–12 kilometers, which was clearly inadequate to check the attack of superior enemy forces.

Engineer preparation of the terrain was also poor. According to covering plans, in peacetime first-echelon rifle divisions outfitted only the first position with trenches for rifle squads and fire means, and also prepared false trenches, communications trenches, dug-outs, and shelters. Battalion defense regions of first positions were created in the immediate vicinity of the border, and in the majority of sectors they coincided with the forward edge of fortified regions, whose construction had not been completed by the commencement of the war.

Troop deployment was also unsuccessful: first-echelon units and formations were located 10–65 kilometers from designated defensive belts and sectors, while the enemy was directly at the border, which made it possible for him to thwart the systematic advance of Soviet forces and their occupation of the defense. Covering armies had to create a defensive grouping under direct enemy pressure during difficult meeting battles while his mobile formations were deeply penetrating, especially on the flanks. In 5th Army's sector, the aggressor's forces had penetrated the tactical defensive zone and advanced to a depth of 30–40 kilometers by the close of 23 June 1941.

Mechanized corps were in no better situation: 22d Corps headquarters, 19th Tank Division and 215th Motorized Division were deployed in Rovno, 150 kilometers from the state boundary, while 9th Mechanized Corps formations were in Novograd-Volynskiy and Shepetovka. They suffered losses while advancing, not only from enemy air strikes, but also because of equipment breakdown (as a result of its being worn out and the lack of adequate repair and evacuation means). Corps were regrouped slowly, and counterstrokes did not achieve their aim, that is, they did not lead to the defeat of penetrating enemy tank and motorized formations which desired to avoid combat against Soviet tank divisions, and, having avoided them, to encircle the *front* main force grouping instead. Mechanized corps had to fight basically against enemy infantry formations, well equipped with antitank means and artillery, and having powerful air support.

Thus, an analysis of the grouping and operation of the Kiev Special Military District's 5th Army (and this was typical for many other armies) provides the grounds for concluding that the first army defensive operations of the initial period of the Great Patriotic War began under conditions of considerable enemy superiority on selected axes. Covering armies were not promptly brought up to strength or deployed in their designated defensive sectors. The tactical zone had, in practice, no successive defensive lines, since there were usually no second echelons in rifle corps.

What were the reasons for the failures of Soviet forces in the first army defensive operations? First and foremost, because the condition of the forces, their deployment, and covering plans did not reckon on a surprise enemy attack. On the eve of the war, Soviet theory unambiguously envisioned the presence of a threatening period. The fact that *the defensive structure of Soviet formations and large formations did not fully take into account the power of deep attacks by German-Fascist forces* also favored successful actions by the aggressor. In the prewar years, Soviet military science developed the progressive theory of deep battle and operations, and methods of maneuver. Unfortunately, German-Fascist forces used these ideas. Requisite attention was not focused on the concrete development and mastery of measures to counter this, or to the creation of a stable defense, for which we paid dearly in defensive battles and operations, especially during the initial period of the war. The experience of this period demonstrated *the decisive role of rifle formations in executing defensive tasks. However, their shock force, maneuverability, and capabilities for fighting against enemy tanks and aviation were inadequate.* The trend for improving these combat qualities was observed throughout the entire war, as well as in local wars of the postwar period.

The surprise Wehrmacht attack, the resulting lack of organization during commitment into battle of the greater portion of Soviet forces deployed near the border, and their first unsuccessful battles had serious morale and psychological consequences. They engendered fear of encirclement, "planeo-phobia," and "tankophobia" among the forces and staffs, which negatively affected their steadfastness in the defense. *The condition of command cadres* also did not correspond to the requirements of combat operations. The practice of Armed Forces deployment in 1939–41 and unjustified repressions led to formations and units in border military districts not even being fully manned or outfitted. Command cadre manning of mechanized corps divisions was especially low. For example, 37th Tank Division of Southwestern Front's 15th Mechanized Corps, equipped with 85 per cent of its tanks, had only 41.2 per cent of its requisite officer cadre.[4] Only 4.8 per cent of the officers had higher military education, 46 per cent had military high school education, 35 per cent had completed accelerated courses, and 13 per cent had no military education at all. An absolute majority of command personnel was quickly raised several steps up the service ladder, but they had neither appropriate theoretical knowledge nor practical skills.

Poor command personnel and staff training was a reason for the poor organization of reconnaissance and many shortcomings in control. When organizing the defense, army and formation commanders attempted to cover the entire defensive sector (usually quite wide) with their forces without having information about the enemy, and so scattered their limited forces and means. This made it impossible to create a deeply echeloned defense or form reserves capable of countering enemy mobile formations which had penetrated into the depth.

In contrast with Soviet forces, the enemy had considerable advantages – fully outfitted units and formations, high mobility, and coordination of control organs; almost two years of experience in a victorious war in Western Europe, which had great morale and psychological significance; early and systematic deployment of shock groupings, surprise of attack and delivery of deep, isolating attacks, which thwarted mobilization and Soviet force deployment plans.

In addition, the experience of combat operations at the beginning of the war demonstrated that where forces entered battle in an organized fashion and formation and unit commanders acted creatively and with initiative, the enemy was unsuccessful, despite his advantages. Thus, several days before the war, the commander of 5th Army's 87th Rifle Division, Major General F. F. Alyabushev, under the guise of an exercise, brought division units up to their designated covering sectors and conducted considerable work to organize cooperation and the defensive fire system. This was prompted by the extremely exacerbated situation on the border. According to information acquired from border troops and army headquarters, it had become certain that the enemy was moving forces forward, deploying them in the immediate vicinity, laying out ammunition, and removing their engineer obstacles along the border. However, on 20 June 1941, an order arrived from army head-quarters to withdraw the division from the border and place it in a camp east of Vladimir-Volynskiy. The division commander carried out the order, but on his own initiative left one rifle battalion with artillery from each regiment in the forward defense area. Reliable communications were organized with the battalions, subunits of fortified regions, border troops, and reconnaissance posts sent out from the units.

These measures made it possible for the division commander to obtain objective information on the situation and act accordingly. During assembly of units after the alarm, General Alyabushev received information from border troops on the enemy's penetration in the region of Ustilug. Consequently, he decided not to move regiments forward to the border but to attack the penetrating enemy, defeat him, and then occupy the defensive sector designated by the plan. The attack surprised the aggressor. He was thrown back to the border, and units reached their sectors and occupied the defense. By noon, having renewed the attack, the enemy had penetrated 16th Rifle Regiment's right flank and captured Ustilug. At 1300, he began to commit 14th Tank [Panzer] Division into battle through the existing breach. General Alyabushev moved two direct-fire artillery battalions forward into the enemy penetration sector. Under their cover, 283d Rifle Regiment (the division's second echelon), together with part of 16th and 96th Rifle Regiments' forces, counterattacked the penetrating enemy grouping, threw it back, liberated Ustilug, and thwarted the commitment of the enemy division.

Initiative and operational actions, originality in thinking on the part of the division commander, and troop decisiveness and stubbornness are instructive even for today. All this should, *first of all,* be reflected in attempts on the part of commanders at all levels of the first operational echelon, especially of covering forces, to relate their decisions on defense to actual terrain conditions and to organize systems of fire and cooperation carefully. *Second,* they must also always be ready for unexpected actions, unforeseen in plans, to repel enemy aggression.

Analysis of the conditions for preparing and conducting first army defensive operations during the initial period of the Great Patriotic War makes it possible to draw the following conclusions. Covering force operational plans should envision several of the most probable variants for joining battle upon the commencement of aggression, first and foremost in case of a surprise enemy attack. The defensive grouping of forces and means necessary for this must be created beforehand and deployed at a distance from regions, sectors, and belts designated for defense, so that it can success-fully occupy these positions before the enemy reaches the state border. Units and formations allocated to resolve this mission must be fully manned and outfitted, and ensured reliable air cover. The army combat composition must be capable of creating a deep operational formation which can counter enemy attacks not only from the front, but also from the flanks and rear, and to fight against his aviation, air-assault forces, and diversionary-reconnais-sance groups. As the enemy groupings and their degree of combat readiness increase, it is necessary to increase the combat composition of covering forces and the level of their combat readiness, to prevent the unleashing of surprise aggression.

Taking into account the defense's advantages, engineer preparation of its principal elements must begin as early as possible, under the guise of exer-cises and classes. Particular attention must be focused on creating false objectives, deceiving the enemy, and exhibiting military stratagems at all stages of preparing and conducting defensive actions. The defense should be dynamic, commander and staff actions should exhibit initiative and be creative and steadfast, and those of the forces should be stubborn, bold, and decisive. However, counterattacks and counterstrokes cannot be viewed as the only way to exhibit dynamism in the defense. According to recent war experience, these achieve their aim only if they are well prepared and succeed not only in stopping the enemy, but also in exhausting him by a stubborn defense and changing the correlation of forces and means with respect to the main indices.

In subsequent periods of the Great Patriotic War, army defensive opera-tions were, as a rule, conducted under more favorable conditions. Several weeks to several months were allotted for their preparation, which made it possible to organize systematically both the replenishment of formations and units with forces and means, and their training; to plan carefully operations and battles; and to conduct basic preparatory measures on the terrain, especially the organization of fire destruction of the enemy and cooperation of forces and means participating in the battle and operation. The depth of the tactical and operational defense and the density of forces and means increased. The system of defensive belts, positions, and regions developed along the path of shifting from outfitting one belt and separate regions in the depth to creating in an army three belts comprising two to four positions each. In essence, antitank defense and its engineer preparation – a system of trenches and communication trenches – occupied a central place in the defense. The role of rifle divisions, which comprised the basis of not only the first, but also the second echelon of an army, increased. The dynamism of the defense increased as a result of improving its structure, conducting an artillery counterpreparation, delivering counterattacks and counterstrokes, widely maneuvering fire and forces, boldly combining real and deceptive actions, and employing tank (antitank) ambushes and mobile antitank lines.

These were the principal trends for improving the art of organizing and conducting the defense using formations and large formations during the Great Patriotic War.

OFFENSIVE OPERATIONS

During the initial period of the Great Patriotic War, Soviet forces, having suffered considerable losses, were unable to conduct extensive offensive operations. Dynamic offensive force operations were basically carried out in the form of *front* and army counterstrokes. More than a few army offensive operations were conducted within the framework of the Battle of Smolensk (10 July–10 September 1941). An important element of it was the Yel'nya offensive operation by the Reserve Front's 24th Army (30 August– 8 September 1941). During the battle, two tank, one motorized, and seven enemy infantry divisions were destroyed. Army formations and units exhibited exceptional bravery, courage, and heroism, for which two army rifle divisions (100th and 127th) were the first to receive the designation of "Guards" (1st and 2d Guards Rifle Divisions). The army's merit rests in its shifting to the offensive without an operational pause, under conditions of unceasing enemy action and his overall superiority in forces and means.

Analysis of this and other offensive operations conducted in summer and autumn 1941 makes it possible to draw a conclusion concerning the importance of dynamic offensive operations when conducting a strategic defense. In other words, under conditions of the defensive orientation of the USSR's military doctrine, commanders, staffs, and troops must be prepared not only to conduct defensive operations and deliver counterstrokes, but also to execute counteroffensive and offensive operations. If a counteroffensive operation will most probably be conducted after the enemy is struck decisively during a defensive engagement, then an offensive operation can be conducted simultaneously with a defensive operation, but on a different axis, where the enemy is shifting to the defense.

In subsequent war years, conditions for preparing and conducting army offensive operations and their content and scope changed considerably. This was connected, first and foremost, with improvement in the technical outfitting and organizational structure of the combined-arms army, and with a transformation of enemy views on the defensive formation. The process of completely saturating the army with automatic weapons, more powerful artillery, tanks and self-propelled artillery, and other arms was one of the principal factors resulting in an increase in their combat capabilities. As a rule, the army operational formation consisted of two echelons. When there were five to seven divisions in an army, the second echelon was made up of two or three divisions. *The mobile group was a new element in the operational formation.* At first it was created from several tank (motorized) brigades (regiments), united under a single command; later it consisted of a tank or mechanized corps. *The scope of army offensive operations also increased.* If in the first period of the war they were planned for a depth of 20–65 kilometers with an average tempo of 6–15 kilometers per day, in the second period this increased to 65–100 kilometers with a tempo of 12–15 kilometers per day, and in the third period they were planned for a depth of 120–150 kilometers with a tempo of 10–15 kilometers per day for rifle forces, and 25–35 kilometers per day for mobile groups.

An important factor having considerable influence on the nature and scope of operations and their preparation and conduct was the change in the enemy's defense. If in 1941–42 it was structured on a system of strongpoints and did not exceed two or three kilometers in depth, then in winter 1942/43 the Wehrmacht command concluded that such a defense could not counter Soviet forces' increased offensive might. Hitler's forces were instructed to create an especially strong defense by improving positions in an engineer respect. It became multi-belted and deeply echeloned. By summer 1943 the depth of the main belt increased from two–four to four–five kilometers, and that of the tactical zone from 8–10 to 12–15 kilometers. An army belt was prepared 16–25 kilometers from the forward edge of the defense, and a rear defensive belt was 50–80 kilometers from the forward edge. The density of forces and means increased, and positions and belts were saturated with a large quantity of antitank means and engineer obstacles. This required an increase in tactical and operational densities of shock force groupings, especially in penetration sectors, and improvement of the form for conducting combat actions and, first and foremost, the implementation of a penetration and mobile group actions in the operational depth. The significance of penetrating intermediate lines and forcing water obstacles from the march increased.

Analysis of conditions of preparing and conducting army offensive operations makes it possible to draw the following conclusions. The initial period of the war was characterized by extensive use of not only defensive, but also offensive operations, whose preparation and conduct did not, for the most part, correspond to prewar requirements. However, this did not lessen their significance in repelling aggression. On the contrary, the incredibly complex conditions for execution and achieved results are not only of great cognitive, but also of practical significance for today: how to teach soldiers to fight and win in an unusual circumstance and in critical situations; and when, where, and how to conduct counteroffensive and offensive operations.

The development of the theory and practice of army operations in the

Great Patriotic War proceeded by way of improving prewar views. Its main trends were the following: changing the system of fire destruction, shifting to the continuous, comprehensive resolution of this task with employment of all fire means and aviation, and increasing the depth of simultaneous destruction of the enemy defense's principal elements; increasing the shock force and mobility of the penetration echelon by increasing the number of tanks and self-propelled artillery, and by continuously increasing the employment of forward detachments and raid groups; reinforcing the composition of the echelon for developing success, from isolated tank, motorized, and cavalry formations to mobile groups consisting of more mobile, better controlled tank or mechanized corps, whose actions were continuously supported by aviation.

An army's operational formation was characterized by the creation of those elements which ensured reliable fire destruction of the enemy, penetration of his main defensive belt by first-echelon forces, rapid commitment of a mobile group into the penetration and its swift forestalling actions in the operational depth, intensification of efforts by introducing the second echelon into battle, and allocation of various types of reserves to resolve suddenly arising tasks. These trends maintain their importance today as well, with the single difference that the maneuver potential of the contemporary mobile army group must be considerably greater than that of motorized rifle divisions; this can be achieved by using assault-storm formations and units, as well as army aviation.

The role of rifle divisions in an offensive operation was determined by their place in an army's operational formation and their assigned missions. In operations of the initial and first periods of the war, they were, as a rule, the only means for creating first and second echelons; they were also assigned the mission of penetrating the enemy defense and developing the penetration; under favorable conditions, cavalry and tank formations were attached to resolve the latter mission. In subsequent periods of the war, the place of rifle divisions in an army offensive operation did not especially change, but their role increased, since demands for penetrating the enemy defense at high tempos increased. First-echelon divisions began to be reinforced by a quantity of tanks and artillery considerably greater than before. Second-echelon rifle divisions were used more often under these conditions to increase the strength of mobile groups and create an internal front of enemy encirclement.

In army offensive operations, tank and mechanized corps were usually employed as mobile groups. However, because of the insufficient shock force of rifle divisions, they were often used to complete the penetration of the enemy defense, and then to exploit success into the depth; they then suffered considerable losses, which weakened their capabilities to resolve their designated principal mission. In improving the organizational establishment structure of rifle formations after the war, the following was taken into account: tank-self-propelled regiments [*tankosamokhodnyy polk*] were introduced into their composition, while mechanized divisions were introduced into rifle corps. This trend was reflected under contemporary conditions as well: motorized rifle divisions replaced rifle divisions, whose shock force and mobility were higher not only than the mechanized, but also the tank corps of the Great Patriotic War.

In Great Patriotic War army offensive operations, the problem of air defense was not resolved. Today it is acquiring special significance in connection with the role the enemy has given to the use of aviation, including army aviation, in battle and operations. The trend to increase the role of air defense can also be clearly seen in postwar local wars. Air (rocket) defense has become one of the important elements of the content of combined-arms battle and operations, with respect to combat and operational support.

Thus, everything stated previously makes it possible *to formulate the following trends in the development of tactics and operational art*:

First. Continuous growth in the quantity of varied, increasingly complex weapons employed in battle and operations requires an improvement in engineer training of combined-arms commanders and staffs, as well as operational-tactical training of the branches of the Armed Forces, combat arms, and services.

Second. The spatial scope of combined-arms battle and operations is increasing as a result of using air space not only for maneuver, but also for delivery of a strike against objectives in the depth. There is great force dispersion in connection with the increased independence of combat actions not only of units, but also of subunits.

Third. The role of fire destruction has increased, and aviation is widely used to resolve combat missions of units and formations. At present, combat actions are unthinkable without long-range fire power. According to local war experience, the significance of radio-electronic suppression of enemy radio-emission objectives has sharply increased. Under conditions of extensive use of radio-electronics and guided weapons, radio-electronic suppression is becoming one of the principal components of battle and operations, called upon to disrupt enemy troop and weapons control.

Fourth. The role of maneuver in combined-arms battle and operations is increasing. This is conditioned by high force mobility and the introduction of flying vehicles into ground forces formations and units. In this connection, maneuverability and dynamism of combat operations have increased, and the problem of educating creative, dynamically thinking officers who act with initiative in non-standard ways is raised once again. It is also necessary to develop a new theory of combined-arms battle tactics – *the tactics of deep group air-land battle* – which would reflect all its new elements: radio-electronic suppression (electronic strike); deep fire destruction employing all types of high-precision weapons, including aviation; extensive use of tactical air assaults, raid detachments, and special groups; and dynamic and decisive operations of combined-arms subunits and units simultaneously from the front, flanks, and rear. We do not want penetration in narrow front sectors practically in linear combat formation of subunits and even units, which we often observe in troop and unit exercises, but rather *simultaneous deep attacks along axes by several small groupings*, including subunits and units of various combat arms and army aviation (and naval infantry on coastal axes), coordinated with respect to front and depth.

Fifth. The influence of moral-psychological training of officers, staffs, and troops, and their professional expertise on the course and outcome of battle continues to increase. The trend toward ever increasing dependence of success in battle and operations on the level of commander and staff training was clearly observed during the Great Patriotic War and local wars of the postwar period. It still maintains its significance under modern conditions.

Sixth. The independence of all control levels; soldier initiative and creativity in resolving assigned missions; the organizing role of combined-arms commanders and staffs and chiefs of combat arms and services in preparing for battle and operations and in troop control during their conduct, and their personal contact with and practical assistance for subordinates are increasing. Improvement in work methods for controlling formations and units on the basis of automating processes requires improving our officers' computer literacy. A deep understanding of these trends will, in our opinion, facilitate the development of promising methods for conducting battle and operations, and the improvement of commander, staff, and troop training.

NOTES

1. V. G. Reznichenko, "Podgotovka i provedeniye armeyskikh operatsiy," *Voyennaya mysl'* [Military thought], 1 (1991), pp. 19–27.
2. A. V. Vladimirskiy, *Na kiyevskom napravlenii* [On the Kiev axis] (Moscow: Voyenizdat, 1989), pp. 19–21.
3. Ibid., pp. 22–7.
4. Central Archives of the Ministry of Defense, f. 229, op. 3814, d. 7, l. 221.

On Several Tenets of Soviet Military Doctrine

COLONEL GENERAL I. N. RODIONOV[1]

Soviet military doctrine today is attracting a great deal of attention from military and civilian specialists, both within the country and abroad. This is explained, to a great degree, by the fact that at the end of the 1980s a qualitatively new stage in its development commenced. Conditions of the situation (both domestic and foreign), as well as objective reasons which conditioned the appearance of a series of new directives and tasks, were stated in detail in addresses by the Minister of Defense of the USSR, Marshal of the Soviet Union D. T. Yazov, and by Chief of the General Staff of the Armed Forces of the USSR, General of the Army M. A. Moiseyev, and were disclosed in print, first and foremost in the journal *Voyennaya mysl'* [Military thought]. In this article, the author states a number of personal opinions on some tenets of Soviet military doctrine for the purpose of their broad discussion.

ON THE SIGNIFICANCE OF MILITARY DOCTRINE FOR DEVELOPING AND IMPLEMENTING DEFENSE POLICY AND ENSURING DEFENSE SECURITY

The definition of Soviet military doctrine, its structure, and its content were fully stated in the plan for the document, "On the USSR's Military Doctrine."[2] Analysis demonstrates that it touches *all aspects of government activity* in the realm of defense policy and the creation of necessary conditions for the reliable defense of the Motherland. What, then, are the bases for such a statement?

First, *the political aspect of military doctrine* reflects the state's attitude toward problems of war and peace, the military-political war aims, missions for preventing it, reinforcement of defense, and security of the country.

Second, it is very important that the military-technical aspect of doctrine specifies *on the basis of fundamental political aims* the main trends for Armed Forces development, and forms and methods for repelling aggression and training troops and forces to resolve their assigned missions. It must be clearly understood that the state's military-political aims should be adequately reinforced by its economic, socio-political, and spiritual capabilities and the corresponding combat potential of the armed forces. In other words, military doctrine stands on firm ground only when the aims and missions stated in it correspond to available forces and means, that is, if it truly reflects the combat capabilities of the armed forces in its military-technical aspect, and views concerning the methods for preparing and conducting military operations correspond to objective conditions and have an adequate material foundation.

Third, it is necessary to consider that *the content of documents on military doctrine is formulated by the country's higher military-political leadership.* In addition, its primary conceptual aims are legally affirmed by the highest organs of state authority. Consequently, its tenets concern the activity of various ministries, departments, and installations dealing with the development and practical implementation of both the Soviet Union's domestic and foreign policy. Military doctrine also directly affects the improvement of the country's defense potential. It comprises a large number of components, and depends on various factors: political, economic, spiritual, and, of course, military. The latter is most clearly manifested through the Armed Forces' combat potential.

The profound transformations currently underway in the country were, naturally, also reflected in the substance of the factors. Together with the progressive orientation of ongoing changes and those positive results which should be achieved during *perestroyka*, one also cannot fail to note negative trends taking place in today's activities. The manifestation of political instability in the USSR and of elements of nationalism and separatism in its regions, the economic difficulties associated with the shift to a new management system, the destruction of society's moral principles, and a number of other processes have inflicted serious damage on the country's defense potential. Under existing conditions, the Armed Forces are one of the most stable bulwarks on which the state's defensive might is maintained. Further collapse of the Soviet Army and Navy's combat potential can seriously complicate the achievement of political aims as specified in contemporary military doctrine.

At the same time, the practical realization of military doctrine's aims requires precisely organized and coordinated efforts. Unfortunately, attempts are being made in several mass media sources to oppose the activities of the Ministry of Defense of the USSR, the General Staff of the Armed Forces of the USSR, and a number of branches of the defense industry on the one hand, and the Ministry of Foreign Affairs, various parties, social organizations and movements on the other. I think that this is an extremely dangerous and unproductive path. Obviously it would be much more useful if all discussions were conducted to seek better mutual understanding and to define precisely the place and role of each structural element of the state and society in resolving the very complex problems of *perestroyka*. It is a matter of ensuring that general efforts improve the USSR's defense capabilities and strengthen its Armed Forces. In this regard, attempts to pull apart the Soviet Army and Navy according to "national headquarters," insufficiently considered calls for reducing defense expenditures, and a campaign to discredit the USSR Armed Forces are cause for alarm.

For example, of what value is the idea of creating "national" armed forces? Their organization, composition and arms, principles for manning and outfitting, and training and indoctrination in any state depend on political aims and missions, the country's socio-political and economic situation, views of the military-political leadership on the nature of a possible war, an analysis of their combat capabilities and those of potential enemies, the presence of means for armed struggle, and other factors. Doctrinal aims are worked out on this basis, which form the foundation for the development of the army and navy and their improvement, both in peacetime and wartime. Consequently, it must be a matter not of a one-act process of creating armed forces, but of their normal continuous functioning. This is indissolubly connected with problems of training national military cadres, personnel and materiel mobilization resources, development of an infrastructure (albeit a minimal base for the defense industry), creating strategic reserves of raw materials and food, etc. Can any state permit multifold duplication of all the given measures? Sometimes one gets the impression that advocates of "national (republic) armed forces" have simply not thought these issues through. The idea of creating such armed forces is understandable only under conditions of their formation as a counterbalance to central organs of power, to satisfy personal ambitions of the leadership of individual union republics.

If we are to speak seriously of preserving the USSR as a strong, indivisible state, then there must be a uniform military doctrine in the country, a uniform Armed Forces, uniform principles of outfitting, manning, training, and educating them, centralized leadership, and uniform views on their employment.

Until now we have essentially touched upon only the normative functioning of Soviet military doctrine as a system of officially accepted, fundamental views concerning policy and the development of the Armed Forces and military art. Without speaking about the significance of doctrine on a broader plane, one cannot fail to mention its informative function. This is expressed in its cognitive and educational role with respect to the population and Armed Forces personnel in the interests of their correct understanding of missions in the realm of the state's defense policy and reinforcement of its defense capabilities. In addition, an open statement of doctrinal principles informs the entire world community of the essence of the USSR's military policy. At the same time, it also serves as a warning to a potential aggressor of the inevitability of retaliation in case of an attack against the Soviet

Union. All these issues have acquired particular immediacy at the current turning point in the development of the international situation and profound transformations in Soviet society.

What are the innovations of the USSR's military doctrine? The answer to this question is of no little importance, partly because, although recently the epithet "new" has been used very often, we are emphasizing that our military doctrine has "defensive orientation." This, in turn, presupposes that the "old" doctrine had a different, that is, offensive orientation. But is this so?

Analysis of the evolution of the Soviet Union's doctrinal tenets demonstrates that over the country's entire history there have never been aggressive political aims or ambitions, there has been no doctrine whose political aspect had an aggressive offensive orientation. However, at separate stages of Soviet social development, based on principles of class struggle, Soviet military doctrine was excessively ideologized. In the 1920s and 1930s it often seemed to be stated that offensive actions and a strategy of annihilation were inherent to the nature of the first revolutionary class state. At the same time, its military-technical aspect for achieving political and strategic aims gave priority to dynamic, offensive methods of Armed Forces actions. In the prewar period, this was most clearly manifested in the laconic statement "beat the enemy on his own territory." In military art, the main form of military operation was considered to be the offensive, and questions on organizing and conducting the defense were undervalued and, therefore, inadequately worked out. The latter was especially characteristic for the operational and strategic scales.

In the postwar period, based on the experience of the Great Patriotic War, Soviet military doctrine, in accordance with political directives that the USSR intended to attack no one, proceeded in questions of ensuring state security from the creation of an adequate threat to the most important military and economic objectives on the territory of the potential enemy. Therefore, in the 1950s and 1960s, the concept of rocket-nuclear war was a priority. Its essence lay in the defeat of an aggressor by dynamic forms of armed struggle employing nuclear and conventional means of destruction. This was a consequence of underestimation, not only by military specialists, but also by the country's highest political leadership, of the role of nuclear weapons and the consequences of their employment. It was not by chance that the belief existed at this time in the possible victory of socialism in a third world war. In 1961, it was officially stated: "If imperialist aggressors are so bold as to unleash a new world war, the nations will no longer tolerate a system which would plunge them into a devastating war."[3] Such an approach also required seeking corresponding methods of defeating the aggressor, developing the most dynamic types, forms, and methods of conducting military operations, and finding adequate means for developing the Soviet Armed Forces, especially their technical outfitting.

As a result of the arms race, by the end of the 1970s a situation had unfolded in which deterrence of aggression by both sides had been achieved by the threat of guaranteed nuclear destruction of the most important enemy objectives. The basis of Soviet military doctrine's political aims were *the inadmissibility of nuclear war and the necessity of renouncing first use of nuclear weapons.* Thus, it turned out that the political aspect of doctrine had a defensive orientation, while its military-technical aspect, as before, gave priority to the offensive as the principal type of military action. A clear contradiction appeared between political doctrinal aims and methods for their practical realization. As a result, there was a lack of trust of Soviet policy and a misunderstanding of it in the international arena; this, in turn, intensified confrontation and the arms race.

Only in the second half of the 1980s did a new approach to assessing the world situation make it possible to reassess the primary significance of missions for strengthening the country's security. Ideas and tenets of new political thinking lie at its foundation, whose essence, in the realm of international relations, reduces to recognition of the priority of common human values and introduction of peaceful alternatives to confrontation accompanied by an arms race: strengthening measures for trust, mutual understanding, cooperation, and disarmament. The logic of socio-political development in the contemporary world, the accumulation of enormous reserves of nuclear means, and the sharply increased destructive properties of conventional weapons have objectively advanced to the foreground a vitally important problem for all humanity, that is, preventing a new war, which, if started, would place a question mark on the fate of all civilization. This was one of the main reasons making it necessary not only to define clearly the content of Soviet military doctrine, mainly its military-technical aspect, but also to introduce a series of new purposes, aims, and tenets. In my opinion, the most fundamental of these are the following.

The first aspect consists of the fact that in the USSR's modern military doctrine, priority has been given not to preparing for war, but to preventing it, and to strengthening international security. Once again we will emphasize that the Soviet Union previously had never pursued aggressive plans and aspirations, nor did it attempt to unleash war. However, in addition, never before in doctrinal tenets had war prevention been so unambiguously stated as the primary mission. Today, political measures remain the priority for its resolution; however, they should be coordinated precisely with measures of a military nature. This primacy in no way means the dictate of politics. At the current level of development of armed struggle, political solutions and practical measures must, as never before, take into consideration possible military consequences. And strict coordination of the efforts of all interested parties is necessary for this in developing political initiatives, be they in the realm of foreign or domestic policy.

Past experience and present events attest to the necessity of joint political and military efforts in the matter of war prevention. Let us recall, for example, the Soviet leadership's activities on the eve of the Second World War and the Great Patriotic War. At that time it was manifesting exceptional dynamism in the realm of foreign policy, and had signed various agreements, some of which even had to be concealed from its own people; nevertheless, war was not successfully avoided. One of the reasons for this, in my opinion, was that, despite these efforts, the level of the country's defense capability did not appropriately support foreign policy efforts in war prevention. Moreover, everyone is familiar with the enormous losses the Soviet people suffered when the war did begin. The Armed Forces and the state as a whole were inadequately prepared for it.

Another example is the development of the situation in the Persian Gulf. The most dynamic diplomatic and economic efforts directed toward achieving the withdrawal of Iraqi forces from Kuwaiti territory and preventing an even more dangerous development of the situation in this region were undertaken by all the world's leading states and the five permanent members of the UN Security Council. In addition, these efforts were reinforced by measures of a military nature. Such actions were dictated by the dynamics of the situation. New political thinking and new principles of mutual relations among different states were still only opening a new path. Far from all states had renounced politics from a position of strength. Sources of military danger still exist, ready to develop into a direct military threat. It is important to emphasize that under modern conditions the problems of the essence of the concepts "military danger" and "direct military threat," the establishment of their interconnection and interdependence, and an analysis of factors which allow for the outbreak of war have acquired particular currency and require universal and thorough investigation.

A second aspect is the linkage of a defensive orientation to the military-technical aspect of military doctrine. One often hears that our doctrinal aims, directing the USSR's Armed Forces mainly to conduct essentially defensive retaliatory actions at the commencement of a war, virtually place us on the brink of destruction beforehand. Events of June 1941 are most often recalled. Any military specialist understands how complex the problem facing the Soviet Union is in connection with new aims. However, citing 1941 is, at the very least, incorrect. In the prewar period, priority in the military-technical aspect of military doctrine was given to the offensive, proclaiming the principle of "beat the enemy on his own territory." Therefore, the main thing, in my opinion, is not that we intend to defend ourselves, but that we are now (in peacetime) already preparing for the commencement of military operations to repel aggression. Of course, additional difficulties are arising, but they should not prompt a feeling of doom; on the contrary, they should mobilize soldiers to seek more effective actions under these complex conditions. For this, the quality of scientific research and operational and force combat training must be raised to a new, fundamentally higher level.

The orientation of the Soviet Armed Forces toward conducting pre-dominantly defensive actions at the commencement of a war does not at all mean renouncing the counteroffensive and offensive. It is very important, however, not to go to extremes here. Whereas until the mid-1980s troops and control organs unjustifiably focused little attention on questions of defense, especially at the operational and strategic levels, now, more often than not, these questions prevail over offensive questions. Army and naval personnel must be thoroughly prepared to conduct all types of combat operations.

Of course, one cannot reduce innovation to only the two above-mentioned aspects. It is much more varied, and encompasses all spheres of the daily activities of the Armed Forces, as well as of the country as a whole. After all, the implementation of the most important doctrinal aims is a national matter requiring coordinated efforts of various socio-political forces. It is especially important to take this into consideration now. Whereas in the past military doctrine

> specified a model of actions for the country and armed forces after "D" day, that is, when war had become a fact, then now it is a matter of shifting emphasis to armed forces actions on this side of a fateful "D" day to prevent a horrible catastrophe.[4]

It is difficult not to agree with this tenet.

How, then, is Soviet Armed Forces participation seen in implementing the most important doctrinal war prevention aims? The Soviet Army and Navy can and must make their main contribution in resolving doctrinal aims by maintaining a high degree of combat readiness to repel aggression in any situation. Raising the question of the necessity for further strengthening the Armed Forces, it should be noted that some circles may interpret this as forcing militaristic attitudes and lack of faith in the ability to prevent war. However, this is not so. One cannot fail, however, to focus the reader's attention on the fact that the Armed Forces (as an instrument of the state), by its readiness to carry out its constitutional duty for armed protection of the Fatherland, plays a powerful deterring role and participates in the resolution of missions for preventing war. The nation maintains an army and navy for this, so that they are ready to protect it. New political thinking has not yet become predominant throughout the entire world, and war prevention is still posed only as a mission, for whose implementation all must work. An imprecise understanding of these tenets, especially by the officer corps, can have very serious negative consequences.

Under modern conditions, a one-sided orientation of social opinion only on war prevention often results in ultrapacifist attitudes predominating in a specific portion of the population. As a result, calls are heard for unilateral disarmament, and the question is posed concerning the expediency of the Armed Forces' very existence. Moreover, in individual regions of the country there are attempts to thwart the army and navy draft, and to make the daily activities of troops (forces) and their operational and combat readiness difficult.

And there is more. The necessity of intense work on improving the Soviet Armed Forces' combat potential does not mean a call for their quantitative increase. It is a matter of qualitative parameters of troop (force) groupings, whose composition is determined by the higher state leadership in accordance with international treaties and agreements reached. In addition, it must be emphasized that peacetime ground and naval force groupings are not able to execute all missions in the event of a possible war against the Soviet Union. Consequently, measures are necessary to improve the mobilization readiness of the USSR's Armed Forces and the country as a whole.

Together with maintaining the army and navy at constant combat readiness to repel aggression, their representatives are charged with executing a number of important functions. The first is participating in preparing the country's initial positions in conducting negotiations on questions of disarmament or military actions, and in expert assessment of their intermediate and final results. The second is participating in verification of the implementation of agreements reached and treaties signed in the military realm. The third is seeking optimal directions for development. The fourth is the most important mission of developing theoretical foundations and directions for practical activity in employing the Armed Forces to resolve the entire set of missions confronting them both in peacetime and in wartime; this is specifically charged to the country's higher military leadership and military scholars. In addition, this category of servicemen deals with developing the principal requirements and recommendations for the higher organs of authority in the realm of foreign policy, economics, science, and social and other spheres of society's daily activities.

There is one more aspect: the problem of USSR Armed Forces participation in resolving war prevention missions, which has elicited ambiguous assessments. I have in mind the possibility of using a military contingent to conduct peace-keeping actions in accordance with a decision by the United Nations Security Council. This tenet is reflected in the proposed document "On the USSR's Military Doctrine."[5] During discussions at the USSR's IV Congress of People's Deputies, both supporters and ardent foes of such an approach came forth. Events in the Persian Gulf are a particular case. The given problem must be examined more broadly. Similar development of a situation may be repeated in other world regions. The Persian Gulf War demonstrated how fragile and interconnected the world is.

The actions of a special contingent of the Soviet Armed Forces in similar situations to counter the escalation of armed conflict will be appropriate for the requirements of Soviet military doctrine on war prevention. The USSR – a permanent member of the UN Security Council – also bears responsibility for keeping peace on the planet. One can speak of the inhumanity of risking the lives of Soviet soldiers and officers in such situations, but if one takes into account that this is justified by the preservation of the lives of a much larger number of civilians, including women, the elderly, and children, then one can hardly call this inhuman. In addition, the Soviet Union's position in such situations as the Persian Gulf crisis must be more consistent. When conducting its foreign policy, the Soviet Union and its political leadership must constantly maintain a balanced course with respect to all regions, calculated for the long-term and taking into consideration possible changes in the military-political situation in all regions of the world. In addition, in each concrete instance it is necessary to consider what degree of participation of the Armed Forces of the Soviet Union in operations under the aegis of the UN will correspond to the Soviet Union's interests, and what the consequences of such actions may be for its defense capability. It is categorically inadmissible to use soldiers and officers to satisfy someone's personal ambitions and gain superficial "political authority," as has happened in the past in the USSR.

In this regard, when examining the question of allocating a Soviet military contingent as part of UN forces it is very important to work out a precise legal mechanism for making appropriate decisions. It is necessary in all instances to preclude the possibility of making these decisions *in camera*, in violation of Soviet laws and norms of international law. If such a mechanism is created, the question of determining principles for manning such contingents (in my opinion this should be voluntary), the method of outfitting them, and procedures and methods of using them can be seriously raised. The fact itself of their employment in such an instance is not a renunciation of the defensive orientation of Soviet military doctrine, nor does it contradict its principal aim of war prevention; rather, it only suggests the probability of more dynamic actions in the interests of achieving this aim.

One may object that these questions are not directly connected with the USSR's defense. It is certain, however, that the destructive power of different weapons of mass destruction knows no boundaries. Obviously, there is not a single country in the world that will be able to "sit it out in the trenches" if large-scale local conflicts arise. It seems to us that these questions cannot fail to affect directly the Soviet Union's security as well.

This article shows only a few approaches to resolving the problem of war prevention. The tenets of military doctrine on preparing the country and Armed Forces for war and methods for conducting armed struggle to defend the Fatherland are very important for further research and practical implementation. The significance of these tenets are predetermined by the development of the contemporary world, in which, as before, reasons and sources for the outbreak of war still exist. Inasmuch as individual arguments bear a polemical nature, they obviously do not leave the reader indifferent; consequently, their discussion will make it easier to resolve the problems raised in this article.

NOTES

1. I. N. Rodionov, "O nekotorykh polozheniyakh sovetskoy voyennoy doktriny," *Voyennaya mysl'* [Military thought], 3 (1991), pp. 2–9.
2. *Voyennaya mysl'. Spetsial'nyy vypusk* [Military thought. Special edition], 1990, pp. 24–8.
3. *Materialy XXII s"yezda KPSS* [Materials of the XXII Party Congress] (Moscow: Gospolitizdat, 1961), p. 364.
4. A. A. Kokoshin and V. V. Larionov, *Predotvrashcheniye voyny: Doktriny, kontseptsii, perspektivy* [War prevention: Doctrines, concepts, prospects] (Moscow: Progress, 1990), p. 34.
5. *Military thought*. Special issue, p. 25.

Developmental Trends of Armed Struggle

COLONEL A. N. ZAKHAROV,
CANDIDATE OF MILITARY SCIENCES[1]

The increase in the number of types of arms and military equipment in Armed Forces services and combat arms, and the broadening of their functional capabilities are resulting in the *emergence of increasingly newer linkages between the principal elements of armed struggle.* Here, the specific manifestation of laws at each of the levels (tactical, operational, and strategic) speaks of their systemic interconnection on a global (restricted to terrestrial civilization) scale, points to the complexity of the process under examination, and necessitates the employment of a multi-criteria assessment.

Consequently, in the interests of revealing the most general trends, it is expedient to represent armed struggle as a system which would reflect the entire complexity of the interconnections of scope, form, and content of military actions at the *tactical, operational, and strategic levels.*

A system formulated according to the principle of qualification of armed struggle by *several groups of characteristics,* making it possible to determine the direction of changes of its principal indicators as dependent on the development of military equipment and armaments, obviously corresponds to these requirements. It is clearly expedient to characterize the *scope* of armed struggle by *space and time: first, by duration and the number of spheres* encompassed by military actions; *second, by duration, consistency, and irreversibility.* For corresponding scales, *form* characteristics can be the *duel battle, the group battle, combat actions, and the operation*; content characteristics are the *subject, object, means, and methods (procedures)* of conducting armed struggle.

Such a system considers armed struggle as essentially a process of successive *synthesis* of the combat actions of simple work and robot systems into increasingly more complex systems: subunits, units, formations, etc. Here, depending on the natural regularity of interaction between military equipment and armaments of formations of various sizes, three levels of synthesis can be distinguished in the process under examination: *tactical, operational, and strategic.*

The *first* (standard) is opposition of crews (teams), subunits, units, and formations basically employing uniform equipment, that is, tactical combat actions. The *second* (generic) is opposition of large formations employing groups of varied military equipment of a single combat arm, that is, mostly operational combat actions. The *third* (specific and branch) is opposition of large formations employing groups of military equipment of combat arms of a single armed forces service, as well as large formations of other armed forces services.

It should be emphasized that in the process of synthesis there is not only a *quantitative* intensification of the properties of indicators with respect to levels, but also the appearance of *new qualities* at each level. Based on this assumption, we note that both indicators of armed struggle and its developmental trends are synthesized according to a single principle: *the successive ascent from indicators (trends) of the process of opposition of crews, to analogous indicators (trends) from units, to the armed forces of states during war.*

As a whole, the system under examination, which makes it possible to judge with comparative objectivity changes in the scope, form, and content of armed struggle as dependent on the development of military equipment and arms, is indicated in Figure 1.[2] It is structured as follows: *vertical hierarchy* – levels (tactical, operational, and strategic); *horizontal division* – groups of scope, form, and content characteristics. This makes it possible to consider all possible variants of the synthesis of indicators (trends), specifically: *successive synthesis* – from the lower to higher level through all others; *discrete synthesis* – from the lower to higher level, omitting one level; and *direct synthesis* from the lower to higher level, excluding intermediate levels.

Comparing the principal characteristics of existing means of armed struggle of different armed forces services and combat arms with those anticipated by the end of the twentieth and beginning of the twenty-first centuries, on the basis of maximum formalization of their properties, made it possible to reveal the most general features of the *developmental direction of armaments*. Among the principal ones are increase in range; increase in effectiveness of strike, basically through an increase in precision of reconnaissance and delivery of warheads to the target; increase in structural and technical complexity of weapons through an increase in combat support systems (especially information); an increase in autonomy, the level of robotization, and mobility; improvement of processes of preparing for combat employment; increase in the number of types of weapons of all spatial spheres, with an increase in the role of "weapon, air, sea, and space"; sophistication of weapons at the standard, generic, and specific levels; increase in mutual influence of various weapons; expansion of the sphere of employing computer technology and means for automated troop and weapons control; reduction of the degree of human participation in the process "reconnaissance – target indication – strike"; and deepening of the intra-generic, intra-standard, and intra-branch unification of weapons.

Assessing changes in scope, form, and content of an armed encounter at all levels, conducted by employing the established criteria, made it possible to reveal the most general *trends of armed struggle* for the period to 2005–2010 (Figure 2). Seven trends will for the most part determine the nature of operations at the end of the twentieth and beginning of the twenty-first century:

First – an increase in the degree of mutual influence of the results of combat actions in various spheres, and a shift from actions primarily "on land" to armed struggle on land, at sea, and in the air, with an increase in the latter's significance.

Second – reaching the depth of the operational zone by means of simultaneous combat actions.

Third – striving for simultaneity (action to strike an object or grouping at one time) and reducing the period of irreversibility (the time for troop formations to arrive at a "critical mass of losses").

Fourth – a shift at all levels and in all spheres to combined-arms combat actions, based on massed, grouped, and concentrated strikes by different combat arms.

Fifth – an increase in the level of simultaneity of actions by troops and weapons, with an increase in the role of weapons complexes and systems in each sphere in the process of any operational mission.

Sixth – displacement of the principal mass of force actions from military equipment and armaments directly participating in the strike, through a system of control on military equipment of support and information systems.

Seventh – reduction of times and expansion of the arsenal of methods for unleashing military (combat) actions.

We will examine each of these.

The first trend reflects the continual growth of the quantity of air and naval forces and means used to strike ground forces groupings, since the capabilities of ground forces to defeat the enemy are becoming clearly inadequate. Confirmation of this is the war in the Persian Gulf. Ground troops of the multi-national forces there commenced dynamic actions only after air and naval strikes lasting many days against Iraqi ground objectives (even under conditions of complete air and naval superiority). Consequently, success in operations, especially at the beginning of a war, will be directly dependent on the enemy's carrying out effective air and naval strikes, and gaining and retaining superiority in the air and at sea.

As a whole, in preparing an operation, this trend assumes, with the commencement of repulsion of aggression, the planning of successive

Figure 1. System of criteria of basic characteristics of warfare

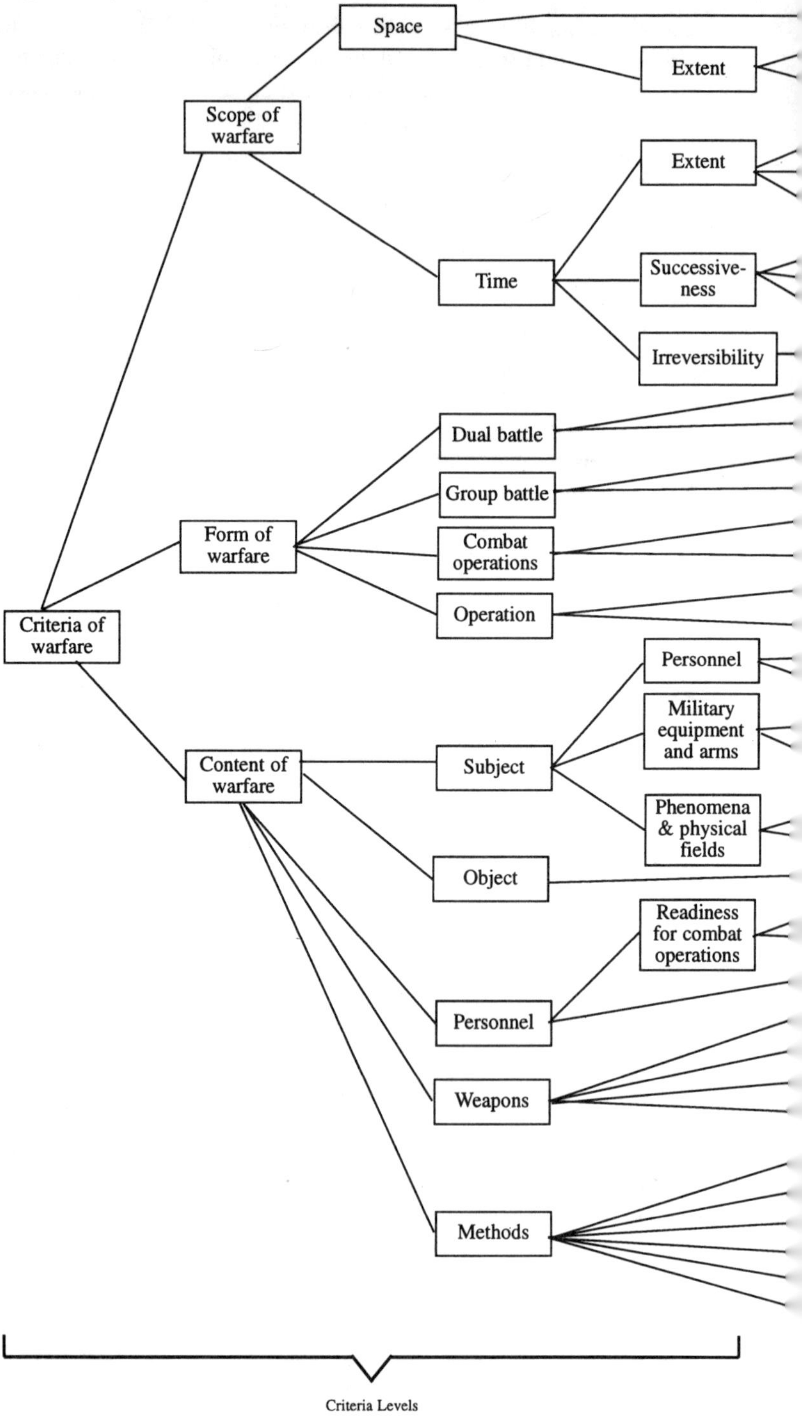

Criteria Levels

Criteria	Indicators
Number of spheres	Single sphere, Dual sphere, Multiple spheres, Fraction of unit
Correlation of range of reconnoitering a target and reach of weapons	Fraction of unit
Degree of achievement of depth of tactical, operational and strategic zones of responsibility by simultaneous operations	Minute, hour, day
Time of preparation for initiation of military operations	Second, minute, hour
Time of "reconnaissance-target designation-engagement" cycle in tactical, operational and strategic zones	Second, minute, hour
Time of "engagement" cycle	Simultaneity, Succession, Discreteness
Degree of simultaneity	Continuousness, Time difference
Degree of continuousness	Synchronism
Degree of synchronism	Second, minute, hour
Time for building up "critical mass (threshold value) of losses"	One type, Comprehensive
Nature of weapon effect	Single, Multiple
Kind of effect	One type, Combined-arms
Nature of interworking of weapons	Single strike (fire), Group strike (concentrated fire)
Kind of effect	Deliberate effect
Nature of coordination of forces	Single arm, Combined-arms
Kind of effect	Group strike, Massive strike, Deliberate effect
Nature of coordination of troops	Independent, Combined-arms
Kind of effect	Group strike, Massive strike
Role of man in warfare	Degree
Protection	Degree
Number of types of military equipment and arms participating in warfare	Units, tens, hundreds
Contribution of each type of military equipment and arms to corresponding potential of force grouping	Fraction of unit
Number of phenomena and physical fields whose properties are realized in process of warfare	Units, tens
Contribution of each phenomenon and physical field to corresponding potential of force grouping	Fraction of unit
Role of destruction of particular potential in achieving success in warfare	Degree
Type of force element	Full strength, Reduced strength
Level of combat effectiveness	Fraction of unit
Nature of table of organization structure of troop units of all levels	Single arm, Combined-arms
Degree of influence of type of weapons of warfare on results of combat operations	Fraction of unit
Density of combat formations	Units, tens/km^2
Degree of mutual influence of weapons and troop units	Fraction of unit
Importance of individual and collective protection	Degree
Level of automation and robotization	Fraction of unit
Level of capability for surprise beginning of battle	Fraction of unit
Degree of mutual penetration of methods of operations	Fraction of unit
Arsenal of methods for beginning combat operations	Units, tens
Degree of integration and simultaneity of effect	Fraction of unit
Degree of systemization and centralization	Fraction of unit

Criteria

Indicators

Figure 2. System of Most Important Trends of Warfare

Level/Characteristic		Tactical (type)	Operational (arm)	Strategic (Branch)	Strategic (Sectorial)
Space	No. of spheres	Transition from one-sphere to two-sphere	Transition from two-sphere to multisphere	Expansion of multisphere nature	
Space	Extent	Increased range of reconnoitering target to limits of weapon reach	Increased degree of mutual influence of results of combat operations in different spheres	Movement from warfare in a limited space in one sphere to warfare in an unlimited extent in several spheres	
Space	Extent	Reaching depth of tactical zone by simultaneous operations	Reaching depth of operational zone by simultaneous operations	Approaching global scale	
Space	Extent	Expansion of "intersphere boundary zones" through increased depth of mutual penetration of weapon kill zones of contiguous spheres (multipurpose weapons)		Reaching depth of strategic zone by simultaneous operations	
Time	Extent	Increased degree of readiness for combat employment	Shortening time periods for initiating combat and military operations		
Time	Extent	Shortening time of "reconnaissance" and "engagement" cycles	Bringing "reconnaissance-target designation-engagement" cycle nearer real time		
Time	Extent	Increased transience of battle	Establishing unidimensional nature of cycles for performing engagement missions in tactical, operational, strategic zones	Increased transience of the operation	
Time	Extent		Increased transience of combat operations		
Time	Successiveness	Expansion of simultaneity	Striving for simultaneity		
Time	Successiveness	Drop in level of discreteness	Rise in level of continuousness and synchronism		
Time	Irreversibility	Increased probability of guaranteed target kill	Shortening of period of irreversibility – time for accumulating "critical mass (threshold value) of losses"		

SCOPE OF WARFARE

TRENDS

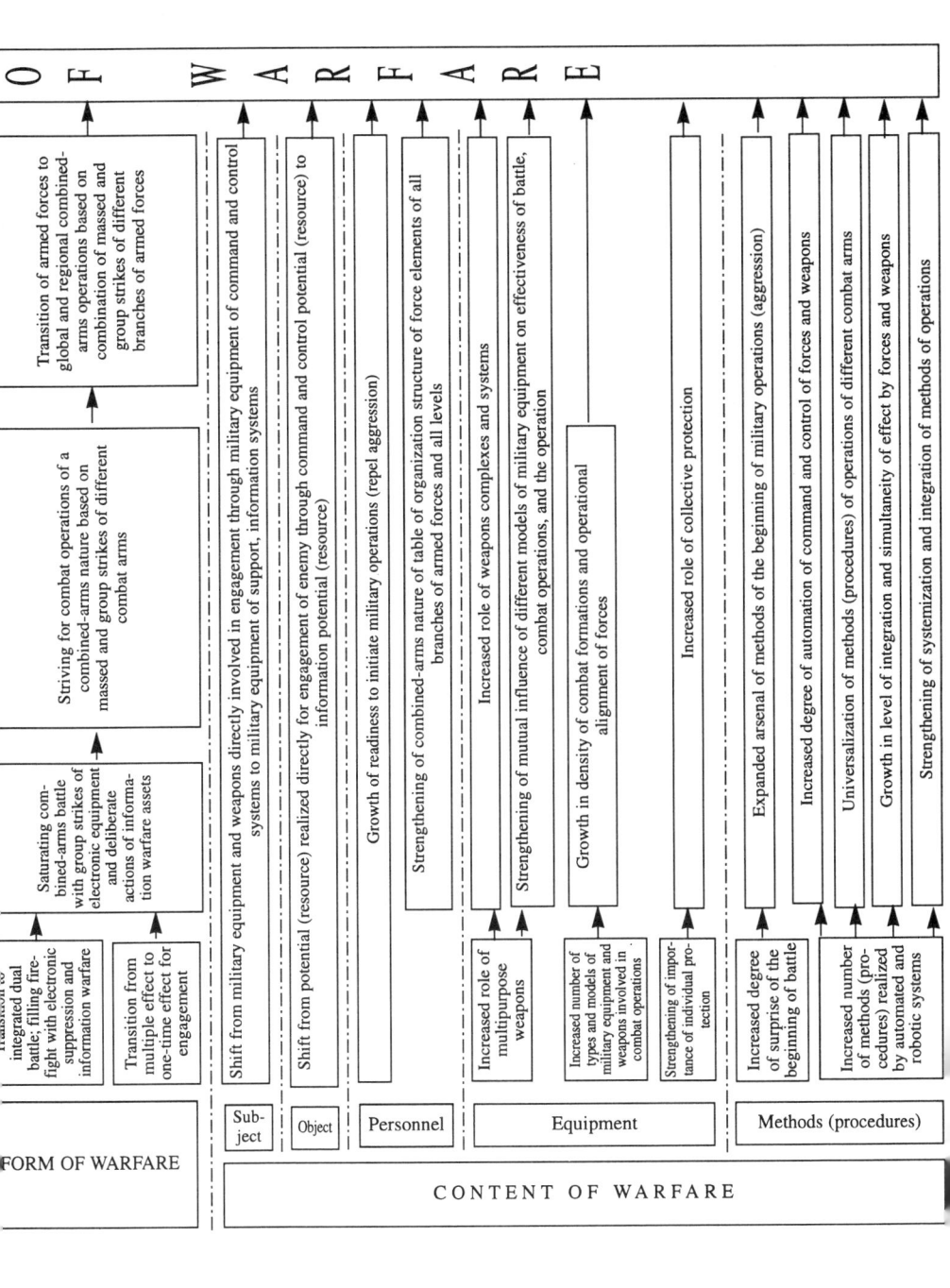

concentration of efforts to seize the initiative at first in the air, then at sea, and only after this on land, and requires close cooperation of forces and means, simultaneously carrying out combat missions in all spatial spheres, while conducting combat operations. In this regard, the necessity of reinforcing ground forces groupings with powerful air and naval echelons, and shifting from the designation of *zones* of combat actions for troop formations to specification of *ranges and combat space*, and zones and regions of responsibility for various forces in them is being closely examined.

The second trend is conditioned by the continuously increasing range of destruction of weapons complexes of all types of basing, the quantitative and qualitative growth of airborne forces, the conduct of air-storm operations, and the employment of special operations forces. This means that the zone of employment of combat means is shifting into the depth of the operational structure of opposing groupings. The intensity of combat operations in the zone of direct contact is not decreasing. Analysis of local military conflicts demonstrates that, under modern conditions, any one of the opposing sides is able to envelop a large formation's defensive belt by simultaneous combat operations. This presupposes creating defensive groupings and an operational force formation capable of implementing, with differentiation (depending on means), protection, envelopment, and defense of principal stationary strategic objectives, not only of ground forces, but also of other armed forces services and technical and rear support systems; and of ensuring the timely destruction of airborne and air-mobile forces between defensive lines.

A complex situation may unfold upon commencement of an operation if the *third trend* is manifested to a considerable degree. This reflects the process of the constant increase in might of practically all means and systems of destruction being developed to demolish individual and even group objectives with a single strike. This makes the first and subsequent massed strikes of aviation, the navy, long-range artillery, and RSZO employing high-precision munitions catastrophically dangerous. According to calculations by US military experts, during the first massed strike lasting 2.5–3 hours, all principal command posts of the first operational echelon's defending forces can be destroyed, and, consequently, control at the operational-strategic level can be disrupted or even thwarted. It is necessary to consider possible manifestations of this trend when preparing and during an operation.

The fourth trend demonstrates that by the end of the 1990s the employment of all combat arms and armed forces services will be implemented by complexes in each operation, or even in an *independent operational mission*. Thus, when striking ground objectives by strategic aviation with the employment of conventional means of destruction, participation of tactical fighters, sea-based cruise missiles, pilotless aircraft, reconnaissance airplanes, and radio-electronic warfare, which will ensure bombers' penetration of the air defense system, final target reconnaissance, protection of the region for launching guided missiles (dropping bombs), and suppression of enemy air surveillance systems, should be expected as well. It is possible to foresee something similar in conducting military operations on land as well, for example, when routing armored groupings. Apparently, remote terrain mining means, airplane-helicopter groups, air- and sea-based cruise missiles, recce-strike complexes, RSZO, long-range antitank rocket complexes, radio-electronic warfare means, airborne forces, and special operations forces will participate. In addition, the high accuracy of new weapons complexes and their fast action will make it possible to deliver strikes only against objectives *selected* for destruction and at a *specific moment in time.* Consequently, with respect to form, the operation will become the totality of massed, group, and concentrated strikes by aviation, rocket forces, naval artillery, radio-electronic warfare means, combined-arms formations (units), etc.

The *fifth trend* is closely linked with the preceding two, differing with respect to means, objectives of destruction and means of protection, and place and time of troop actions in the operation.

Therefore, on the one hand, during the planning of the operation, when determining each operational mission (massed strike), it is obviously expedient to specify the "central asset" – the "leader" – toward whose maximum effectiveness the actions of all other forces and means should be directed. It should be emphasized that, in the future, the role of "leader" will most often be played not by a combined-arms formation, but rather by a "base" fire means – a recce-strike complex, the strike echelon of cruise missiles, an airplane strike group, or an RSZO grouping. On the other hand, the defender's principal efforts must be concentrated in the interests of protecting troops from the actions of the enemy "leader" during a strike.

The *sixth trend* is conditioned by the ever increasing significance of timely reception of information concerning objectives to ensure the required effectiveness of means of destruction. This means that achievement of success in operations will, to a great degree, depend on the effectiveness of the struggle against reconnaissance and information systems. This trend requires dual action when preparing and conducting military actions. *On the one hand*, when planning to hit the enemy, commanders and staffs should at first focus principal attention on forces and means of acquiring (reconnaissance), transmitting (communications), processing, and storing information (automated control systems), then on forces and means of redistribution (command post personnel and combat equipment, communications), and only then on means of destruction. *On the other hand*, it is necessary to undertake all measures to conceal and distort information being carried and destroy information being emanated by troop objects.

The *seventh trend* results from the continuous growth in the number of forces and means capable of delivering powerful and deep destruction by conventional munitions (B-2 airplanes, sea-based cruise missiles, recce-strike complexes, etc.), and by an increase in the degree of *constant readiness* to deliver strikes. Essentially, this trend cautions us that with each year the side which proclaims a "non-aggressive" military doctrine will have fewer capabilities (with respect to both time and combat-ready means) to repel successfully a carefully planned attack if the first defensive operation (or preparation for it) commences only after aggression has been detected. From this ensues a minimum of three principal requirements for future operations:

First – planning and preparing the first operation beforehand, with designation (within the framework of the area of each troop formation's combat space) of zones and regions of responsibility for hitting the enemy's most dangerous combat systems and conducting measures for protecting one's own most important objectives against their actions, with allocation of sufficient on-call forces and means to resolve this mission.

Second – planning an operation on the basis of determining the most dangerous variant for one's forces which the enemy can use to unleash aggression, with consideration of the features of all other variants.

Third – implementing the greater portion of measures for practical preparation of an operation, whose conduct is permissible with respect to operational-strategic conditions of peacetime troop deployment, as well as those which require the strictest *maskirovka*, but which can be kept secret.

And one thing more concerning one facet of the latter trend. No one can deny that even with the highest degree of weapons readiness to deliver a strike, a variant can be forecasted where the process of the enemy's preparation and unleashing of aggression takes on an *irreversible* nature. Consequently, in a theoretical plan the possibility is granted to begin a defensive operation with *preemptive strikes* to thwart aggression, without violating one's obligations (in accordance with military doctrine). In examining the trend from this point of view, one draws a conclusion concerning reduction in the period of irreversibility, and that in the near future preemptive strikes may be the *single means for thwarting aggression and successfully commencing a defensive operation*. Therefore, today it is obviously necessary to recognize the time requirement for expediency in planning the commencement of operational-strategic defensive actions with delivery of preemptive strikes against those enemy means whose combat employment at a specific moment would take on an *aggressively irreversible nature*. In addition, the time is logically arriving when the period of irreversibility will be so small that it will be impossible to avert enemy actions, even with the help of preemptive strikes, *without stepping on the path of aggression oneself.* To resolve this contradiction, it is already necessary today to speak of the radical path of considering the requirements of this trend: *preventing the very moment* of irreversibility, which can be achieved only by its qualitative, quantitative, and spatial restrictions, without the violation of which the aggressor cannot implement his plans for a surprise attack. In addition, the magnitudes of restrictions must be such that, even in case of an aggressor's violation of them, the defender would not be faced with the fact of a surprise attack.

NOTES

1. A. N. Zakharov, "Tendentsii razvitiya vooruzhennoy bor'by," *Voyennaya mysl'* [Military thought], 11–12 (1991), pp. 9–15.
2. Translator's note: the translated content of the two figures in this paper has been taken from JPRS UMT-92-005-L, 23 March 1992.

Conclusion

Since its creation as a distinct realm of study in the 1920s, the Soviet definition of operational art has changed little. In theory and in practice, identification of the operational level, its use in planning and conducting war, and its utility of studying the nature of war, retrospectively or as a vehicle for foresight and forecasting, has proved its worth. In this sense, Soviet operational theorists have contributed not only to their own military development, but to the health of military establishments of other nations who appreciated and adopted the Soviet approach. It is no coincidence that Western study of the operational level as a distinct and valid subject in its own right burgeoned in the 1970s and 1980s with positive results.

The contents, scope, and importance of operational art has evolved over time in consonance with the changing nature of war. Most importantly, study of the operational level has fostered better understanding of the impact of technological change on warfare at all levels. At times, technological changes have increased the importance of operational art (as in the 1930s and 1970s), and at other times major technological innovations (atomic, nuclear) have tended to lessen the importance of operational art relative to strategy. Today, as we confront a new technological revolution in weaponry (high-precision weapons and weapons based on new physical principles), we must again anticipate what impact these weapons will have on the importance of operational art.

Likewise, technological changes have altered the relative balance and importance of the offense and defense within the operational level. The tank and airplane of the 1930s unfettered the offense and made blitzkrieg and deep operations supreme. Corresponding development of antitank defenses during the Second World War restored the viability of the defense until new combined-arms concepts empowered the offense with new strength and vigor by war's end. In much the same way, ATGMs of the 1970s seemed to reinvigorate the defense, while operational and tactical maneuver concepts seemed to restore the power of the offense. Today, the effect of high-precision weapons again casts doubt on the viability of tank-based offensive concepts.

These incessant dialectical changes have accorded the operational realm a dynamic and ever-changing character, and have impelled constant study on the part of military establishments if they hope to master the complexities of operational art. The historical development of operational art eloquently attests to the necessity for continual sound and imaginative study if military establishments are to adjust, survive, and master future war.

The 1990s promise to be a decade of such challenges. Russian and other theorists in the republics of the former Soviet Union themselves must lead the way in military analysis if the Russian Federation or any other Soviet successor state is to continue to play an important role in military affairs. It is clear that study is going on, as evidenced by the recent theoretical debate regarding doctrinal defensiveness as juxtaposed against more traditional Soviet offensive strategic, operational, and tactical concepts.

It is reasonable to assume, and in fact discern from recent military writings, that Russian military theorists will, while addressing defensive topics, also incorporate elements from their offensive military analysis, which so dominated their attention through 1985 and persisted in some forums until 1987. This synthesis of old and new should prompt Russian analysis of at least the following topics (probably, for obvious political reasons, primarily in closed forums):

- the employment of operational maneuver groups in the defense and, in particular, in the counteroffensive, counterstroke, and counterattack;
- the use of airborne and air assault forces in defensive battles and operations and in offensive counteractions;
- raid tactics in defensive combat;
- the future evolution of land-air battle and development of the air echelon;
- the future development of non-linear warfare;
- the modernization, reorganization, and proliferation of artillery systems, organizations, and tactics.

Whether or not political and economic developments permit further development of operational art in the Russian military to occur in orderly fashion, it is clear that these very questions will also challenge the military establishments of other nations which have more recently developed a keen appreciation of the importance of operational art in future war. An acute understanding of operational issues, set within the context of strategy, will continue to provide the cornerstone for mastery of future war and the attainment of national security. This survey as to how one nation adjusted to operational changes over time attests to the nature and importance of that crucial process.

Index

advance guard echelon, 32
air assault, 17, 18, 25, 28, 31, 32, 33, 35, 36,
  39, 42, 109, 114, 115, 117, 130, 134, 142,
  149, 154, 164, 166, 172, 174, 175, 176, 177,
  183, 184, 189, 191, 195, 207, 208, 224, 228,
  230, 242, 252, 255, 256, 257, 258, 259, 263,
  269, 270, 272, 289, 290, 297, 305, 320, 329,
  334, 357
airborne, 258, 259, 260, 261, 270, 301, 303,
  357
air-land operations (battle), 122, 254, 257,
  264, 277, 279, 299, 301, 308, 318, 319, 334
air-mobile forces, 175, 176, 258–60, 261, 301,
  304, 307
Alksnis, Ya. A., 167, 195
Alyabushev, F. F., 328
Ammosov, S. N., 111
amphibious assault, 100, 142, 154, 207, 208,
  226, 228, 230, 301
annihilating battle *see* annihilation
annihilating blows *see* annihilation
annihilating engagement *see* annihilation
annihilating operation *see* annihilation
annihilation, 1, 11, 12, 13–14, 16, 17, 24, 28,
  54, 56, 59–60, 62, 66, 71, 75–9, 81, 83, 84,
  110, 115, 117, 126, 128, 167, 170–1, 199,
  215, 252, 269, 271, 277, 278, 289, 291, 295,
  296, 319, 338
anti-assault operation (defense), 207, 208,
  226, 228
Armor Academy, 35
army defensive region, 116
artillery offensive, 97, 102, 169, 187, 227
artillery preparation, 97, 102, 159, 168, 169,
  172, 187, 198, 295, 296, 297
atomic attack (strike), 131
attrition, 1, 13, 14, 31, 55, 56, 59, 65, 75–9
automated control, 306

Bagramyan, I. Kh., 45
Balaton Operation, 104, 152
Baltic Sea, 80, 82
Bazarevskiy, A. V., 11, 54, 66
Belgorod–Khar'kov Operation, 96, 185
Belitsky, S. M., 111

Belorussian Military District, 35, 117, 192,
  195
Belorussian Operation, 103, 170, 232–3, 235,
  236, 241, 243
Belorussian–Polish Theater, 41
Belorussian Theater of Military Operations,
  63
Belov, P. A., 113
Beloy, A. S., 54
Berezina River, 245
Berlin Operation, 242
Berzin, Ya. K., 247
Bezkhrebtyy, M. N., 122, 123, 222–44
Black Sea, 80, 82
blitzkrieg, 17, 49, 60, 63, 77, 110, 356
Blyukher, V. K., 3, 35, 182
Blyumental', F., 61
Bobrov, 35
Bobruisk Operation, 158, 199
Bogdanov, A. A., 57
Bogomyakov, S. N., 35
Brezhnev, L. I., 211
Bronch-Bruyevich, M. D., 54
Bryansk Operation, 185
Budapest Operation, 158
Bubnov, A. S., 11, 16
Bulow, G., 214–15, 217

Cambrai (Battle of), 151
Cannae, 15
Chaykovskiy, K. A., 26
Chemical Defense Academy, 35
Cherednichenko, M., 121, 125–37
Chervonobab, V., 121–2, 149–61
Civil War (Russian), 4, 5, 6–7, 8, 9, 10, 11,
  24, 54, 55, 56, 57, 58, 67, 69, 72, 73, 79,
  112, 114, 118, 152, 163, 179, 180, 181, 182,
  223, 245–6, 255, 256, 266, 288
Clausewitz, 4, 14
cleaving strike (attack), 102, 186
Cold War, 188
concentration, 98, 99, 104, 118, 121, 123, 133,
  135, 143, 146, 151, 152, 153, 154, 156, 166,
  168, 180, 181, 184, 198, 204, 213, 215, 271,
  295, 297, 301, 302, 303, 305, 324, 325